Participant Observer

PARTICIPANT OBSERVER

An Autobiography

William Foote Whyte

ILR Press
Ithaca, New York

Text design by Kat Dalton

Library of Congress Cataloging in Publication Data

Whyte, William Foote, 1914–
Participant observer : an autobiography / William Foote Whyte.
p.   cm.
Includes bibliographical references and index.
ISBN 0-87546-324-X (cloth). — ISBN 0-87546-325-8 (pbk)
1. Sociologists—United States—Biography.   I. Whyte, William
Foote, 1914–   .   II. Title.
HM22.U6W48   1994
301'.092—dc20
[B]   93-47550

Copies may be ordered through bookstores or directly from

ILR Press
School of Industrial and Labor Relations
Cornell University
Ithaca, NY 14853-3901

Printed on acid-free paper in the United States of America
5 4 3 2 1

*To Kathleen, who has enriched my life
in so many ways for so many years*

Contents

Photographs appear between pages 158 and 159.

Acknowledgments

For helpful criticisms and suggestions, I am indebted to the following people, who read one or more of the chapters of an earlier draft: Jennie Farley, Corey Rosen, John Seybold, John Whyte, Martin King Whyte, Joyce Wiza, and James C. Worthy. I am especially indebted to Martin King Whyte, who wrote me detailed notes on the first twenty chapters of that earlier draft. John Seybold read chapters of my early life up through the college years and provided his own recollections of me at Swarthmore College.

Individuals involved in my later field projects contributed not only infomation but insights and ideas that reshaped the design of my research. In that sense, many of those projects can be called by a now-popular term participatory research.

Finally, my last field project; a study of the Mondragón cooperative complex in the Basque country of Spain, led me to the most remarkable man I have ever known, José María Arizmendiarrieta. A Catholic priest whose idealistic vision combined with a highly pragmatic view of the world, he provided the basic design and early orientation for that extraordinary social and economic invention. He died before I could involve him as a full participant in my research, but after our initial meetings in 1975, I continued to learn from him through interviews with his closest associates and by reading what he wrote and what was written about him. The Mondragón project also led beyond participatory research to the development of participatory action research when Cornell anthropology professor Davydd J. Greenwood teamed up with José Luis González, personnel director of the FAGOR group of cooperatives, to organize a project in which fifteen members of the cooperatives worked with them to reshape their personnel program on the basis of data they gathered and analyzed themselves.

Although I abandoned fiction long ago, that early ambition influenced my career planning. Growing up the son of a college professor, I found myself on the way to an academic career, yet I did not reconcile myself to that fate until close to the end of my first research project. I tried to broaden my social experience so that I could write about people whose backgrounds were not upper middle class like my own. For many years the life of a college professor seemed too dull for me. I had to learn from my own fieldwork that an adventurous life need not be beyond the reach of an academic.

I have always felt both a pressure to specialize and a strong desire to explore a wide range of fields. At various times in my career, I could have been typed as an urban sociologist, a rural sociologist, an industrial sociologist, or a student of the sociology of science. My longest ongoing commitment has been to industrial sociology or, as I prefer to call it, organizational behavior, which suggests its interdisciplinary character. In my fieldwork and writing, I have collaborated with social anthropologists, social psychologists, economists, political scientists, engineers, and plant, animal, and soil scientists, as well as practitioners in industrial management and labor.

If there is a common theme in my work, it is my commitment to social exploration. Fieldwork fascinates me. I want to explain what is out there. In the first stage of exploration, everything seems new and strange, but eventually I see

1. Introducing Myself

The titles of my other books have always come to me last, after a long struggle. Not so in this case. "Participant observer" not only conveys the research style for which I am best known, but in a sense, it also describes who I am and have been: an active participant in a variety of scenes at home and abroad, yet an observer—and not only of other people. This is a book on what I have learned from observing myself.

My Ph.D. is in sociology, but I am often identified as a social anthropologist. Over the years, I have strived to create my own niche as a behavioral scientist, concentrating on the study of organizations, while working to gain the recognition of mainstream colleagues. That tension remains unresolved.

I have aimed to be a scientist, yet at the same time I have felt the urge to put what I learn to practical use. That is not a common combination of commitments among social scientists. I have acted on my reform urges within the university and also on the national scene, with modest practical results in both fields of action.

I once hoped to become a writer of novels and plays. That ambition has long since been cast aside, yet the tension between science and humanism continues to influence my work. I do not want the people I study to become submerged in my data so that readers get no sense of the human struggles I describe and analyze.

Looking back on my field studies, I can think of several individuals who made the transition from passive informants to key informants and finally to active participants in my research. Ernest Pecci (the man I called Doc in my book *Street Corner Society*) became my guide and interpreter of life in the North End slum district of Boston. And Pecci introduced me to Angelo Ralph Orlandella, whom Harvard paid a one hundred dollar grant to help me figure out the structure of corner gangs in his neighborhood. He may well have been the first high school dropout ever paid for his help with such research.

3

Participant Observer

a pattern that seems to make sense. Once I have described that pattern in writing, I lose interest in seeing the pattern repeated again and again and look for a new field to explore. I have done my share of supervising students' thesis research, and I always envied those who were out exploring the field. When I was actively involved in directing a project, even when most of the data were being gathered by students, I felt a need to do at least some small portion of the fieldwork myself so that the scene and the people would come alive in my own mind.

Since my explorations have taken me from North America to Latin America and Spain, I can claim to be an internationalist, although I do not conform to the most common model followed by sociologists with an interest in international issues. In that model, sociologists link up with fellow sociologists abroad who help the foreigners carry out research comparable to what they have done at home. This is an important and legitimate research strategy, but it was not my style. When abroad, I did not avoid associating with fellow social scientists, but I wanted to get more directly involved in the fieldwork myself. I was more interested in talking with the managers, union leaders, engineers, workers, farmers, and agricultural professionals myself—in their own language if possible—than in collaborating in survey research with social scientists in the host country.

In what follows, I shall focus on the interconnections between my personal experiences and my scientific and professional work. That means recalling from memory or from notes those experiences that led me to decide what and where to study, what research methods to use, what theoretical frameworks to use as guides, and how my own ideas on theory and research methods developed and changed over more than half a century of fieldwork. I shall describe not only decisions that paid off but also the blind alleys I sometimes followed and the theoretical misconceptions that led me astray

This introduction may give the impression that I have been unfocused, going in many different directions at once. That raises the key question: Is there a central core to Bill Whyte? I shall try to answer that question in the chapters that follow.

2. Getting Started

I was born on June 27, 1914, at the end of one era and the beginning of another. The next day, the heir apparent to the throne of Austria-Hungary was assassinated, thus triggering the series of moves and countermoves that led to World War I.

I was the only child of John and Isabel Van Sickle Whyte. My birthplace was Springfield, Massachusetts. I had the good fortune to be born into a happy marriage. I don't recall any serious arguments between my parents throughout my growing-up years—or later.

John Whyte and Isabel Van Sickle had met in Germany when they were both abroad on fellowships. John Whyte was not conventionally handsome, but his face radiated an animated and warm personality that drew people to him. He had a brilliant mind that got him through college well ahead of his age-mates, and he was musically gifted. He played the violin and had an exceptional bass-baritone singing voice. In fact, his voice teacher in Germany once told him that he might be able to make it as an opera singer—but only if he abandoned teaching to put all his efforts into developing his voice. He decided that teaching had to come first. Still, I remember that voice, especially as he sang Negro spirituals. As I write this, I can hear him singing "Deep River" and "Swing Low, Sweet Chariot."

John Whyte was a great teacher. In the mid-1920s, the student newspaper at the City College of New York, where he taught German, conducted a student survey of all the professors and graded each one. They were very hard markers, for even some of the professors with the highest reputations among their colleagues received failing grades. Among all the hundreds of teachers, John Whyte was one of only ten who were given A's.

I do not take after my father in build, athletic ability, or temperament. In my early teens, I had grown up to a thin six feet three inches. John Whyte was a robust five feet eight. He was also a natural athlete. In baseball, he was good enough to attract the interest of a semiprofessional team—but joining would have required him to play on Sundays, which at the time was contrary to his religious beliefs. In tennis, he was a crack doubles player, so good that he and his partner could compete with some of the best in the country.

John Whyte was full of nervous energy. I think of him as a coiled spring, ready to jump into action. My own reactions are much slower. In that regard, I am much more like my mother.

I remember Isabel as a lady—it seemed natural to think of her in those terms—a serene and lovely lady. Her honey-blonde hair contrasted with John's black hair, and her emotions were less close to the surface than his. Like John, she was a top student. She worked on an M.A. in German while he was getting his Ph.D. She seemed to be a gentle person, but she knew her own mind and did not hesitate to express her opinions, politely but firmly, even when opposed by persons of great prestige.

My family was solidly upper middle class and, like many such families of its day, strongly committed to high Culture (with a capital C, meaning literature and the arts) and dedicated to intellectual achievement. As I look back on the places we lived in my growing-up years, I see shelves loaded with books. Although few of those books were ever open after a first reading, we treasured them as if they were an indispensable part of our beings. Once, in my teenage years when I brought a girl home, her first remark upon entering the house was, "So many books! Are they all yours, or did they come with the apartment?" My father thought that was one of the funniest things he had ever heard.

I was named for my grandfather, who came to America from Scotland when he was three years old. The family settled in Watertown, a small town in Wisconsin between Madison and Milwaukee. Grandpa Whyte became a country doctor and later was president of the Wisconsin State Board of Health. He married Florence Adelaide Kohn, the daughter of a Jewish father and a mother of English extraction. She was a skilled pianist and a smart business manager, a necessary complement to a doctor who did not have the heart to press people to pay their bills.

The descendant of early Dutch settlers, my maternal grandfather, James H. Van Sickle, was a schoolteacher and later superintendent of schools in North Denver, Baltimore, and Springfield, Massachusetts. Known as an educational innovator, he was an early believer in the idea of the junior high school. He married a former high school pupil, Carolyn Valentine. The name suggests that she was of English extraction. My mother, Isabel, was the second girl of the family, followed by two boys.

In political orientation, the Whytes and the Van Sickles had much in common in the early years of this century. The Whytes were enthusiastic supporters of the Progressive party senator from Wisconsin, Robert M. La Follette—until he filibustered on the Senate floor in a vain attempt to block our entry into World War I.

The Van Sickles were great admirers of the Democratic reform president Woodrow Wilson. My parents followed in this tradition until the election of 1920, when, in reaction to what they considered Wilson's betrayal in abandoning his Fourteen Points and "peace without victory" stand, they rejected James Cox, the Democratic presidential candidate. Isabel voted for the Socialist labor leader Eugene V. Debs and John for the Republican candidate, Warren G. Harding.

As the incompetence of President Harding became generally recognized, John's 1920 vote became a source of some amusement in our family. That vote represented the only defection of the Whytes from their liberal and Democratic orientation. John and Isabel became enthusiastic supporters of Al Smith in 1928 and of Franklin D. Roosevelt in 1932 and throughout the New Deal years.

In religious orientation, my grandparents were very different. The Whytes were dedicated members of the Presbyterian church, and my father remembered having to go to church or Sunday School five times every Sunday. While a graduate student in Germany, he fell away from the church, much to the distress of his parents. He used to say that those early years had stored up enough church to last him a lifetime. Later, John rarely attended except for when he was a paid soloist in the choir of one of the major churches in Manhattan.

Grandmother Van Sickle went to the Christian Science church, but she was hardly a true believer. When anyone in the family was sick, she did not hesitate to call a doctor. If Grandpa Van Sickle went to church at all, I don't recall hearing about it.

When I was old enough to learn about such matters, I gathered that my parents were agnostics. If I wanted to go to church, it was up to me.

Since my parents did not believe in original sin, they saw no sense in baptism, but they yielded to my father's parents, who had returned from a visit to the Holy Land with a bottle of water from the Jordan River. Thus, at the age of two, I was baptized—but not before Mother boiled the water because it looked dirty. Question: Does boiling remove the holiness from holy water?

During elementary school, in Caldwell, New Jersey, my friend Robert Vogel tried to recruit me into the Methodist-Episcopal Sunday School. For a couple of years, I went with him during the fall and early winter, but I dropped out in January. As my parents pointed out, I stopped going shortly after bringing home the Christmas presents that were distributed to all the Sunday School children.

I had a Catholic friend, Ed Bennett, but he never tried to convert me. From my parents, I got the impression that Catholics were superstitious people who needed the hocus-pocus of the mass to sustain their beliefs. They had no objections to my associating with Catholics, but they did point out that, if I should marry one, I would have to agree to raise my children in the Catholic church.

In Caldwell, most of the parishioners in the St. Aloysius Church were poor working people, but Mother told me that in Baltimore and New Orleans the social elite belonged to the Catholic church. She also told me that she had a warm spot in her heart for a famous Baltimore churchman, Cardinal James Gibbons. When her father was the target of an eventually successful political fight to oust him and bring in a superintendent willing to disregard the qualifications of teachers from elsewhere to conform to their slogan, "Baltimore for Baltimoreans," the cardinal made an unannounced visit to the Van Sickle home to express his support for my grandfather. Not knowing the proper form of address, Grandma fixed on the highest-sounding title she could think of: "your majesty."

Many years later, when my own children were growing up, I got the family involved with a Presbyterian church, but my relationship to organized religion remained ambiguous and uneasy. I was repelled by preachers who concentrated on saving individual souls. And although I was attracted by ministers who preached a social gospel, I did not want to go to church to hear a thinly disguised lecture on current affairs. I needed to feel some sense of moral uplift as well as hear a message that made intellectual sense to me. Still, I admired religious leaders of any faith who strived to advance what I conceived to be social justice.

I was brought up to believe it was immoral to discriminate against people for reasons of race, ethnicity, religion, or social class. I learned early that I should not speak of "niggers" and that I should not call Brazil nuts "nigger toes," as many of my friends did.

As I was growing up, Mother spoke with pride about what her father had accomplished with the Negro schools in Baltimore. In his era, integration was out of the question, but James H. Van Sickle ended the practice of dumping on the Negro schools any white teachers thought not competent enough to teach white children. He was determined to staff the Negro schools with the best talent he could attract from anywhere in the country.

There were few Negro families in Caldwell, New Jersey, in my early years, but there was a Negro boy in my grade in school, and we became friends. He once proposed that if he could walk to school with me, he would fight off any boy who dared to attack me. That seemed a good deal to me. Being usually the loser in fistfights I could not avoid, I had no lust for physical combat, and I liked my protector. Besides, I took pride in demonstrating to the community that I did not discriminate against Negroes.

My family tree inoculated me against anti-Semitism. According to family records, seven-eighths of my ancestry goes back to England, Scotland, and Holland. The remaining eighth is traceable to a great-great grandfather who was a rabbi. His son settled in rural Wisconsin, where there were no synagogues, married a gentile, and raised his children in Protestant churches, which meant that Jewish religious beliefs and traditions did not survive in my family. Further, the Jewish name passed out of our family line when Florence Adelaide Kohn married my grandfather. Not so with her brothers. Although they were no more Jewish in blood or customs than he was, my father's Kohn cousins encountered discrimination John Whyte never experienced.

I never knew my father to mention his Jewish ancestry outside the family. Not having been brought up in the Jewish religion, he felt no need to identify himself as part Jewish and thus invite discrimination. Once, in speaking to my wife, Kathleen, and me shortly before we were married, he advised us not to mention his Jewish ancestry. I should add, however, that during the Hitler dictatorship, he served as chairman and executive officer of the Committee in Aid of Displaced German Scholars for the Modern Languages Association. Of course, most of those displaced were Jewish.

My parents were quite class-conscious, while at the same time opposing discrimination against individuals based on their social class. I learned that upper-class people had superior social prestige but that that did not mean they were better people than the upper-middle-class Whytes. I would hear disparaging remarks about the "idle rich" and about business executives who were only interested in money and were unconcerned with the higher values of the arts, literature, and the intellectual life.

My closest contact with people of other cultural backgrounds was through our next-door neighbors, the Boucles. Mr. Boucle was a foreman in a printing plant of the American Book Company. There were two sons in the family, both of them older than I.

My parents never suggested that I limit my contacts with these boys, but I did become aware of the cultural differences between our families. My parents were devotees of classical music and looked upon jazz as cultural pollution. For a brief period, when the boys next door were trying to develop a jazz band, they frequently practiced in the evenings. Although they resented the loud and unpleasant sounds, my parents never complained to the neighbors.

My mother discovered another cultural difference between our families once when Mrs. Boucle was sick in bed. When Mother took over a bowl of home-made soup and a book for her to read, she noticed that there was only one book in the whole house. Imagine that! Although Mr. Boucle worked for a book printer, their bookshelves were bare. Later, when my mother was sick in bed, Mrs. Boucle came over with her contribution of soup. She now reciprocated by lending their only book, an autobiography of a ship captain who had given a copy of his book to the Boucles.

In my growing-up years, I felt a sense of pride whenever I thought of the Whyte–Van Sickle family lines. From what I knew of those in the two generations before me, no one was socially or politically prominent or wealthy, but they were all upright, hard-working citizens who had achieved goals aspired to by their families and their communities. That was a comforting thought, and it also gave me something to live up to.

3. *Family Upheaval*

World events directly affected my family life during first grade. The house we lived in, on Wiegand Place in the Bronx, belonged to the University Heights campus of New York University (NYU), which was right next door and where my father taught German. In the hysteria of World War I, NYU closed the German department and discharged all of its professors, forcing us to move.

The only housing we could afford was a fifth-floor walk-up in the Bronx. Mother found those stairs exhausting.

That winter, my mother came down with what was first diagnosed as bronchitis, for which her doctor recommended she get away to a warm climate. Leaving Father behind, she and I moved to Dade City, Florida, to live with Uncle Irwin and Aunt Belle Schuyler. Mother took over my first-grade lessons.

Uncle Irwin taught high school and also owned a farm with citrus fruit and cattle. I had no one to play with, but I became good friends with a calf that enjoyed licking my fingers. I thus discovered one advantage of associating with cattle: it eliminated the need to clean my fingernails. But soon the calf began to turn into a bull, and, instead of sauntering up to me as I approached him, he pawed the ground and charged. I just barely escaped up a tree. That ended our friendship. With the help of Cooperative Extension, Uncle Irwin slaughtered my friend. I refused to eat him. I knew that charging me was not his fault.

During that period, I encountered religion in its most concentrated form. Uncle Irwin said grace eloquently and at great length before every meal. One evening when Uncle Irwin was away, Aunt Belle had started serving us when I asked her, "Aren't you going to say grace?"

She replied, "I don't know how."

Mother was startled. "For thirty years you have been listening to Uncle Irwin say grace, and . . ."

Aunt Belle nodded and, with a sheepish smile, said, "I guess I haven't been listening."

I stepped into the breach and said grace myself. I concluded an appropriately long-winded thanks to the Lord with the exhortation "Be men!"

When Mother questioned this unorthodox ending, I explained, "Since 'amen' doesn't mean anything, I thought it would be better to finish with 'be men' because that does mean something." Mother cherished this early evidence of my creativity—or was it a manifestation of male chauvinism?

When we returned to the Bronx in the late spring, Isabel was still coughing. Finally, the correct diagnosis was made: tuberculosis. At the time it was thought that the clearer air in the mountains was conducive to recovery, so Mother went to a sanitorium in Colorado Springs, close to Denver where she had grown up. My father had to remain in New York, where, after several months of unemployment, he had landed a job with the National Association of Credit Men. I was too young to be left alone when he was at work, so for more than a year I was farmed out to relatives.

My first stop was Springfield, Massachusetts, where I stayed with the family of James H. Van Sickle. Three of the four children of James and Carolyn had long since left home, but the family included their daughter Helen and Carolyn's divorced sister, Mame, who had been married to what we then called a drunkard. Helen had had polio as a small child and thus remained dependent on her family all her life. Having no children of her own, she looked upon me as her special child. Besides taking care of Helen, Aunt Mame played with me, told me stories, and read aloud to me. I was well cared for but in an adult world.

I started second grade in Springfield. When Grandma discovered I was bored with the work, she arranged to have me tested and then advanced to third grade. Mother was upset with this move, since she felt it was important socially for me to remain with pupils my own age. I encountered no intellectual problems in third grade, but neither did I make any friends, and some of the boys in that class enjoyed roughing me up on the way to school.

When the school year ended, my father took me to East Orange, New Jersey, to stay with his sister, Effie, and Homer Watt, who was a professor of English at New York University. For the first time during my exile, I was in a family with children: Harold, three years older than I; Bill, a year and a half older; and Jean, a couple of years younger. And now that I was lodged nearby, my father came out to join us some weekends.

I had no problems fitting in with the Watts except on Sundays. We children had to go to church and Sunday school. But that was not the worst of it. Homer and Effie believed it was sacrilegious to have fun on Sundays. We were confined to the house and yard. Card games were banned because they were thought to lead to gambling, which in turn led to all kinds of other sins.

The only game allowed was Authors, in which players sought to acquire a matched set of cards for a particular author. Cousin Bill evaded the ban by marking the deck. As we played Casino with the Authors cards, Aunt Effie would come out on the front porch to inspect now and then, and she would beam at us for our dedication to culture.

I enjoyed the Watt children and during my stay with them cemented a friendship that has lasted over the years. The only problem I had in their neighborhood was with Joe, a boy older and tougher than I, who enjoyed picking on me. Indirectly and temporarily, cousin Harold solved that problem for me. He was a nature lover, a collector of rocks, fossils, butterflies, and garter and milk snakes. One day Joe approached me from the rear when I was holding a garter snake. When I turned around, he was terrified. As he backed away, he promised to be my friend if I would not unleash the snakes on him.

The truce lasted until the incident with the walnuts. One day we were sitting on the steps of his front porch. Joe had two pants pockets full of walnuts. While we talked, Joe would pick walnuts out of one pocket, crack them, and eat them. I thought it would be nice if we shared the nuts as well as the conversation. My left hand was close to Joe's right-hand pocket. How many nuts could I transfer from his pocket to mine before he caught on?

I tried the first nut, and it was easy. So it went until I got down to the last nut, which was deeper in his pocket than the others. I did not need it, but I could not resist the challenge. As I reached for it, Joe caught me. After taking back his nuts, he beat me up and chased me home. End of friendship, although I could still fall back on Harold's snakes for protection in our yard.

I have wondered what lesson I should draw from the walnuts incident. Crime does not pay, or quit while you're ahead?

Although I was fond of Aunt Effie, there were aspects of her behavior that I found hard to understand. Many years later, one memory of her stood me in good stead during the Vietnam War. I was reading about a hearing before the Senate Armed Services Committee. The senators were questioning the general in charge of our bombing operations over North Vietnam and wanted to know if the bombing was helping us win the war.

The general's account of the excellent job he was doing recalled a trip I had made with Aunt Effie and the Watt children many years before. On that occasion, we had gotten off schedule and were approaching an unknown town when it was already after lunchtime. Effie stopped the car in front of a restaurant. With us trailing behind her, she marched in and demanded to see the proprietor. When he presented himself, she looked him in the eye and asked, "Do you serve good food?"

It occurred to me that the general's answers to the senators' questions were just as credible as the answer the restaurant owner gave Aunt Effie. The two incidents inspired me to write "The Brass and My Aunt Effie," which was published in the *Nation* and later reprinted in the *Congressional Record*.

I suffered no serious deprivations during my times with relatives. I had the loving care of grandparents and aunts and uncles. Still, it was not the same as being in my own home. My most vivid memories of that period suggest what I was missing.

Every few weeks, the Watts received a visit from Homer's sister, Dora. The Watt children looked forward to her visits since she always brought them presents. Because I was not a member of her family, she never brought me anything. The presents were of little value, but this symbolic exclusion from the family upset me. I did not like Aunt Dora.

Also during this period, we spent several weeks in the summer in an old resort hotel in Wading River, on Long Island. The high point for me was the two weeks my father spent with us. I remember how he walked down the road to the Long Island Railroad at the end of his vacation. I walked a bit with him, and, when he embraced me to say good-bye, I was crying. He looked back once while I was still standing there, and there were tears in his eyes too.

When it was time to go back to school and Isabel was expected home from Colorado Springs, my father decided to move us to Caldwell, New Jersey. Why Caldwell? Because it had the highest elevation of any town within commuting distance of New York City, and it advertised itself as the third healthiest spot in the country. I never learned which towns Caldwell conceded to be even healthier than, but at least they were not within commuting range.

Although Mother returned home, my time with her was limited for at least a year because of her illness. My parents had twin beds on a sleeping porch at the back of the house, and I slept on a porch at the other end of the house. Most of the time there was no one between us except a live-in Finnish maid, and I felt very much alone. As I looked up to the horizon beyond Central Avenue, I used to imagine monsters coming down the hill to get me. Since I knew monsters did not exist, I never confessed my fears to my parents, but still I could not banish those fantasies. During the day, I could stand at the door of the sleeping porch and talk to Mother, but any closer contact was ruled out. If something had upset me, she would try to console me in words, but she could not take me in her arms.

This disruption of my family life must have had profound effects on me. Mother thought that perhaps throwing me on my own resources forged me into a self-reliant and self-sustaining person. She used to say with pride that, although I enjoyed my friends, I was able to make life interesting for myself. Perhaps, but I did feel lonely or bored more often than she realized.

The disruption also may have had important effects on my emotional development. I grew into a person who kept his feelings to himself. I found it difficult to tell anybody what I was feeling. Since I could not readily articulate my feelings, I sometimes wondered if the feelings were really there. In my adolescent years, I developed semiserious attachments to several girls, but I was unable to say "I love you" to any of them. When I tried to say it, I would wonder if I really meant it, and that would stop me. Even in the early years of my marriage to Kathleen, I found it hard to say those words—an omission I later made up for many times as our relationship grew and deepened over more than fifty years.

4. Growing Up

Since I was an only child, my parents were especially concerned about not spoiling me. They wanted me to feel loved—and I did—but not to become highly dependent on them. They did not believe in corporal punishment. Their strategy was to "reason" with me.

I was what they considered a "good boy." I seldom disobeyed them. In fact, my transgressions were so few that I can remember most of them.

One incident occurred when I was too young to remember—just a few months beyond my second birthday—but Mother would never forget it. At the time, we were still living in the Bronx, where I played with a Kiddie Kar, a little three-wheel vehicle that could be propelled only by the foot power of the rider on the pavement. That must have seemed like hard work, so I lugged the Kiddie Kar to University Avenue, a main thoroughfare that led down to Gun Hill Road, another busy street where the streetcars ran. I pushed off down the hill, picking up speed as I went. My mother had little athletic ability, but on this occasion she outdid herself. She spotted me from the top of the hill, sprinted, and caught me just as I was reaching the Gun Hill Road intersection. I never wandered off again, but I like to think the incident was an early manifestation of an adventurous spirit.

My father used to boast that he had never spanked me. He had forgotten an incident that is still a vivid memory for me. One afternoon, when I was a few months beyond four, Isabel was out, so John was in charge. I was out playing with my closest friend. I felt a bowel movement coming on, but I was having such a good time that I did not go inside, and nature took its course.

After John had cleaned me up, he put me over his knees and gave me several whacks on the bottom, which was, after all, the offending part of me. The spanking worked. Fifty years would pass before I again dumped in my pants.

The next memorable transgression did not occur until I was eleven. My friend Ed Bennett and I had seen some of our classmates smoke cigarette butts, so we decided to pool our money and buy a pack of Fatimas. My parents did not catch me in the act, but as Ed was smoking our last cigarette on our front porch, we heard my father approaching from inside the house. Ed quickly placed the half-spent cigarette behind him. My father followed the wisp of smoke to the cigarette, picked it up, snuffed it out, and remarked, "My, did I leave my cigarette here?" We did not answer his rhetorical question, but it told me we had been found out—which took some of the fun out of a pastime I was not enjoying much anyway.

Some time later, my grade-school class got a lecture on the evils of smoking, and the speaker asked those who had ever smoked to raise their hands. I assumed many hands would go up, but mine was the only hand raised. Now when anyone asks me if I smoke, I can truthfully answer that I gave up cigarettes at the age of eleven.

When I was twelve, I was allowed to ride anywhere on my bicycle except on Bloomfield Avenue, the main artery for cars and streetcars between Caldwell and Newark. The day I violated that rule, it was misty and the avenue and the car tracks were getting slippery. To get around a double-parked car, I turned into the middle of the street. As I tried to turn back, my front wheel stuck in the streetcar tracks and I fell right in front of an oncoming Ford Model T. The woman driver was unable to stop, but she had the presence of mind to keep going straight, and I just lay there between the wheels as the car passed over me. I suffered nothing but bruises. The bicycle was a total wreck.

I was given credit for having the presence of mind to lie low and not move. I appreciated the credit, but I did not deserve it. I had simply frozen on the spot—which was the best thing I could do.

I realized that I could have been killed and did not have to be told that I had been a bad boy and deserved to be punished. My parents rejoiced at my narrow escape and got me to renew my promise not to ride on Bloomfield Avenue—a sacrifice I was happy to make. And then they bought me another bicycle.

Although my parents were happy that I was generally such a good boy, there were times when I wondered whether I was being too good to be considered what we then called a "regular fellow." I worried about that one day when Grandma Whyte casually remarked that she wondered if I had enough "spunk" because I never seemed to get into "mischief." The very next day, in one of my eighth-grade classes, I was presented with just such an opportunity for mischief. In my desk I found a very overripe banana. When the boy across from me left his seat momentarily, I slipped the banana onto it. When he sat down, he was outraged. I laughed, but nobody else did, and then suddenly I realized that what I had done was not really funny. It was just a dirty trick—and on a boy who had never done anything to deserve it. I don't recall being punished. The teacher seemed less annoyed than confused by this uncharacteristic act of a "good boy," and my victim never made good on his threat to make me pay to clean his pants. Nevertheless, the incident brought on its own punishment. I was embarrassed. I realized then that I was not good at making mischief, and that perhaps I'd better reconcile myself to being good.

My parents wanted to help me discover whatever talents I had, but they believed it was up to me to decide what I was good at and what I wanted to do. They assumed that anyone in our family would have some talent in music, until I proved otherwise. When my first piano teacher would not let me get beyond scales and other finger exercises, they assumed that my lack of progress was due to her approach. They switched me to a more "progressive" teacher who got me playing simple tunes, but after five years, when I was still not much beyond "The Happy Farmer," they let me drop the lessons.

I appreciated my father's wonderful singing voice and hoped to emulate him. When I was in high school, I tried out for a leading role in the Gilbert and Sullivan operetta *The Pirates of Penzance*. When I sat down after my tryout, a friend said sympathetically, "I guess you haven't had much chance to practice." I accepted the excuse, but lack of practice was not the problem. If you can't carry a tune, you are unlikely to become a good singer. I have wondered why my father did not simply tell me that I would never be a good singer. I assume he was sticking to his belief that I had to learn my strengths and weaknesses myself.

Writing was a different matter. Mother occasionally wrote poems, and in 1924 she won a gold watch in an annual contest run by Franklin P. Adams, a columnist in the *New York World*. I never had much interest in poetry myself, but I started writing stories, first for myself, when I was eleven years old. My parents encouraged me, and they always wanted to read whatever I wrote, but they never criticized my writing, although Mother did say that people write best about familiar situations and experiences.

Father was so strongly committed to nonintervention that, shortly before Kathleen and I got married, he took her aside to tell her that she must not criticize my writing because it was important for me to develop independent judgment. We laughed about that. We assumed my character was firmly enough formed at twenty-four that my writing style was not likely to be corrupted by my wife. In fact, over the years she has played an increasingly important role as copy editor and critic and even as collaborator. In particular, she has provided a healthy restraint on the increasing verbosity of an old man.

In growing up, I experienced the best and worst of both public and private school education. I encountered the worst of public schools in the first grade in the Bronx. Even though the class met in temporary storefront quarters, the five rows of desks and seats were screwed to the floor, as was the custom in that era.

The teacher was a strict disciplinarian who had unbounded faith in the virtues of competition and in her ability to make razor-sharp discriminations in pupil performance. First thing every Monday morning, she would have us all stand in the back of the room before directing us to take our seats in the order of our performance in the previous week. The ranking system began with the first row on her right. After delivering her customary exhortation, whose contents I quickly forgot, she would call out the names by rank, beginning with number one. After each name, she would pause to give the child time to take his or her assigned seat.

Ranks shifted from week to week, with one exception. Always the same boy was left standing alone until he could slink into the last seat in the last row. Having been "left back" on a couple of occasions, he was older and taller than any of us. He also had an unfortunate tendency to wet his pants.

On the basis of no evidence, the teacher started me in the last seat of the second row. About eight weeks later, I had moved up to the middle of the first row. But even then, I was fully aware of my mixed feelings about the system. I felt sorry for the children consigned to low ranks and especially for the boy who had won permanent possession of the last seat in the last row. I also heartily disliked the teacher. Nevertheless, I allowed myself to be trapped by the system. I worked hard and climbed the ladder, rung by rung.

While I was in elementary school, Mother became interested in the "progressive education" movement. This led her into discussions with parents in Essex Fells, another part of town, who were establishing the Caldwell Country Day School. I was about to enter sixth grade in West Caldwell School and had no desire to leave my friends. Assuring me that I could go back to West Caldwell if I wished, she and my father persuaded me to give the new school a try. After one day, I was hooked.

Caldwell Country Day School had freestanding desks and chairs that could be moved around. We also had much smaller classes, with enthusiastic teachers who gave us a good deal of individual attention.

My most vivid memory of that school was of the weekly council ring, in which we gathered around one of the teachers to read aloud poems or stories we had written, to show pictures we had drawn, or to describe recent experiences. I got started on a long-continued story called "Toby Timber," about a boy who ran away from home because his parents were cruel to him. Over many weeks, I followed his adventures until he finally wounded up in the Azores. Why there? Because one day while perusing a map, I discovered that there actually were bits of land between America and Europe.

Through "Toby Timber," I became something of a celebrity. Everybody wanted to know what was going to happen in the next episode. Claiming that authors of continuing stories never gave out such advance information, I refused to tell. A more honest answer would have been that I hadn't yet decided. The mother of one of my classmates had a theory that the story projected my hostility toward my parents. We laughed about that. In fact, I had casually thought of running away to have adventures, but my parents were too good to me. Besides, how would I manage to find places to eat and sleep?

During my three years at Caldwell Country Day School, I experienced both the best and the worst of progressive education. The worst came in my final year with a new teacher named Form—an incongruous name because he did not believe a teacher should provide form or structure. He was dedicated to "self-initiating creative activity," based on the romantic notion that children were so endowed that the main responsibility of teachers was to avoid suppressing their creative impulses.

While Mr. Form would sit at his desk waiting for us to initiate some creative activity, we sat there determined not to oblige him. Sometimes we would ask him to read aloud out of books he obviously did not approve of. Sometimes we went out on the playground to try to entertain ourselves, while we complained about how bored we were.

During my years at Caldwell, I lived in four social worlds. The first was the adult world, centered around my parents. When they had friends in, I joined them at the dinner table. I was not expected to take an active part in the conversation, but they did not exclude me. When I asked a question, they answered with the respect due to an adult. Fascinated with the discussions of current affairs and the arts, I would mull over such conversations and sometimes follow up with questions that occurred to me after the guests left. The same pattern persisted during summer vacations in Pennsylvania's Pocono Lake Preserve. The cottage we stayed in was designed and partially built by Grandpa Van Sickle, and the house brought together a larger adult and children's world revolving around my Van Sickle grandparents.

The second social world was centered around Steve Branigan, the half-brother of Joe Boucle, who lived next door. Polio had left Steve with shriveled legs in braces, but his chest and arms were powerful. To move himself around, he sat in an improvised vehicle put together from an orange crate, a two-inch-by-four-inch board, rollerskate wheels, and a rope for Joe or others to pull him along the sidewalk. In spite of his physical handicap, Steve dominated the group of boys two or more years older than I. In that group, we talked mainly about sports, particularly major league baseball.

My third social world was concentrated on Overlook Road, two blocks away, where several of my classmates lived. My best friends were Ed Bennett and Robbie Vogel, and our activities centered on a vacant lot between their homes. Both Ed and Robbie could run faster than I and were generally more athletic. I could outdo them only in schoolwork. I must have shown some intellectual arrogance until one day when they taught me a lesson.

That day, we were playing in the Vogel home when the conversation turned to lakes, boating, and canoeing, topics on which I considered myself an authority since I went to Pocono Lake Preserve every summer and they had had little if any experience at lakes. I found myself explaining that you could not only "row a boat" but that it was also correct to say you could "oar a boat." The moment I said it, I realized it did not sound right, but, before I could back off, they jumped on me—figuratively. Trapped, I stubbornly insisted that I was right until they began attacking with cries of "Billy know-it-all." Unable to stop this chorus, I retreated downstairs to the kitchen to strike up a conversation with Mrs. Vogel and ask for a glass of water. I delayed my exit, hoping they would forget about me, but, as soon as I started for home, "Billy know-it-all" followed me until I was out of earshot.

I was crushed. I thought I had lost my friends forever. The rift was soon patched up, but I learned from it: You could be ever so smart in school and still do very stupid things outside.

Switching to Caldwell Country Day School got me into the fourth social world. Here, my social activities centered around Dick Colman, who later became football coach at Princeton University. He was not only the best athlete among us; he was also the most popular with the girls. In fact, whenever I got interested in a girl and confided that interest to Dick, he would find her more attractive than he had previously, and soon she would be "Dick's girl." That went on until I switched my interest to one of Dick's cousins. The family relationship protected me from competition, but, as soon as Dick told her about my interest, she became very elusive.

Long before the era of Little Leagues managed by adults, we organized and controlled our own activities. Most afternoons and some evenings during the summer, we would gather on the vacant lot on Overlook Road to play baseball or touch football. (None of us had the helmets and padded uniforms for what we called tackle football.) We never had the eighteen or twenty-two boys needed for two baseball or football teams, but we adapted the games for however many showed up. We made our own rules and more or less lived by them.

Since none of us could pitch the ball over the plate regularly, we dispensed with balls and strikes and therefore had no need for an umpire. The rule was that a batter could swing or not as he chose. This often led to arguments, with the pitcher yelling, "What are you waiting for?" and the batter yelling, "Come on, get it over the plate!"

Since none of us owned a catcher's mask, nobody was willing to stand right behind the plate. We took turns farther back, trying to catch the ball on the first bounce. Since this would have made it too easy to steal bases, we made a rule against stealing.

I was never the leader of any boys' group, but I did demonstrate some ability to link up groups. The high point of my organizing activity came when I got together a baseball team by linking up boys from Overlook Road and boys from Caldwell Country Day School. I even went beyond those two groups and recruited the best pitcher in the eighth grade at West Caldwell School.

I had chosen Dick Colman as captain, since he was the best player except for our pitcher. Then disaster struck. On the day I had scheduled a game with another informally organized team, Dick had to go on a Boy Scout hike. I was stunned to think that a key player would let his team down for Boy Scouts. I had been a Boy Scout myself. In fact, the scoutmaster had told me that I had done better on the Tenderfoot test than any boy he knew, but after that triumph, I rested on my laurels and eventually dropped out.

I refused to let Dick's defection cancel the game. This would be real baseball, since we now had a pitcher who could find the plate and a catcher with a catcher's mask. That meant recruiting an umpire, and I found an adult willing to serve. As the tallest among us and therefore the best target, I played first base. I didn't distinguish myself at bat or in the field, but the game did go on—and we won!

My father encouraged my interest in sports. On several occasions he took me to the national tennis championship matches at Forest Hills, in Queens, so I got to see the great players of the 1920s, from Bill Tilden and Billy Johnson, to the Frenchmen René Lacoste, Henri Cochet, and Jean Borotra, who took the Davis Cup away from the Americans. My father took me to one New York Giants game and to one when the Yankees were playing the St. Louis team then known as "the hapless Browns." That game was disappointingly one-sided, but I saw both Babe Ruth and Lou Gehrig hit home runs.

I realized early on that I would never be the athlete that my father was. It was only in tennis that I was better than other boys my age—and that mainly because none of the boys I knew played the game as regularly as I did.

I never had any urge to become a boxer, but, if I was not to be considered a "sissy," I would have to learn to fight. When I was about ten and not getting along with my friend Robbie Vogel, the older boys next door tried to toughen me up by promoting a fight between us. When neither of us struck a blow, they pushed us together, and then Robbie hit me hard on the nose. End of fight. As I struggled to hold back the tears, Robbie turned to run away. While I cried out that it wasn't fair, Joe Boucle caught up with Robbie and beat him up.

Some time later, Robbie, Ed, and I picked a fight with another boy our own age and size. My uncle John was visiting at the time, and I was trying to explain to him why this was a fair fight. It was not really three against one, I said, because we had taken turns hitting the other fellow. Uncle John acted as if he did not understand and asked me to explain. By the time I had told the story the second time, I realized I had not even convinced myself.

I concluded that I would have to find some way of becoming a man without mastering the "manly art of self-defense." Fortunately, I seldom encountered situations when fistfights were forced upon me.

5. High School

My father returned to teaching in 1924, at the City College of New York (CCNY) in the Bronx. A few years later, he took a position at Brooklyn College. Unfortunately, when its new campus was built, at the end of the subway line, John faced a daily commute of at least five hours. He and my mother decided to move from Caldwell.

My parents were determined to move to the community offering me the best education available within commuting range of Brooklyn College. And for social as well as financial reasons, my parents preferred a public school.

The choice was Bronxville, in Westchester County. Under the leadership of Superintendent Willard W. Beatty, who later became U.S. commissioner of Indian Education, the Bronxville schools enjoyed a reputation as one of the best and most progressive public school systems in the country.

Bronxville was a marked contrast to Caldwell. Bronxville's population of about six thousand was all wedged into one square mile, tucked in between Yonkers and Tuckahoe. Bronxville had its tree-lined streets and lawns around its houses but hardly any open spaces except for the school athletic fields. I missed the open country spaces surrounding Caldwell. And whereas Caldwell had a heterogeneous population, from farmers and local businesspeople to commuters, Bronxville was overwhelmingly a town for commuters.

Bronxville was said to have the highest average per capita family income of any town in the country. But it also had a few moderately priced duplex homes and apartments for people of "modest means." My parents did not like the idea of settling among so many rich people, but the appeal of the school was decisive.

I began life in Bronxville with a head start. Through my Uncle John, who had worked under Edmund Ezra Day at the Rockefeller Foundation, we met the Day family. My parents and the Days became close friends and frequently got together to play bridge. Emerson Day became my best friend and frequent companion on the tennis courts. I met other friends through him, but he was a year older and a grade ahead of me, so that my social circle was not based in my own class. The girl I found most attractive was also in the class ahead of me. Continuing the pattern I had established with Dick Colman in Caldwell, she was attached to Emerson Day.

We brought a dog with us from Caldwell. I told my younger friends that Jolly was a triple breed—which impressed them until their parents informed them that such a lineage was no distinction. He was a handsome animal, with the brown color of a collie, the short hair and build of a German shepherd, and just a touch of bulldog, which showed in his slightly bowed legs. He had a white streak between his ears, four white paws, and a white tip on his tail. Jolly was the friendliest dog in Bronxville. Since dogs were not allowed in school, I tried to keep him away, but one morning he sneaked after me, on the other side of a long hedge, and I did not spot him until I was across the street from school. After that, he would find his way there on his own and follow me to classes. Since he would just lie down beside me, the authorities made an exception for him.

Bronxville had a much better extracurricular program than Caldwell. In sports, there were intramural teams below the varsity level for boys of all ages and weights. I was tempted to go out for football, but at six feet three inches in height and only 130 pounds at sixteen, I was persuaded that football was not a sensible sport for me. I was a reasonably good shooter in basketball—but only if no defenders were around to disturb my concentration. When Bronxville established interscholastic tennis in my junior year, I played number 1 on a mediocre team.

I did attract the attention of the head of the physical education department with a long interview in the school paper with Bronxville resident John Heisman, who had introduced the forward pass to football and whose name is attached to the annual award given to the best college player.

In dramatics, I played the male lead in *The Romancers*, a slight one-acter by Edmond Rostand, author of *Cyrano de Bergerac*. My parents told me I had acted very well and shouldn't worry over my one mistake. That came at the climax of the play, when the heroine is about to be abducted in a sedan chair. Hearing her cries for help, the hero dashes in, vanquishes the abductors in a sword fight, and wins the girl. Waiting in the wings, ready to bound on stage when I heard the heroine scream, I reached for my sword—only to discover I had left it in the dressing room! I dashed downstairs, grabbed the sword, and raced back a minute late for my entrance.

Schoolwork provided few frustrations and many satisfactions. The teachers sought to stimulate us intellectually and to encourage individual initiative. In some subjects, they laid out the lessons for a whole year in advance. By accelerating our learning, we could gain time for other studies or to pursue other interests within school. Covering four years of French in two years gave me time in my senior year for my most valuable learning experience.

The *Bronxville Press*, which appeared on Tuesdays and Fridays, was edited by Paul Lambert, who had been a reporter on the daily newspaper the *New York World*. Each year he hired a high school senior to cover school news. When I got this job, it provided me with a great opportunity and also taught me the valuable discipline of meeting deadlines: Sunday night for Tuesday's paper, Wednesday night for Friday's paper. Paul Lambert was an ideal editor and boss. He guided me into the craft of journalism and encouraged me to write more and to expand the scope of my coverage. He even suggested that I write personal columns, one on sports, one on other topics. The second column, "The Whyte Line," led me into a role closer to that in my professional career than anything I did in college.

The common pattern of writing personal tidbits about pupils and teachers did not appeal to me. Rather, I pursued the continuing controversy in Bronxville, as elsewhere, between those committed to traditional education and those pressing for more flexible and progressive alternatives. Paul Lambert was on the progressive side, whereas the rival weekly was solidly in the conservative camp.

I suggested to Lambert that I get involved in the controversy by writing about "common misconceptions about Bronxville education." He told me that was a bad idea. It could put the progressive forces in a defensive position and strengthen the enemy. I don't recall whether it was he or I who suggested the alternative, but for the rest of the year I wrote weekly columns based on visits to elementary school classes from kindergarten through sixth grade, where I observed classroom activities and interviewed the teachers.

I never asked permission from the authorities; I simply began visiting classes. At the start of each visit, I would explain to the teacher what I wanted to do. At first, the teachers were surprised, but no one objected. After my columns began to appear, I learned that teachers I had not visited were unhappy over being neglected.

At the end of the school year, Superintendent Beatty told me that he was worried when he first heard that a high school senior was poking into elementary classes, but now he wanted me to know that I had written the best descriptions he had seen of the educational program he and the teachers were trying to develop. Beatty gathered the columns together and printed them in a school bulletin, entitled *Bill Whyte Visits the Elementary School*. Thus, I published my first research report in 1931, at the age of sixteen. On its cover is a photograph of tall, gangling Bill Whyte in knickers, sitting in a first grader's chair behind a circle of little readers, peering between my knees, poised to furnish the word when the fingers moving on the page indicated that a child was stuck. This was a staging of an actual scene when I visited a first grade and was labeled "posed after the event."

Beyond the valuable experience, I also was earning money: eight cents an inch. One month when I got up to full steam, turning in about twenty double-spaced pages of copy every Sunday night, I earned fifty dollars—a lot of money for a high school senior in those days. The experience also paid off in getting me up to speed in touch typing, and it inoculated me against writer's block. Whenever I know what I want to write, the words seem to flow easily onto the page.

One of my news stories, a report on a science lecture, won first prize in the Associated Press's National High School Awards annual contest. That was nice, but publication of *Bill Whyte Visits the Elementary School* meant much more to me. On graduation, I tied with a girl for the highest grade point average, but still my newspaper work was the most rewarding experience of my high school years.

6. Travels in Europe

When my father got back into teaching in 1924, he felt the need to immerse himself again in Germany, so we took summer trips there and to other parts of Europe in 1925, 1927, and 1929. We could hardly afford the expense, but we crossed the ocean tourist class, traveled third class on the continental railroads, and stayed at pensiones rather than hotels.

I was the envy of my friends after my first trip abroad, but now I think I could well have done without these "cultural advantages." The first summer, when I was only eleven, we made a grand tour in which we took in all the noteworthy museums and cathedrals—and some that did not seem that noteworthy to me. Although I found adult conversation more interesting than the average boy my age, I now felt the loneliness of an only child. My memories are a blur of museums and cathedrals, trains, one airplane flight in which I got very airsick, dingy pensiones, and finally three weeks in Leipzig, where the pensione served Wiener schnitzel and cheesecake for lunch every day. I have never overcome my aversion to Wiener schnitzel, and it took many years before I could appreciate cheesecake.

During our 1925 trip, we were joined by the Von Klenzes in Germany. Camilo Von Klenze was then chairman of the German department at CCNY, and it was he who had lured my father back into teaching. During one museum visit, Camilo served as my guide toward an appreciation of impressionist paintings. I was fascinated to find that a painting which, when viewed close up, seemed to be nothing more than dots and splotches of color, could convey such a luminous and lively impression of landscape and people when seen from the appropriate distance.

The highlight of each trip to Europe was the final two weeks, when we visited my third cousins in Bromley, just outside London. My mother had made the connection with this branch of the Whyte family when she and my father were studying in Berlin. Isabel told John that a Marjorie Whyte was staying in her pensione and wondered whether they were related. They were delighted to discover that their ancestry traced back to the same couple in Kinross, Scotland.

The Whytes were an extraordinary family. Mrs. Whyte was widowed and had four daughters in their twenties and thirties, all of whom averaged six feet tall. After dinner, we often moved to the music room of their spacious home, where we would enjoy listening to Mrs. Whyte's daughters as they played in a string quartet and my father sang. The daughters also played a good game of tennis.

During the 1929 trip, Emerson Day came with us. That provided me with a friend, a tennis partner, and a fellow student, since Father had promised the Days he would give us German lessons throughout the trip. He ran an advertisement in the Baden-Baden paper for a German to give us the lessons, and although the pay was modest, he received more than twenty replies. Albert Bauer, a schoolteacher, clinched the job by offering us the friendship of two sons, Helmut and Willi, about Emerson's and my age. As I wrote later for the *Bronxville Press*,

> We arranged to take a walk with them every afternoon, in which we would talk only German. During the month in Baden-Baden, we got good practice with them in conversational German, but even more important, Helmut and Willi became our good friends. With them we walked all around the heights surrounding Baden-Baden, visited ruined castles, swam in clear mountain pools, and ate lunch in the woods. Those weeks were the happiest I had ever spent in Europe.

Although my school grades were never as good as my father's, he generally assumed that I was doing my best. Now, whereas Emerson was giving him errorless exercises, my own were sprinkled with mistakes. Once he took me aside to say that my errors were not due to lack of ability but to simple carelessness. If I took pains to review my work carefully before turning the papers over to him, I would also do flawless work. Buckling down, I found that he was right. From then on, I got everything right—at least on my German exercises. And the incident did not lead me to think my father was expecting more of me than I was able to deliver.

My father had his sabbatical in 1931–32 so we went abroad for the whole academic year. I was ready to enter college, but, since I had skipped a grade in elementary school, delaying college a year only put me back to where Mother thought I should have been all along, with my age-mates.

When I told my *Bronxville Press* editor, Paul Lambert, about our travel plans, he asked me to write a weekly column from Europe about anything that interested me. I agreed but suggested that I might be entitled to a 25 percent raise—from eight to ten cents an inch—and Paul agreed. As a result of my column, now called "Personally Conducted," I became the first (and last) foreign correspondent for the *Bronxville Press*.

The assignment was ideal. I wrote about my personal experiences, about our German friends, and about the political and economic trends and problems of a nation in the depths of the depression and bitterly divided between those supporting the Nazis and those favoring the Social Democrats, who were struggling to block the impending dictatorship of Adolf Hitler.

We first settled in Partenkirchen, a beautiful mountain town in Bavaria, which would be the site of the 1936 Winter Olympics. We stayed in the Hospiz, a small hotel-pensione on the edge of town, next door to a boys' private school, the Jugendlandheim Tatkraft. (*Jugendlandheim* means "country home for youth," and *Tatkraft* means "energy.")

The school director agreed that I could sit in on whatever classes I thought I could handle, beginning with earlier grades and moving in with boys my own age when my German permitted. At first, I felt somewhat at sea and participated little in class, but the boys and teachers seemed to accept me as a welcome novelty. Thinking I would have an advantage in a Shakespeare class, I volunteered to read a passage aloud. I was greeted first by suppressed giggles and then by roars of laughter. The teacher had learned his English in England, and my American accent seemed funny.

My first efforts at reciting in German—a poem I had memorized—also provoked amusement. I resolved then that I would have to struggle to sound more like a German.

The Jugendlandheim was reported to be progressive, but I was impressed with the formality of teacher-student relations and the tight control over artistic expression. When the bell rang and the teacher entered the classroom, all the boys stood up and remained standing until the teacher sat down. In my first art class, we had a leaf in front of us, yet the teacher instructed us mechanically to first draw a pentagon and then, step by step, to fill in the details according to instructions.

In my columns for the *Bronxville Press*, I interpreted what had happened to Germany following the loss of World War I, the near-starvation years of the allied blockade, the catastrophic inflation of the early 1920s, which wiped out people with fixed incomes, and then the Great Depression, deepening into the

1930s. I personalized my stories by concentrating on three families: the Von Hausens, the Cossoneaus, and the Bauers. My father had met the first two in his student days. We had met the Bauers during our trip to Germany in 1929.

The Von Hausens had risen from a precarious lower-middle-class position to higher status and greater affluence by taking advantage of the inflation and contacts with relatives who were farmers. While so many others were close to starvation, the Von Hausens received enough food from relatives to survive and even to begin a business of canning vegetables, fruits, and jellies. As the business grew, the family bought two small factories and a store, for which they paid only trifling sums as the currency depreciated. Even in the depressed economy of the early 1930s, the Von Hausens were rich.

The Cossoneau story was one of family tragedy. On his death, Herr Cossoneau had left his wife and daughter, Marguerite, with investments sufficient to maintain an upper-middle-class way of life. The family's money had been in what were then thought to be the safest investments: city, state, and national government bonds. Germany's inflation had practically wiped these out, so that some were reinstated at only 10 percent of their former value.

Marguerite had never held a job, but she pieced together a very small income with sewing jobs and by occasionally selling a short story to a magazine. In a few years, the money from the bonds would be used up.

Frau Cossoneau once said to us, "Every day that I live now, I take away from Marguerite money she could live on. I might as well die today as tomorrow or a year from now. To me it makes no difference, but to my daughter—I am robbing her of her chance to live."

When we returned to Baden-Baden, I renewed my contact with the Bauer family. The father still had his teaching job, but he was a staunch Social Democrat and worried about what could happen to him and his family if Hitler came to power.

Willi had completed three years of study to become a schoolteacher. He had four more years of practice teaching and further study before he would be eligible for a state teaching position. He estimated that he would have to wait six more years after that before there would be a job opening.

Helmut had good academic grades and wanted to study economics in the university but had been denied admission because the field was already overcrowded. He had one more year to go in the university and then had a year of training as a practice teacher in Baden-Baden. After that, he would return to his studies for three more years. He would be qualified to teach public school then but expected he would have to wait six more years to secure an opening.

Willi and Helmut were typical of German youth who were striving for professional careers. In practically any field, the applicants far outnumbered the jobs that were available.

I realized that I could convey the condition and problems of a nation much better through such personal stories than through simple accounts of facts and figures. This storytelling mode carried over into my professional career as I focused on particular individuals and groups to explain the functioning of industrial and agricultural organizations.

Over the years at home, I had heard my parents, relatives, and their friends discussing German history, politics, and economic development. I could have passed any examination on the main clauses of the Versailles Treaty—and on what was wrong with it—from the German point of view. I knew that Germany had not only lost its African colonies but also territory in the heart of Europe: the provinces of Alsace and Lorraine to France, although the majority of Alsatians were ethnic Germans; the Sudetenland of German-speaking people to what was becoming Czechoslovakia; and the Polish corridor, giving a revived Poland an outlet to the sea; and it had temporarily lost the Saar Valley, the heart of German heavy industry. The treaty also imposed enormous reparations on Germany—sums that could be paid only if the victorious allies opened their markets to German imports, which, of course, they were unwilling to do. I knew also that the treaty required the demilitarization of the Rhineland and finally—the ultimate indignity—required Germany to assume full responsibility for causing the First World War.

As I settled down in Partenkirchen, I began learning how the Germans themselves regarded the treaty and the subsequent course of their history. My teachers at the Jugendlandheim were so bitterly divided between pro- and anti-Nazis that they had agreed not to discuss politics even among themselves, but they seemed to welcome the opportunity to unburden themselves to an outsider. I also found occasion to interview men I met through the Hospiz.

I got the impression that Germans were unanimous in their convictions regarding what was wrong with the Versailles Treaty but were sharply divided over what to do about it. I was particularly struck with the depth of feeling attached to the "war guilt" clause. This gained the allies nothing in money or territory and yet the Germans would use it as a great rallying cry among those thirsting for military revenge.

Focusing on the current scene, I paid special attention to Adolf Hitler and his National Socialist party. Besides reading the newspapers and interviewing Germans of all political persuasions, I read a biography of Hitler by one of his sympathetic followers and then wrote four columns on the Führer, his program, and his party.

What I read and heard did not win me over to Hitler, but at least I did take him seriously. After the first two columns appeared, Ignatius D. Taubeneck, my high school social studies teacher, who was also a popular public lecturer on current events, told the *Bronxville Press* that readers of my columns had learned more about Hitler and his program than they could have picked up in two months of reading the fragmentary pieces that appeared in the daily newspapers. With due regard to his hometown bias, Taubeneck might have been right. When we left for Europe late in the summer of 1931, American newspapers had not yet started taking Hitler seriously. They paid more attention to the outrageous things he said than to the serious possibility that this wild man might take power in Germany.

Although I gave full coverage to Hitler's anti-Semitic policies, I was not convinced that, once in power, he would actually implement his program. Like many Germans, both pro- and anti-Nazi, I thought his program might be mainly political demagoguery, useful for gaining power but less extreme when he had to face the problems of governing the country. It was hard to imagine a political leader who would become so fanatical that, toward the end of World War II, he would divert troop trains from the Eastern Front so as to maximize the number of Jews he could ship to "the final solution" in the gas chambers.

I struck up a most interesting conversation with an old German count at the Hospiz. A strong nationalist, he had no use for Hitler personally yet saw him as a means of restoring Germany as a great power. The count predicted that a Hitler-led government would send German troops into the Rhineland.

I asked, "If Germany moves troops into the Rhineland, what will France and Britain do?"

"Nothing," he replied. Unfortunately, he was right.

To improve my German, I had resolved not to read anything in English. I weakened when my parents received as a Christmas present a new best-seller, *The Autobiography of Lincoln Steffens*. That book influenced me more in my eventual professional work than anything else I had ever read. The famous political muckraker had grown up in an upper-middle-class family, sharing much of the same cultural milieu as I had experienced, and he had the same commitment to political and economic reform that I had absorbed from my parents. Still, as he was investigating city politics, he was able to get "corrupt politicians" to talk freely and with apparent frankness. Without abandoning his own ethical standards, he was less interested in condemning individuals than in understanding how they saw the world and how they explained their behavior. He even found that, without approving of their behavior, he could like and respect some of them—and also learn from them. Maybe someday I could get such people to talk to me.

7. College Life

My parents selected Swarthmore College for me, and I did not object. They had been attracted by a great innovator in higher education, Frank Aydelotte, Swarthmore's president in the 1920s and 1930s. He introduced the honors program to the college.

Swarthmore is a small coeducational college founded by members of the Society of Friends and strongly supported by Quaker families. There is a Quaker meetinghouse on campus, but, in my period, at least half the students were non-Quakers, and the college exerted no religious pressures on its students. Although I never joined the Society of Friends, I had a high regard for their religious and social values.

Swarthmore, located in the suburbs of Philadelphia, was blessed with a beautiful campus. A spacious lawn and tree-lined walk sloped up from the suburban railroad station to Parrish Hall, where rustic woodlands dropped down to Crum Creek on the other side of the campus. Academic and social life revolved around Parrish Hall's administrative offices, classrooms, recreation area, and two floors for women freshmen and sophomores. Parrish was flanked by the library and by Clothier Hall, for large meetings.

My parents would have found the money to finance my education, but Swarthmore awarded me a five hundred–dollar-a-year scholarship, which it gave to five incoming students each year regardless of their families' ability to pay. Swarthmore agreed to hold the scholarship for me until I returned from Europe in 1932.

My parents had succeeded in raising me to be independent and self-sufficient—perhaps too self-sufficient, as I look back now on my early years. In just about three hours on the Pennsylvania and New York Central railroads, I could have been home for almost any weekend, yet I went home only for college vacations.

Besides mailing my laundry home, I wrote weekly letters. I described not only what I was doing but also how I felt about everything from my studies and athletic activities to girls. I asked Mother and Father to keep my letters— probably an unnecessary request to doting parents—because I might sometime later want to reflect on this period of my life. If I could write best from my own experience, as Mother had told me, then it seemed important to document that experience while I was living it. Thus, I was really writing to myself as much as to my parents.

In college, I found myself pulled between two competing urges: the need to establish my own identity and the desire to be accepted by my fellow students. As a freshman, to symbolize my individuality, I sometimes wore a beret. No other student wore such headgear. Furthermore, my beret was not of the conventional black or dark blue but a bilious light green, which was visible hundreds of yards away. If I had it to do over again, I would junk that beret and find some less blatant way to establish my identity.

A major clash between my competing urges occurred just a few weeks into my freshman year, during the fraternity rushing period. Swarthmore had five national fraternity houses on campus and one local fraternity house off-campus. My egalitarian values did not fit with an institution that took some men in and excluded others; further, there was no need for fraternities to house students since nearly all the male students lived in Wharton Hall, an old U-shaped three-story building. Still, fraternities were a focal point of much of the college's social life.

During rushing, which began soon after college started, I set aside my reservations about fraternities—but then received only two bids: one from the off-campus fraternity, the other from Phi Sigma Kappa, neither of which was my first choice. Disappointed, I wavered over my decision but finally accepted the bid from Phi Sigma Kappa. The local fraternity had an interesting group of intellectuals, and two of my friends, John Seybold and Earle Edwards, accepted its bid, but with its off-campus location, it was too peripheral to campus activities. I liked the Phi Sig men, and I even found that two of them, Dick Hubler and Barry Freeman, shared my interest in writing.

Through my freshman year, I remained ambivalent about fraternities. I was troubled that there seemed to be such a sharp separation between our studies and our social lives. Since my friends and I did not live in the house, we generally went there only one evening a week for a business meeting, which was mainly dull and routine. I proposed that we shorten the meeting and devote most of our time to a discussion, to be led by one of our members on a topic of interest to

37

him. The proposal was accepted, and it did seem to liven up the meetings and lead later to informal discussions among smaller groups.

I entered sophomore year with a wholehearted dedication to making Phi Sigma Kappa a better fraternity. I got three Bronxville High School seniors interested in Swarthmore, and all three were admitted. Besides their intellectual qualifications, two of them were on the Bronxville tennis team, and the other was a star on the school baseball team.

I plunged into rushing with enthusiasm and high hopes, but the outcome was a great letdown. My fraternity made a respectable showing, but none of my Bronxville recruits accepted our bids. Their best freshman friends were pledging another fraternity—the one that had been my first choice. The letdown brought on some soul-searching and pangs of conscience. I realized that I had been so involved in the rushing process that I had engaged in some negative campaigning by running down rival fraternities. Not only was that unlikely to be effective, but, more important, it did not fit with my conception of myself. Rushing had distorted my sense of values. How could I have felt that building up my fraternity was such a vital part of my life? The experience did not turn me against Phi Sigma Kappa, but it did make me ambivalent again. The experience also indicated that I had a tendency to get so committed to an activity that my perspective on life got distorted. In the future, I would have to use better judgment to control the enthusiasm driving me toward particular objectives.

Events outside college jarred me out of my ambivalence. By sophomore year, my best friends were fellow classmates John Seybold, Earle Edwards, and Bob Greenfield. We all shared an interest in politics and social reform, and John and I shared an interest in writing.

In the late fall of that year, Earle told me about a Quaker project to invite Swarthmore students to spend a weekend at a settlement house in a Philadelphia slum district. I went along with John and Earle and several other Swarthmore students.

We managed to strike up a conversation with a man on the street, and he invited us into his home and that of a neighbor. Their houses, like others in the area, were three-story, wooden walk-ups that were poorly insulated and that lacked indoor plumbing. We saw people so poorly clothed that they could not go outdoors in the cold weather of early March, people going hungry on the inadequate home relief allotments, and a very sick man whom a premed student diagnosed as having tuberculosis but who was receiving no medical attention.

Returning to the comforts of Swarthmore, I could not get the slum and its people out of my mind. I called the settlement house and asked them to get a doctor for the sick man, but what more could I do?

I recorded the events in the slum in a 4-page single-spaced letter to my parents (March 10, 1934), by far the longest letter I had ever written. This was my conclusion:

> It is foolish to think of helping these people individually. There are so many thousands of them, and we are so few. But we can get to know the situation thoroughly. And that we must do. I think every man owes it to society to see how society lives. He has no right to form political, social, and economic judgments, unless he has seen things like this and let it sink in deeply.

After some days of soul-searching, I decided to resign from my fraternity. I informed Dave Davis, my roommate and fraternity brother, of my decision, and he urged me to take time to reconsider. I insisted on going ahead and even heightening the drama by reading a statement, "Resignation from the Fraternity System," at our next meeting.

The statement began by explaining that I had entered the fraternity with serious doubts but had tried to be a good member as long as I could. I had enjoyed my association with Phi Sigma Kappa and valued the friendships I had made. I then described the weekend in the slums, leading to the conclusion that we in college were too isolated from "actual life." My ambition was to become a writer, and I did not want to "write nice genteel stories about my own class," so I had to get to know and understand poor working people and the unemployed. While disclaiming any desire to become a social reformer, I said "I simply want to spend one day a week in helping as much as I can and learning as much as I can in the city."

The brothers of Phi Sigma Kappa responded more generously than I expected. They said I had been a good member, and they wanted to maintain contact with me. But my commitment to "actual life" lasted only a few weeks. College work was pressing, and I realized that I was not doing anything of much use to either Philadelphia or myself. I decided I would have to wait for a later opportunity to make a full-time commitment to slum life.

My junior year began with an anti-rushing campaign. Since thirteen men had resigned from their fraternities the year before and fraternity men were afraid that their whole system might be falling apart, some of us saw this as the time to strike the fatal blows. We arranged for evenings of discussion on fraternities, college life, and national and international affairs. Since the fraternities pledged only half their usual numbers that year, we may have had some impact, but they later regained their appeal and went on as before.

I directed my next reform efforts to the cause of eliminating dinks, the undersized colored caps freshmen were required to wear. Some of us managed to get the issue submitted to a total student body vote. We lost, but a few years later the dinks quietly passed away.

By now I had become a prime target of those I called "the rah-rah boys." I returned one evening to the room I shared with Earle Edwards to find that our mattresses had been thrown out the window, the beds overturned, and drawers emptied out and their contents strewn around. This only reinforced my commitment to undermine the campus social establishment.

In the spring of my junior year, I hatched a plot against the Book and Key, the senior honorary society. This was a self-perpetuating organization, entirely independent of the college administration. Member qualifications were secret, but it was easy to infer them from those chosen: athletes and big activity men. Book and Key met in a windowless, reddish stucco building on the edge of campus. Every Thursday night in the Parrish Dining Hall, at precisely seven minutes to 7:00, the seven members of Book and Key would suddenly rise from their chairs and march in a line out and over to the society's house.

Selection of new members was carried out ceremonially in front of Parrish Hall amid a crowd of students gathered for the event. On the appointed evening, at precisely seven minutes to 7:00, the seven members of Book and Key would march single file from the Clothier cloisters until they reached the crowd. They would then split up and weave through the crowd until one of them had tapped a junior and run with him back to Clothier Hall, followed by the other Book and Key members. They repeated the ritual every seven minutes until they had tapped all seven recruits.

I had decided that if I could add one more touch of foolishness to the ceremony, Book and Key might appear as ridiculous to everyone else as it did to me. Armed with a tin can attached to a long string and a fishhook, I took up a position in the crowd behind a man I was sure would get tapped, slipped the hook onto the back of his coat, and waited. When the moment came, he and his tapper ran off to Clothier with the tin can bouncing behind him, while a fellow conspirator recorded the event with a movie camera. I escaped unnoticed. The event provoked some discussion, but Book and Key survived for some years after me.

My next reform effort was also directed at campus social life. I had been troubled by the pattern prevailing at the regular Saturday-night record dances.

Dances followed the cut-in custom, which divided the women into two classes: a very few who were so popular that they could not dance more than a few steps before being cut in on and the others, who tended to be left out because whoever danced with them might be "stuck" with them for a long time. Part of my concern was personal: I had no skill at "small talk" and so was at a loss as to what to say when I did cut in on a popular girl.

I may never have taken any action had Osmund Molarsky not involved me in one of the most embarrassing experiences of my campus social life. He liked a girl I shall call Alice, but she did not like him. He did not think she deserved to be on the social sidelines. If I would take her to one of the Saturday record dances, he said, he would guarantee that I would not get "stuck" with her.

Halfway through our first dance, someone cut in on me. With Oz manipulating the stag line, the pace of the cutting in accelerated until I could hardly say a complete sentence to Alice before someone took her away from me.

Although I knew the cause of Alice's sudden popularity, I nevertheless found myself caught up in the spirit of the evening. Now Alice looked more attractive and desirable than ever before, and I felt frustrated because I had so little time with her.

Oz was not content to let well enough alone. During the dance, he had asked some of the men who had cut in on Alice for feedback on their experience. There was general agreement that she was attractive, and she certainly was popular. Still, they were puzzled. She seemed at a loss for small talk, and the fellows did not know what to make of her.

The next day, Oz congratulated Alice on her popularity but then said he wanted to offer her a lesson in small talk. This upset Alice, who countered, "I guess I did all right at the dance without any help from you." That upset Oz, and he blurted out the story of how he had manipulated the stag line.

I could not bring myself to face Alice after that, but I did brood over what this incident indicated about the inhumanity of the prevailing social pattern. My brooding led me to write a letter to Swarthmore's weekly newspaper, the *Phoenix* (January 26, 1936), which I signed "Median." I argued against the complete separation in boy-girl relations between the intellectual and social sides of college life. Although my letter provoked a response or two caricaturing my position as advocating a ban on all social activity except intellectual conversation, I did strike a responsive chord among some of the students. And when the editor leaked my identity, one of the most popular girls came to me to express her agreement with my position. We invited some other students to meet with us to discuss what might be done, but we were all at a loss for ideas. That meeting ended my campus reform efforts.

During college, I limited my athletic participation to tennis. In my freshman year I managed to win the number 6 position. In later years, I moved up to the number 3 and 2 positions in singles and played on the number 2 doubles team.

Writing continued to be one of my chief interests. I considered trying out for the *Phoenix*, but after my experience with the *Bronxville Press*, that seemed a comedown.

The *Manuscript*, the literary magazine, presented an opportunity, however, that kept me involved throughout my college years. Those interested in writing stories, plays, and poems met for an evening every two weeks in the home of English professor Robert E. Spiller. A quiet and unassuming man, Spiller was uninspiring in the classroom, but warm, understanding, and encouraging with one student or a small group. On those evenings at Robert Spiller's we would read aloud pieces we had written and discuss their strengths and weaknesses. Students took the lead in the discussions, but Spiller would pull the threads of discussion together and add words of his own on how the story or poem might be improved.

I became editor of the *Manuscript*, but my most vivid memories take me back to things I wrote—particularly a one-act play I called *The Outsider*. Every spring our drama teacher organized a one-act play-writing contest. Judges selected four to be produced, and, during my junior year, *The Outsider* was one of them.

According to the rules of the contest, it was up to the playwright to recruit his own director and actors. My leading character, Tim, was a student whose intellectual and artistic interests left him out of the mainstream of college life. My first choice for Tim was Allen Tucker, who had had a good deal of acting experience. He tried out for other roles, but I managed to talk him into playing Tim. All went well until just a few days before the performance, when Allen told me he had to drop out. Tim was too much like himself, and he couldn't stand reinforcing that image on campus. I decided to play the part myself.

The play went well, and our drama coach told me my job of acting was one of the best she had seen by a college student. But then I discovered that some of the students didn't think I was acting at all; they thought I was just playing myself. I had put too much of Bill Whyte into the part and had mistakenly assumed that the other side of me—the varsity tennis player—would protect me from being seen as the Outsider.

In my senior year, John Seybold and I teamed up to write a play about the problems of Swarthmore women who were left on the social sidelines. With an all-female cast, it was a challenge to make the plot and dialogue seem real. During my college years, I entered three plays in the writing contest, but only this one won first prize. The female reviewer of the *Phoenix* reported that the play was an authentic portrayal of an important aspect of college life, though she added that the climax, in which our leading character threw herself out a third-story window, seemed overdrawn. (A year earlier, a girl had thrown herself in front of a train, after her long-term relationship with a Swarthmore man had broken up.)

I got further encouragement for my fiction-writing ambitions from *Story*, a magazine with the prestige in literary circles to attract some of the best work of aspiring young authors. In fact, some then well-established authors of novels had been published first in *Story*. The magazine had announced that it was having a short story competition for college students and that it would award two cash prizes, plus publish the winning stories. I submitted "The Outsider," a story reworked from my one-act play. I did not win, but the magazine awarded me with an unannounced third prize of ten dollars. Much more important than the money, *Story* promised to publish "The Outsider."

For years after leaving college, I waited in vain for the publication of my story. When I inquired, co-editor Martha Foley assured me that the magazine planned to publish it but that somehow it had not fitted into any issue so far. And then the magazine went out of business.

Among all my other activities, I did find time, off and on, to pay attention to several girls. None of these relationships developed into serious long-term commitments—with that limitation being at least as strong on the female side as on mine. I encountered the now-familiar pattern that the girls I liked best liked someone else more. I also did not plan my social life well enough to build my relationships. I would become so absorbed in my studies that I would fail to call a girl for a Saturday-night date until the last moment, when it was embarrassing for me to call and embarrassing for her to admit that she had not already been asked out by someone else. A girl whom I went out with over several weeks accused me of being more interested in my studies than in her—and I had to admit that she was right. Worried about my relations with girls, I wrote this interpretation in a letter home:

> Around here I have the reputation of being unusually stable emotionally. John Seybold calls it emotional complacency. I am steady and methodical. I am afraid there isn't anything exciting about me. I can bore a girl stiff—and I probably often do. I can't cut loose. I think everything out, and when I have thought a problem out, it is too

late to act, or else I act so methodically that there is no spirit in it. I have never been in love. Perhaps I need that. Perhaps I need to have someone come along and smash down my emotional defenses. This problem of temperament worries me. If I married a girl of my own temperament, I should die of boredom. But if I married a girl at a different temperamental pole, she might do the same. I don't know that this temperament rule always works out. I hope not. The case of Grandpa Van Sickle and Grandma is certainly encouraging. [He was silent, reserved; she was vivacious.]

I remember my senior year as a relaxed and sociable period. I could not think of any more aspects of college life that needed reforming. I had to study for the final examinations, but I felt well prepared. I had confidence in my own study methods and did not cram. I remember my father saying that, the night before winter examinations at the University of Wisconsin, he would go out skating on Lake Mendota. In my four college years, I never stayed up past 10:30 studying.

During my senior year, my social life revolved around a house on the edge of campus, which had been converted to provide rooms for about twenty-four senior men. I roomed with John Seybold and Earle Edwards and came to enjoy my association with the other men also. Social life at the house centered on the game of Monopoly, to which our economics professor had introduced us, claiming that it would help us understand capitalism. Whatever the game's educational merits, we enjoyed it on many evenings.

I assume I annoyed many of my fellow students and made even more uncomfortable, but, of course, most of them simply ignored me. Even my best friends found me strangely different from my peers. Upon reading an early draft of this book, John Seybold wrote:

> What I didn't know about your early childhood was your mother's absence for a prolonged period, due to TB, and then your isolation from both parents due to your sleeping arrangements [on the far porch]. I wonder if that had something to do with your disposition toward analytical introspection, which is more pronounced in you than in anyone I have ever known—almost as if you decide what your emotions ought to be under given circumstances, and turn them on accordingly, perhaps after sharing this indecision with your associates.

Still I like to think that my more relaxed senior year helped humanize a too rigid and self-righteous Bill Whyte. As we talked and played together, I found I came to like many of those I had opposed on campus issues, and they seemed to warm up to me.

8. College Studies

On entering college, I thought I would major in political science. My only memory of political science takes me back to my first course with Robert C. Brooks, then known as a leading authority on the government and politics of Switzerland. Brooks was also a great enthusiast for everything Swiss. One of his first class assignments called for a brief paper on whether we would be citizens of Switzerland or of the United States.

My answer had nothing to do with the virtues and defects of the two governments and political systems. I reported that I did not want to become a big frog in a little pond. I aspired to be a big frog in a big pond.

I soon tired of R. C. Brooks, and a course in political theory further diminished my interest in political science since it seemed to consist of philosophical theorizing with little relation to political behavior. More than two decades would pass before Swarthmore would create a department of sociology and anthropology.

I never considered majoring in English. My interest in writing drew me to Professor Spiller, but I felt I could get what I wanted from him and his colleagues without concentrating on their field. I did pursue literary interests to the extent of taking a course on Goethe and one on French literature.

Introductory psychology seemed too miscellaneous to hold my interest, and I did not know there was such a thing as social psychology.

Philosophy baffled me. The introductory course was taught by an idealist, which meant I was trying to grapple with a picture of the world as if it all existed in the human mind.

My interest was turning to economics, even though the introductory course was not open to freshmen. Professors Clair Wilcox and Patrick Murphy Malin were well known on campus not only for their teaching but also for their commitment to linking social equity with economic progress.

In my sophomore year, a two-semester course provided my introduction to economics. I had learned that Professor Malin practically never gave any student an A. Although I had no sympathy for that perfectionist standard, I resolved to extract an A from Malin. I also figured out how to do it.

Malin gave open-book examinations, and he always drew his questions from recent stories in the *New York Times*. He would reproduce the lead paragraph of a story and then pose a question that required us to analyze the economic issues underlying the news item. I began developing my own clipping service. Like the other students, I came armed with my economics books for quizzes and examinations, but I also brought a set of folders holding my newspaper clippings. After scanning the questions, I would check my files and pull out the clippings to match each question. The task would then be easy since my clipping would give me the balance of the story, in which the reporter had invariably done the analysis. Whatever the academic backgrounds of the reporters, they were better equipped to provide well-informed and sophisticated analyses than I was in an introductory course. Now all I had to do was put the interpretation in the newspaper into my own words. I took pride in adding a twist or two that I had figured out.

I got an A from Pat Malin but then felt guilty about it. Although I had broken no rules, my triumph did not reflect an exceptional command of economics but rather my ability to figure out a system to beat the professor.

No other class lent itself to my system, but the experience did help me develop a strategy for preparing for quizzes and examinations in other courses. If I knew in advance the questions I would have to answer, I would be prepared to write better answers. In several courses I organized my exam preparation around questions I asked myself. For each such question, I then outlined or wrote out my own answer. Generally, about half the instructor's questions paralleled my own. I found taking this active stance toward exam preparation improved my grades, but, more important, it gave me a stronger sense of having mastered the information and ideas in my courses.

Even with these study strategies, my grades for my first two years at Swarthmore were good but not outstanding. My average for the first two years was just slightly above B—including a well-deserved C in organic chemistry.

In my junior year, I entered the honors program, which freed about half of us from classes, substituting seminars that met once a week, often in the homes of professors. Each honors student took two seminars a week for a total of eight in the junior and senior years. We chose one major and two minor subjects, distributing the seminars among the subjects on a 4-2-2 or 3-3-2 basis. We had no midterm or final examinations for these seminars. Instead, toward the end of the senior year, honors students took comprehensive written and oral examinations given by outside examiners.

Instead of having each of our professors teach us and then determine what we had failed to learn, honors seminars were structured so that professors and students were on the same team, preparing to face the outside examiners. Of course, the examiners had to consult with our professors to determine the content of our studies, but our professors had no control over the selection of questions. In effect, the professors, as well as the students, were tested by the outside examiners. Final grades were given by the examiners: highest honors, high honors, honors, and pass in course.

For a student who did not need close supervision, this was an ideal program. Each seminar was organized around discussions of what we had been reading and of one or two major papers each student wrote during the semester. Other than the six hours a week in seminars, our time was entirely our own. The professor would give us some general guidance on readings, but we then had to work up a bibliography especially designed to focus on the topic we had selected. Now, for the first time, I could pursue problems in depth, and I enjoyed the supportive and stimulating experience of working with a professor and a small group of students. I decided to major in economics and minor in political science and American history.

The first semester's honors seminar with Clair Wilcox, "Government and Business," was my most absorbing college learning experience and also the one that had the greatest impact on my subsequent career. Each of us wrote two long papers for that seminar. The second was supposed to be on some topic in the field of state or local finance. Since I found none of the proposed topics interesting, I asked Wilcox if I could write on financing New York City. Wilcox agreed but said he could refer me to only one book on the subject.

I arranged to leave early for Christmas break so I could spend eight to ten days in the New York Municipal Library going over budgets and official reports. I followed up with the Citizens' Budget Commission, a privately financed watchdog agency, well equipped with its own documents and knowledgeable employees. I did not have the nerve to try to interview the mayor, but I did manage to conduct fairly productive interviews with several heads of city departments as well as with people at the commission.

My paper was due in the final seminar after Christmas vacation. Trying to figure out what I wanted to say and get it down in an eighty-eight-page paper—by far the longest I had ever written—made this a very high-pressure project. I just barely got the paper done in time to get a copy to Wilcox and carbons to the students so they could read it before the seminar meeting.

When Wilcox spent the first ninety minutes of the seminar on a general discussion of state and local finance, without any mention of my paper, I began to have doubts. But then, as I wrote home (January 19, 1935),

> Wilcox said, "Now we come to New York City." Thereupon he opened the paper and said, "This is a swell paper." Wilcox rarely gets enthusiastic. But after he had thought it over some more, he went on. "This is better than many Ph.D. theses I have seen at Penn. Of course, some of those theses aren't much good, but then . . . This is really a remarkable piece of work from someone spending part of his time for six weeks."

A few days after the seminar, Wilcox told me that the paper had the makings of something worth publishing, so that I should go ahead with revisions I already had in mind. On February 17, I wrote home:

> For the past ten days I have been spending part of my time reworking my paper on New York City. First I read the thing over carefully and made independently an outline of the logical sequence of sections. Then I rewrote certain sections, for which I had new material, and brought the whole thing up to date. As I finished each part, I handed it to the stenographic office to work on. Yesterday morning they finished it. The revised paper is 106 pages long, not counting bibliography. The typing bill was $20.63. You can thank God and the Economics Department that you don't have to meet that bill.

The typist provided me with eight copies, which I put in the best bindings I could find. I turned over three to Wilcox, one to be passed on to the president of Swarthmore, and another that the president had promised to send to Herbert Lehman, then New York's governor. I sent one to Walter Latzer of the Citizens' Budget Commission, who had helped me with the project. He responded with enthusiasm and asked for another copy.

Soon, I received another letter from Latzer, telling me that others on the commission had read the paper and were as enthusiastic about it as he was. He went on to predict "a very fine future" for me and offered to recommend me for a job with the commission after college. Governor Lehman also wrote, saying, "I shall read [the paper] at the first opportunity with very great interest. I have glanced through it and have already seen enough to make me confident that it is well done and that I shall enjoy reading it."

Wilcox suggested that I send a copy to the American Academy of Political and Social Science, publisher of the *Annals*, which also put out monographs. He knew the editor, Thorstein Sellin, and telephoned to see if he could interest him in my project.

In mid-May, Sellin informed me that *Financing New York City* would be the next bulletin in their series. He added that this was the first time the *Annals* had published anything by an undergraduate. After publication, I was told that I was the youngest author to have a manuscript in the New York Public Library.

Financing New York City led me to a summer job with the Citizens' Budget Commission, where I worked under George Bullock, the commission's director of public relations. He proposed that I undertake a study of the financing of the New York City colleges. Since my father taught at Brooklyn College, I realized that this could lead me into some awkward situations, but I naively assumed that I could avoid problems by getting the facts straight.

Soon after beginning to work with the administrative office of the city colleges, I encountered the problem that would derail me. Officials pointed out that their faculty salaries were indeed higher than those prevailing in most colleges but that professors in the city system also carried much higher teaching loads. The general pattern at the city colleges was five classes a week, they said, or fifteen teaching hours, whereas the pattern at most other colleges was nine to twelve hours.

It seemed to me that a systematic and objective study should not be limited to comparisons of salaries but should include equally solid comparisons of teaching loads. I suggested that the scope of my project be expanded. Bullock scoffed at the idea. Although I tried to make him see that college teaching required far more working time than classroom hours, he kept coming back to those fifteen teaching hours.

I tried to get around Bullock by writing letters from home to a number of colleges, requesting information on their teaching loads. I gave my home address, but one or two responses were addressed to me at the commission. When he discovered my duplicity, Bullock was furious.

I cannot now recall whether I quit or was fired, but my assignment never led to anything productive for me or for the commission. I departed with mixed feelings of self-righteousness and guilt. I felt I had tried to make my project an honest one, but I also realized I had let down Walter Latzer, who had helped me so much in preparing *Financing New York City* and had recommended me for the job, and I had deceived my boss.

Returning to Swarthmore, I had to think seriously about what I would be doing after college. Aydelotte was then president of the trust that administered the Rhodes scholarships, and he took it for granted that I would apply. When he heard to the contrary, he invited me to lunch to try to sell me on the cultural advantages of two years at Oxford, plus travel on the continent of Europe, plus the honor and prestige. I was flattered but not persuaded. My economics professors told me there was no outstanding economist attached to Oxford and that if I wanted to study in England, I should apply to the London School of Economics. Besides, I told Aydelotte, having already spent three summers and a full year in Europe, I had had far more cultural broadening than the average student. What I needed now was to deepen my understanding of my own country.

Fortunately, Aydelotte did not lose interest in me. In fact, he sent a letter and a copy of *Financing New York City* to a friend, Ralph J. Baker, a Harvard Law School professor. Baker was impressed with the publication and showed it to colleague Felix Frankfurter, then a distinguished Harvard Law School professor and later a justice of the Supreme Court. Naturally, they both assumed that I would want a career involving municipal finance and municipal government. In that case, they thought I should study at the London School of Economics. In a letter to Aydelotte, Baker went on to detail two other alternatives he had discussed with Frankfurter. One was to apprentice myself to A. A. Berle, then chamberlain of the New York City government. The other was to apply for a junior fellowship at Harvard.

On that last alternative, Baker, in a letter to Aydelotte, commented:

> I think that Felix puts this third because he does not feel that at this time there is any man here in this particular field to be of special value to Whyte. Of course, he would have complete freedom and a reasonably wide opportunity for associations and for study. The question is whether there is any one individual around whom his work would center for inspiration and guidance.

Students were not free to apply for the fellowship directly, but Baker advised Aydelotte to write a letter for me to Charles Curtis, one of the senior fellows involved in selecting the junior fellows.

Other career opportunities were now opening up for me. I was invited to Albany to discuss a possible job in New York State government, and Harold Phelps Stokes, then editor of the *New York Times*, invited me to lunch. He made no mention of a job offer, but I assumed our discussion could lead to one. I had thought seriously about journalism, and the *Times* would have been ideal for such a career.

This high-level attention was certainly flattering, but much of it was based on a false assumption: that I was interested in municipal finance. That was the topic Wilcox required for the paper. I was interested in New York City but not in municipal finance in general. I had enjoyed working on my finance project, but I did not see myself pursuing a career in the field. Other aspects of economics interested me more, and I was still not prepared to abandon my dreams of writing novels or plays.

The more I learned about the Society of Fellows, the more I was attracted to it. The society provided three years of support at the salary level of a Harvard instructor and complete freedom to work out my own study plans. A junior fellow could take any course or seminar at Harvard but at that time could not work for a Ph.D. while on the fellowship. That restriction was an advantage to me, since at the time I had no interest in an academic career; it seemed too dull to provide the adventures I still dreamed of. At the same time, since I came from an academic family and had been doing so well on the academic track, I might well have been sucked into accumulating credits toward a Ph.D. if I had been allowed to do so. The junior fellowship would free me to do what I really wanted to do: a close-up study of a slum district and let me get to know people and problems unfamiliar in my upper-middle-class environment.

When I won the fellowship, I learned that I was the first junior fellow in the four years since the Society of Fellows had been created to be selected straight out of college.

9. The Society of Fellows

I accepted Harvard's junior fellowship, but then, as if to hedge my bets, I spent the summer with my parents in Greensboro, Vermont, finishing the novel I had started in college. Since this could well have been my last chance to find out if I had what it took to be a professional writer of fiction, I stuck with the task until I could type "THE END," although I was beginning to realize that I did not have a publishable novel. Writing it reinforced the lesson I should have learned before: I could not write good fiction on a theme remote from my experience.

I moved to Harvard in 1936 before the opening of the fall semester so as to take in the Tercentenary, celebrating the three hundred–year history of the oldest university in the United States. The Tercentenary included formal speeches and seminar sessions presented by some of the world's most eminent natural and social scientists. I had looked forward to hearing Bronislaw Malinowski, who was, along with A. R. Radcliffe-Brown, the pioneer in creating a new framework for the study of social anthropology.

Up to that time, social anthropologists had been cataloging culture traits and tracing their diffusion from one tribe to another. Malinowski and Radcliffe-Brown had broken with this tradition in an attempt to develop a holistic view of society and culture, focusing on the interrelations of economic and political activities with family and kinship structures.

I had hoped to hear the great innovator build on his four-year study of the Trobrianders, make a case for his new research strategy—and then suggest some of its implications for the understanding of modern industrial communities. Instead, he focused on whether human nature inevitably doomed mankind to violent conflicts and wars. Citing evidence from various cultures, Malinowski argued that violence and warfare were not inevitable products of human nature but were shaped by cultural and social forces. Changes in cultures therefore could reduce or eliminate armed conflicts. I found this a comforting conclusion, but I was disappointed that Malinowski gave no indications of how social anthropology might help humans understand and change their cultures.

The Society of Fellows provided me with a bedroom, bathroom, and living room in Winthrop House on the Harvard campus. Though the arrangements were generous, I missed the common shower room at Swarthmore, which threw us all together and provided a base for making friends. Here I was surrounded mainly by undergraduates, but I never met any of them. Among them was John F. Kennedy; someone pointed him out to me as the son of the prominent financier and government official Joseph P. Kennedy.

Junior fellows were free to use the common room set aside for tutors, who worked closely with individual students, and I took my meals in the Winthrop House dining room with some of the tutors and with Henry Guerlac, another junior fellow who lived in Winthrop. The most memorable among the tutors was John Kenneth Galbraith, who came to be recognized as a leading economist and later established a reputation as a highly skilled writer and effective figure on the political scene. I enjoyed his sardonic wit and admired the way he could cut through what he called "the conventional wisdom" to reveal the underlying realities of political and economic problems. I also looked up to him physically, as he towered four inches over my six feet three.

The Society of Fellows was created by a small group led by a biochemist, Lawrence J. "L. J." Henderson. Others in that group were A. Lawrence Lowell, president of Harvard during the planning discussions for the society; John Livingston Lowes, professor of English; and Alfred North Whitehead, professor of philosophy. According to George C. Homans and Orville T. Bailey (1959: 5)

They felt that the heavy formal requirements for the [Ph.D.] degree were so many encumbrances on the best young scholars, and trammeled the most productive years of their lives. The ablest was stamped by the same press as the merely able. The Ph.D. program was a good school of apprentices, a poor school of originators. In our graduate schools, Lowell wrote, "We have developed into a mass production of mediocrity." Elsewhere he said, "I do not want to depreciate the Ph.D., but to diminish it as the sole road to teaching in an institution of higher learning. Nor do I wish to diminish the study for the Ph.D., but to provide an alternative path more suited to the encouragement of the rare and independent genius." For such men, both Henderson and Lowell thought, freedom was the best discipline.

The planning group looked abroad for ideas and particularly studied the Cambridge University Prize Fellows Program at Trinity College and the Fondation Tiers in France, but what they designed was not a copy of any existing program. (The Trinity College fellows were selected entirely from among undergraduates in that college, whereas the Harvard program was not limited to students at Harvard. To be sure, applicants from Harvard did have the inside track; fifty-seven out of the first eighty-five junior fellows were at Harvard at the time of their selection.)

The planning committee submitted its report in 1926, but the program could not be implemented without substantial financing. Lowell had been extraordinarily successful in raising money for Harvard, but he had failed to attract funds for the new program. As he was completing his long term as president, the Society of Fellows meant so much to Lowell that he refused to allow anything to block its establishment. As he later wrote, " 'The result was that, there being no visible source of the necessary funds, I gave it myself, in a kind of desperation, although it took nearly all I had' " (Homans and Bailey 1959: 19).

For newly appointed junior fellows, the induction ceremony at our first dinner together consisted of Chairman Henderson reading a statement of our obligations to advance science and scholarship. When I heard it, I had a momentary urge to shout, "Let me out of here." The emphasis on science and scholarship did not offend me, but I was struck by the absence of any reference to an obligation to make our learning useful to society. I said nothing, but I continued to wrestle over a way to reconcile my research interests with my social welfare concerns.

At the beginning of his term, each junior fellow was presented with a handsome solid-silver candlestick, based on a bronze design found in Holland by L. J. Henderson. The fellow's name was engraved into its base, along with the date of appointment. When one of us got married, the other junior fellows clubbed together to buy a second candlestick. This custom had been begun by the junior fellows themselves, since Henderson discouraged marriage until one was established in his career, and he did not consider the fellowship as constituting such establishment.

The only requirement of a junior fellow was that he attend Monday-evening dinners with the senior fellows, hardly an onerous duty. We met in quarters in Eliot House, reserved for such gatherings long before the society was established.

The dinner meetings followed a regular pattern. For the junior fellows, the action began with the tossing of salad in the pantry. George C. Homans and his special friends were in charge of this ritual and acted as if special expertise and occult knowledge were required.

Before dinner, senior and junior fellows, and sometimes invited guests, would meet in the living room over sherry, crackers, and cheese. After about a half-hour of sipping, munching, and conversing, a waiter would announce that dinner was served. Chairman Henderson would lead us into the dining room, where we sat on both sides of the U-shaped table. There were no fixed places, but it was an unwritten rule that senior fellows would not sit together, so that we juniors could take full advantage of the wisdom of our elders. Since I found most of the senior fellows interesting and stimulating, I appreciated the arrangement.

With the main course, we were served a Burgundy wine bought by Henderson on one of his trips to France. Following dessert, waiters passed around a box of Havana cigars, selected, of course, by Henderson. After dinner, port wine was served.

I enjoyed the food, wines, and above all the conversation. The physical and social arrangements made me feel privileged but also conveyed the message that I had to achieve something important.

The senior fellows were an impressive group, but Henderson stood out among them. For me and probably most of the junior fellows, he was the dominant figure. Earlier, he had been known to students as "old pink whiskers." By 1936, the pink had faded to gray, but whiskers, goatee, and sideburns still set off his round face, and he fixed his piercing eyes on all those who, he assumed, needed his firm guidance.

Having established his reputation as a scientist (his research was on the chemistry of blood), Henderson was also a self-appointed expert on sociology. His discovery (in French translation) of the works of the Italian economist and sociologist Vilfredo Pareto had led him into this field. Each year, Henderson taught a seminar on Pareto, and he also organized a course he called "Concrete Sociology." The title reflected his conviction that sociology was a fuzzy field and needed to be brought down to solid realities. The course consisted of lectures on cases drawn from experience and were presented by their principal actors. The most memorable such actor was Chester I. Barnard, who had been president of the New Jersey Bell Telephone Company. Encouraged by Henderson, he had written, and in 1938 published, *The Functions of the Executive*, considered an important contribution to organizational sociology. I was also impressed by Elton Mayo's account of the pioneering research at the Western Electric Company on morale and productivity, given some months before the 1939 publication of the classic *Management and the Worker* by Fritz J. Roethlisberger and William J. Dickson.

Although we had no course requirements, it was assumed that any social scientist would take Pareto's seminar, and some of the junior fellows in other fields also took it. Henderson conducted it as if it were a Bible lesson. He would read aloud from the text assigned for the day and then elaborate on its profound implications. Students participated in discussion but at some risk. If one's contribution seemed stupid to Henderson, he did not hesitate to point that out. There was no escape, for if we did not contribute, he would assume we were empty-headed, so we had to prepare our remarks carefully in advance.

"Concrete Sociology" provided no theoretical framework, but it did offer an ideal definition of the sociologist that I often referred to later: "The sociologist, like the physician, should have first, intimate, habitual, intuitive familiarity with things; secondly, systematic knowledge of things; and thirdly, an effective way of thinking about things."

Insofar as medical researchers benefit from experience in clinical practice, Henderson's definition suggested that the sociological researcher should also become involved in practice. Henderson rejected that conclusion, drawing on the first principle of the early Greek physician Hippocrates: "Do no harm." I said that this seemed to mean "Do nothing." Henderson denied that inference and claimed most sociologists had learned practically nothing worth knowing, which led back to the conclusion to "Do nothing."

When I told Henderson that my interests were shifting away from economics toward sociology or social anthropology, he advised me to consider the example of George Homans, who had gotten into sociology through research in history. Henderson regarded history as being built on solid foundations and therefore as providing valuable discipline to a budding sociologist. I read Homans's book *English Villagers of the Thirteenth Century* and found it a solid work, yet taking his route to sociology seemed to me to be a detour not worth the time and effort.

I was also at odds with Henderson on national politics. He was a staunch conservative and had no use for the man whom he insisted on calling "Frank Roosevelt." Henderson had a low regard for politicians in general, but particularly for liberal politicians, whom he saw as driven by sentimentality. The country would be better off, he believed, if it were led by "sensible engineers." When I pointed out that Herbert Hoover was an engineer and was generally considered an unsuccessful president, Henderson was unmoved.

Henderson was particularly impressed with "practical men" who interpreted the world on the basis of personal experience. I found it hard to counter such arguments. And except for Harry Levin, so did the other junior fellows. As I wrote home, Harry's triumph occurred during an evening discussion Conrad Arensberg, Henry Guerlac, and I were having with Henderson:

[Henderson] was summing up his reasons for opposing Roosevelt. "I voted for Frank Roosevelt in 1932 because I thought he was a clever politician." (Henderson is a great admirer of Machiavelli.) Then he went on to give his main reasons for changing his vote. "I have heard from people whose judgment I respect and who know Roosevelt personally that Frank Roosevelt is a vindictive person. One of them said that Frank Roosevelt was the most vindictive person he knew. I mentioned this to Walter Lippman, who agreed with that judgment. . . . And then I heard another story about the head of the law firm that first employed Frank Roosevelt. A member of his family quoted him as saying "I wouldn't trust Frank Roosevelt with a $25 lawsuit." He answered, "I object to being misquoted in my own house. What I said was that I would not trust Frank Roosevelt with a $10 lawsuit."

Thereupon Henderson leaned back and had his little chuckle. I couldn't think what to say. Then Harry Levin, who hadn't said much so far, spoke in a quiet voice. "I have a story about Roosevelt too. You know, he is a very enthusiastic philatelist. Now I have heard that when he trades stamps with little boys, he cheats them!" Suddenly the atmosphere exploded in gales of laughter. It was quite a while before the laughter subsided. I'll say this for Henderson. He laughed too.

This emphasis on his prejudices and blind spots does not do Henderson justice. He had an extraordinary ability to see through the biases and prejudices of other people and to tear apart any reasoning not based on empirical data or scientifically grounded theory. Henderson represented the ultimate challenge. We could not accept his view of the world, yet he challenged us to subject our own views to rigorous questioning.

After Henderson, the next most memorable figure was A. Lawrence Lowell, Harvard's president from 1911 until 1931. Although in his early eighties, he was still physically active and mentally alert.

I knew what the Lowell name meant in Boston society and was startled one Monday night to hear another junior fellow, James G. Miller, quote this old jingle in Lowell's presence:

> Here's to Boston, home of the bean and the cod,
> Where Lowells speak only to Cabots,
> And Cabots speak only to God.

Lowell was somewhat deaf, so he did not have to respond to something he did not care to hear, but I could not imagine anyone higher than A. Lawrence Lowell.

I knew that Lowell had been involved in the Sacco and Vanzetti case and I had looked forward to hearing his account of the case. In the 1920s, in response to widespread claims that Sacco and Vanzetti had not received a fair trial, the governor of Massachusetts had appointed a three-man committee that had included Lowell and the president of the Massachusetts Institute of Technology to review the evidence and the trial. The committee had found no solid grounds for overturning the guilty verdict. Along with millions of others, I had believed that Sacco and Vanzetti were not guilty of murder and had been convicted because of their views and activities as anarchists.

Harry Levin had told me that Lowell would not be reluctant to discuss the case, and an opportunity came on a Monday evening. As several of us gathered around, Lowell went through the evidence, step by step. As his story unfolded, I found my confidence in my interpretation being shaken. My knowledge was drawn from newspaper accounts and family discussions, whereas Lowell had seemed to weigh all the evidence dispassionately. Furthermore, he had had no axe to grind and had been reluctant to get involved. He had agreed to serve on the committee only at the urging of some of his Harvard colleagues.

I raised all the questions I could think of, without finding any holes in Lowell's story. When I was stuck, Harry Levin pointed out that Sacco and Vanzetti had testified that they were elsewhere when the murder took place, and other individuals had testified in their defense. Lowell replied that there was always a question of weighing conflicting evidence, and added, "You know, Italians always have an alibi."

Fifty years after the execution, when all the records of the Sacco and Vanzetti case were opened for public scrutiny, *Harvard* magazine ran an article suggesting that the records did not provide solid grounds for reversing the conviction. After checking with Harry Levin on my memory of our evening with Lowell, I wrote a letter to *Harvard* recounting our conversation. They did not print my letter nor did I ever get an answer.

I learned another bit of evidence later on from P. A. Santosuosso, editor and publisher of the weekly *Italian News*. At the time of the murder, he was a reporter on the *Boston Globe*. When the news had come in, he had gone to Braintree, where the murder took place, to investigate. The murder had occurred in a payroll office on the ground floor of a factory. The factory workers were on the second floor. When they heard shots, some of them rushed to the windows and saw two men running by. When Santosuosso asked them to describe the two men, they replied that it was twilight so that they could not see well enough to provide useful information. Nevertheless, during the trial, workers testified that these two men looked like Sacco and Vanzetti. After the trial, Santosuosso asked his editor if he should make public what he had been told by the workers on the scene. His editor ordered him not to get involved.

I found the junior fellows an impressive group, and many went on to gain worldwide scholarly and scientific reputations. Of those I knew during my term, four won Nobel prizes: John Bardeen (physics), Ivan Getting (physics), Paul Samuelson (economics), and Robert B. Woodward (chemistry). Arthur Schlesinger, Jr., won a Pulitzer Prize in history and became a leading American historian. Among my closest friends, Henry Guerlac achieved recognition as a leading authority on the history of science, and Conrad M. Arensberg was elected president of the American Anthropological Association. Harry Levin gained recognition as the leading authority on James Joyce and for his studies in comparative literature.

In early 1937, I decided to move out of Winthrop House to the North End. I was fascinated by the contrast in scene and points of view from the Haymarket Square subway station where I got on to Harvard Square. In half an hour, I could go from the bottom to the top of society.

One Monday evening, I tried to connect the two worlds—at least in conversation. As I was walking toward the subway, I encountered two old men talking on a street corner. One of them was a Mr. Chase, the only Yankee who had continued to live in the North End after it had become an Irish district and then almost 100 percent Italian-American. Chase hailed me and introduced me to a stately silver-haired gentleman: John F. Fitzgerald, known locally as "Honey Fitz," a former mayor of Boston, father-in-law of Joseph P. Kennedy, and grandfather of John Fitzgerald Kennedy. Honey Fitz immediately launched into an account of recent family history.

He recounted how Joseph P. Kennedy had broken with ethnic traditions, which called for a rising Irish Catholic to go to Boston College or Holy Cross. Kennedy's Harvard degree had led to a job in a Boston investment firm. Starting at the bottom, he had seemed to be progressing up the ladder of success. But then the son of one of the partners had flunked out of Harvard and come to work in the firm. A few months later, the partner's son was promoted ahead of Kennedy.

This moved young Kennedy to call a meeting of the Fitzgerald and Kennedy clans to assess what the event meant for his career. The conclusion: Kennedy should seek his fortune elsewhere. So he had moved to New York, where he had soon become a millionaire. The moral of the tale: The economic decline of Boston and New England was traceable to the unwillingness of the business leaders to make way for able young men who were sons or grandsons of immigrants.

As I later learned, the Fitzgerald tale was a rather oversimplified version of family history, since Joseph P. Kennedy had become president of a Boston bank before moving to New York. At the time, though, I thought there was some merit in the thesis—and I still do. In any case, I resolved to try it out on Lowell that very evening. Managing to sit next to him at dinner, I told him the story and then asked, "Don't you think that New England would be more prosperous today if the Yankee owners of business and industry had made more of an effort to advance promising young Irish-Americans and Italian-Americans?"

Lowell answered, "But those were family businesses. They owned the businesses."

I had asked a sociological question, and he had given me a legal answer. Apparently it had never occurred to Lowell to question the effects of Yankee domination of the New England economy.

In Winthrop House, my closest friend had been Henry Guerlac, who also contributed to my research, albeit in unorthodox ways. After I moved into the North End, I used his place on Monday afternoons to take a weekly bath before our Society of Fellows dinner. Later, when I began to write notes on the rackets, my folders seemed too sensitive to be stored in my North End room, and Henry let me keep them in an old suitcase under his bed.

Henry had won the junior fellowship on the basis of his research in biochemistry, but his interest had shifted to French history and the history of science. When he decided to abandon biochemistry, he had gone to Henderson to relinquish his fellowship. Henderson said that the society was betting on the individual. Since he would now need more time to prepare himself in this new field, the Society would grant him another three-year term. When I contemplated a much less radical shift, from economics to sociology or social anthropology, Guerlac's case provided the assurance that my fellowship would not be in jeopardy.

John Howard had been appointed to the fellowship as a physicist, and then found his interests shifting toward sociology. For a couple of years, he did some fieldwork with me in the North End, but then his interests shifted again. He got a law degree at the University of Chicago. I encountered him years later when he was an executive in the international programs of the Ford Foundation.

With Harry Levin, I shared an interest in writing, and I looked up to him as the only junior fellow able to come out ahead when he crossed swords with Henderson. Conrad Arensberg became not only a close friend but also my guide and mentor for field research as I was beginning my North End study.

One junior fellow I did not like was George C. Homans—although I recognized that he was a man of ability. By the time we met, he had already published two books, the one on the thirteenth-century English villagers, and the other an interpretation of the theories of Vilfredo Pareto, which he wrote in collaboration with Charles P. Curtis, a prominent Boston attorney with elite social connections.

A direct descendant of Presidents John Adams and John Quincy Adams, Homans enjoyed a top social position. At our Tuesday luncheons for junior fellows, he would talk loudly with a couple of his special friends about the parties they had enjoyed over the weekend. I had learned from my mother that it was impolite to talk about a party in the company of those who had not been invited. I told myself that I did not really want entrée to high society, but I was annoyed over these reminders of what I was missing.

I was also annoyed by George's booming voice. Wherever you sat at the Monday dinners, you could not avoid hearing his pronouncements. It was hard to concentrate on anything else when Homans was in the room. During this period, he never displayed the slightest interest in my slum district study. In fact, he did not even remember what part of Boston I was studying.

Years later, my relations with Homans changed after he published *The Human Group*, in which he used much of the material in my book *Street Corner Society* as one of his major cases for analysis. In the meantime, he had served as commander of a small naval vessel during World War II. Although that service took up only a small part of his life, he devoted a large part of his autobiography, *Coming to My Senses*, to his war years. I like to think that our friendly relations in later years were not due simply to his belated interest in my work but that the navy had a humanizing influence on George Homans.

Years later I also learned that George had outgrown his attachment to Vilfredo Pareto. I once said to him, "You know, George, I found Pareto interesting reading, but I have never found any way of using his theoretical framework in my own research."

"Neither have I," George replied.

10. *Planning My Slum Study*

I started my junior fellowship with a vague idea that I wanted to study a slum
district. Boston provided several possible choices. In my early weeks at
Harvard, I walked up and down the streets of Boston and sought advice in
social agencies.

I made my choice on very unscientific grounds: The North End best fitted
my picture of what a slum district should look like. I had developed a picture
of rundown three- to five-story buildings crowded together. The dilapidated
wooden-frame buildings of some other parts of the city did not look quite genu-
ine to me. One other characteristic recommended the North End on a little more
objective basis: It had more people per acre than any other section of the city. If
a slum was defined by its overcrowding, this was certainly it.

The North End was also rich in history. One of the earliest areas of settlement
in Boston, it became predominantly Irish in the latter half of the nineteenth
century and almost 100 percent Italian-American by the early 1930s. The North
End has colorful landmarks of the American Revolution: Paul Revere's home
and the old North Church, whose lanterns signaled to Paul Revere the routes of
British troops before the battles of Lexington and Concord. On the southern
edge of the North End is Faneuil Hall, where revolutionary leaders sometimes
met. Finally, the harbor by the North End was the scene of the Boston Tea Party.

The North End also figured prominently in political history in the nineteenth
and early twentieth centuries. It was located in the Third Ward and at that time
was dominated by the Hendricks Club in the West End, the area later studied
by Herbert Gans in *Urban Villagers*. There, Lincoln Steffens's favorite ward
boss, Martin Lomasney, held sway through the early decades of this century.
When I began my study in 1937, Lomasney had passed on, and, under the
leadership of John I. Fitzgerald, the Irish-dominated club was struggling to
maintain its power against, or in alliance with, Italian-American politicians.

Although slums had been given much attention in sociological literature, no real community study existed of a district like the North End. As I set out to organize my study, I was thinking of something along the lines of the Lynds' *Middletown*. In the process, I began to think of myself much more as a sociologist or a social anthropologist than an economist.

I was formally introduced to social anthropology in a course on American communities, jointly taught by Eliot D. Chapple and Conrad Arensberg. It was a good course, but much more important to me was the association with Arensberg through the Society of Fellows. He took a personal interest as my slum study developed, and we had many long talks on research methods and social theory. He also volunteered to read my early notes and encouraged me with both compliments and helpful criticisms.

I was particularly impressed with what I learned from Arensberg and Chapple on methods and theories for studying the interactions of individuals. When Arensberg returned to Harvard from a study of a rural Irish community, he and Chapple began working together to devise a methodology and theoretical framework that would be so firmly grounded scientifically as to withstand the critical onslaughts of L. J. Henderson. Their interaction framework was their fifth try and the only one Henderson was not able to tear apart. Anything that survived that supreme test naturally attracted me.

Their framework was designed to focus on objectively observable behavior, thus bypassing the subjectivity inherent in methods that focused on the interpretation of what people say. Arensberg argued that, whenever the same individuals interact over a period of time, a structure for that interaction emerges. That structure can be determined through direct observation, and that structure will strongly influence what people say, think, feel, and do.

One evening when I was with the Arensbergs, Eliot Chapple came by to show us the first model of his interaction chronograph, designed to enable an observer to make micro-measurements of the actions and inactions of two individuals in a standardized interview, which he had also developed. Impressed as I was with the micromeasurements of this methodology, I was not inclined to pursue this type of research myself. I was more interested in field research focusing on larger units of interaction.

Arensberg impressed upon me the importance of distinguishing between *pair events* (between two people) and *set events* (among three or more people). In determining patterns of informal leadership, the observation of pair events provided inadequate data. At the extremes, one could distinguish between an order and a request, but between those extremes it was difficult to determine objec-

63

tively who was influencing whom. In contrast, the observation of set events provided infallible evidence of patterns of influence. The leader was not always the one to propose an activity, although he often did. In a group, where a stable informal structure has evolved, a follower may often propose an activity, but we do not observe that activity taking place unless the leader expresses agreement or makes some move to start that activity. If the observer does not observe any single individual playing this leadership role consistently, this means that two or more individuals are contending (consciously or unconsciously) for the leadership role or else that the informal group has not been in existence long enough for a stable pattern to emerge.

This proposition on the structure of set events seems ridiculously simple, yet I have never known it to fail in field observations. It gave me the theory and methodology I needed to discover the informal structure of street corner gangs in Boston's North End.

The early outline for my research included plans to study the history of the North End, the economics (living standards, housing, marketing, distribution, and employment), the politics (the structure of the political organization and its relation to the rackets and the police), the patterns of education and recreation, the church, public health, and—of all things—social attitudes. Obviously, this was more than a one-person job, so I designed it for about ten people. With this project statement in hand, I went to seek the support of L. J. Henderson.

> We spent an hour together, and I came away with my plans very much in a state of flux. As I wrote to a friend at this time: Henderson poured cold water on the mammoth beginning, told me that I should not cast such grandiose plans when I had done hardly any work in the field myself. It would be much sounder to get in the field and try to build up a staff slowly as I went along. If I should get a ten-man project going by fall, the responsibility for the direction and co-ordination of it would inevitably fall upon me. . . . How could I direct ten people in a field that was unfamiliar to me? Henderson said that, if I did manage to get a ten-man project going, it would be the ruination of me. . . . Now, the way he put all this it sounded quite sensible and reasonable.

I shall always be glad that I went to see Henderson and thanked him for having given me painful but invaluable advice.

Although I abandoned the ten-person project, I was reluctant to come down to earth altogether. In view of the magnitude of the task I was undertaking, I thought I needed at least one collaborator, and I began to cast about to see if I could interest my college friend John Seybold in joining me in the field.

During the winter of 1936–37, I made several revisions of my outline of the study and had numerous interviews with Harvard professors who might help me get the necessary backing.

Among those I consulted was the head of the new Department of Sociology, Pitrim Sorokin, whom Harvard had attracted from the University of Minnesota. He had been secretary to President Aleksandr Kerensky in the brief period between the fall of the czar and the Bolshevik revolution. Since Sorokin was a grand theorist in the old-world tradition, I did not expect any useful guidance from him, but I thought it would be polite to consult him. He responded by giving me a lecture on the futility of doing community studies.

I also consulted Talcott Parsons, then a young assistant professor, making a transition from economics into sociology. He first made his mark with *The Structure of Social Action*, published in 1937. I had met him when he was Henderson's guest at our Monday dinners. An interest in Pareto had brought them together.

I had given Parsons copies of my first research reports on my slum study, and he had passed them around among his younger colleagues. That eventually led to my meeting the sociology instructors: Robert K. Merton, Kingsley Davis, Wilbert Moore, Edward C. Devereux, and Nicholas J. Demareth. They were an impressive group and were to have major influence in the development of sociology. I wished then that I had not allowed Sorokin to turn me off to pursuing sociology at Harvard, since there was a great deal I could have learned from them.

As I read over the various outlines years later, what was noteworthy about them was their remoteness from the actual study I carried out. As I went along, the outlines became gradually more sociological, so that I wound up the planning phase intending to conduct a sociometric study in which I would ask people who their friends were and in that way identify the social structure of the district. I did not do even this, of course, for I learned that I could examine social structure directly by observing people in action. Only a few months after I began my fieldwork, I found North End life so interesting and rewarding that I no longer needed to think in large-scale terms.

I began my first fieldwork while I was sitting in on John Ford's course in slums and housing. As a term project, I decided to study one block in the North End. To legitimize this effort, I got in touch with a private agency involved with housing and offered to give it the results of my survey. With that backing, I began knocking on doors, looking into flats, and talking to the tenants about their living conditions. This brought me into contact with North End people, but it would have been hard to devise a more inappropriate way to begin the study I eventually made. I felt ill at ease, and so did the people. I wound up the study of the block and wrote it off as a total loss.

I subsequently made another false start — if so tentative an effort can even be called a start. I had met an economics instructor who had impressed me with his self-assurance and his knowledge of Boston. He had once been attached to a settlement house and he had talked glibly about his associations with the tough young men and women of the district. He had also described how he would occasionally drop in on some bar and strike up an acquaintance with a girl, buy her a drink, and then encourage her to tell him her life story. He claimed that the women he encountered in this way were appreciative of the opportunity to tell him about their lives, and there was no further obligation.

This approach seemed at least as plausible as anything I had thought of. I picked a place in Scollay Square, which was on the edge of the North End. With some trepidation, I climbed the stairs to a bar and entertainment area and looked around. There I encountered a situation for which no adviser had prepared me. There were women present all right, but none of them was alone. Some were there with men, and there were two or three pairs of women together. I pondered this situation briefly. I had little confidence in my skill at picking up a woman, and it seemed inadvisable to tackle two at the same time. Still, I was determined not to admit defeat without a struggle. I looked around again and now noticed a threesome: one man and two women. It occurred to me that here was a maldistribution of females that I might be able to rectify. I approached the group and opened with something like this: "Pardon me. Would you mind if I joined you?" There was a moment of silence while the man stared at me. He then offered to throw me downstairs. I assured him that this would not be necessary and demonstrated as much by walking right out of the bar.

I subsequently learned that hardly any North Ender ever went into this bar or spent much time in Scollay Square. If my efforts there had been successful, they would no doubt have led somewhere but certainly not to the North End.

11. Learning to Be a Participant Observer

T he North Bennett Industrial School now seems a very unpromising place from which to begin a study of a slum district. Nevertheless, the settlement house proved the right place for me, for it was here that I met Ernest Pecci, the man I called Doc in my book.

I had talked to a number of the social workers at the settlement house about my hopes of getting acquainted with the people and studying the district. In spite of the vagueness of my request, the head of girls' work understood what I needed. Ernest Pecci, she said, was a very intelligent and talented person who had at one time been fairly active in the house but hardly ever came in anymore. He would understand what I wanted, and he undoubtedly had the contacts I needed. She frequently encountered him as she walked to and from the house and could make an appointment for me to see him one evening. I jumped at the chance.

In a sense, my study began on the evening of February 4, 1937, when the social worker called me in to meet Pecci. She showed us into her office and left. He was a man of medium height and spare build. His hair was a light brown, quite a contrast to the more typical Italian black, and it was thinning around the temples. His cheeks were sunken. His eyes were a light blue and seemed to have a penetrating gaze.

I asked him if the social worker had told him about what I was trying to do.

"No, she just told me that you wanted to meet me and that I should like to meet you."

I said that I had been interested in congested city districts in my college days but had felt very remote from them. I hoped to study the problems in such a district. I felt I could do very little as an outsider. Only if I could get to know the people and learn their problems firsthand would I be able to gain the understanding I needed.

Pecci heard me out without any change of expression. Then he asked, "Do you want to see the high life or the low life?"

"I want to see all that I can. I want to get as complete a picture of the community as possible."

"Well, any nights you want to see anything, I'll take you around. I can take you to the joints—gambling joints. I can take you around to the street corners. Just remember that you're my friend. That's all they need to know. I know these places, and if I tell them you're my friend, nobody will bother you. You just tell me what you want to see, and we'll arrange it."

The proposal was so perfect that I was momentarily at a loss as to how to respond. We talked a while longer, as I sought to get some pointers on how to behave. He warned me that I might have to take the risk of getting arrested in a raid on a gambling joint but added that this was not serious. I only had to give a false name and I would be bailed out by the man who ran the place, with only a five-dollar fine. I asked whether I should gamble in the joints. He said it was unnecessary and, for a greenhorn, inadvisable.

At last I was able to express my appreciation. "You know, the first steps of getting to know a community are the hardest. I could see things going with you that I wouldn't see for years otherwise."

"That's right. You tell me what you want to see, and we'll arrange it. When you want some information, I'll ask for it, and you listen. When you want to find out their philosophy of life, I'll start an argument and get it for you. If there's something else you want to get, I'll stage an act for you. Not a scrap, you know, but just tell me what you want, and I'll get it for you."

"That's swell. I couldn't ask for anything better. Now I'm going to try to fit in all right, but, if at any time you see I'm getting off on the wrong foot, I want you to tell me about it."

"Now we're being too dramatic. You won't have any trouble. You come in as my friend. When you come in like that, at first everybody will treat you with respect. You can take a lot of liberties, and nobody will kick. After a while, when they get to know you, they will treat you like anybody else—you know, they say familiarity breeds contempt. But you'll never have any trouble. There's just one thing to watch out for. Don't spring [treat] people. Don't be too free with your money."

"You mean they'll think I'm a sucker?"

"Yes, and you don't want to buy your way in."

We talked a little about how and when we might get together. Then he asked me, "You want to write something about this?"

"Yes, eventually."

"Do you want to change things?"

"Well—yes. I don't see how anybody could come down here where it is so crowded, people haven't got any money or any work to do, and not want to have some things changed. But I think a fellow should do the thing he is best fitted for. I don't want to be a reformer, and I'm not cut out to be a politician. I just want to understand these things as best I can and write them up, and if that has any influence . . ."

"I think you can change things that way. Mostly, that is the way things are changed, by writing about them."

That was our beginning. I found it hard to believe that I could move in with him so easily. But that indeed was the way it turned out.

While I was taking my first steps with Pecci, I was finding a place to live. I had been commuting from Harvard to the North End. Technically, that was possible, but socially it was impossible. I would always be a stranger if I did not live there. I was also having difficulty putting in the time required to establish close relations in the North End. Life there did not proceed on the basis of formal appointments. To meet people, to get to know them, to fit into their activities required spending time with them—a lot of time day after day. While I was commuting, I might come there on an afternoon or evening only to discover that the people I intended to see were not around. Even if I did see them, I might find the time passing entirely uneventfully.

Finding a place to live in the North End was not easy. A spare room was practically nonexistent. I got my best lead from the editor of the *Italian News*, P. A. Santosuosso. I had talked to him before and had found him sympathetic. He directed me to the Orlandi family, which operated the Capri restaurant. I went there for lunch and later consulted the Orlandis' son, Averaldo. He was sympathetic but said they had no place for an additional person. I came back several times just to eat. On one occasion I met Santosuosso, and he invited me to his table. At first, he asked me some searching questions about my study: what I was after, what my connection with Harvard was, what the university expected to get out of this, and so on. My answers seemed to satisfy him, and he told me that he had already spoken in my behalf to people who were suspicious that I might be coming in to "criticize our people."

I mentioned the possibility of living in a settlement house. He nodded but added: "It would be much better if you could be in a family. You would pick up the language much quicker, and you would get to know the people. But you want a nice family, an educated family. You don't want to get in with any low types. You want a real good family."

At this, he turned to Averaldo and asked, "Can't you make some place for Mr. Whyte in the house here?"

Averaldo paused a moment and then said: "Maybe we can fix it up. I'll talk to Mama again."

They did find a place. In fact, Averaldo turned his own room over to me and shared a double bed with the son of the cook. I protested mildly, but everything had been decided—except for the rent. They did not know what to charge me, and I did not know what to offer. Finally, after some fencing, I offered fifteen dollars a month. Avy said that was too much, and they settled for twelve.

The room was simple but adequate. It was not heated, but when I began to type my notes there, I got a small oil burner. There was no bathtub in the house, but I used the facilities of the great university for a weekly bath.

The room provided me with more than just a physical base. I had been taking many of my meals in the restaurant and sometimes stopping in to chat with the family before I went to bed. Then, one afternoon, I was at Harvard and found myself coming down with a bad cold. Since I still had my room there, I decided to stay overnight.

The next day when I was back in the restaurant for lunch, Avy greeted me warmly and said that they all had been worried when I did not come home. Mama had stayed up until two o'clock waiting for me. Avy told me that Mama had come to look upon me as one of the family. I was free to come and go as I pleased, but she wouldn't worry if she knew my plans. I resolved thereafter to be as good a son as I could to the Orlandis.

At first, I communicated with Mama and Papa primarily in smiles and with gestures. Papa knew no English at all, and Mama's knowledge was limited to one sentence, which she would use when some of the young boys on the street were making noise below her window during her afternoon nap. She would then poke her head out the window and shout, "Goddam-sonumabitcha! Gerou-tahere."

I had begun working on Italian with the aid of a Linguaphone, a method combining a textbook and records. One morning Papa came by while I was repeating what the instructor was saying on the phonograph record. He listened for a few moments as he tried to make sense out of this peculiar conversation. Then he burst in on me, fascinated. We sat down together while I demonstrated the machine and the method. After that, he delighted in working with me, and I called him my language professor. In a short time we reached a stage where I could carry on simple conversations, and, thanks to the Linguaphone and Papa, the Italian that came out apparently sounded authentic. He liked to try to pass me off to his friends as *paesano mio* — a man from his own hometown in Italy. When I was careful to keep my remarks within the limits of my vocabulary, I could sometimes pass as an immigrant from the village of Viareggio in the province of Tuscany.

Since I was concentrating almost exclusively on learning about the younger, English-speaking generation, a knowledge of Italian was unnecessary for research purposes. Schoolteachers and social workers had worked in the North End for as long as twenty years and had made no effort to learn Italian. Nonetheless, my efforts at Italian probably did more to establish the sincerity of my interest in the people than anything I could have told them about myself and my work.

I got up around nine o'clock every morning and went out to breakfast. Avy told me I could have breakfast in the restaurant, but, for all my desire to fit in, I never could take their breakfast of coffee with milk and a cold slice of bread.

After breakfast, I returned to my room and spent the morning typing up my notes on the previous day's events. I had lunch in the restaurant and then set out for the street corner. I was back for dinner and then out again for the evening.

Usually I came home again between eleven and twelve o'clock, when the restaurant was empty except perhaps for a few family friends. I would sometimes join Papa in the kitchen to talk as I helped him dry the dishes, or join in a family conversation around one of the tables. There I had a glass of wine to sip, and I could sit back and mostly listen but occasionally try out my growing Italian on them.

The pattern was different on Sunday, when the restaurant was closed at two o'clock and Avy's two brothers and his sister and the wives, husband, and children would come in for a big Sunday dinner. They insisted that I eat with them on Sunday as a member of the family and not pay for my meal. It was always more than I could eat, but it was delicious, and I washed it down with two tumblers of Zinfandel wine. Whatever strain there had been in my work would pass away as I ate and drank. I would then go to my room for a long afternoon nap, which completely refreshed me, so that I could set forth again for the street corners.

Although I made several useful contacts in the restaurant and through the family, that was not why the Orlandis were important to me. There is a strain in doing fieldwork. The strain is greatest when you are a stranger and are constantly wondering whether people are going to accept you. As long as you are observing and interviewing, you have a role to play, and you are not completely relaxed. It was a wonderful feeling at the end of a day's work to be able to come home to relax and enjoy myself with the family.

Pecci and I met for our first outing one evening at the North Bennett Street Industrial School and set out for a gambling joint a couple of blocks away. I followed him anxiously down the long, dark hallway at the back of a tenement building. The door opened into a small kitchen almost bare of furnishings and with the paint peeling off the walls. I took off my hat and began looking for a place to hang it. There was no place. Here I learned my first lesson in participant observation in the North End: Don't take off your hat in the house—at least not when you are among men. It may be permissible, but certainly not required, to take your hat off when women are around.

Pecci introduced me as "my friend Bill" to Chichi, who ran the place, and to Chichi's friends and customers. I stayed with Pecci part of the time in the kitchen, where several men sat around and talked, and part of the time in the other room watching a crap game.

There was talk about gambling, horse races, sex, and other matters. Mostly, I just listened and tried to act friendly and interested. I had wine and coffee with anisette in it, which the fellows chipped in to pay for. (Pecci would not let me pay my share on this first outing.) As he had predicted, no one asked me about myself, but he told me later that, when I went to the bathroom, there was an excited burst of conversation in Italian and that he had to assure them that I was not a government official. He told them flatly that I was a friend of his, and they let it go at that.

We went to Chichi's gambling joint several times together, and then I dared to go in alone. When I was greeted in a friendly manner, I felt that I was beginning to find a place for myself in the North End.

When Pecci did not go to the gambling joint, he spent his time hanging around North Bennett Street, and I began hanging out with him. At first, the street was only a place to wait until I could go somewhere else. Gradually, as I got to know the men better, I found myself becoming one of the Bennetts.

When the Italian Fellowship League was formed in the North Bennett Street Industrial School, Pecci was invited to join, although many of the members were in college or in postgraduate professional programs. He maneuvered to get me into the club, and I was glad to join, since I could see that it represented something distinctly different from the corner gangs.

I also met some North End girls. One I took to a church dance and then back to her house. The next morning, the fellows on the street corner were asking me, "How's your steady girl?" This brought me up short. I learned that going to a girl's house was something you just didn't do unless you hoped to marry her. Fortunately, the girl and her family knew that I did not know the local customs, so they did not assume that I was committed. This was a useful warning, however. After that, even though I found some girls exceedingly attractive, I never went out with them except in a group, and I did not visit any others at home.

Life in the North End was not nearly so interesting and pleasant for the young women as it was for the men. A young man had complete freedom to wander and hang around. The women could not hang out on street corners. They had to divide their time between their own homes, the homes of girl friends and relatives, and a job, if they had one. Many of them had a dream: Some young man from outside the district, with a little money, a good job, and a good education, would come and woo them and take them out of the district. I could hardly afford to fill this role.

As long as I was with Pecci, no one asked me who I was or what I was doing. When I circulated in other groups, people were much more curious.

I began with a rather elaborate explanation. I was studying the social history of the North End—but I had a new angle. Instead of working from the past up to the present, I was seeking to gain a thorough knowledge of present conditions and then to work from the present to the past. I was quite pleased with this explanation, but nobody else seemed to care for it. I gave the explanation on only two occasions, and each time, when I had finished, there was an awkward silence. No one, myself included, knew what to say.

I soon found that people were developing their own explanation: I was writing a book about the North End. This might have seemed entirely too vague an explanation, yet it sufficed. Ultimately, my acceptance in the district depended on the personal relationships I was developing. Whether it was a good idea to write a book about the district depended entirely on people's opinions of me personally. If I was all right, then my project was all right; if I was no good, then no amount of explaining could convince them that the book was a good idea.

My relationship with Pecci changed rapidly during our first few months together. At first he was simply a key informant—and my sponsor. As we spent more time together, I ceased treating him as a passive informant. I discussed with him quite frankly what I was trying to do, what problems were puzzling me, and so on. Much of our time was spent in discussing ideas and observations, so that Pecci became, in a very real sense, a collaborator in the research.

Pecci's awareness of the nature of my study stimulated him to recount incidents he thought I would be interested in. Often when I picked him up at the flat where he lived with his sister and brother-in-law, he would say to me, "Bill, you should have been around last night. You would have been interested in this." And then he would go on to tell me what had happened. Such accounts were always interesting and relevant to my study.

Pecci found this experience stimulating and enjoyable, and yet the relationship had its drawbacks. He once commented, "You've slowed me up plenty since you've been down here. Now, when I do something, I have to think what Bill Whyte would want to know about it and how I can explain it. Before, I used to do things by instinct."

Without any training, Pecci was such a perceptive observer that he needed only a little stimulus to help him make explicit much of the dynamics of the social organization of the district. Some of the interpretations I came up with were more his than mine, although it is now impossible to disentangle them.

I did little formal interviewing. Rather, I strove to participate in the everyday life of the people and the community.

Although I avoided expressing opinions on sensitive topics, I found that arguing on some matters was simply part of the social pattern of the North End and that one could hardly participate without joining in the arguments. I often found myself involved in heated but good-natured discussions about the relative merits of certain major league ballplayers and managers, for instance, and whenever girls would walk down the street, the fellows on the corner would make mental notes and later discuss them. These evaluations were largely based on their shapes, and here I was glad to argue that Mary had a better "build" than Anna, or vice versa. Of course, if any of the men on the corner happened to be personally attached to Mary or Anna, no such comments would be made.

Sometimes I wondered whether just hanging out on the street corner was an active enough process to be dignified by the term "research." I wondered whether I should be asking questions. One has to learn when to question and when not to, however, as well as what questions to ask.

One night in the early months, I was with Pecci in Chichi's gambling joint when a man from another part of the city started regaling us with a tale of the organization of gambling activity. I had been told that he had once been a very big gambling operator. He did most of the talking, but the others asked questions and threw in comments, so at length I began to feel that I had to say something to be part of the group. Finally, I said, "I suppose the cops were all paid off?"

The gambler's jaw dropped. He glared at me. Then he denied vehemently that any policemen had been paid off and immediately switched the conversation to another subject. For the rest of that evening I felt very uncomfortable.

The next day Pecci explained the lesson of the previous evening. "Go easy on that 'who,' 'what,' 'why,' 'when,' 'where' stuff, Bill. You ask those questions, and people will clam up on you. If people accept you, you can just hang around, and you'll learn the answers in the long run without even having to ask the questions."

As I sat and listened, I learned the answers to questions that I would not even have had the sense to ask if I had been conducting formal interviews. I did not abandon questioning altogether. I simply learned to adjust the sensitiveness of the question to the strength of my relationship with the informant.

When I had established my position on the street corner, I got the data I needed without making an active effort. Only now and then, when I was concerned with a particular problem and felt I needed more information from a certain individual, did I find it necessary to get someone alone and carry on a more formal interview.

At first I concentrated on just fitting into the North End, but a little later I had to face the question of how far to immerse myself in its life. I confronted that problem head-on one evening as I was walking down the street with the Bennetts. Trying to enter into the spirit of the small talk, I cut loose with a string of obscenities. The walk came to a halt as they all stopped to look at me. Pecci shook his head and said, "Bill, you're not supposed to talk like that. That doesn't sound like you."

I explained that I was only using terms that were common on the street corner. Pecci insisted that I was different and that they wanted me to be that way.

The people in the North End did not expect me to be just like them; in fact, they were pleased to find I was different, so long as I took a friendly interest in them.

My behavior was nevertheless affected by street corner life. When John Howard first started working with me in the North End, he noticed that I talked differently than I did at Harvard. It seemed natural to me, but what was natural in the North End differed from what was natural at Harvard. I found myself talking much more animatedly, dropping terminal *g*'s, and gesturing much more actively. My vocabulary was also different. When I was most deeply involved in the field, I found myself rather tongue-tied when I visited Harvard. I simply could not feel at ease in discussions about science and international relations.

Throughout my time in the North End, I tried to avoid influencing the group, because I wanted to study it as much as possible as though it were unaffected by my presence. For instance, I avoided accepting office or leadership positions. The one exception was when I was nominated secretary of the Italian Fellowship League. My first impulse was to decline, but then I recognized that the secretary just takes minutes and handles correspondence. I realized that I could write a very full account of the progress of the meeting under the pretext of keeping the minutes.

I tried to be as helpful as a friend was expected to be. When one of the boys had an errand downtown and wanted company, I went along. When somebody was trying to get a job and had to write a letter about himself, I helped him compose it, and so on. Most such situations presented no problems, but, when money was involved, my course was much less clear. I spent money on my friends just as they did on me, but what was I to do about lending them money? I lent money on several occasions, but I always felt uneasy about it. Naturally, a man appreciates a loan, but how does he feel later when he is not able to repay it? I tried to reassure the individual and tell him that I knew he did not have it just then and that I was not worried about it. Sometimes I even told him to forget about the debt. But that did not wipe it off the books; the uneasiness remained. I learned that it is possible to do a favor for a friend and yet cause a strain in the relationship. I know of no easy solution to this problem. On the one hand, there will be times when it is ill advised for a researcher to refuse to make a personal loan. On the other hand, whatever his financial resources, he should not look for opportunities to lend money and should avoid doing so whenever he gracefully can.

If the researcher is trying to fit into more than one group, fieldwork becomes more complicated. There may be times when the groups come into conflict, and he will be expected to take a stand. There was one awkward occasion when I was with the corner boys and one of the college boys stopped to talk to me. At one point, he said, "Bill, these fellows wouldn't understand what I mean, but I am sure that you understand my point." I told him that he greatly underestimated the boys and that college men were not the only people who were smart.

The remark was in keeping with my feelings, but it was also justified from a strictly practical standpoint. My answer did not shake the feelings of superiority of the college boy or disrupt our personal relationship. As soon as he left, it became evident how deeply the corner boys resented his statement. In venting their feelings about him, they told me that I was different and that they appreciated it and that although I knew much more than this fellow, I did not show it.

I had been in the North End only a few weeks when Pecci said, "You're just as much of a fixture around this street corner as that lamppost." But the event that signaled to me that I was accepted was the baseball game Frank Luongo organized against a group of North Bennett Street boys in their late teens. Frank assigned me to a regular but not a key position on the team, but at least I was in the game. When it was my turn to bat in the last half of the ninth inning, the score was tied, there were two outs, and the bases were loaded. As I reached down to pick up my bat, I heard some of the fellows suggest to Frank that he put in a pinch hitter. Frank answered in a loud voice that must have been meant for me, "No, I've got confidence in Bill Whyte. He'll come through in the clutch." With his confidence bucking me up, I went up there, missed two swings, and then banged a hard grounder through the hole between second and short.

That night Gillo (Danny) presented me with a ring for being a regular fellow and a pretty good ballplayer. I was impressed with the ring, which Gillo had made for me from a clear amber die discarded from a crap game. He had used his lighted cigarette to burn a hole through it and to round the corners to form a heart shape on top. I assured the fellows that I would always treasure it.

In the early stage of my North End study, I simply put all my notes in a single folder. Since I was studying a number of different groups and problems, this was very awkward. I had to subdivide the notes. I could organize them topically, with folders for politics, rackets, the church, the family, and so on. Or I could organize them by the groups I was observing: the Bennetts, the men in the Italian Fellowship League, and so on. Without really thinking the problem through, I began filing material in this way.

As the material in the folders piled up, I realized that organizing them by social groups fitted in with the way my study was developing. For example, a college boy had said, "These racketeers give our district a bad name. They should really be cleaned out of here." And a corner boy had said, "These racketeers are really all right. When you need help, they'll give it to you. The legitimate businessman—he won't even give you the time of day." If I filed these quotes under "Racketeers, attitudes toward," they would have only shown that there were conflicting attitudes toward racketeers. Only a questionnaire (which is hardly feasible for such a topic) would have shown the distribution of attitudes in the district. Furthermore, how important was it to know how many people felt which way on this topic? It seemed of more scientific interest to relate the attitude to the *group* in which the individual was a part.

I spent July and August 1937 with my parents. Perhaps I was just too accustomed to the family summer vacation to remain in Boston, but I rationalized that I needed to get away, do some reading, and get some perspective on my study. The perspective was not easy to come by. I still did not see the link between my study of the life of the North End and intensive studies of groups.

I decided that I must somehow broaden my research. That could have meant losing my contact with the Bennetts and the Italian Fellowship League to participate more heavily in other areas, but fortunately it did not happen that way. I decided that studying the league took only one evening a week, so there was no great pressure to drop that, and although the Bennetts took much more time, it meant something to have a corner and a group where I felt at home. Only as I began to see changes in these groups did I realize how extremely important it is to observe a group over an extended period of time.

While retaining my early group ties, I decided to expand my study to include the political life of the community, since street corner activities and politics were inextricably intertwined. There were several political organizations seeking to build up their candidates. I could gain the best inside view of the political system if I aligned myself actively with one organization, although I was afraid this might limit me in dealing with its rivals.

The problem solved itself. In the fall of 1937, there was a Boston mayoralty contest. Former mayor and governor James Michael Curley was running again. Among the Yankees, Curley was the personification of corruption. In the North End, however, he had a reputation as a friend of the poor and the Italians. Most of the local politicians were for him, and he was expected to carry the district by a tremendous majority. I decided that it would be good to get my start in politics working for this man.

The local connection I needed was Joseph Langone, a state senator who represented our ward and two others. At the Orlandis' restaurant, I met Paul Ferrante, who was working for Langone as a volunteer, hoping it would lead to a political job.

After a little preliminary discussion, I enlisted as the unpaid secretary of the unpaid secretary of the state senator for the duration of the mayoralty campaign. When Curley lost the election, I reenlisted, since there was a special election for a vacant seat in Congress and Langone was running for it. All the other local politicians were at least officially for Langone, since he was running against several Irishmen.

As a campaign worker for the state senator, I was a complete anomaly. Most workers in such campaigns can at least claim to be able to deliver substantial numbers of votes; I could not pledge but my own. On one occasion, Langone gave me a ride up to the Massachusetts State House, in the course of which he asked when I was going to deliver the endorsement of the Italian Fellowship League. This was a touchy topic in the club. All the members were interested in seeing an Italian-American advance to higher office, but they were embarrassed at being identified with Joe Langone. The language he used in public was hardly refined. Once while a woman was testifying against a bill Langone had introduced, he had gotten angry and threatened to throw her off Tea Wharf if she ever set foot in his district. On another occasion, the newspapers had carried a picture of Langone with a black eye, which he had received in a fight with a member of the state parole board.

I explained that it was against the policy of the club to endorse candidates for public office. Although this happened to be true, it was hardly a satisfactory explanation for the senator. He did not press the matter further, however, perhaps because he recognized that the support of the Italian Fellowship League did not count for much anyway.

I sought to make myself useful by running errands and doing various odd jobs, such as nailing up Langone posters. Although I was of little help to the senator, I was not doing any harm, so I was allowed to hang around in the combination political office and funeral parlor. I found this an unpleasant place, because I never was able to gain scientific detachment. One of my most vivid memories stems from this period. After one of the senator's constituents died, the deceased was laid out for viewing in the back room of the funeral parlor. Unfortunately, he was laid out in two pieces, since he had had his leg amputated shortly before his death. The rest of his body had been embalmed, but there was no way to embalm the detached leg, which gave off a sickening odor. While family and friends came in to pay their last respects, we sat in the front part of the office trying to keep our attention on politics. Now and then, Paul Ferrante went about the room spraying perfume. The combination of perfume and the stench of the gangrenous leg was hardly an improvement. I stayed at my post through the day but finished up a trifle nauseated.

Since the politicians did not know what to do with me, I developed my own job description. Before one of the meetings of the political workers, I suggested to Tina Langone—the candidate's wife and the real brains in the family—that I serve as secretary for such meetings. I then took notes and typed her summaries. (Carbon paper enabled me to retain copies.)

Actually, my notes were of no use to the organization. Although the meetings were officially supposed to be to discuss political strategy and tactics, they were more pep rallies for the second-string political powers supporting Langone. I never got in on the top-level political discussions where the real decisions were made; however, my note-taking at the lower-level meetings did give me a fully documented record of one type of activity. I went to large-scale political rallies as well, where I sought to record on the spot the speeches and other activities of Langone's leading supporters.

On Election Day, I voted as the polls opened and then reported for duty at the candidate's headquarters. I had been assigned to work with Langone's secretary in East Boston and spent the first part of the day following Ferrante around.

At two o'clock I asked to leave and return to my ward. When I got home, I heard alarming reports from the home ward about the Irishman who was Langone's chief rival. He had hired a fleet of taxicabs to cruise about the area of Charlestown so that some of his supporters could vote in every precinct of the ward. If we did not steal the election ourselves, this low character would steal it from us.

Langone had secured the backing of John I. Fitzgerald (no relation to "Honey Fitz"), boss of the Hendricks Club in the neighboring West End. At about five o'clock, one of Langone's chief lieutenants rushed up to a group of us hanging on a corner to report that having John I's support meant that our ward was now wide open for repeaters. The senator's lieutenant did not ask for volunteers; he simply directed us to get into waiting cars that would take us to the polling places. I hesitated, but I did not refuse.

That evening, I was standing on North Bennett Street when one of the politician's henchmen asked me to go into my home voting place. I explained that I had already voted there under my own name. I was assured that I had nothing to worry about since a new shift was now on duty. I was to use the name Frank Petrillo. They told me that Petrillo was a Sicilian fisherman who was out to sea, so that we were exercising his democratic rights for him. The voting list indicated that Petrillo was forty-five and five feet nine. I was twenty-three and six feet three, so this seemed implausible, but they insisted that this made no difference since those inside the polling place were John I's people. I was not completely reassured, but I lined up to wait my turn in the rush hour before the polls closed.

I gave the name, and the woman at the gate checked me in. I picked up my ballot, went back to the booth, and marked it for Langone. As I was about to put the ballot into the box, a woman looked me over and asked me how old I was. Suddenly the ridiculousness of my masquerade struck home. I couldn't say forty-five, so I compromised on twenty-nine. She asked how tall I was, and again I compromised and said six feet. They had me, but still the questioning went on. The woman asked me how I spelled my name. In the excitement, I spelled Petrillo wrong. The other woman checker now came over and asked me about my sisters. I thought I had recalled seeing the names of some female Petrillos on the list, and, in my case, if I invented names that did not appear, they could be names of women who were not registered. I said, "Yes, I have two sisters." She asked their names. I said, "Celia and Florence."

She leered at me and asked, "What about this Marie Petrillo?" I took a deep breath and said, "She's my cousin." They said they would have to challenge my vote and called for the warden in charge of the polling place.

I had a minute to wait before he stepped forward. I saw before my eyes large headlines on the front pages of Boston's tabloids — HARVARD FELLOW ARRESTED FOR REPEATING. This was an ideal man-bites-dog newspaper story. In that moment I resolved that I would not mention my connection with Harvard or my study when I was arrested.

The warden stepped up, said he would have to challenge my vote, and asked me to write my name on the back of the ballot. I went over to the booth. By this time, I was so nervous that I forgot what my first name was supposed to be and put down "Paul." The warden took my ballot and looked at the back of it. He had me swear that this was my name and that I had not voted before. I did so. I went through the gate. He told me to stop. He looked at the book of registered voters. He turned back to the booth, and for a moment his back was to me. Then I saw him scratch out the name I had written on the back of the ballot. He put the ballot into the box, and it registered with a ring of the bell. He told me I could go, and I tried to walk out in a calm and leisurely manner.

When I was on the street, I told the politician's lieutenant that my vote had been challenged. "Well, what do you care? We didn't lose anything by it." Then I told him that the vote had finally gone through. "Well, so much the better. Listen, what could they have done to you? If the cops had taken you in, they wouldn't hold you. We would fix you up."

I did not eat well that night. I did not feel nearly so guilty until I thought that I was going to be arrested. Up to that point, I had just gone numbly along. After supper, I went to look up a fellow member of the Italian Fellowship League. As I had walked into his home precinct to repeat, I had encountered him coming out of the polling place. As we passed, he grinned at me and said, "They're working you pretty hard today, aren't they?" I immediately jumped to the conclusion that he knew that I was going in to repeat. Now I felt that I had to see him as soon as possible to explain what I had been doing and why. Fortunately for me, he was not home that night.

As my anxiety subsided, I recognized that, simply because I knew my own guilt, it did not follow that he knew what I had done. I confirmed this indirectly when I talked with him later about the election. He raised no question concerning my voting activities.

I did confess my crime to Pecci. He agreed that repeating was a serious mistake, but he did not tell anybody about it.

What did I gain from my performance on election day? I had seen how repeating was accomplished. But this was really of very little value, for I had observed similar activities at quite close range before, and I could have gotten all the data I needed without taking any risk. More important, I had risked jeopardizing my whole study. Although I escaped arrest, crimes like mine are not always fixed as firmly as the politician's henchman think they are. A year later, when I was out of town at election time, somebody was arrested for voting in *my* name.

Repeating was fairly common in our ward, but only a few people engaged in it, and they were generally looked down upon. Knowledge of my repeating never went beyond some of the key people in Langone's organization. I had not been observed by anyone whose opinion could damage me. Furthermore, I was just plain lucky that I did not reveal myself to the member of my club; in fact, I was lucky at every point.

The experience posed problems that transcended expediency. I had been brought up to be a respectable, law-abiding, middle-class citizen. When I realized I was a repeater, my conscience troubled me. Such behavior was not part of my picture of myself. I could not laugh it off as a necessary part of fieldwork. I could have refused. Others had.

To be accepted by people in a district, you do not have to do everything just as they do it. In fact, in a district where there are different groups with different standards of behavior, it may be a matter of very serious consequence to conform to the standards of one particular group.

I also learned that the field-worker cannot afford to think only of living with others. He has to continue living with himself. If the participant observer finds himself engaging in behavior that he thinks is immoral, then he will wonder what sort of a person he is. Unless the field-worker can carry with him a reasonably consistent picture of himself, he is likely to run into difficulties.

Langone lost the special election for Congress, and I gradually phased out my relations with the political organization and became more active once again on North Bennett Street. Then, one Saturday night in April 1938, I stumbled upon one of my most exciting research experiences. It was the night the owner of the bowling alley put up prize money—the biggest bowling night of the whole season. I recall standing on the corner with the boys while they discussed the upcoming contest. Pecci, Frank, and Gillo were making their predictions on the order in which the men would finish. At first, this made no particular impression upon me, as my own unexpressed predictions were exactly the same. I was convinced that they were right and yet I wondered why the scores should approximate the leadership structure of the gang, as they predicted. Were the leaders simply better natural athletes? That made no sense, for George Vitale had won the promise of a tryout with a farm team of the Boston Braves. Why should he not outdo us all at bowling? Then I remembered the baseball game we played against the younger crowd on North Bennett Street. I could see the man who was by common consent the best baseball player of us all striking out with long, graceful swings and letting the grounders bounce through his legs. And then I remembered that neither I nor anyone else seemed to have been surprised at his performance. Even George himself was not surprised, as he explained, "I can't seem to play ball when I'm playing with fellows I know like that bunch."

At the alleys that night, I was fascinated and a bit awed by what I witnessed. Here was the social structure in action right on the bowling alleys. It held the individual members in their places—and me along with them. I did not stop to reason then that, as a close friend of Pecci, Frank, and Gillo, I held a position close to the top of the gang and therefore was expected to excel. I simply felt myself buoyed up by the situation. My friends were for me, had confidence in me, believed I would bowl well. I felt supremely confident. I have never felt quite that way before—or since. I was feeling the impact of the group structure upon me. It was a strange feeling, as if something larger than myself was controlling the ball as I went through my swing and released it toward the pins. And then I won the prize money!

When it was all over, I looked at the scores of all the other men. I was still somewhat bemused by my achievement, and now I was excited to discover that the men had actually finished in the order Pecci, Frank, and Gillo had predicted.

Even as I was learning the power of the group structure, I could not restrain my impulse to gloat over my triumph. I claimed I had really become a good bowler and would not give the group credit for my victory. Pecci countered by setting up a contest, me against Slim (Long John), the lowest-ranking member of the leadership subgroup. With Pecci, Frank, and Gillo cheering for Slim and telling me that I had been bowling "over my head," I lost a one-sided contest. I settled for a sociological discovery.

As I later thought about the bowling contest, I became convinced I had discovered something important: the relationship between individual performance and group structure. I believed then (and still believe now) that this relationship can be observed in all manner of group activities.

The other point that impressed me about the bowling contest involved field research methods. I had the scores of the men on that night, and this one set of figures was certainly important, for it represented the performance of the men in the event that they all looked upon as the climax of the year. But this same group had been bowling every Saturday night for many months. It would have been easy to keep a record of every string bowled by every man on every Saturday night of that season. This would have produced a set of statistics that would have been the envy of some of my highly quantitative friends. I kept no record of these scores, because at the time I saw no point to it. I was looking upon Saturday night at the bowling alley as simply recreation for myself and my friends. At the same time, I was enjoying the bowling so much that I felt a bit guilty about neglecting my research. Only after passing up this statistical gold mine did I suddenly realize that the behavior of the men in the regular sessions at the bowling alley was exactly what I should have been observing. Instead of bowling in order to be able to observe something else, I should have been bowling to observe bowling. I was learning that the day-to-day activities of these men constituted the basic data of my study.

12. Kathleen: Discovery and Rediscovery

It took me eleven years from the time of our first meeting until I married Kathleen King, but most of that long time should not be charged against me. When we met on the *S. S. Belgenland* en route to Europe in the summer of 1927, I was thirteen and hardly in a position to propose marriage.

We met in the most unpleasant surroundings: a dirty ship with tourist-class cabins far below the waterline, along dingy corridors that smelled stiflingly stale. The ship's sole redeeming features were the presence of a group of boys and girls about my age and of Clarence and Alice King and their children. I was fascinated by the Kings' adventurous spirit. The family, which included Kathleen (age 13) and her three brothers, ranging in ages from 9 down to 2, was setting off on a six-week walking trip through rural England. They were traveling with a vehicle specially designed by a basketmaker which consisted of a long rectangular basket on baby carriage wheels. It held the smallest child and all the camping gear.

The Whyte and King families hit it off from the moment they met. My father learned he had been in the same class at the University of Wisconsin as Clarence—who preferred to be called Jim. Jim had a law degree from Columbia but at the time we met was director of Community Chest drives in Bridgeport, Connecticut. Alice King had a beautiful contralto voice.

I found myself drawn to Kathleen immediately. She had coal-black hair, cut in what we then called a boyish bob, but she still seemed very much the young woman. She was vivacious and seemed completely at ease in the group of youngsters we socialized with or alone with me.

Kathleen was the first girl who did not play hard-to-get as soon as she discovered that I was interested in her. She had grown up playing with boys, so it seemed natural to view them as friends. With her, there were no pretenses to break through. She was just her natural self. When I was with her, I felt a warmth and understanding I had never felt before. Between group games, we had many long and serious talks about our beliefs and aspirations.

I got up very early in the morning to see the Kings off at Plymouth, and we continued on to Bremen. I was sad to see the Kings go. I thought then that I would never forget Kathleen.

While ours was not exactly an arranged marriage, it seemed that fate and our parents were conspiring to throw us together.

After our meeting on the boat, I saw little of Kathleen since she lived in New Canaan, Connecticut, and I in Bronxville, New York. My parents enjoyed driving around the countryside and visiting old friends, and that brought us to the Kings' now and then; but during high school, several years passed when we did not see each other. When I was old enough to begin thinking about marriage, I thought that, before taking such a step, I must look up Kathleen to see if my attraction to the girl on the *Belgenland* might grow into a life-long love.

Then, during college, a strange coincidence led me to her. One day I was visiting a friend in his dormitory room when I saw a picture of Kathleen on his bureau. I asked if she was his girlfriend. He said no and explained that their families were friends. Recognizing that I had more than a passing interest in her, he invited me to visit him at the end of the school year, promising we would see Kathleen.

During that weekend we were all invited for lunch and a swim in the Kings' pond. Fate seemed to be working against me, for I soon discovered that Kathleen was engaged to a young man she had met at the Arts Students League, where she was a student. Still, we had a lot to catch up on, and her fiancé allowed me to monopolize her as we swam. As it was becoming a bit chilly, my rival went back to the house. As Kathleen and I lay close together on a raft, half submerged, we became so absorbed in our conversation that we didn't notice the cold or that, after a few minutes, we were entirely alone.

We talked about love and marriage—but not between us. I told Kathleen that I had been attracted to a number of girls but had never really been in love. Could she tell me what it was like? She said it came down to wanting to take care of the one she loved. For example, when her husband was about to leave the house on a rainy morning, she wanted to be there to remind him to take his rubbers.

I became convinced that Kathleen should not marry her fiancé. The love she described seemed to fit a mother more than a wife.

As we lay on the raft, close but not touching, I was sorely tempted to kiss her.

We seemed so close, so oblivious to the rest of the world, that it seemed natural. Why did I hold back? I don't believe it was because it was not good form to kiss a girl who was engaged to another man. If I had been prepared to offer myself in his place, nothing would have stopped me.

During the summer of my junior year in college, when I was working with the Citizens' Budget Commission, I encountered Kathleen by chance in Grand Central Station. I learned that she was living in Greenwich Village and still studying at the Art Students League. I asked when we could get together, and she invited me to lunch. That was the only occasion when we were not completely at ease with each other. Somewhat diffidently, she managed to slip in the news that she was no longer engaged. I was pleased, but I was not yet prepared to go on from there. Once more, we lost touch.

In the fall of 1937, my parents drove to Connecticut to arrange for my Great-Aunts Mame and Belle and Aunt Helen to settle in a nursing home. They stopped at the Kings on a weekend when Kathleen was home. Unbeknownst to me, my father was equipped with clippings on the exploits of his only son. He told them about my North End study and must have provided quite a vivid picture. This inspired Kathleen to write me. She wrote about the months she had spent in England studying calligraphy, how she had enjoyed it and yet how she understood why it was important for me to know my own country better.

The letter could not have arrived at a more opportune time. I was getting lonely. I had more friends than ever before, a few among the junior fellows and more among the corner boys in the North End, but I was now twenty-three years old, and there were no girls in my life.

Through Harvard friends I had met girls who seemed attractive enough to take to the movies or to dinner and dancing, but no one had stirred me to undertake a romantic campaign. Furthermore, I found that when I got interested in girls from the Harvard-Cambridge world, I was so occupied with my fieldwork that I would forget to follow up with further invitations—a bit of carelessness that indicated even to me that I was not becoming seriously involved.

Shortly after the letter from Kathleen, I received one from her father, who was now teaching at the New York School of Social Work, later attached to Columbia. He invited me to speak to his community organization class. The class was on a Friday afternoon, and the invitation included a weekend with the Kings in New Canaan.

From time to time over the years, Kathleen and I would ask her father whether the invitation to address the class was an excuse to arrange our marriage. His only response would be a grin, followed by a change of subject.

After I gave my report on my North End study in Jim King's class, he and I took the train to New Canaan. When we arrived, Kathleen was upstairs. I remember the feeling of anticipation as I stood at the foot of the stairway. She remembers too the feeling of awkwardness as she realized I could see her feet, knees, and waist before she could see me. The embarrassment was only momentary. We found we had much to talk about, from the North End to England.

The next afternoon, Kathleen drove me to see my aunts. When we were leaving, Aunt Mame followed us to the head of the stairs and called after me in a horse whisper, "Bill, is it serious?" We both laughed, but I was beginning to suspect it was.

We returned to the Kings' home in the cool of the early fall evening when the dew was beginning to settle on the grass. Kathleen paused to look at the first stars, and it was then that I should have kissed her, but I was slow as usual. That night after supper as we talked alone, the barriers came down and we found ourselves in each other's arms.

A week later I telephoned the Kings to say that I wanted to visit again: Would Kathleen be home that weekend? They arranged it. By then we both knew we were getting serious. After that second visit, in October, I wrote my parents that I might be marrying Kathleen.

Our marriage plans became firm during the Christmas season — but in two stages. During the holidays I was invited to visit the Kings and to stay as long as I liked. Kathleen and I found ourselves talking ever more seriously about marriage, but it still seemed indefinite and far away.

I told her I was still unclear about my career plans. The only thing I was sure of was that I would not become a college professor, since I craved something more adventurous than the academic life. She said she could live with uncertainty until I found my way. So that she would know the worst about me, I told her about my election day repeating. She was shocked but persuaded herself that this one crime did not presage a criminal career.

Money seemed a serious barrier. At the time, I had lent three hundred dollars to North End friends. It would be at least a year before I could save up enough money to get married. Kathleen said somewhat diffidently that we could count on her money as well as mine. She received a thousand dollars a year from a trust fund set up by her grandparents. We talked it over, and I found I could not object. If I had been determined to marry for money, I would have aimed higher.

During this visit, we talked as if we were going to get married, but I had not committed myself completely. One thing still held me back, and I even had the temerity to tell Kathleen what it was. There was a girl in Caldwell to whom I had once been quite attached. Before making an irrevocable decision, I felt I had to see her again. At this point, Kathleen should have told me to go to hell, but she didn't. Why did I not just tell her I had some business to attend to and that we could talk further when I returned? I was having such a good time visiting the Kings that I could not think of any good excuse for leaving, and I could not lie to Kathleen.

I drove out to visit the girl in Caldwell. She was pleasant enough, but she did not strike fire in my heart, and besides, it was clear she had become interested in someone else. We had a rather awkward conversation and then I drove back to New Canaan. Now at last I was prepared to make my commitment, and happily Kathleen was ready to take me with open arms.

Kathleen made two visits to Boston before we were married. She claims I had to get the approval of the boys on the corner. I said I wanted her to be sure she could live happily in the North End, for we never gave any thought to starting married life anywhere else. In any case, the corner boys' enthusiasm for Kathleen seemed spontaneous. We took her along for our regular Saturday-night bowling and for coffee-ands, and she joined in as if she were perfectly at ease with old friends. They found her charming and attractive, and several commented admiringly that she did not use much makeup.

I also took her to meet my junior fellow friends, who responded to her much as the boys on the corner did. We were invited to an evening at the home of Alfred North Whitehead and his wife. Later, the eminent philosopher made a point of telling me how charmed he was by Kathleen and said I must bring her again. I wrote her in detail about these triumphs.

In late winter, we arranged for my parents to visit the Kings so we could announce our intentions. But then something came up that I felt urgently required my presence in the North End that weekend—I can't remember now what it was, and it could hardly have been as important as I thought. I wrote Kathleen to excuse myself and tell her that I had written my parents to inform them of our marriage date and plans. Kathleen was deeply hurt by my decision. She had every right then to call everything off, but, thank God, she didn't.

Kathleen was embarrassed at having to face John and Isabel Whyte, who were about to lose their only son in marriage, without their son standing beside her, but my mother immediately put her at ease, saying they had always wanted a daughter. My father gave her a great bear hug. Kathleen knew from the beginning that her in-law problems were bound to be minimal.

On Kathleen's second visit to the North End, that spring, the main task was to find a place to live. We could not expect to find the comforts of middle-class living, but neither did we want to demonstrate our commitment to slum life by finding the slummiest apartment available. The district was exceedingly crowded, and there were few vacancies. We looked at one depressing flat after another with dark, gloomy rooms that smelled of moldy plaster. We knew we might have to settle for an apartment without a bath because only about one out of twelve flats in the North End came so equipped, but we did want to hold out for our own toilet. At the time, it was common in the North End to have on each floor a toilet that was shared by two or three families, none of whom was responsible for cleaning it.

When the leads provided by my friends had led nowhere, Kathleen and I just wandered around looking for vacancies and inquiring of people on the street. Toward the end of Hanover Street, less than a block from the waterfront, we noticed an old brick building that was being remodeled. We went in to number 477 and found the owner supervising the work. He told us that one of the three flats was unrented and showed us around. It had not only an indoor toilet but also a bathtub. There was a large kitchen at the back, a large living room in the front, and a modest-sized bedroom off the living room. The apartment was freshly painted, and the floors were in good shape. It was light and airy, with windows on Hanover Street and also in the back toward the harbor, so it was reasonably cool and airy in the summer.

There was no central heating, which was even rarer than bathtubs, but we could make the place livable with a combination gas and kerosene stove. During the winter we would use the kerosene burners to heat the apartment and also to do some of our cooking. With the kerosene burners on, the kitchen would heat up to about seventy-five degrees Fahrenheit. If we left the door from the kitchen to the bathroom open, the bathroom was reasonably comfortable. The living room stayed in the sixties on cold days. The bedroom was farthest from the heat, but bearable under the covers.

The rent was twenty-seven dollars a month, less than half what our Harvard friends were paying. We took it on the spot.

Our end of Hanover Street was populated predominantly by Sicilians, and our friends on North Bennett Street warned us that we were moving into a very tough part of town. While upper-class Yankee Bostonians and the Irish-Americans looked down on Italian-Americans, without making any distinctions among them, in the North End, regional distinctions were still very much alive. The northern Italians, few of whom remained in the North End by the time we arrived, looked down on the immigrants from the villages around Naples, and they in turn looked down upon the Sicilians, who brought with them the reputation of the Mafia. In fact, many of the leading gangsters and racketeers of the prohibition era *were* of Sicilian extraction.

In the two years we lived at 477 Hanover Street, I never saw anyone pull a knife or shoot a revolver, nor did I see as much as a fistfight. Kathleen could go anywhere on Hanover Street or anywhere else in the district at any time of the day or night, completely safe not only from physical attack but even from embarrassing remarks.

Having settled on the apartment, we bought the equipment we needed (stove, water heater, secondhand refrigerator, and light fixtures). Since my parents slept in twin beds, I had assumed that was the thing to do, but Kathleen wanted a double bed, and I have always been glad I let her have her way—though being six feet three, I did hold out for a bed six feet nine inches long. I had a studio couch, bought for my Winthrop House room, and the rest of our furniture was a mix of Kathleen's few antiques and King castoffs.

In this era, one was expected to set up a front room in style, to be used only on special occasions. North End decor called for overstuffed easy chairs and couches and brocaded draperies that fell in folds on the floor. Further, one was expected to have many little ornaments on shelves and in corners.

We did not feel bound by local customs, and we could not afford to buy furniture and knickknacks. We set ourselves up in a faintly colonial style, the most distinctive feature being fishnet curtains, which Kathleen bought by the pound from a ship's chandler. We spent much of our time in the kitchen, and I had my files and typewriter in the living room.

Just a few weeks before our marriage, I fell ill, for the first time since beginning work in the North End. I went to the infirmary at Harvard and was told I had flu and was run-down and had better stay there for a few days.

I suspect that my problems were as much psychological as physical. No longer dependent upon my parents, I had become very self-sufficient. Now, suddenly, I was about to lose my independence. Was I sure I was deeply in love? Up to this point, my idea of love had come largely from the movies and fiction, so I assumed a man who was really in love would lose his appetite and pine so in the absence of his loved one that he would find it hard to concentrate on anything else. None of this applied to me. I had developed a taste for Italian cooking, washed down with red wine, and the fare at the Capri restaurant never lost its appeal. Kathleen was much on my mind, yet I had no difficulty concentrating on my work, and that made me wonder about the depths of my devotion.

I reflected upon our relationship. Having gone deeply into the study of interpersonal relations in my research, I wondered how our interaction patterns would fit together. Kathleen was naturally more talkative than I and much quicker to jump into a conversation. I concluded that this made for a good fit, as I tended to withdraw into my own thoughts and often was at a loss for something to say. I remembered one girl I had taken out in Cambridge who not only was physically attractive but also seemed to share some interests with me. It did not work out because she tended to be as silent and slow in speech as I, so I felt constantly under pressure to do the talking. With Kathleen, there was no such problem. At times, I wondered if I would get a word in edgewise, but she learned to observe when the words were starting to come forth, and she was always interested in what I had to say. Later on, I developed an unconscious means of gaining entry into conversations. Before I had the words quite ready, I would open my mouth and emit a low hum. This was a signal that I had started the motor and that I would produce words at almost any moment. Then, once I got started, I could keep up the pace.

Whatever the individual features of our relationship, underlying it all was a feeling of warmth in Kathleen's company that I never experienced with anyone else. It had been that way when we had first met at the age of thirteen. That such a feeling of belonging together could last over eleven years seemed to augur well for our future together. So, although I still had moments of anxiety right up to the day of our wedding, I reassured myself that getting married was what I wanted and what I needed. To what extent I was "really in love" when we married now seems hardly a question worth asking, for I find myself much more in love with Kathleen after more than fifty years together than I was when we made our vows.

There was one part of our plans then that would have been problematic if we were approaching marriage today. After leaving the Art Students League, Kathleen had taken a course at Columbia with George Salter, a refugee from Hitler's Germany, who was a leading book jacket designer, and she had studied calligraphy with Alfred Fairbank in London. In the spring of 1938, two of her jackets had been accepted by New York publishers, so she was just getting her start professionally. For someone interested in designing book jackets, New York was obviously the place to be. Kathleen reasoned that there were two publishers in Boston, so she might get some work there. Had we faced this situation as a young married couple in the 1970s or later, we would probably have considered having her remain in New York and getting together on weekends. At the time, neither of us gave a thought to that option. Although she realized she was risking her career in commercial art, Kathleen wanted to be with me and to share in the adventure of the North End study.

On May 28, 1938, we had a small family wedding in the home of the Kings. The wedding breakfast was in the garden, with lilacs and irises in bloom.

The Kings had lent us their Chevrolet coupe for our honeymoon and the rest of the summer. Against tradition, we had spent the hours before the wedding loading it with the last of our household effects. After the reception, we drove to a hotel in New Bedford, Massachusetts, and the next day we took the ferry to Nantucket Island, where the Kings lent us a small cottage. This seemed like a pleasant and economical arrangement, for the cobblestone streets in the center of town, the stately mansions (built at the time of the whaling boom) along the main streets, and the moors and beaches of Nantucket provided an ideal setting for romance.

As it turned out, the start of our married life was hardly auspicious. I was still rather run-down from my illness, and I came down with the flu again. For several days, our honeymoon consisted of visits in the little hospital in Nantucket.

By the time I was well enough to leave the hospital, our vacation was almost over, so we went back to Boston. After a couple of weeks getting settled in the North End, we drove up to Greensboro, Vermont, for a visit with my parents. This might have been a pleasant visit for all of us, since Kathleen was fond of my parents, but tennis got in the way. The previous summer, I had attained the greatest heights of my tennis career. I had won the number 2 ranking in Vermont in the state championship at Burlington. Then I had come home to Greensboro and had won the championship there, beating my father for the first time in the finals.

My father assumed I would again enter the Vermont State Championship, but I should have known better. I had played little or no tennis all that spring, and during our honeymoon and the two weeks in Boston, I had not been on the courts. I lost in singles in an early round, and my father and I didn't do much better in doubles. Father and I had to drive more than an hour each way to the tournament and all the while talked endlessly about how I had done on the court and what I should have done to do better. Then friends and relatives would come around to greet the newlyweds, and the socializing would go on late into the evening. Kathleen bore up through it all, but this was a very poor way to begin married life.

Returning to the North End at the end of the summer, we began to settle in. There was a couple from Genoa upstairs and a couple from southern Italy downstairs. Both women welcomed Kathleen, and each took pride in teaching her how to cook her regional dishes. She even learned to make pizza, which was then unknown beyond Italian neighborhoods. There was a bakery next door and they baked bread in the evenings. Kathleen would go down and buy five cents worth of dough, bring it up to our apartment and bake it, with all the fixings of pizza on top.

We had two minor problems in that apartment. At first, there were mice. For a time, I made a game of it. I would find a mouse hiding in our kitchen cupboard and fake a move toward it, which would send it running away around the three sides of one of the cupboard shelves. I learned to time their moves so that, as one was approaching the end of the third side of the cupboard, behind a metal canister, I would bang my fist hard against the canister and knock it out. I would then pick it up and drop it out the window. Kathleen thought the drop from the window might not be enough to end the mouse and it might come back. I met this challenge by putting some paint on the tail of each mouse before dropping it out the window. I was gratified to find that no mice with painted tails reappeared in our apartment. Still, there were enough mice with unpainted tails to be a problem until we adopted a more traditional solution: We got a kitten, which also saved the canisters from further dents.

Later, when Kathleen and our first child came home from the hospital, we were suddenly overrun with bedbugs. They did not attack me, so Kathleen assumed she had hives, until they attacked baby Joyce. Soon there were swarms of them. The people in the adjoining building had moved out, and the enterprising bugs had worked their way through the wall to us. We had to call in an exterminator.

From my friends on the corner, I had learned that a good husband devoted one night a week to his wife and spent the other nights with the boys. I did indeed spend several nights a week out on the streets, but I would not have been happy following the corner boys' pattern. Besides, work now involved more writing than fieldwork. I spent much of my time typing, and then I would read what I had written to Kathleen and we would discuss it. Thus began a pattern whereby she became an active participant in my writing, a pattern that has continued to this day.

I look back on the period in Boston as a happy and carefree time—especially Sundays. Then we would sleep late, have a big breakfast, and set out to explore the Boston area—by foot, in the subways, and on trolleys. We spent a day at the Arnold Arboretum, at the end of one trolley line, and another time we took the subway out to Jamaica Plain, where Boston merged into open country.

During our last year on Hanover Street, we bought America's first mini-car, a $375 Crosley. After that, we could explore farther and invite up to two friends to go with us. When Kathleen was about nine months pregnant, we made quite a spectacle when we got out of the car, as I rose vertically on my long legs and Kathleen spread out horizontally.

At first when Kathleen came home from the hospital with baby Joyce, I would hold her only when I was sitting on our bed, so there was no chance of dropping her. But soon I got used to fathering her—even to the extent of helping Kathleen change her diapers. That was a small price to pay for starting a family.

13. Rethinking and Reshaping
My North End Study

I was doing fieldwork in the North End for eighteen months before I knew what I was doing. I had the general idea that I was conducting a community study as a nonparticipating observer, but as I became accepted into the community, I found myself becoming almost a nonobserving participant. I got the feel of local life, but that meant that I took for granted what my friends took for granted. I was immersed in their life, but I could as yet make little sense of it. I had the feeling I was doing something important, but I had yet to explain to myself what it was.

I also faced a very practical problem. My three-year fellowship would run out in the summer of 1939. Applications for renewal, for a period up to three years, were due in the early spring of 1939.

To apply, I would have to write something. I had several months in which to do the writing, but the task at first appalled me. What data was good enough to write about? I pondered this and talked it over with Kathleen and with John Howard, who was working with me in the district.

I knew very little about family life in the North End, and my data were very thin on the church, although John Howard was beginning to work on that area. My room at the Orlandis' had overlooked the corner where Joe Lombardi, reputed to be New England's racket boss, sometimes was seen with his followers. I had looked down upon them many times from my window, but I had never met the man. Racketeering was of obvious importance in the district, yet all I knew about it was the gossip I picked up from men who were only a little closer to it than I. I had much more information about the political life and organization of the district, but even in this area I felt there were so many gaps that I could not yet put the pieces together.

What did I have to present? As I thumbed through my folders, it was obvious that the ones on the Bennetts and the Italian Fellowship League were fatter than the rest. If I knew anything about the North End, I knew about these groups.

Gradually, a pattern for my research emerged. I realized that I was not going to write a community study like *Middletown*, which is about the people in that community in general. Individuals and groups do not figure in the story except as they illustrate the Lynds' points.

The Lynds accomplished their task admirably. I now realized that my task was different. I was dealing with particular individuals and with particular groups.

There was another difference. I had assumed that a sociological study should present a description and an analysis of a community at one particular point in time, supported of course by historical background. I now realized that time itself was one of the key elements in my study. I was observing, describing, and analyzing the groups in the North End as they evolved and changed through time.

I could say something significant about the individuals and groups in the district if I saw the individuals and groups in terms of their positions in the social structure. Furthermore, I had to assume that, whatever the differences among individuals and groups, there were also basic similarities. Thus, I did not have to study all the corner gangs to make meaningful statements about them.

I needed no additional data on the Italian Fellowship League. Most of the few college men in the North End were in the league, so that this one group represented an important sample.

I now saw the connection between my political study and my case study of the Bennetts. Politicians did not seek to influence separate individuals; consciously or unconsciously, they sought to gain the support of group leaders. Men like Pecci were the links between their groups and the larger political organization.

Nonetheless, there were still important gaps in my study. The gap that worried me the most was in the area of the rackets and the police. I had a general knowledge of how the rackets functioned but nothing to compare with the detailed interpersonal data I had on the Bennetts.

I finished writing my first two case studies—one on the Bennetts and one on the league—and submitted them as part of my application for a three-year renewal of my fellowship. When I learned the fellowship was renewed for only one year, I tried to appeal the decision, but an encounter with L. J. Henderson only worsened the pain. He told me that the Society of Fellows had appointed someone better than I for a three-year term but that that fellow had asked to start his term a year later. I should consider myself lucky to have received the one-year renewal.

I was bitterly disappointed. Since I was just beginning to get my bearings, I did not see how it would be possible to finish an adequate study in the eighteen months that remained of my fellowship.

I now believe that this deadline was very good for me. A community study has no logical end point. The more one learns, the more there is *to* learn. If I had had three years instead of one, my study would have taken longer to complete. Perhaps it might have been better, but knowing I had just eighteen months to go, I had to settle down and push ahead much more purposefully with the research and writing.

The most important step I took in broadening my study began with one of my periodic efforts to get Pecci a job. I had heard that the North End Union had gotten a grant to open three storefront recreation centers, and I sought to persuade the director, Frank Havey, to put local men like Pecci, who were leaders in their groups, in charge. He had planned to staff the center with trained social workers. I could see Havey was tempted by the idea and afraid of it at the same time. My plan almost backfired when I brought Pecci in to meet him, for, as Pecci told me later that day, he had had a dizzy spell in the office and was in no condition to make a favorable impression.

By this time, I had figured out the probable cause of these spells. When Pecci did not have any pocket money to spend with his friends, he could no longer participate with them in his role as leader. I expected that a steady job would enable him to resume his customary pattern of social activity and cure him of his neurotic symptom. But I could hardly explain this to Havey. As a last-ditch effort, I gave Havey a copy of my case study of the Bennetts, which must have made the difference. Havey agreed to hire Pecci.

In the meetings to discuss the plans for the centers, Pecci was passive and apparently apathetic. Nevertheless, almost from the moment Pecci's center opened, it was apparent that it would be a success. (The other centers, staffed by trained social workers, had to close down within two weeks. The social workers were simply unable to maintain discipline.)

During one of my early visits to Pecci's center, he introduced me to Angelo Ralph Orlandella, whose friends called him Ralph. On the night the center had opened, Ralph's gang had been hanging around outside, looking the place over. Ralph came in, talked to Pecci, and then brought his gang in. By the next night, Ralph had become Pecci's lieutenant. Pecci knew a few people in the part of the district where the center was located, but Ralph knew everybody.

Having learned that Ralph had been keeping a scrapbook of newspaper accounts of North End activities and some personal material on his gang, Pecci suggested that Ralph could help me with my study.

I invited Ralph to my apartment. The scrapbook was completely miscellaneous and unfocused, but it did have one part that particularly interested me: a section on Ralph's gang, which contained one page for each member. At the top of the page was a line drawing (from memory) of the individual and then such information as his age, address, education, job, and ambition. (Usually Ralph had written "none" opposite the heading "ambition.")

I told Ralph that, while it was fine to look upon these men as individuals, it was even better to observe them in their relations with each other. I had only begun my explanation when Ralph got the point and accepted it. This was the sort of thing he knew; he had so taken it for granted that its importance had not occurred to him. From this point until the end of my North End study, Ralph was my research assistant. I even managed to get Harvard to pay him one hundred dollars for his services.

Ralph and I began by analyzing his gang, the Thatchers. We also looked at other gangs that came into the recreation center. In this I had the great advantage of having two sharp observers commenting on the groups. I was reassured to find that Pecci and Ralph were in complete agreement on the top leadership structure of each gang—with one exception. Pecci claimed that Carl was the leader of one gang; Ralph argued that it was Tommy. Each presented observations in support of his choice. The following morning, I heard Ralph pounding up the stairs to our flat, where he breathlessly delivered a bulletin: "You know what happened last night? Carl and Tommy nearly had it out. They got into a big argument, and now the gang is split into two parts, with some of them going with Carl and the rest going with Tommy." Thus, their conflicting views of the gang both turned out to be accurate representations of what was taking place.

As I worked on these gang studies, I assumed that I had finished my research on the Bennetts. Still, I kept in close touch with Pecci, and, just for recreation, I continued to bowl with them on some Saturday nights.

With my attention directed elsewhere, I failed to see what was happening to the Bennetts until Pecci told me about Slim's mental health problems. He was having trouble getting to sleep at night, and, when he did drop off, he would awake suddenly in a cold sweat, with the sheet covering his face. Pecci had learned that when Slim was six years old (in Italy), he had been stricken with pneumonia and given up for dead, only to waken with a sheet drawn over his face.

I believed that Pecci was on the right track in tracing the origin of Slim's symptoms, but why were they coming out now instead of earlier? Perhaps the problem had to do with the drastic changes in his interaction patterns? When the Bennetts had been together on their corner night after night, Slim had been close friends with the top leadership subgroup of Pecci, Gillo, and Frank, although he did not have the respect of the followers. Now that Pecci was hanging out in Spongi's gambling joint, the Bennetts were no longer gathering every night on their corner. When Slim showed up on the Bennetts' corner, he was subjected to disparaging remarks by the remaining members. When Slim dropped into Spongi's place, nobody paid much attention to him. The Bennetts continued to get together for Saturday-night bowling, but now Slim was bowling poorly and was increasingly subjected to razzing by the other members.

When Pecci told me about Slim's problems, it was as if he set off a flash in my head. Suddenly, all the pieces of the puzzle fell together. The previous season, I had stumbled upon the relationship between position in the Bennetts and performance at the bowling alleys. I now saw the three-way connection between group position, performance, and mental health—and not only for Slim. Pecci's dizzy spells seemed to have precisely the same explanation: they occurred when he was unable to pursue his customary pattern of social interaction.

If my diagnosis was correct, then the therapy was clear: Reestablish something like Slim's preexisting pattern of interaction, and the neurotic symptoms should disappear. Although I now had a real opportunity to test my conclusions on group structure, and embraced them with enthusiasm, I still did not know how the therapy could be implemented.

I was awestruck when Pecci started carrying out the therapy. Whenever he dropped into Spongi's, he would look around and ask the fellows if they had seen Slim, and that got them asking each other when they had last seen him. Then, when Slim came in, Pecci would give him a big welcome. Soon Slim was included, along with Pecci, in any small group that went out from there with Spongi. Without telling anybody what he was doing, Pecci also changed the social situation on Saturday nights at the bowling alley. Whenever Slim prepared to bowl, Pecci would call out that he was once again the good bowler he had been before. Soon, Gillo and Frank were also cheering for him. As a result, Slim received much less razzing.

In response to this treatment, Slim not only lost his neurotic symptoms but also closed out the season by winning in the final bowling contest. His five-dollar prize was a nice bonus in the development of interaction theory.

Also during this period, I finally got to meet Tony Cataldo, the prominent North End racketeer. I had dropped in one afternoon at the Capri. Hector, Avy Orlandi's older brother, was grumbling about a pair of banquet tickets he had had to buy from a local policeman. He said that his wife did not want to go to banquets; perhaps I might like to accompany him.

I asked what the occasion was. It was in honor of the son of the local police lieutenant, who had just passed his bar examinations. It was obvious what sorts of people would be present at the banquet: mostly policemen, politicians, and racketeers.

At the banquet hall, we encountered Tony Cataldo and one of his employees, Rico Deleo. Hector knew Tony slightly, and Rico lived right across from me on Hanover Street. Rico asked what I was doing, and I said something about writing a book on the North End. Tony said he had seen me taking photographs of the saint's day *feste* on Hanover Street the previous summer.

We went to a banquet table together, where we had to wait more than an hour for our food. We munched on olives and celery and sympathized with one another about the poor service. After dinner, we went downstairs for bowling. By this time, Tony was quite friendly and invited me to stop in at his store any time. (I later paid several visits to the back room of the store from which Tony operated some of his numbers business.)

A week after we met, Tony invited Kathleen and me to dinner. His wife told us later that he had described us as a Harvard professor and a commercial artist. She was upset that he gave her only one day's notice when she felt she needed at least a week to prepare for such important personages. Nevertheless, the food was quite elaborate, and each course seemed like a whole meal. After dinner, Tony drove us out to meet some of his relatives in the suburbs. Then we all went bowling together.

We had dinner twice at their home, and they came to ours twice. On each occasion, apart from the small talk, we talked some about the *feste*, about the club life of the *paesani* from the old country, and other such things that Tony associated with my study. Then, I gradually eased him into a discussion of his business. The discussion seemed to move naturally in this direction.

After our first visits together, Tony seemed to lose interest in us. I was worried by this sudden cooling-off. I am not sure I have the full explanation, but I think there were at least two parts to it.

During this time, Tony ran into a business crisis. Some men broke into his horse room one afternoon, held it up, and took all the money from the customers and from Tony. It was a traumatic event for him and for his family. In the middle of the holdup, his six-year-old son came into the room; thinking he would join in the game, he pointed his toy gun at the holdup men and made "bang-bang" noises. They grabbed him and locked him in a closet.

To maintain good relations with his customers, Tony had to reimburse them for the robbery. It was also frustrating, because, as the men were making their getaway, Tony could look out the window and see them running right beneath him. He had a clear shot at them, yet he could not shoot, because he knew that a shooting would close down gambling in the North End. As long as business was done quietly, the "heat" was not likely to be on.

The other possible reason for the interruption in our relations may have been my social status. The Cataldos were highly status-conscious. They did not allow their young son to play with the local riffraff, and they explained that they lived in the district only for business reasons. When we were their guests, they introduced us to friends and relatives who lived in more fashionable parts of the city. When the Cataldos came to our house for dinner, they just met us and nobody else. Furthermore, Tony saw me associating with men on Hanover Street who were distinctly small-fry to him. At first, he had thought his contact with me was important; now, perhaps, he considered it insignificant.

I was aware of this risk and thought of having Harvard friends to dinner with the Cataldos. I had been keeping the two worlds apart. One of the junior fellows, W. V. O. Quine, a symbolic logician, had once asked me to introduce him to a crap game. He explained that he had figured out mathematically how to win. I explained that my crap-shooting friends had reached the same mathematical conclusion by their rule-of-thumb method, and I begged off.

I was hesitant about mixing my Harvard friends with those in the North End. I did not worry about what the North Enders would do to my friends from Harvard, but I did worry that some Harvard friend might say something that would make things awkward for me or act in a way that would make the North Enders feel ill at ease. Since I kept the two worlds separate, Tony could not improve his social standing by associating with us.

Tony was a member of the Hanover Association, which was right across the street from our apartment. I joined the club to renew my pursuit of Tony Cataldo.

At first, I was disappointed. Tony was rarely in the clubroom. I considered dropping out of the club, and perhaps I would have done so if there had been other research areas demanding my attention. At least I recognized that the club presented some new angles for my research. It was far larger than any corner gang I had studied. Here was an opportunity to carry further the observational methods I had used on the Bennetts.

I also began looking around for *the* leader. I did not find him. If Tony was not around much, then somebody had to take over in his absence. The club had a president, but he was just an indecisive nice guy who obviously did not amount to much. I did not find the leader because the club consisted of two factions with two leaders and—just to make matters more confusing for me—the leader of one faction was not even a member of the club at the time I began my observations.

To observe a club of fifty members, I would have to develop more systematic procedures than I had used with a small group of men. I began with positional mapmaking: making a record of the groups I observed each evening in the club. To some extent, I could do this from the front window of our apartment. I simply adjusted the venetian blind so that I was hidden from view and looked down and into the storefront club. Since our flat was two flights up, I could not see past the middle of the clubroom. To get the full picture, I had to go down there.

When evening activities were going full blast, I looked around to see which people were talking together, playing cards together, or otherwise interacting. I counted the number of men in the room so I would know how many I had to account for. Since I was familiar with the main physical objects of the clubroom, it was not difficult to get a mental picture of the men in relation to tables, chairs, couches, the ratio, and so on. When individuals moved about, or when there was some interaction between groups, I sought to keep that in mind. In the course of an evening, there might be a general reshuffling of positions. I was not able to remember every movement, but I tried to observe which members were the first to reshuffle. When another spatial arrangement developed, I went through the same mental process.

I managed to make a few notes on trips to the men's room. At first, I went home once or twice for map-making during the evening, but, with practice, I got so that I could retain at least two arrangements in memory and do all of my notes at home after the evening sessions.

The link between the social structure of the club and the racket organization became clear during a political campaign. Tony had been trying to persuade the club to invite his Irish candidate to address us, although nearly all the members were for an Italian. At this point, I committed a serious blunder. I said that, although we were all for Fiumara, it was a good idea to hear what other politicians had to say. The vote was taken shortly after I spoke, and it went for Tony.

That led to a rally for the Irish candidate in our clubroom and to the most serious dissension within the club.

At the time, I was still hoping to reestablish close ties with Tony, and I wanted to make some move in that direction. So I sought to do the impossible: to take a stand that would not antagonize the members but that Tony would appreciate. It was a foolish and misguided idea. I antagonized Carlo, the leader of one faction, and he forgave me only on the assumption that I had acted out of ignorance. That being preferable to treachery, I accepted the excuse.

My effort to win favor with Tony was a complete failure. Before the political crisis, he had hardly known Carlo and had not recognized his position as leader. When Carlo opposed him vigorously and effectively, Tony made every effort to establish closer relations with him. Since I had taken a position on his side, Tony needed to make no efforts to establish closer relations with me.

My action was not only unwise from a practical research standpoint but also a violation of professional ethics. It is unethical for a researcher to establish his social position on the assumption that he is not trying to lead anyone anywhere and then suddenly throw his weight to one side in a conflict.

Up to this point, I had also been trying to submerge my reformist urges in the supposed interests of science. In the summer of 1939, I gave in to the urge to do something.

In all my time in the North End, I had heard again and again about how the district was forgotten by the politicians, how no improvements were ever made, and how the politicians just tried to get themselves and their friends ahead. But perhaps the bitterest complaint concerned the public bathhouse, where, in the summer of 1939, as well as in several earlier summers, there was no hot water available. In a district where only 12 percent of the flats had bathtubs, this was a serious matter.

If we could not get action from the local politicians, why not go direct to the mayor—and on a mass basis? If the corner gang leaders were able to mobilize their gangs for action, then it should be possible, by working with a small number of people, to organize a large demonstration.

I talked this over with Ralph Orlandella, who was enthusiastic and ready to act at once. He promised the support of his section of the district. For the North Bennett Street area I called on Pecci. For the area around Langone's headquarters, I picked one of the local leaders. And, with my new acquaintances on Hanover Street, I was able to mobilize that end of the district.

Then began the complicated task of bringing the groups together and getting them ready to march at the same time. Since I was the connecting link among most of the corner gang leaders and since I had begun the organizing activity, I was the logical man to lead the demonstration. The problem was that I was not prepared to depart so far from my role as observer. I agreed that I would serve on the organizing committee, but we would have to have a different chairman. I proposed Pecci, and everyone agreed.

Although he was happy to participate, Pecci was not prepared to be the leader. I then proposed Frank Luongo, and he too was acceptable to the planning group. Frank said that he would conduct a public meeting to get people together for the march but that the chairman should be elected by the representatives of the different corners who were there assembled. We agreed on this.

Another problem arose, however, when Ralph brought representatives to the meeting, whereas a large part of the Hanover Street section came en masse. Thus, when there were nominations for chairman, a man from Hanover Street, who had previously had no part in the planning, was nominated and elected. Ralph's friends were annoyed by this, for they felt they could have elected one of their candidates if they had brought in all the gangs from their area. Ralph also suspected that the chairman would try to turn the demonstration to his personal advantage, and I had to concede that that was a good possibility. From this point on, our committee worked to hem in the chairman so that he would have no opportunity to go off on his own tangent.

On the morning of the march, we assembled in the playground in front of the bathhouse. We had had mimeographed handbills distributed throughout the neighborhood the day before, and the newspapers had been notified. Our committee was ready to lead the march, and the playground was pretty well filled with marchers. Some of the older generation were there lining the sides of the playground. I assumed they would be marching with us, but they didn't. We should have realized that, if we wanted to get members of the older generation to participate, we had to work through their leadership too.

Most of the demonstrators were men, but a few young women did join us— including Kathleen and several pushing baby carriages. As we set off for city hall, young boys from all over the district thronged in among us carrying home-made banners. We had the satisfaction of stopping traffic all along the route, but not for long, since the parade moved very fast. It seemed that everybody was trying to get to the front, so that we leaders were almost stampeded. Some of the women pushing baby carriages were unable to keep up.

We had no opposition from the police, who were concerned only that the demonstration remain orderly as we assembled in the courtyard below city hall. The ten committee members went up to the mayor's office, while the rest of the marchers sang "God bless America," accompanied by an improvised band. We had known the mayor would be out of town, so we had agreed to talk to the acting mayor. Treating us seriously and respectfully, he got our names and a list of our grievances. Then, as our committee members began to speak, I heard Ralph say in a low voice, "Get out of here, you cheap racketeer." I turned to see a local politician elbowing his way in and saying, "I would like to add my voice to the protest as a private citizen." Ralph interrupted: "He's got nuttin' to do with us. He's just trying to chisel in." Frank Luongo reiterated Ralph's remarks, and the acting mayor ruled that he would not listen to the politician. While committee members spoke, I distributed a prepared statement to the reporters. At the end of our session, the acting mayor promised that all our protests would be seriously considered and that action would be taken.

We then marched to the bathhouse playground, where we told our supporters what had taken place. Once again, the politician tried to address the crowd, but we elbowed him out.

The next day the newspapers carried big stories with pictures of our demonstration. The various papers gave us credit for having three hundred to fifteen hundred marchers. Everyone happily accepted the latter figure, but I suspect three hundred was closer to the truth.

The day after the demonstration, engineers examined the boilers in the bathhouse, and in less than a week there was hot water. The street cleaning and garbage collections also seemed to improve, for at least a while. For all the mistakes we had made, the demonstration had brought results. Now the problem was, What next? We had gotten an organization together, and we had staged a demonstration. Somehow, we had to keep the North Enders working together.

In this we were unsuccessful. Several committee meetings petered out without any agreements on concerted action. The committee members were not accustomed to working together, and we had started off with such a sensational performance that anything else would be an anticlimax.

I realized that any overall street corner organization would have to be built around a continuing activity. The softball league we developed the following spring met this need to some extent. In fact, I worked with the men on the committee to set it up so in a sense the march on city hall did have ongoing benefits, although they fell far short of our hopes.

I had justified my intervention in getting Pecci the job at the recreation center in purely scientific terms. I was testing an idea, and the test provided evidence of the soundness of that idea. The protest march was different. I was not testing an idea, just yielding my urge to reform. Still, that adventure did no harm to my project, and I did learn something from it—although it was peripheral to my research plans: I was still struggling to learn how best to combine research and action.

Through the spring and summer of 1940, I spent most of my time writing the first draft of *Street Corner Society*. I already had the case studies of the Bennetts and the Italian Fellowship League. I followed these with three sections that I called "Politics and the Social Structure," "The Racketeer in the Cornerville S. and A. Club," and "The Social Structure of Racketeering."

As I wrote, I showed the various parts to Pecci and went over them with him in detail. His criticisms were invaluable in my revisions. At times, he would smile and say, "This will embarrass me, but this is the way it was, so go ahead with it."

When I left the district in the midsummer of 1940, the Hanover Association had a farewell party for me. We sang "God Bless America" three times and the "Beer Barrel Polka" six times. I have never felt so much as though I were leaving home. The only thing that was missing was a farewell from the Bennetts, and that was impossible, for they no longer existed by this time. Their disappearance made me feel that I had lost my closest friends.

14. *Graduate Work in Chicago*

The junior fellowship was supposed to carry such prestige that it would not be necessary to get a Ph.D. Two of my contemporaries, Harry Levin and George Homans, had distinguished careers on the faculty of Harvard without doctorates. With Pitrim Sorokin heading the sociology department, I saw no possibility of moving from the Society of Fellows into a Harvard appointment. Much as I dreaded the prospect of formal graduate study after the exciting years in the North End, I decided I had better get a Ph.D.

The sociology department at the University of Chicago had an outstanding reputation, but that was not what attracted me. On the advice of Conrad Arensberg at Harvard, I chose Chicago so I could study with W. Lloyd Warner, who had left Harvard in 1935 after completing the fieldwork for several books that came to be known as the Yankee City series.

I was granted a $600-a-year assistantship. Since the tuition was $100 for each quarter, that was nowhere near enough for a couple and a baby to live on, and quite a comedown from the $2,250 I had received in the final year of my junior fellowship. Fortunately, we had been able to save enough during the North End years to survive for a year in Chicago.

We found an apartment at 6102 South Dorchester Avenue in the Woodlawn district, just a block from the Midway—a park that separated Woodlawn from Hyde Park, where the University of Chicago was located and where many faculty families lived.

Since Warner had joint appointments in both the anthropology and sociology departments, having him for my major professor did not determine my program. I was eager to finish graduate work as soon as possible, so I decided on my program on a very pragmatic basis. There was substantial overlap in the requirements of the two departments. Beyond those core areas, both departments would require me to study topics in which I had little interest—physical anthropology and archaeology or the family, delinquency, and crime—but those areas in anthropology would require more time to learn. I also assumed there would be more job opportunities in sociology. (In fact, I was offered only one job when I was finished, at the University of Oklahoma.)

Warner chaired my Ph.D. committee, and I soon asked Everett C. Hughes to be a committee member. I had known nothing about Hughes, but he had recently completed the fieldwork for *French Canada in Transition* (1943), an outstanding study of a Quebec industrial city. When I was interviewed for admission to Chicago, he was immersed in reading my North End materials, and he greeted me warmly. Like me, Hughes operated on the borderline between sociology and social anthropology.

Hughes and Warner were close friends and had many interests in common. Lloyd and Mildred Warner and Everett and Helen Hughes accepted Kathleen and me with open arms, treating me more as a colleague than a student.

As Warner's research assistant, I had an assignment designed to enrich his and my knowledge of French sociology and anthropology. Some of Émile Durkheim's books had been translated into English, but he and his associates had published many articles in *L'Anné Sociologique*, and those had not been translated. Warner asked me to abstract some of those articles.

I was out of step with the other students beginning their graduate studies since I arrived with the first draft of my Ph.D. thesis in my trunk. This had both advantages and disadvantages. On the one hand, I could evaluate anything published in urban sociology based on my own intense experience in the North End. On the other hand, it was difficult to avoid giving the impression that I claimed to know more than the recognized experts. Nonetheless, I did make some friends among the sociology students. John Clausen has remained a good friend to this day.

The sociology department was marked by professional rivalries that were reflected in the faculty members' somewhat strained interpersonal relations. I found myself in one camp with Warner and Hughes. From students closer to Louis Wirth and Herbert Blumer, in the other camp, I got the picture of Warner as a big-name newcomer who was more a showman than a serious scholar. It was now more than four years since he had finished the fieldwork for his Yankee City series, and he had nothing in print to show for it. He could not be criticized for long, however, for the first volume of the series appeared in 1941 and the other volumes appeared in 1942, 1945, 1947, and 1959, followed by a one-volume abridged edition in 1962.

I found Warner an exciting teacher. He brought into the classroom the joys of social exploration, and I admired him for his commitment to new fieldwork, even as he was writing up the Yankee City studies. I could have been part of that project, but Lloyd advised me to push ahead with my doctoral thesis and the other requirements for the Ph.D. Still, I envied the students working with him and had mixed feelings as I talked with them: I shared their interests yet felt excluded.

From students outside the Warner/Hughes camp, I got the impression that Hughes was a bumbling professor who was incapable of presenting a systematic picture of sociology. Hughes made no pretensions about presenting grand theory, but I found his lectures and discussions fascinating for the insights he brought to bear on the most mundane situations.

Students in the Warner/Hughes camp learned to be on guard against Blumer and Wirth. I contrasted the two pairs in terms of their involvement in fieldwork. Blumer had done none since he had worked on his doctoral thesis on children's responses to movies, and Wirth had done none since publishing *The Ghetto*. Both had built their reputations on their sharp criticisms of the work of other scholars. When I learned that Blumer had supported himself through graduate school by playing football for the Chicago Bears, I was fascinated, but I was disappointed to learn that he made no use of this experience in his teaching.

Louis Wirth seemed to be coasting along on his scholarly reputation. He was heavily involved in Jewish causes and interethnic relations. He often was so unprepared for his classes that he was still organizing his notes when it was time to start the lecture.

The three other major members of the department were apparently not aligned with either of the two camps. William F. Ogburn was department chairman and best known for having invented the concept of cultural lag. He taught a course on cultural change, which seemed not to go much beyond the notion that cultural change tends to lag behind technological change. I also took his statistics course. He presented the subject clearly and systematically, and I should have taken to it more than I did. Ogburn also made special efforts to get to know the students and show that he was interested in them.

Sam Stouffer taught the more advanced statistics courses. I found him a lively teacher, full of interesting ideas. I took to him personally but failed to profit from his class. I was still not ready to get into survey research.

The veteran of the department, Ernest Burgess, was a bachelor who lived with his sister and taught courses and did research on the family and courtship patterns. Burgess had been a protégé of Robert E. Park, who had gone from journalism into sociology and had been a major figure in stimulating and guiding the department's studies of the city. Burgess and Park had collaborated on a sociology textbook.

I found Burgess a friendly old man who encouraged my interest in urban studies. I am indebted to him for introducing me to Clifford Shaw, who was then based with the Illinois Institute for Juvenile Research. It was Shaw who introduced me to the Near North Side of Chicago, which I was fascinated to find was as familiar as the North End.

Harvey Zorbaugh, in *The Goldcoast and the Slum*, had described the area as one where people did not really know each other and had few close ties. I wondered how Zorbaugh had come to that conclusion. Then I remembered a time when I had gone looking for Chichi in a part of the North End that was unfamiliar to me. I had his address but not the number of his flat. I asked at several doors if Chichi lived there. Everyone denied knowing him until Chichi himself heard my voice and came out to greet me. Of course, everyone in Chichi's building knew him, but he was the only one who knew me. Was this the way Zorbaugh had determined that the Near North Siders did not know each other?

The differences in points of view within the sociology department were not unhealthy from the students' standpoint, and we wanted to get those differences openly discussed. The most popular debate at the time was over the value of statistics versus that of the case study. We had Blumer and Stouffer debate, and that argument was extended nationally in a meeting of the American Sociological Association, where Blumer squared off with George Lundberg. That was such a sharp argument that when the two shook hands at the end, it conveyed the misleading impression that there were no hard feelings.

I was ambivalent during the Blumer and Stouffer arguments. I had no taste for statistics, but I liked Stouffer much better than Blumer. I was dedicated to case studies, but my kind was not really represented in the argument. I was trying to link together individuals, groups, and organizations in the same community and to follow the dynamics of their interrelations over a long period of time. I had not seen such a study attempted in the sociological literature.

While I was pushing to complete my doctorate, I revised my manuscript on the North End for publication. Although I was drifting away from my ambition to write fiction, I was determined to write *Street Corner Society* so that it would be read by a wide audience. I submitted the manuscript first to the publisher Reynal and Hitchcock, which was sponsoring a competition in which it was looking for a nonfiction manuscript based on scholarly research but deserving broad readership. I came in second to a book on philosophy.

With the encouragement of Warner and Hughes, I then submitted the manuscript to the University of Chicago Press. An editor there accepted it, but then the business manager wrote to tell me that I would have to cut the manuscript by a third and put up a thirteen hundred-dollar subsidy, since the book would sell few copies. We were able to live on my fellowship of fifteen hundred dollars, but putting up the subsidy exhausted the money we had saved in the North End. At first, I was more concerned about the revision than the subsidy, because I did not see how I could comply without cutting the heart out of the book. I can no longer remember what I cut, but I believe the condensation improved the manuscript.

The Japanese attack on Pearl Harbor occurred in the middle of my Chicago studies, adding a sense of urgency to finishing graduate school. With a wife and child, I had a family military deferment, but I knew that would not last for long. The war seemed to be a good war, and yet my life experience made it hard for me to imagine myself in the armed forces. Still, I did not feel right about standing aside while others served. I felt I had to complete my doctoral work by mid-1942. The principal hurdles remaining were the field examinations and my thesis defense.

I remember little about the field examinations, except for the section on social anthropology. When I took them, in the spring of 1942, Warner was on leave, but he sent in a question. I had ten days to figure out why some cultures place a high or low degree of emphasis on age grading in their social organization. That caught me unprepared. I knew in general that age grading existed in all cultures, but I had given no thought to the factors underlying different degrees of emphasis on this principle.

As I read up on the topic, I devised two lines of analysis, which I also found useful in later research. First, I figured out the general conditions that might account for the phenomenon in question. Next, I examined cases to check whether there was some degree of fit between the cases and the theoretical assumptions. If so, I then subjected those assumptions to attack by looking for deviant cases: those that seemed to fit the presumed general conditions but that did not show the expected characteristics. An examination of those cases then enabled me to modify and sharpen the theoretical analysis.

I read about African and American Indian tribes in which age grading was an influential organizational principle. Then I concentrated on the Indian tribes of the Western Plains. Although age grading was prominent throughout the

Plains, it was much more dominant among the tribes in the North than among those in the South. In my exam paper, I concentrated on explaining that difference.

Warner was happy with the paper, which encouraged me to think that I might have the makings of a publishable article. Over the next few months, I did some revisions. In 1944, "Age Grading of the Plains Indians" was published in *Man*, the British journal of the Royal Anthropological Society.

In that era, all the members of the department attended and participated in one's thesis defense. Given the divisions within the department and Warner's absence, mine promised to be rough. I could anticipate who my main challengers would be and their main criticisms: that I rejected the orthodox idea that slums were unorganized or disorganized, and that I was presumed to be ignorant of previous slum studies. The Chicago department was known as a leading center of urban studies, with a particular emphasis on slums. As I had read up on the literature, I had come to the conclusion that some of the most highly respected studies were so misleading as to be useless. I had therefore decided not to begin my book, which I was presenting as my thesis, with a review of the literature. Furthermore, my book was completely bare of footnotes. Finally, the university had a requirement—long since abandoned—that all Ph.D. theses had to be printed. Since Kathleen and I had already exhausted our savings to subsidize the publication of *Street Corner Society*, I could ill afford to take on the expense of printing even a few copies of my thesis along with a review of the literature chapter and a full set of footnotes.

The sharpest attack came from Louis Wirth, who had published one of the better studies of slums. He asked me to define a slum. I replied that it was an urban area where there was a high concentration of low-income people living in dilapidated housing under poor sanitary and health conditions. Wirth objected on the grounds that this was not a sociological definition, but I refused to satisfy his conceptual appetite. I said that the conditions I mentioned were what had led me to study the North End and that it was an empirical problem to determine how people lived under those conditions.

After fruitless attempts to get me to define a slum in terms of "social disorganization," Wirth attacked me for failing to cite the generations of sociological literature on slums. This provoked an interchange in which I attempted to demonstrate that I really did know that literature.

At this point, Everett Hughes intervened. He said that the department would accept the book as my thesis provided I wrote a separate review of the literature. This supplementary material could then be printed (at my expense) and bound with the university library copy of my book. That would make my thesis fit into the traditions of the graduate school.

I decided that if I had to write a literature review, I might as well get some published articles out of it. "Social Organization in the Slums" was published in the *American Sociological Review* in 1943, and "Challenge to Political Scientists," a critique of the political science literature on slums, in the *American Political Science Review* in 1944. In that article, I argued that students of urban politics should stop moralizing about good and bad politicians and focus on field studies of political behavior. The article provoked a lively debate, some of which was reflected in a later issue of the *Review* that contained attacks on my article by two political scientists and my rejoinder. A decade or so later, Pendleton Herring of the Social Science Research Council invited me to a small conference, attended by several professors in the University of Michigan Survey Research Center and some young and presumably impressionable political scientists, to discuss how political behavior should be studied.

When I told Everett Hughes that I had had two articles accepted for publication, he persuaded the department to accept them as my literature review and to abandon the formal requirement that they be bound with the book in the library copy. Thus, the thesis defense ordeal produced an academic dividend: I could now launch my career with two articles as well as *Street Corner Society*.

From 1940 to 1942, I let up on my studies only once, to attend the first meeting of the Society for Applied Anthropology (SfAA) at Harvard in November 1941. Connie Arensberg had invited me to come and present a paper based on my North End research.

I could ill afford the time and travel expense, but this seemed too important to pass up. I was committed to the society's aim of discovering ways in which social research and practice could be linked more effectively, and this would be my first chance to present a research report to colleagues.

Since I attended and joined SfAA at the first official meeting, I claim to be a charter member, although I had nothing to do with its creation. SfAA was organized mainly by a small group of people little older than I and only a little better established in the academic world. The sole exceptions were Margaret Mead and her husband, Gregory Bateson. Margaret had come to public attention as early as 1928 with *Coming of Age in Samoa*. From that time and for as long as she lived, she was the anthropologist best known by the American public. She was also a prominent figure in academic anthropology.

Among the twenty-five or so who attended the SfAA's first meeting, Margaret Mead was the queen bee, yet none of us resented her central role. Without being so designated on the program, Margaret assumed the role of discussion leader after each paper. That a person as important as Margaret was with us encouraged us to believe that we were creating something important.

My paper was entitled "The Social Role of the Settlement House." The theme at the time seemed a novel one: that the social workers at the house were not really dealing with the indigenous culture and social organization of the community but were seeking to attract those ready to leave that community behind them.

Years later, with my permission, anthropologist Scudder Mekeel copied my article, which had appeared in the first issue of *Applied Anthropology*, to make the same points regarding the relations between the Bureau of Indian Affairs (BIA) and American Indian tribes. He had only to substitute BIA officials for social workers and the Indian tribe for the slum community, and he could reuse "The Social Role of the Settlement House" almost exactly as I had written it. This encouraged me to believe that I had come upon uniformities of social relations of quite general significance.

15. Teaching Schoolteachers Sociology

I n a long career, a six-week summer school teaching job would hardly seem worth mentioning, but it may have been the best teaching I have ever done, and it still brings back vivid memories. The summer school program, supported by the Kellogg Foundation and conducted in Charlotte, Michigan, was designed to enrich the experience and ideas of elementary school teachers. The program director believed that the teachers should be exposed to sociology, and it was my job to provide that exposure.

In the mornings, students went to classes taught by members of the staff, including me. In the afternoon, they observed a demonstration fourth-grade class taught by a very gifted teacher.

For most of my students, this was their first exposure to sociology. Rather than try to give them a very general introduction to my discipline, however, I hoped to teach them some social skills and ways of thinking that would help them understand their communities and the children they were teaching. I decided to get them started right away on interviewing and observing and also on analyzing the community of Charlotte. About half the teachers lived and worked outside the town in a nearby community within the county, so Charlotte was familiar territory.

Teaching the teachers how to interview and observe was slow going. They had trouble separating what the interviewee said from their interpretations of what the interviewee was thinking and feeling. Similarly, they had trouble separating behavior they had concretely observed from their interpretations of what the behavior meant.

To correct these deficiencies, I proposed that they and I observe the demonstration class together and later compare our notes on what we observed. The demonstration class was in an open classroom, where six groups of four pupils each sat around tables. The pupils were free to move their chairs around their table and they were also free to talk to their classmates. I urged my students to pay special attention to the informal organization, particularly the grouping of the pupils and the relations among the children.

The following morning, in a lecture with blackboard diagrams, I laid out what I had observed. I had noted the first names of at least three-quarters of the twenty-four children. I had also sorted them into groups of four, and for several of the groups, I had identified the informal leader.

Although my students had observed the class six or seven times, they did not know the names of any of the pupils or have any idea of the relations among them. Instead of observing the pupils, they had focused solely on the teacher; they had observed the children only when the teacher spoke to one or more of the pupils.

At first, the students were awed, but then I showed them that they were all capable of the same performance. I had begun by drawing a spacial map of the room, including all the desks and chairs, thus providing a general framework within which to place and identify individual pupils. If I heard one child say to another, "Hey, Joe . . ." I could assume that the pupil addressed was named Joe.

To identify the leaders of the groups, I concentrated on *set events*: interactions in which one individual acted and two or more others responded, or two or more individuals addressed their actions and remarks to one individual.

During recess, my students had remained in the classroom, chatting among themselves. I had followed the children out to the playground to observe the interactions and activities that were not formally structured by the arrangement of the tables and chairs. The recess also provided an opportunity to observe interactions among children who were not members of the same table. On this basis, I could develop at least preliminary ideas about the broader leadership pattern in the classroom, although clearly a good deal more time would have been required to determine this pattern conclusively.

For the study of the social organization of Charlotte, I provided some background, through readings and lectures, on social classes and status systems. I also took advantage of two unplanned events.

In the course of one week, two women from Chile came to speak to the summer school students. These women seemed to be talking about two very different countries. One of them told us that Chile was a very advanced nation, culturally as well as economically. She told us that Santiago had a symphony orchestra and that local companies performed operas. The other woman told us about factory workers, who she said were exploited and had to work for low pay under difficult physical conditions.

I asked my students which Chilean had presented "the true picture." When they could not answer, I pointed out that the question was unanswerable. They should try to interpret what each woman said in terms of her social background and personal experience. What had they learned along these lines? They were then able to piece together a coherent picture. One of the women came from an elite family, and her life seemed to revolve around "high culture." The other came from a more modest background and was employed as a doctor in a large factory.

The other event involved a popular high school history teacher whom the superintendent of schools had discharged the previous spring. The teacher had counterattacked by announcing his candidacy for the school board, along with that of one of his supporters. By the time summer school had begun, the teacher and his supporters had organized a campaign. At the time, the board was divided four to one against them. The two incumbents had voted with the majority. If the insurgents won, however, they would have a three to two majority. The election was scheduled for near the end of our summer session.

The whole town was excited about this campaign, and it struck very close to home for the teachers in my class. I asked my students to tell me what they knew about the occupational and social characteristics of those supporting the incumbents and those supporting the insurgents. The major division was between the Main Street merchants and their families and the younger local professionals and those who commuted to work in East Lansing.

I next asked them to identify the candidates in terms of their memberships in associations, particularly the Rotary Club and the Lions. There was general agreement that most of the Rotarians were for the incumbents, whereas most of the Lions were expected to vote for the insurgents. Further, except for one woman who was engaged to be married to a Lion, the students agreed that the Rotarians enjoyed higher status than the Lions.

The campaign came to a climax with a public meeting at the school. At past annual meetings, attendance had rarely surpassed thirty to forty citizens. On this occasion, the auditorium was crowded with more than four hundred.

The meeting began with an open debate on two closely related issues: a teacher tenure act, proposed by the insurgents to limit arbitrary discharges, and the school board election.

I was impressed by the contrast in the speeches of the members of the opposing factions. Those in the Main Street faction emphasized that the schools had an annual budget that topped $1 million a year and that school board members therefore had to know how to manage money and meet a payroll. The speakers for the insurgents pleaded with the audience to "consider the interests of our children."

The teacher tenure act was voted on first, and it lost by a very narrow margin: seven votes. Then came the climactic school board election, which the insurgents won by equally narrow margins. We had witnessed a small-town political revolution!

The following morning in class, with interest and excitement still running high, we had a lively discussion of what had happened and why. Then I asked, "If you were called upon to advise the insurgents on a strategy to retain control of the school board, what would you suggest?" This also provoked a lively discussion. Then I asked another question: "If you were to advise the Main Streeters on a strategy to regain control of the school board, what would you suggest?" That question yielded a stunned silence. I filled the gap by offering my own suggestions.

When summer school was over, I was pleased to find that I had escaped the political pitfalls that the director had feared I would encounter. Further, as I was told later, my notes on political strategies were being studied by members of both factions.

Summer school ended on a high note for me. The teachers seemed enthusiastic, and I shall never forget one woman who said, "I have been going to summer school courses for seventeen years, and I want you to know that you are the best teacher I have ever had."

As much as I appreciated the praise, I wondered if I would receive such accolades in the future. In this case, fate had set up an ideal situation for me: an elementary school class to observe and a heated community conflict coming to a climax just before the end of the summer session.

16. *Oklahoma and the Phillips Petroleum Company*

I taught at the University of Oklahoma for only nine months, but in that brief time, my life changed both personally and professionally. Since we didn't have a car, I was fortunate to find a small home within easy walking distance of the campus, although the house did have a drawback for a mother of a two-year-old and seven months pregnant with a second: the washing machine was in the back yard in a shed that had no hot water. To ease the burden on Kathleen, I carried pails of hot water when I came home for lunch.

We were greeted warmly by the sociology professors and their wives, but we were surprised by their formality. While we were still busy unpacking and arranging things, they began dropping in. Both husbands and wives came with their calling cards, and then they would look around for a silver salver to put them in. We had neither calling cards nor a salver, so the visits got us off on the wrong foot socially. Then there were the Saturday-night affairs at the faculty club, where husbands wore tuxedos and the wives came in evening dress to dance to phonograph records.

There was no hospital in Norman, so Kathleen had to be checked by an Oklahoma City obstetrician, a long trip on an interurban trolley or the Greyhound bus. When labor began in the middle of the night, she woke me up to call the local undertaker, who provided Norman's only emergency transportation. I was so nervous that my knees were knocking together. What would I do if the baby started to come when I was with her in the back of the hearse? I needn't have worried because the labor lasted many hours, as it had with Joyce.

With wartime travel restrictions in force, it was impossible for either of our mothers to join us to take care of Joyce and help me around the house. Before the war, household help had been cheap and available—even though there was an unwritten law in Norman that Negroes could not stay overnight. (There was a rumor that many years earlier an unnamed Negro man had raped an unnamed white woman.) With the wartime economic boom, Negroes were happy to abandon Norman. It was some weeks after Martin was born before Kathleen could find anyone even for one day a week. She finally found a humpbacked white woman, whose physical appearance had made her unappealing to most local residents. Now they wanted her, but she preferred to work for us.

In planning my courses, I met with W. B. Bizzell, who had been president of the University of Oklahoma but, following a fight with the board of trustees, had been bumped back to professor and chairman of the Department of Sociology. I was to teach three courses—a bit on the light side for that era—and Bizzell arranged my schedule so that I had Tuesdays and Thursdays free for fieldwork. Although it was customary to ask a new assistant professor to teach introductory sociology, I didn't have to teach it because one of the other professors refused to give it up. I happily agreed to waive my rights. When I managed to duck that assignment in later years, I became the rare academic sociologist who had never taught introductory sociology.

I had hardly started teaching when I was suddenly appointed acting chair of the Department of Anthropology. All the anthropology professors had left except one, and he had been fired for what would now be described as sexual harassment of a student. No anthropology courses were being taught, but David Baeriss, the sole remaining graduate student, was preparing to submit his master's thesis, and someone had to take charge of examining him. Since I was the only professor who had studied anthropology, the assignment and title fell to me.

Baeriss was majoring in archaeology, an area in which I was entirely innocent, and his thesis involved a statistical analysis of Indian ear spools. In sociology, statistics was my weakest subject, and I had never heard of ear spools. (They are outsize ear ornaments.) I read the thesis aloud to Kathleen, assuming she would be more knowledgeable about ornaments than I, and managed to round up another professor as unqualified as I was to simulate a serious oral examination.

Years later, when David Baeriss was professor of anthropology at the University of Wisconsin, I asked him, "Why were you so nervous? You knew we knew nothing about your thesis topic." He replied, "That's why I was nervous. I couldn't imagine what you would ask me."

I enjoyed my association with Baeriss, and the extra work of being acting chair was a small price to pay for the advantages of the new title. Besides the novel entry in my professional résumé—assistant professor of sociology and acting chair of the Department of Anthropology—the appointment enabled me to move into a much larger office with a half-time secretary. She was Dorothy

Roberts, a college student who could take shorthand, an enormous help when I began dictating field notes. I had only one minor problem with her: She was so well brought up that she could not hear profanities and obscenities, and I had been trained to report what informants said, without alteration. Still, when the transcription read that the informant had said, "The situation is normal—all fluffed up," I had no difficulty reconstructing the actual words.

Since forty-three Indian tribes lived within the state of Oklahoma, Bizzell assumed that I would want to study Indians. I told him that I found Indians interesting but that I wanted to work on something more closely related to the war effort. How about fieldwork in the oil industry? Bizzell liked the idea and said he would do what he could to help me get started. His help proved invaluable.

While he had been president of the university, Bizzell had become well acquainted with Frank Phillips, founder and chairman of Phillips Petroleum and a great industrial entrepreneur. His business was then only about twenty-five years old, but it was already becoming a major oil company.

The basis of their friendship was Phillips's interest in archaeology. After flying to an archaeological site in his private plane, Phillips would go with the university archaeologist to an appropriate spot, where Phillips would hand his coat to his pilot and the archaeologist would hand Phillips a shovel; Phillips would dig, and up would come a pot. While Phillips posed with Bizzell and the pot, the university photographer would take pictures. Phillips would then climb back into his plane and fly back to company headquarters in Bartlesville, Oklahoma. The pot would end up in Phillips's private museum on his ranch estate.

In November 1942, I arrived in Bartlesville with a letter from Bizzell. Phillips greeted me and then said, "I can give you two minutes. Then I have to meet with my board of directors." As fast as I could, I told him I wanted to interview and observe relations among workers and management at Phillips Petroleum.

Phillips asked me two questions: "What experience have you had in the oil industry?" None. "Are you a lawyer?" No. He raised his eyes to the ceiling. During this momentary pause, I claimed that I understood working people and would fit in somehow. At this, he called in Warren Felton, his employment manager—the top position in personnel in Phillips at the time—and left me with Felton without any apparent instructions. Felton took me to his office, where we talked briefly. When I learned that Felton's assistant was about to take off for Oklahoma City, I arranged to accompany him in the hope of establishing a firmer relationship. Finally, Felton's assistant promised to present my proposed study to Al Wenzel, manager of the Oklahoma State Division.

Wenzel and his personnel manager, Jeff Franklin, thought the study was a dandy idea but not right at that time. The CIO was organizing, and they were facing a representation election. If I would just wait until it was over, it would be fine for me to come in. I asked when the election was to take place. "Maybe in a couple of weeks," they said, "but we're not sure." I knew enough not to accept that. In fact, the election took place in mid-April, and, as it turned out, I left Oklahoma in June.

Scrambling for another approach, I said that I knew little about the oil industry, so it would be very valuable if I could sit in the office and go over their personnel records. For three to four weeks, two days a week, I engaged in some of the dullest work of my career. I sat in the office going through personnel records, accumulating an enormous pile of data I later destroyed. At least it gave me an excuse to be there.

The division headquarters were on the edge of Oklahoma City, far from any restaurants. For lunch, Wenzel, Franklin, and their associates would bring in sandwiches. We would eat together, and I would try to be as charming and nonthreatening as possible.

Wenzel and Franklin finally thought of a way to get me out of the office. A personnel man was going to the plants known as Capok to do a job description, and Franklin told me I could go with him. At the main Capok plant, which was making aviation gasoline out of natural gas, I met the plant superintendent and the foreman. While the personnel man interviewed workers, I made notes and began to learn something about the nature of the jobs. But the next week the personnel man was pulled off onto something more urgent.

Since I had never done job descriptions, it seemed impractical for me to continue to do them. Instead, I told the workers and managers what I was really trying to do. The superintendent agreed to let me do my research.

The Capok plants were far from bus and trolley lines, but the superintendent introduced me to Don Brim, an engineer who lived in Norman, and he agreed to drive me to Capok on Tuesdays and Thursdays. His working hours were nine to five. The operators worked on rotating shifts that changed at 7:00 A.M. and at 3:00 and 11:00 P.M., which meant that I could see men on two shifts during each visit and, in the course of several weeks, I would see everybody. Traveling with Don also gave me an inside view of how the local scene looked to management.

The three plants at Capok turned out to be an ideal setting for study. Except in emergencies, the work consisted of watching dials and charts, running tests once an hour, and making occasional adjustments. The workers were bored and glad to talk, and I was glad to listen.

I found myself in the wonderland of what was then high technology. Capok was a self-sufficient plant where natural gas was transformed into high-octane aviation gasoline. One foreman supervised the forty-five workers who ran the three plants: the control room, where the transformation process occurred; the engine room, where six enormous engines powered the transformation process; and the catalyst plant, which produced the chemicals used in the transformation process.

The jobs in the main plant's natural gasoline department were at the highest level of technology. Workers' activities were centered in the control room, which housed charts and meters that were monitored by three operators each shift. The polymerization (poly) operator had overall responsibility and coordinated the work of the hydro-stillman and the fractionator operator. Among them, they controlled the operations of four fractionating columns, several stills, a cracking furnace, and a cooling tower, all linked by pipes and tubes.

During my time at Phillips, I became aware that two opposing symbolic representations of the company existed. Those who opposed the union saw the company as vertically integrated—as sort of one happy family. Those who favored the union did not see themselves as enemies of the company—several of them told me that "Phillips is a good company to work for"—but they did see Phillips as divided into two horizontal segments, with management at the top and the workers at the bottom.

Two attempts to unionize the workers had already fizzled. This third attempt was by far the most serious threat to management. The obvious question was, Why now and not before? A change in the external environment provided part of the answer. By this time, the Wagner Act, which protected workers' rights to organize, had been enacted and withstood court challenges. The other part of the answer had to do with the growth of the company. The company president liked to reminisce about the early days when he signed the paychecks for all Phillips employees, and he insisted that Phillips was still the same company.

Recently, Phillips had lost the strongest supporter for the vertical integration model, Fred Gleason. At the time of his death, Gleason had been general superintendent of field operations, the main link between the Oklahoma division in Oklahoma City and company headquarters in Bartlesville. Gleason had grown up with the company. Without a college education, he had learned on the job. The Capok men remembered him fondly. He knew individual workers and would stop by to chat with them. If anyone had been unfairly disciplined by his foreman, he could take the grievance to Gleason in Bartlesville.

Gleason had been succeeded by Rex McRoy, a former army officer who had no ties to the Oklahoma City workers and did not believe in establishing any. In a crackdown that sent shock waves through the ranks of workers and local management, he fired seven workers for stealing gasoline and he fired a superintendent and several other members of management for failing to maintain discipline and for gambling with the men. When he made his first appearance in Capok with a reconstituted local management and a foreman said something about getting the cooperation of the workers, McRoy was reported to have replied, "To hell with cooperation! All I want out of those men is a solid eight hours of work a day—on their feet." The latter point led to the banning of wooden boxes, which the men in the control room in Capok had been sitting on from time to time while watching the charts and meters.

Poly operator Joe Sloan had not been involved in taking gasoline, but he told me that the McRoy crackdown "changed me from Republican to Democrat and from anti-union to pro-union—overnight!"

In the late 1930s, management had established a new policy requiring all foremen to have college degrees. This change hit the workers in Capok particularly hard, since they had risen rapidly, with the expectation of further promotions.

The horizontal cleavage was exacerbated when the first college-trained foremen, Ed Jones and Tom Fitch, were hired. They insisted on giving the workers detailed instructions on how the plant had to be operated. When following those instructions did not produce the results a foreman demanded, he blamed the results on the workers' incompetence. To protect themselves, the workers resorted to "boiler housing." They would write on the daily operating data sheets the instructions they had been given, but they would then operate the plant so as to get results the foreman wanted. In the hope of finding ways to improve operations, the foremen would make elaborate quantitative studies based on what was fictitious data. Here I encountered the first of many instances of management folly in failing to rely and build on the knowledge workers had gained through experience.

By the time of my study, Tom Lloyd had been appointed foreman in Capok. He was a chemical engineer, yet he did not claim to know plant operations better than the workers. Now, workers told me, there was no need to "boiler-house" the operating records. But although the men told me they liked and respected Lloyd, they noted that McRoy was still in power in Bartlesville.

In the representation election, workers could vote for the company union, a CIO-affiliated union, or no union. Management strongly supported the company union, so as not to divide the anti-CIO vote. The company union had been formed years earlier by management, which also had provided it with a clubhouse. At first, some of the workers had taken it seriously and seen it as an organization through which to appeal a decision by a foreman. But when some members of local management had advised leaders of the company union that their activism could adversely affect their relationship to the company, the company union had become dormant.

Division manager Al Wenzel brought the company union back to life. I happened to be in his office when he telephoned its president to instruct him to write a letter to the vice president of the division *demanding* that meetings to negotiate a new labor contract be scheduled immediately. Furthermore, the union president was told to insist that the new contract be more comprehensive than the old—which had no clauses regarding wages, fringe benefits, or working conditions.

Management and the president of the company union then got together to organize elections for worker representatives to a bargaining committee. In the first election at Capok, Jesus Christ and Joseph Stalin got the most votes. On the second try, a fractionator operator received two votes and was declared the winner.

In a bargaining session, the representative brought up the issue of reclassifying the poly operator job, which he argued required skills equal to those of more highly paid top operators in Phillips's refineries. Management rejected this demand. Later, in informal conversations, McRoy dropped a verbal bombshell that had a more dramatic effect on labor relations than anything I was to encounter throughout my subsequent career. This is how the Capok representative told me the story:

Did you hear what McRoy said about us? He told us we were only watchmen. He said, "Down there in that plant you have got automatic controls and charts. If anything goes wrong with the meters, you just call a meter man. If anything goes wrong with the engines, you just call a repair man. If anything goes wrong with operations, you just call an engineer, and he tells you what to do. There is no skill in that work. You just have to watch the charts."

In the wake of that statement, a union activist picked up fifty pledge cards for the union—some from men who would not even let him talk union to them before. A common view was, "If that is what the company thinks of us, then we need union protection."

Engineers and local managers were embarrassed by McRoy's statement. When an engineer asked a fractionator operator, "What seems to be the problem with the number 4 fractionating column?" the worker replied, "You tell me. You're the engineer." And for a week, the poly operators signed their daily operating data sheets "The Watchman."

Fortunately for management, the union vote was some weeks away. After a cooling-off period, management got negotiations going again.

Phillips was then completing construction of a large plant in Borger, Texas, and was prepared to offer a number of Oklahoma workers transfers, which would increase their pay and opportunities. For several weeks, officials from the main office were in and around Capok for meetings and personal interviews. No worker was required to transfer nor did management have to accept everyone who wanted to make the move.

Up to this point, the union organization drive and the company's counter-moves and blunders were the chief subjects of conversation. Now those topics were submerged by discussions of the move to Borger. These discussions focused workers' attention on their long-term careers with Phillips and thus tended to reinforce the message that "Phillips has been a good company to work for."

The vertical integration message got another boost during the farewell party for the men leaving for Borger. Holding the party was not management's idea, but Wenzel exploited the opportunity when poly operator Tom Walling asked him to provide beer and pretzels and join in the clubhouse festivities to honor the departing workers. I made a point of going so as to observe the "one big happy family" symbolism. Al Wenzel was a very active master of ceremonies, but he gave full public credit to Walling for suggesting the party. Wenzel expressed his own and the company's appreciation for the years of skillful service of the departing workers, and other management people spoke along the same lines. Wenzel announced that no one at this happy event was allowed to mention "coming events." The emphasis was to be entirely on their common membership in the great Phillips company.

After the formal ceremonies, workers and managers settled down to roll dice or play checkers or other games. Managers were mixing with the workers, and Al Wenzel was the biggest mixer of all. His red suspenders drew attention wherever he was, and the booming good fellowship of his voice resounded through the hall.

Just before the election, management and the company union had managed to complete negotiations on a new contract—which now included wages, fringe benefits, and working conditions! Management called a districtwide meeting on company time to promote the proposed contract.

The company union won the election in a very close vote. The CIO union immediately filed a protest, charging that management's meeting to sell the company union contract constituted one among several unfair labor practices. The union protest prevailed, necessitating another vote some months after I left.

What factors influenced individual voters' decisions? I had enough information on how about twenty-five workers probably voted to offer some answers.

I thought first about the nature of the jobs. I noted a striking contrast between the workers in the engine room and in the control room. Whereas the control room workers were predominantly for the CIO, the engine room people were antiunion.

Why this difference? In the first place, the engine room workers had had no problems with the earlier autocratic foremen. Being chemical engineers, foremen Jones and Fitch did not claim to know anything about engine operation, so they left the workers alone.

The social background of the workers also made a difference. All the engine operators had grown up on family farms, whereas the men in the control room had grown up in towns or cities, where they had ample opportunities to mix with groups of boys. On the farm and in school or church, the farm boy was constantly under adult supervision.

The importance of family background was not something I had to figure out for myself. Poly operator Tom Walling, who had grown up on a farm, told me, "When I first went to work in industry, I looked on the foreman like he was my father."

Another factor I identified was the "special personal relationship with management." That seemed to explain the vote of the chief operator of the catalyst plant. His father had worked for Phillips and had lost his life in a plant fire. Every Christmas after that, until the man was old enough to work for Phillips, his mother had received a substantial check from the personal bank account of Frank Phillips—and they still received a Christmas card. Even so, when he had served under Jones and Fitch, he had signed a union pledge card. He was president of the company union when Wenzel revived it, and that special relationship with management reinforced his earlier bond to the company.

I was particularly interested in two waverers: men I had identified as favoring the CIO but who at voting time seemed to be leaning toward the company union. Although the Capok representative insisted that he had not enjoyed the company union negotiation meetings, he confessed that he had been impressed with the "sincerity" of the management negotiators, who had persuaded him that they really did want to make things better for the men. He might vote for the company union, but still he had a lingering doubt: Would management be so good to the men when the pressure from the CIO was off?

Finally, there was a former farm boy, poly operator Tom Walling, who had developed a special relationship with Al Wenzel and other management people after organizing the farewell party. He never told me how he voted, but he did comment that "there is a lot of corruption in unions." He had never raised this point before.

I have told the Phillips story in some detail because my work there led to a major change in my field of study. This first experience inside industry fascinated me. I enjoyed the challenge of trying to fit together company history, labor relations, and the personal stories of the men. As I began to see my way through the puzzles, I would come home after a day in the field to share my intellectual excitement with Kathleen.

This warm glow of satisfaction was abruptly shaken when I made a farewell visit to Al Wenzel. He told me that they could not have beaten the CIO without me. I laughed — but nervously — and asked what I had done. He said that my research reports had been read by F. E. Rice, vice president of the natural gasoline department. My reports did not name any workers, but they had pointed to Rex McRoy as the chief target of worker hostility.

During the final strategy meeting in Bartlesville, Wenzel had found that McRoy was assuming that during the two weeks before the election he would be in Oklahoma City calling the shots. Wenzel objected, "This is a local matter. We know our people. Let me handle it." Rice agreed. Wenzel believed that if McRoy had been observed on the local scene before the election, it would have swung the election to the CIO.

When Wenzel had finished his story, I felt somewhat nauseated. Basically, my sympathies had been with the union, and yet I had to recognize the possibility that I had contributed to its defeat.

❧

In negotiating entry for the Phillips study, I had promised to send my research reports to management. Why had I not waited until after the election? I had sent them before because I was then in the process of figuring out the next move in my career. I might have been able to continue at the university, but this was by no means certain. Married men with children were no longer receiving automatic deferments from the army.

I felt I had to get involved in something contributing to the war effort. A job in the Phillips personnel department might have been a possibility. For that, it was important to show what my fieldwork could produce, and it was already getting late to make a major career move.

When I met with F. E. Rice, it became clear that I was too hot to handle for a job with Phillips. Yet, Rice told me that he found my reports interesting and valuable, and, as a parting bonus, he offered me a check for two hundred dollars. I thought of declining on principle, but I could not think what principle might be involved. I had deceived myself into believing I was carrying out social research while being employed by the company. I had not learned how to do research acceptable to me and at least tolerable to the organization that employed me.

After several failed attempts to land a war industry job, I got a job offer that seemed ideal. At Harvard, Talcott Parsons in sociology and Clyde Kluckhohn in anthropology were involved in planning a training program for military government personnel in preparation for the invasion of Italy. I was to devote half of my time to teaching Italian culture and social organization and the other half to conducting research on Italian culture. The job would take me back to the North End, this time to concentrate on first-generation immigrants. It would also enable me to pursue library studies of the academic literature. Based on earlier readings of parts of the twenty-four volumes of the remarkable Sicilian physician Giuseppe Pitré on the culture of Sicilian peasant communities in the early years of this century, I had written a paper, "Sicilian Peasant Society," that was to be published in *American Anthropologist*.

The Harvard program was about to begin. We packed in a great rush and arranged for a moving company to load our belongings afterward and send them to a warehouse in Boston.

17. Interruption

On the way to Cambridge, we spent a day with the Kings in New Canaan, and Kathleen stayed on with the children. In Boston, I visited the Orlandis, and they invited me to stay with them while apartment hunting. It felt good to be back in the room that had been mine during the first eighteen months of my North End study.

On Friday, June 25, I went out to Harvard to sign my employment contract and have lunch with Kluckhohn and Parsons. They apologized for a delay in getting me my contract; the office preparing it had not yet delivered the promised forms. I agreed to meet them again on Monday.

By that afternoon, my head ached and I felt a bit feverish, and that night I began to feel pain in my legs. I thought I had brought this on myself by going barefoot at the Kings. Since I couldn't sleep, I got up at about 4:00 in the morning and walked several blocks to an all-night cafeteria. Then I walked back and tried, in vain, to get to sleep.

June 27 was my birthday, and Kathleen expected me in New Canaan. I asked Avy Orlandi to call and tell her I would have to wait until my fever subsided.

The next several days are a blur in my memory. Gradually, I recognized that my illness was serious. When I was a junior fellow with access to Harvard's infirmary and medical services, I had never consulted a local doctor. I had heard that one North End doctor, Gerardo Balboni, was on the staff of Massachusetts General Hospital. I knew it was one of the best hospitals in the country and I asked Avy to call him for me.

Dr. Balboni was at first puzzled. He told me to rest in bed and drink lots of liquids. By this time, I was in no condition to get out of bed except to go to the toilet. Soon that trip became more and more difficult. The toilet was a floor below, down a long staircase. Each time I made the trip, I felt weaker than the last time.

I had Avy call Harvard to let Parsons and Kluckhohn know I could not make the Monday appointment. By now, the Orlandis were worried about how to care for and feed me. I could not face spaghetti or any of the other Italian dishes I had come to love. Calling up my childhood memories, I asked Mama to fix me a bowl of milk toast. She asked me, "Don't you want me to put some sugar on it?" I shuddered at the thought and told her I would take it straight.

The Orlandis brought me a bowl to urinate in. By then I was finding it harder and harder to urinate. When I could not urinate at all, I realized I would have to get to the hospital as soon as possible.

I should have had the Orlandis call an ambulance, but Avy offered to get me to the hospital. He and some friends who owned a car carried me down the two flights of stairs, lifted me into the car, and delivered me to the hospital.

Dr. Balboni arrived soon after I had checked in. Now the diagnosis was clear: I had polio. He had been slow to come to that conclusion because polio was still unusual in New England. The epidemic had started weeks earlier in Oklahoma, and I had carried the virus with me to Boston. By this time, I was not surprised by the diagnosis.

I gave Dr. Balboni a phone number to call Kathleen. She asked, "He is going to live, isn't he?" Dr. Balboni replied, "We don't know. You better get here as soon as you can."

When she told him she had a nursing baby and a two-year-old, he told her she could not return to them for six weeks for fear of infection. Just that day Kathleen had begun weaning Martin, but now she had to cut him off abruptly and leave the children and instructions with her mother. She called my parents, and they arranged to take the same train she would catch at South Norwalk. They were shaken by the news. Mother kept saying, "Why did it have to happen to Bill? He has been such a good boy." Mother was not sure that there was a God, but if he did exist, she could not understand why he would let bad things happen to good people.

As the disease advanced, I could not move a muscle below my waist, except in the right big toe—which suggested (correctly as it turned out) that whatever recovery I would manage, the right leg would be stronger than the left. Each day I would wiggle that toe as if that sign of life justified my hopes for recovery. Except for some muscle soreness in my shoulders, the disease did not strike above the waist.

In the early days in the hospital, I experienced constant and intense pain such as I had never felt before. Knowing that the disease was eating away at my nerves and muscles made the pain harder to bear. It seemed as if I could never sleep, but I must have dozed for short periods, accompanied by nightmares. I soon realized that I would never play tennis again, and I wondered if I would ever walk again. I thought of the last time Kathleen and I had made love, coming east on the sleeper, the swaying and bumping of the train adding to the excitement and pleasure. Now I wondered if we would ever make love again. Although I knew polio could be fatal, I did not think I was going to die, but I did brood over how I was going to manage to go on living.

I felt some sense of relief when Kathleen and my parents arrived. While my fever lasted, they were not allowed to come into the room, so we had to communicate rather stiffly from bed to door. Unknown to me, outside the door stood an iron lung, ready if the polio attacked my lungs. Kathleen experienced the worst moment of my hospital stay on the day she came to the quarantine gate and saw that the machine was gone. She had to wait for agonizing minutes, wondering if she would find me in that iron lung. The machine had been removed because my fever had dropped, and the disease would destroy nothing more.

This was a difficult time to be in Boston. Kathleen estimates that she and my parents had to call more than forty hotels or rooming houses before they could find rooms, and these were in two different houses. The day after Kathleen settled in, the landlady learned I had polio and evicted Kathleen immediately. Fortunately, my parents had old friends in Boston who had left for their summer place, and they invited Kathleen to move into their apartment. That would have been ideal except that wartime blackout rules were in force. In the evenings she had a choice of sitting in the dark and brooding but getting whatever breezes were blowing, or shutting the windows and pulling down the blinds so that she could read while enduring the sweltering heat.

If I had come down with polio somewhere else—or anywhere just a few years earlier—the hospital would have encased my legs in plaster casts. Massachusetts General was one of the first hospitals in the country to try out the new treatment pioneered by a remarkable Australian, Elizabeth Kenney. Although a woman and a nurse, she had overcome the resistance of the medical establishment and had convinced physicians that the spasms of polio could be relieved by periodically wrapping the affected parts of the body in hot wet packs. The hot pack treatment was prescribed for every two hours during the day. It was a heavy job, requiring two nurses, one to put heavy woolen blankets in a tub of boiling water and crank them through an old-fashioned hand wringer and another to put me on a rubber pad and wrap the hot blankets around my legs. They relieved the pain and helped me relax, at least temporarily.

Because of the wartime shortage of nurses, it was impossible to count on two when I needed them. Kathleen took over wringing the blankets, the heaviest part of the treatment. That committed her to being at the hospital every two hours. When she wasn't working on me, reading to me, or otherwise trying to take my mind off the pain and my worries about the future, she needed something else to do. She tried to be a volunteer with a hospital Red Cross unit but was rebuffed. The volunteers were young women from the social elite of Boston, and she could not join them unless she was recommended by one of their members.

From a hospital administrator, she learned that there was a supply room where drop-in volunteers folded bandages. Most of them were working men and women who came in to make their contribution to the war effort. Kathleen ended up dividing her time between that work, my room, and the employees' cafeteria. Her volunteering brought us an unanticipated dividend. She was told that since she was now a hospital employee, visiting rules did not apply. She could stay as late as we wanted.

Leaving the hospital, she had a long but pleasant walk along the esplanade bordering the Charles River and occasionally stopped to enjoy a Boston Pops concert in the band shell. Several times she was approached by sailors, but she explained she was in Boston to be with her husband who was in the hospital with polio and that fended them off.

When I was no longer contagious, friends came by to visit. I recall seeing Ernest Pecci and Frank Luongo, as well as Clyde Kluckhohn and Talcott Parsons. Connie Arensberg, now teaching at MIT, and Harry Levin, now in Harvard's comparative literature department, came by, as did Gordon Donald. I hardly knew him, but he brought the news that Eliot Chapple was working in the hospital on a research project and was eager to see me. Such a visit would have meant a lot to me because I had sent Eliot a copy of the manuscript "People in Petroleum," which I hoped would be my second book. When Gordon came by, he would tell me how eager Eliot was to see me, but, in my six weeks in the hospital, he never did find the time to visit.

Parsons asked Kathleen if we needed a loan—an offer she refused with thanks. Officially, Harvard did nothing. At the time, we were so preoccupied with my illness that it did not occur to us that Harvard had any obligations to me. As I looked back upon it later, I felt let down by the institution that had supported me so handsomely as a junior fellow. Since I could not perform my duties, I could not expect Harvard to pay me a year's salary, yet we had gone to considerable expense for Harvard: getting our belongings to Boston, storing our belongings until we were ready to move again, and moving. Shouldn't Harvard had offered to defray at least some of those expenses? If my contract had been ready when I had arrived and I had signed it, would that have made a difference?

Some of the strength gradually came back to my right leg, but it was clear that it would take many months of rest and treatment before I could get back to work. Kathleen consulted the doctors and they recommended the Georgia Warm Springs Foundation, founded by Franklin D. Roosevelt after he benefited from the supposed curative effects of the springs.

Kathleen received word that the foundation could take me in. Since rail traffic was now under military control, complicated arrangements had to be made to get me to Georgia. Kathleen went first to a station ticket office. Rebuffed, she demanded to see the agent's supervisor. Rebuffed again, she repeated her demand and went to someone at the next level. She kept getting the same answer: "Lady, don't you know there's a war on?" Officials tried to dismiss her, but she refused to leave until she got the name of the immediate superior. At last, when she got to the top, the official arranged everything and made it look easy. A friend told her, "You were talking to the man in charge of all the troop movements on the eastern seaboard."

Kathleen and the children could not accompany me because they could not get train reservations, but weeks later they took a plane. She accompanied me as far as New York and then rejoined the children in New Canaan. From New York to Warm Springs, the Kings arranged for a family friend who had been in the medical corps to go with me.

Since I was not able to sit up, I had to travel to the train on a stretcher. To get the stretcher into my compartment, someone had to remove a window. So as to avoid having to transport me from Grand Central Station to Penn Station for the train that would take me to Warm Springs, I had to take the one train a day from Boston that entered New York City over the Hell Gate Bridge. Between trains at Penn Station, I was moved out through my window into an infirmary to wait. Someone then had to perform another window-removal operation to get me into my compartment on the train heading south. That train stopped at Atlanta and then had to make an unscheduled stop at Warm Springs. Finally, after another window-removal operation, I was lifted out into an ambulance that took me to the foundation.

The village of Warm Springs is in a valley. The foundation facilities are on top of a hill, among tall pine trees. At the time I arrived, the buildings were arrayed around the green grass of a quadrangle: hospital buildings; medical and business offices; a recreation hall, where movies were shown two nights a week, plus a matinee for children; a dining hall; and a treatment building, containing a waist-deep swimming pool supplied with warm water. Everything was accessible by ramps.

My physiotherapist gave me two treatments a day, the first in bed and the second in the pool, where I was wheeled on a stretcher and lifted down by an orderly. The treatment was based on a theory that the disease damaged or destroyed some of the connections between nerves and muscles so that the body had to be "reeducated" to restore them. The physiotherapist would run a finger lightly along the lines of the hoped-for nerve-muscle connection while helping me to respond. The response never came easily. I had to relax, concentrate on thinking about what I wanted to do, and then try—but not too hard, since this was thought to be a very delicate process. Gradually, I was able to get more and more response out of the right leg. The left leg deceived us by now and then showing what seemed to be a flicker of response, which we were never able to build into anything useful.

I was surprised that the foundation was such a cheerful place. Perhaps it was because all the patients were there after the disease had done its worst damage and now they could hope to gain back some strength, and for some, recovery could be almost complete. Nearly all of us could look around and see people worse off than we were. I realized that I fell somewhere between those who would have a nearly complete recovery and those who would have lifelong disabilities.

The saddest case was a Canadian soldier, who was there with his fiancée and his mother. The disease had reduced him almost to a skeleton. Confined to a wheelchair, he was nearly helpless. What could he expect of the pleasures of life, love, and marriage? And what could his fiancée expect?

At the other extreme was my roommate, a soldier who had been stricken in Fort Benning, Georgia. He had had the type of polio that strikes the lungs and upper body and is often fatal. At the most critical point, he had been completely paralyzed, unable to move a muscle, yet he remained conscious. He heard the doctors discussing whether they should fly him to a major hospital where he could get better care. The decision: "No, he would never make it." As he prepared to leave the foundation, he had only a slight weakness in his back and was walking without any apparent handicap, while I, who was never so close to death, would have a substantial physical handicap for the rest of my life.

The business manager of the foundation had told Kathleen not to come because there would be no place for her and the children. But the patient representative wrote that she could rent a place in the village of Warm Springs for a while, until one of the foundation cottages opened up.

Living conditions were difficult in the little house Kathleen rented. It had been a cotton pickers' cabin and had only screen doors with hooks instead of locks. Kathleen did not think she was prejudiced but was shaken by the constant warnings about the Negroes. The doors would rattle at night, probably because of animals. She took to sleeping with a flashlight and planning how she would escape with the children through one door if someone came to the other.

To visit me, Kathleen had to walk in the heat for more than a mile through woods and up a hill, pushing a baby carriage with nine-month-old Martin and riding herd on three-year-old Joyce. While I was still flat in bed, Kathleen would take me out on a wheeled stretcher. I have vivid memories of looking up into the tops of the pine trees and on into the clouds and the warm summer sky. I could see and touch Kathleen from this position, and she would lift the children up beside me so I could feel that the family was together again.

About two weeks after Kathleen came to Warm Springs, I was able to sit up and get around in a wheelchair. I was also beginning to get up on my feet, at first with help from the physiotherapist. During my attempts at walking again, I found it difficult to keep my balance. The signals from the soles of my feet did not help me as before, and I had to relearn how to stand up. With the help of the physiotherapist and supported by crutches, I began to take a few halting steps. Gradually, the right leg became strong enough to support some of my weight, and I began trying steps, holding on to railings.

We consulted the doctor about the possible extent of recovery. He assumed that the left leg would remain so lifeless that I would have to be equipped with a full-length leg brace, a heavy contraption made of leather and steel. He had one made for me, and I used it clumsily for a couple of weeks. Then that leg surprised us and started showing enough improvement to indicate that I could get along without the cumbersome brace, with just the support of a toe strap, which extended from above the calf and attached to the lowest shoelace, to keep the toes from dragging. That change was a great relief.

The doctor said that, after another six to nine months of rehabilitation, I might be ready to go back to work. He added that it would take another year before the muscles not struck by polio would regain full strength. Sexual relations? He said there was no reason I could not make love when I felt ready to do so.

At last, a foundation cottage did open up. Kathleen and the children moved in, and soon I was able to join them. From there, an orderly wheeled me to my daily physiotherapy.

I shall never forget that first night in bed together. Weak as I was, we embraced and made love—completely and gloriously. As I lay back, exhausted but happy, I felt that life was beginning anew for me. Unfortunately, that experience was deceptive. When I tried again, I could not follow through. We tried again and again without success. Finally, we had to agree to forego lovemaking until I had more strength. That time would come some weeks after I was back at work.

Depressed as I was over my plight, I tried to look on the bright side. First, getting polio had resolved my ambivalence about war service. At the foundation, I received a letter from my draft board, reclassifying me as eligible to be drafted. A letter from my doctor settled that.

Second, getting sick gave me an opportunity to make another try at writing a novel. I decided to write about the North End and to model the leading character after Ernest Pecci. When I was still flat on my back, I began writing in longhand, holding the paper on a clipboard over my head. When I was able to sit up, I got back to my typewriter. By the end of March 1944, when we were getting ready to leave the foundation, I had finished the manuscript. Even then I had an uneasy feeling that it was not very good. Later, I tried it out on a literary agent, who confirmed my judgment. She reported that parts were well done but that it did not measure up as a novel. Perhaps I had said what I had to say in *Street Corner Society*. (In a sense, I did sell that novel. Years later, we had a minor house fire that destroyed the manuscript. The insurance company asked me to place a value on the loss; I said it was worth one hundred dollars.)

While in Warm Springs, I experienced both highs and lows in my attempts at publication. The high came when we received the first copies of *Street Corner Society*. The low came when I received a letter from Warren Felton informing me that, although "People in Petroleum" was an interesting manuscript and useful to the company, it would not be in the best interests of Phillips to permit it to be published. In talking my way into that study, I had foolishly promised to let the company have the right to clear any manuscript based on my work there. I am not sure such a pledge was necessary, but I was stuck with my promise.

Science did not suffer from the suppression of the Phillips manuscript, however. Disguising the name of the company, I included much of the material in the following decades in articles and books. Nonetheless, the company's decision was very depressing at the time because I believed I had written a book that would be recognized as an important contribution to the newly developing field of human relations in industry — now more commonly called organizational behavior.

By the end of 1943, it appeared that I might be ready to go back to work by May or June of 1944. There was no chance of going back to Harvard since American military government personnel might already be in Italy. Everett Hughes, at the University of Chicago, suggested I might be interested in pursuing a study of human relations in the restaurant industry that he knew could get funding. The National Restaurant Association (NRA) had been negotiating with the business school at Chicago to establish a master's degree in restaurant administration. The university had agreed to establish the degree on the condition that the NRA provide some money for research. When the contract was signed, the dean discovered that no one on his faculty had any interest in research on the restaurant industry.

George Brown of the business school brought the problem to the Committee on Human Relations in Industry, of which he was a member. The committee had been created in 1943 with Lloyd Warner as chairman and Burleigh B. Gardner as executive secretary. It also included Everett Hughes, Frederick Harbison (in the Department of Economics) and Allison Davis and Robert Havighurst (from the Department of Human Development). Hughes suggested I direct the study.

They could not hire me sight unseen, so I had to travel to Chicago to meet with the committee. That was a frightening prospect. The trip was scheduled for February, and I would have to go alone, since Kathleen had no one with whom to leave the children.

By this time, I was getting about with two canes. The muscles in my left hip were still not functioning, but the muscles in my upper left leg had regained enough strength so that I could raise the leg off the ground. That made it possible to abandon the long leg brace for everyday use, but the doctor ruled that, for safety's sake, I would have to use it on the trip. I was getting daily practice in going up and down steps without the aid of railings, but I did not yet feel secure.

I went on a sleeper from Atlanta to Chicago. Everett Hughes met me at the Englewood Station on the southwest side of the city on a snowy February day. He drove me to his home in the Hyde Park district, just a few blocks from the university. I shall always be especially grateful to Everett and Helen Hughes for their support at this critical time.

My only memory of that visit is of the beginning of my lunch with the members of the Committee on Human Relations in Industry in the Quadrangle

Club, for University of Chicago faculty. To get from the lobby to the dining room, I had to go down two steps without railings. Probably no one in the dining room was watching me, but I felt that all eyes were on me. I imagined myself falling down, thereby demonstrating that I was not fit to take the job. I took a deep breath and pushed out—unsteadily but successfully. After that, everything else seemed easy. The job was mine when I was ready for it.

In mid-March, Kathleen and I left Warm Springs to spend two months at the Kings' home in New Canaan. For many months, Kathleen continued the physiotherapy by running her fingers along the routes of the injured nerves. I had to manage the rest of the recovery process by myself, which I did by going up and down stairs, without leaning on banisters, several times a day. I had mixed feelings about those tasks. It worried me that no one stood by to offer me a hand, yet at the same time I knew I had to learn to do it all myself. At first, Martin had more trouble with stairs than I did. He had learned to walk in Warm Springs, where there were no stairs, so now he just bumped against a bottom step and fell down.

In mid-May, we set off for Chicago. My time out had finally come to an end. Oklahoma had changed my life by providing me with an opportunity to get involved in an intensive organizational study and then sending me on my way with the polio virus.

18. *The Committee on Human Relations in Industry*

Kathleen and I and the children arrived in Chicago in June 1944. Everett and Helen Hughes had arranged for us to rent a furnished apartment owned by Robert Redfield, my former social anthropology professor at Chicago.

The apartment was ideally located—just two blocks from my office in the Social Sciences Building, far enough for me to get some exercise yet not too far as to tax my strength. The apartment was on the ground floor, but the entrance to the building presented a problem: I had to go down four steps, without a railing. There were just two steps down out the back door, and there I could lean against the door frame if I needed support. Still, I had been trained at Warm Springs to manage stairs without railings, and I had practiced during the weeks in Connecticut. If I wanted to regain my physical independence, I had to master those front steps, so I went out that way except when the weather was especially bad.

Before taking the first step off into the void, I would carefully line up my feet on the edge, place my canes on the next step down, take a deep breath, and push off. To avoid falling forward, I would overcompensate and lean back, which increased my chances of falling backward. Kathleen would watch me from behind a curtain until I was safely down. If I fell backward—which I did now and then—she would wait to see if I got up. The occasional bumps were more damaging to my pride than to my bottom.

I also had to adjust to people trying to be helpful. The rather heavy doors to the Social Sciences Building opened inward, so I had to lean forward and throw my weight against them. Once, when I was preparing to do this, someone dashed in front of me and swung the door open. It was all I could do to avoid falling on my face. When someone grabbed hold of me to get me into a car, I resisted, but not because of stubborn pride. I would explain, "I know what I am going to do, but I don't know what you are going to do, so please let me do it."

I did not object to people trying to be helpful, but I wanted to be free to accept or reject the help—with thanks. I have always appreciated those who ask, "May I help you?"

To get into the field, I had to figure out how to get around Chicago. The station for the Illinois Central Railroad was a very long walk from our apartment, and the elevated was about the same distance. I would need a car with automatic transmission. With the war still going on, no new cars were available. At that time, only Cadillac and Oldsmobile made cars with hydramatic shifts, so we asked a dealer to find us a secondhand Oldsmobile. The car he found had fifty-one-thousand miles on it, but we settled for that. We arranged to have the brake pedal lowered so I could reach the brake and the accelerator without having to lift up my right foot.

Since my appointment was in the Department of Sociology, I shared an office with the executive secretary of the Committee on Human Relations in Industry, Burleigh Gardner. He and I were the only committee members working full time on research. As a very junior member of the committee, I felt privileged to be part of this path-breaking enterprise. The passing years reinforced that conviction. In its 1982 meeting, the Division of Management History of the Academy of Management had a symposium on the committee. The committee lasted for only six or seven years, yet it made intellectual history by developing intimately detailed case studies of the working lives of individuals and work groups.

I date the emergence of organizational behavior as a field of study to the 1920s, when the Western Electric Company started its research program, which culminated with the publication of *Management and the Worker*, by Fritz Roethlisberger and William Dickson, in 1939. There were personal links between the Western Electric research program and the emergence of research and teaching in organizational behavior through the Committee on Human Relations in Industry. Critical to these links were W. Lloyd Warner, formerly in the anthropology department at Harvard, and Elton Mayo in its business school.

Mayo, whose name has become synonymous with the Hawthorne program, had nothing to do with it in the beginning. The program began with a physical focus, with tests to see how changes in lighting affected workers' productivity.

Mayo, a psychologist from Australia, became interested in the Western Electric research program when a company official consulted him about an experiment in which the productivity of a group of five women relay assemblers continued to increase even when the stimuli of rest periods and refreshments were withdrawn. Mayo became involved when the researchers could not make sense of their data, and it was he who moved the program toward studies of psychological and social factors.

Warner persuaded Mayo to organize an intensive study of one group of men in the bank wiring room who were operating under ordinary, nonexperimental conditions. Their productivity was recorded in a straight line.

The apparently strange behavior of the women in the relay assembly experiment captured the attention of professors and students and came to be attributed to the "Hawthorne effect"—the friendly attention the women were receiving from the research observer, who was with them throughout every working day. But, as Conrad Arensberg (1951) has pointed out, the men in the bank wiring room also had constant, friendly attention from a research observer. The difference was that the bank wiring workers were managed in a conventional manner, characterized by frequent contacts with a foreman and an inspector, whereas the relay assemblers operated in what would now be called an autonomous work group; they saw their foreman only when they picked up materials or delivered their output.

Since Roethlisberger later presented seventeen explanations or partial explanations for the behavior of the relay assembly women (Dickson and Roethlisberger 1966), the case hardly merits the scientific attention it has received. Yet it has always seemed to me that the bank wiring room study ranks as one of the best work group studies ever done. But since it showed no dramatic results and yielded no obvious clues as to what might be done to increase productivity, the case has been overshadowed by the relay assembly experiment and a psychological explanation substituted for a sociological analysis of the relations among the workers and between the workers and management.

I suspect that Mayo latched onto the Hawthorne effect because it confirmed predictions he had made in earlier factory studies, in which he had focused on the monotony and boredom of mass-production work and the "obsessive reveries" these conditions produced among workers. Pursuing that theme, in what I later called (1978) "one of the most monumental misunderstandings of the implications of social research in the course of intellectual history," Mayo persuaded the management of Western Electric that the research demonstrated the need to establish a personnel counseling program through which friendly counselors could encourage workers to talk out their personal problems.

The establishment of the counseling program marked the end of systematic social research at Hawthorne. The researchers attached to the program were limited to the notes the counselors brought in from their interviews with workers and supervisors. They were barred from making any follow-up studies of problems mentioned in the reports.

Harvard also failed to capitalize on its pioneering efforts at Hawthorne. By the time the counseling program was established, Mayo was approaching retirement. Roethlisberger was a gifted field interviewer and interpreter of field situations, but he was highly dependent on Mayo for initiating new research projects.

When I was at Harvard (1936–40), I gathered that Roethlisberger was doing important work, but you would never have gotten that impression from listening to him in group situations. He talked little and mainly listened—sympathetically and with a twinkle in his eye. Until a new group came to the business school with Paul Lawrence in the 1950s, Harvard left this emerging field of research to the Committee on Human Relations in Industry—and to other groups that followed Chicago's lead.

After working with Lloyd Warner on the Yankee City studies and a community study with Allison Davis of Natchez (*Deep South* 1941), Burleigh Gardner moved to the Chicago area as director of research for the Hawthorne personnel counseling program. While the ground rules prevented him from doing any solid research, his observations and reading of counselors' reports on their interviews did have one major payoff. Gardner wrote *Human Relations in Industry* (1946), the first textbook on organizational behavior, for which most of the case materials were from his Western Electric experience.

Gardner began teaching a course in human relations in industry in the downtown evening executive program of the University of Chicago Business School. The 1982 report of the Academy of Management's management history division seminar on the committee (Muhs 1989) quotes Gardner as saying that after five years at Western Electric, "I got my Five Year pin, and I looked around and I thought, my God, is there any job in this plant I want?" Gardner left Hawthorne to try his hand at management consulting and to look for support for the Committee on Human Relations in Industry. He invited Warner and Robert Havighurst to join him as partners.

One of the first people they approached for support for the committee was Walter Paepke. Paepke's intellectual interests extended far beyond the bottom line of the Container Corporation of America, where he was the CEO. He was also on the board of trustees of the University of Chicago and would later found the Aspen Institute. Paepke responded by saying, "This committee belongs in the university." With that encouragement, the three men set up the Committee on Human Relations in Industry in 1943.

The committee was supported by thirty-six hundred dollars in annual contributions from companies. The committee members met about every six weeks with top officials of the supporting companies for dinner and discussions of human relations research.

Why did the companies support the committee? Was it because they wanted the committee members to do research inside their plants and to advise them how to make improvements? On the contrary, during the first year of the program, Gardner was unable to get permission for any in-plant studies. He had to settle for sending graduate students house to house in working-class neighborhoods, doing interviews on what made a job good or bad.

In the wartime economic boom, companies were concerned about the high rates of labor turnover and absenteeism and might have thought that exchanging ideas on workers' job attitudes could be useful. The annual fee was a trifling sum, and perhaps the opportunity to exchange semiphilosophical views with the professors had some appeal.

The breakthrough to in-plant studies occurred in one meeting at which Walter Paepke challenged Gardner: "Things are so screwed up in our 35th Street plant that you couldn't possibly make things worse. Why don't you come in and see if you can help us."

That was the beginning, although in-plant access was still difficult to arrange when I came to Chicago in 1944. There were two common answers to my requests: Either "the situation is so tense in our plant that introduction of any outsider could set off an explosion" or "Things are running smoothly, and we are afraid that an outsider coming in to ask workers how they like their jobs could just lead them to think of reasons to complain."

Plant managers had no interest in what people from the "ivory tower" might contribute. They would fend us off by demanding, "Have you ever met a payroll?" Personnel managers were more approachable, but in general they were interested in gimmicks: "What we would like to know is how to make workers *feel* they are participating." The discussions would end when I told them that we were not into impression management, that the only way to make workers feel they were participating was to invite them to get involved in decisions of importance to them.

One person with a conspicuously different attitude was James C. Worthy, the personnel manager of Sears Roebuck and Company. He got involved with the committee program through David G. Moore, then a part-time doctoral candidate in sociology at the University of Chicago. After working as a personnel counselor at the Hawthorne works, he had applied for a personnel job at Sears. Worthy hired him and assigned him the task of making sense out of the data gathered by a consulting organization for a Sears morale survey. Worthy felt that the surveys conveyed some general idea of the state of morale but revealed little about the factors that were causing morale to be high or low.

As Worthy reported, "Davė did begin to make some sense out of these [survey] numbers. At one point Dave said, 'You know, there is somebody you ought to get to know, a fellow by the name of Burleigh Gardner. I used to work with him over at Western Electric.' "

Gardner, Moore, and Worthy worked together to build a survey that went beyond the assessment of morale to provide basic data on the factors influencing employees' responses to Sears, from satisfaction with pay to relations with supervisory personnel. They also worked out a feedback procedure to help store managers use the survey results to improve their own performance.

Worthy had a strong intellectual interest in social research and contributed to our understanding of the relations between morale, organizational structure, and the personality of store managers. The surveys of the B stores (of intermediate size) revealed systematic differences in morale and business performance related to structure: The stores with flatter structures (fewer levels of authority) had higher morale and were performing better than the stores with longer hierarchies. This seemed to suggest a policy to promote flatter structures, but the answer was not that simple.

Follow-up studies revealed a relationship between the structure and store managers' personality. On the one hand, store managers who had faith in their subordinates fitted well with a flat structure. Furthermore, if they were transferred to a store with a longer hierarchy, they would soon report that they did not need all those levels of supervision, and some time later the researchers would find that they were once more managing a flatter organization. On the other hand, managers who told the researchers how hard it was to get good people and how they had to check carefully to get anything done, would soon report that they needed additional supervisory personnel when they were placed in a store with a flat structure. If they continued in that job, they would create the long hierarchy with which they were comfortable.

Such research provided an important counter balance to our overreaction to Frederick W. Taylor and the scientific management school. We had been concentrating so heavily on what we called the "informal organization" that the formal organizational structure seemed to have been disregarded.

The Sears studies brought formal structures back into focus, but now as part of a larger system of relations that took into account the personality of executives and informal relations at work. That made the field of organizational behavior more complex but also more interesting to study.

This was a time of intellectual ferment at the University of Chicago—and somewhat later elsewhere—as more and more professors and students dedicated themselves to the new field of organizational behavior, which seemed to focus on some of the key socioeconomic problems of the times.

The reaction among professors in related fields was much less enthusiastic. Up to this time, research and writing about social problems in industry had been monopolized by labor economists, by industrial psychologists (measuring job aptitudes), and by Frederick Taylor and his associates in scientific management, and many of our colleagues in these camps seemed concerned about our invasion of their territory.

I encountered three reactions among sociologists. When I told William F. Ogburn that I was thinking about studying human relations in industry, he commented, "I thought Frederick W. Taylor and his associates had taken care of that field." When I explained how our approach was different from Taylorism, he seemed willing to concede that it was sociologically legitimate. Some other sociologists reacted by calling the new field "industrial sociology" and tracing its origins back to Max Weber—but his work had not generated new teaching and research programs such as those that grew out of the Western Electric program. There were also those who accused us of studying "managerial sociology," which, because it was one-sided, could hardly be considered a scientific discipline.

Some labor economists wrote articles attacking us on both ethical and scientific grounds. Since our financial support came from management, they assumed that workers would not talk freely with us. When we studied one of the rare cases of union-management cooperation, some critics claimed that by cooperation we meant simply having the union go along with management policies and programs.

There were exceptions among fellow social scientists. Some industrial psychologists reacted with interest and began redefining their field as "industrial social psychology." Likewise, some labor economists found our approach both novel and interesting. In this regard, I think particularly of Frederick Harbison (who joined our Committee on Human Relations in Industry) and Charles Myers of MIT.

The differences in the scale of studies contributed to the problems of interdisciplinary understanding. When a labor economist undertook research, he would think, for example, of studying relations in the steel industry. If he considered something on a smaller scale, he might limit himself to a study of union-management relations in U.S. Steel. For us, a really large-scale study would focus on a single plant, and we were more likely to concentrate on a single department or even a small work group.

Such differences in scale also tended to separate sociologists. Those identifying with Max Weber tended to focus on the major structural determinants of behavior rather than on the behavior itself.

Those operating on the larger scale criticized us for neglecting macro influences on worker behavior, while we claimed that failure to study worker behavior directly led to invalid assumptions about what was causing such behavior. As I look back on that debate, it seems that there is some validity to both arguments—suggesting a need to link micro and macro studies.

Now, fifty years after those initial arguments, it is possible to evaluate them dispassionately. The ethical attacks were clearly based on misunderstandings about our relations with workers. When we began a study in any plant, we always let it be known that we had the financial support of management. And before contacting workers, we would meet with union leaders to explain the objectives of our study and to ask their advice on how to proceed. We expected that this approach would be met with some suspicion, and we did not assume that workers would immediately talk freely with us. After the researcher had been around for a while and there were no negative consequences workers could attribute to us, most of them did begin to talk more freely and frankly about their problems at work. Even union leaders would say to us, "We have complained about this problem again and again, and management has not taken any action. Now you talk to management. Can't you get them to see our problems?"

Some critics were concerned because they feared that our research would have powerful influences on managerial behavior. In fact, few leaders of management paid any attention to us. I thought then that we were unable to communicate well enough to influence management. I now feel this was a misconception. We were working in a period when the "great arsenal of democracy" was achieving enormous productivity to win World War II. For those years and the early postwar years, American manufacturing had such enormous prestige that managers did not want to consider conducting studies that might point out deficiencies. In fact, in the early postwar years, Japanese managers paid much more serious attention to social research than did American managers.

A leading student of Japanese management, sociologist Robert Cole, claimed that the strong interest of Japanese managers in American organizational behavior research was due to a "creative misunderstanding." When Douglas McGregor, Rensis Likert, and others were writing about participative management, the Japanese mistakenly assumed that the leading American companies were striving to move in this direction and the Japanese would have to do likewise if they wanted to compete.

19. *From Restaurant Research to Hotel Action Research*

After several failed attempts to gain access to study a case myself, it occurred to me to tackle Stouffer's restaurant. Since Vernon Stouffer was on the National Restaurant Association Committee, which sponsored the restaurant teaching and research programs at the University of Chicago, he could not turn me down. Thus, for three months, I put in three days at Stouffer's, observing and interviewing, particularly during the time after the lunch hour and before the "guests," as customers were called, began coming in for dinner.

The National Restaurant Association grant provided funds for research assistants. Margaret Chandler was with the project from the beginning. She had gotten started in the field at a cafeteria where she had been a customer. She volunteered to do odd jobs, and she soon had opportunities to do some interviewing.

Edith Lentz had been working in factories and had not finished her undergraduate program. I did not see how I could hire her, yet she impressed me enough that I was reluctant to turn her down. I suggested that she could be a participant observer at a restaurant while supporting herself with a part-time job as a waitress. She agreed. I suggested she apply at Harding's, which was similar to Stouffer's, except that Harding's had a 15 percent service charge instead of tips.

At Harding's, the woman who interviewed her said, "I think you will enjoy working here. We don't hire any Jews or Negroes." Edith was a devoted Quaker, firmly opposed to any form of discrimination. I asked, "Did you take the job?" She nodded. That confirmed my hunch that she would be a good fieldworker. After several weeks on the job, I found her notes valuable enough to hire her full time as a research assistant—which paid as much as the job at Harding's.

Stouffer's was a new world to me: a combination production and service organization; food production was in the basement, and service was provided on the first and second floors. Dieticians supervised the food preparation and the service pantries; a directress of service supervised the hostesses and waitresses.

During the noon rush hour, Stouffer's served a large volume of customers, who were seated, served, and sent on their way all in about twenty minutes. The dieticians had to make sure that food trays were ready to replace empty trays in the pantry, yet avoid having food left over. They also had to pay close attention to weather reports, which influenced the volume of shoppers in the loop district.

There were three means of communication linking the work areas: the TelAutograph (which transmitted a written message to a receiver tape), the house telephone, and direct person-to-person speech. When the pace became particularly hectic, mechanical means did not suffice; during the rush hour, I would often see a dietician running up and down between the kitchen and the service floors to check on what was needed and when.

In my previous work in industry, I had concentrated on the worker-boss relationship. Now I had to broaden my focus to include interdepartmental relations and the impact of technology on human relations.

I concentrated much of my interviewing on the waitresses and hostesses. Waiting tables was considered a low-status job and one requiring minimal skills, but, in such a high-volume restaurant, serving well requires considerable social skills. While being officially subservient to the guests, the skillful waitress learns how to manage them and how to organize a constantly changing set of orders and people. I was also seeing the impact of supervision on the stresses experienced by the waitresses. Some hostesses devoted all their attention to the guests, whereas others constantly observed the waitresses so as to recognize and deal with emerging problems.

In some busy restaurants, we found a good deal of friction if several waitresses arrived at the service counter at about the same time and were clamoring to be served—especially when the service pantry workers were men. When being ordered around by women became too much for some of them, the men would back away and simply leave the waitresses fuming. In Harding's, management had eliminated this problem by placing a spindle on the service counter. Waitresses would place their orders on the spike, and the counterman would pull off each order form from the bottom. In this way, the spindle served as an automatic queuing mechanism. This simple technology got a lot of attention in the academic literature, and some scholars thought I invented it. In fact, Edith discovered it.

The Stouffer's project also gave me the opportunity to study the effects of a change in managers and in directresses of service. A few weeks before I arrived, Mr. Potter had left to become manager of the restaurants in Marshall Field's department store, and he had been succeeded at Stouffer's by Mr. Lathrop. Shortly after, Mrs. Lewis, directress of service, had resigned and been succeeded by Miss Stanton. The waitresses—and particularly the younger and less experienced women—were unhappy about these changes.

Potter had spent at least half of every day out on the floor, observing and chatting informally with employees and supervisors. He gave no direct orders but later discussed any problems he observed with supervisors. Employees felt he was interested in their problems. Lathrop spent most of his time in his office. When he did come out, employees had the impression that he was looking for something that was wrong and for somebody to blame.

A similar contrast characterized the shift from Lewis to Stanton. The waitresses felt that Lewis wanted to help them do a better job and did not hesitate to bring problems, criticisms, and suggestions to her. They regarded Stanton simply as a disciplinarian with no understanding of the problems they faced.

These observations led me to my next case study. I moved across the street to study Potter, to understand how he had developed such a supportive relationship with employees—without undermining the authority of the supervisors.

It took me six months to do the fieldwork at Stouffer's and Marshall Field's and to write up my case study of Stouffer's. Since I had only twelve months to do all the fieldwork and deliver my research to the NRA, I worried about the time it was taking to finish just these two cases. I was thus especially pleased to discover that after my fieldwork I had the framework for my book *Human Relations in the Restaurant Industry* (1948).

Members of the sponsoring committee of the National Restaurant Association decided that it would be a good idea for me to get out of Chicago and give some of the other NRA members an idea of what I was finding out. I talked in Columbus, Ohio, and Minneapolis on human elements in supervision and was very well received. This was in marked contrast to the reaction I received from the committee to the first draft of my book. One critic expressed the committee's unhappiness: "I thought the idea of working with the University of Chicago was to raise the status of the restaurant industry. If this book is published, it will have the opposite effect. Therefore, it should not be published."

The contract with the NRA did not give the committee veto power over the manuscript, but I wanted to make the research useful to people in the restaurant industry. Lloyd Warner assured me that I would be the final judge of what was published, and he would explain academic freedom to the NRA committee.

There followed a long, painful process of negotiation and mediation. I recognized that having Warner as mediator greatly enhanced the prospects of agreement. Still, that role cast Warner as the respected senior social scientist and me as the irresponsible upstart. I felt I should have been mature enough to deal with the criticisms face to face, but I had sense enough not to object to Warner's role—and I recognized that he was playing it with superb skill and understanding.

The NRA critics were also upset by my discussion of the stresses of waiting tables in a busy restaurant where management emphasized fast service. I had emphasized that point by focusing on "the crying waitress."

My discussion of status also upset them. I could not leave the status question out, however, since interviews with employees had made it clear that the low status of their occupation was a substantial concern, although I had tried to make my points in ways that were not offensive to managers.

After the committee had gone through the second draft, we met for a final negotiation session. My critics now recognized that I had tried to meet their objections, but there was still one statement that the critics found particularly offensive: "You can't be a man when you are a waiter. That's right. You aren't a man. You are just a servant." I believed that this and similar quotations expressed more convincingly how many waiters felt about their jobs than any words of mine could. The committee members were not persuaded, and I was not willing to yield.

At this impasse, Charles Rovetta (representing the School of Business) asked if my critics would accept the book if I put the objectionable quotations in an appendix. They looked relieved. I said I would accept this suggestion—under the condition that I could indicate in the text where the quotations could be found. Thus, appendix B is entitled "Job Attitudes." A more accurate title would have been "Job Attitudes the NRA Sponsoring Committee Could Not Accept."

The book was finally published, along with a foreword by the NRA Faculty-Industry Committee that read more like a disclaimer than an endorsement: "This book is not a study of the restaurant business as such, but rather a scientific approach to human relationships in business under abnormal wartime conditions. The experiences and problems encountered in this project might apply equally well to other lines of endeavor."

I was happy to get the book out with even this minimal endorsement. It never sold well, but I cannot blame that on the NRA. Committee members had warned me that "restaurant managers don't read books." Still, the book or parts of it have been used in teaching restaurant and hotel administration.

During my NRA trip to Minneapolis, Byron Calhoun, vice president and general manager of the Radisson Hotel, asked me to recommend a personnel manager who could support the kind of human relations I was describing. When I learned that there had been three personnel managers in the preceding year, I was not inclined to propose anyone to fill the position. I made a counterproposal. I would find him a personnel manager, provided the appointment was tied in with a research project financed by the hotel.

Meredith Wiley, a student in human relations in industry at the University of Chicago who had just received his master's degree, became personnel director of the Radisson. Edith Lentz was hired as a researcher. She sent copies of her research notes to me and shared them with Wiley. Every month I spent two days at the Radisson, going over the research and the action planning with Lentz and Wiley and discussing plans and progress with Byron Calhoun. Once a month, Edith came to Chicago for further discussions.

We began the research in familiar territory, the Radisson's three restaurants. In the course of a year, Edith moved on to studying the housekeeping department and the front office.

Our strategy was to promote and facilitate group meetings in which supervisors discussed problems with the employees they directed. That required preliminary coaching of the supervisors by Wiley. Edith observed each of these meetings and afterward interviewed some of the employees. Then she met with the supervisor to discuss how the meeting went and to make suggestions for improvement.

A meeting between the chef and the coffee shop waitresses proved to be a turning point in interdepartmental relations. It began with a barrage of complaints from the waitresses, but the atmosphere changed from adversarial to problem-solving as the waitresses suggested changes that might improve their relations with the kitchen.

What did we accomplish with this project? We achieved one major objective: a change in the role of the personnel director. Previously, the person in charge of personnel at the Radisson (and elsewhere generally in that era) was responsible for maintaining the employment records, recruiting and selecting new employees, and dealing with union grievances. Although he had no special training in human relations or any systematic data to guide him, he was also supposed to advise line management on human relations problems. Wiley delegated most of the work on employment records and recruitment and selection so that he could concentrate on improving relations within the hotel and between the hotel and the union. Employees and supervisors came to recognize that Wiley had an intimate knowledge of what was going on at the Radisson—and that he was using it to help them do their own jobs better. They also trusted Edith Lentz and talked freely with her, knowing that what they told her would not be used against them.

Soon, we could see major improvements in relations and services in various departments of the hotel, but unfortunately we had limited success in dealing with top management. The resident manager, Bernard Kozel, was in his mid-fifties and a former officer in a European army. For years he had worked with a hotel accounting organization, going over the financial records and telling top management whom to fire and how to push the organization to greater efficiency. The Radisson job was his first experience in management. He worked long hours and spent at least half of every day roaming the hotel, issuing orders to anyone, with no regard for the chain of command. He believed it was sometimes important to "read the riot act" to keep people on their toes, and both employees and supervisors hated and feared him.

Our first approach with Kozel was a flat failure. We hoped that by skillfully interviewing him, we might lead him to acknowledge some of his problems and give us openings to help him. I made one try at this strategy over dinner, but Kozel spent our time together simply describing the great things he had accomplished. I was tempted to say, "We're finding that the employees think you are a very disruptive influence, and we suspect Mr. Calhoun is concerned about this problem. What are we going to do about it?" But I could not bring myself to do it.

Wiley tried the same approach. Kozel refused to be interviewed. When our research revealed that Kozel was telling supervisors, "Don't talk to Wiley. He's a dope," it became clear that a new approach was required. Wiley set up an appointment in Kozel's office and used the occasion to state firmly his understanding of the way he (and Calhoun) expected Wiley and Kozel to cooperate. Wiley illustrated his points by citing cases in which Kozel could have avoided being disruptive if he had consulted Wiley before taking action. Kozel exploded at several points during this long session, but, as Wiley sketched out projects in which they could work together, Kozel calmed down. When the encounter was over, Kozel shook Wiley's hand and said, "I'm glad you came in. I think we have this straightened out now."

Kozel stopped reading the riot act, and the frequency of his disruptive interventions decreased. This was hardly a transformation of his leadership style, but perhaps that degree of change was all we could expect.

Calhoun liked what we were doing, but he seemed to regard it as just one of many possible personnel projects. When we had barely started, he talked to me about having Wiley start a company magazine, an employee recreation program, and various other ideas. I pointed out that, if Wiley responded to all those suggestions, he would have no time to help supervisors and managers improve their performance. Late in our program, Calhoun contracted with a consultant for twelve hundred dollars a year to supply a monthly packet of posters and accompanying inspirational messages for the employees. I shall never forget one poster that featured a reigning movie star dressed in a maid's uniform, reaching down to pull her stocking way up her shapely thigh. I did not believe the Radisson's maids would be likely to see her as a role model.

Byron Calhoun embodied the American dream. As a teenager, he had worked in a hotel as a dishwasher, had risen to become CEO and part owner of the Radisson—and would become CEO of the Intercontinental Hotels chain. Employees and supervisors stood in awe of his knowledge and demonstrated success, and yet they feared him. He failed to involve others in his vision for the hotel, so they did not know where he was going or what to expect. He recognized that, in group meetings, subordinates never ventured to question any of his ideas, but he did not know what to do about it. Like Kozel, he sometimes gave orders without regard to the chain of command.

When I talked with Calhoun about how things were going in the hotel's various departments, I refrained from discussing his own leadership style. I felt insecure in confronting the tycoon and set the problem aside, reasoning that I would take up the issue after we had reached an agreement on whether to pursue the research project for a second year. This decision meant nothing to me financially, since I was not paid for my services, but I saw an agreement to continue as a sign of success.

Calhoun expressed great satisfaction with our work and said he would extend the contract if Edith was willing to continue with the field research. Quite sensibly, Edith decided it was time to go back to college. (She eventually followed me to Cornell, where she got her Ph.D., played a major role in studies of hospitals, and then served on the faculty in hospital administration at the University of Minnesota.)

When it became evident that the project would not be continued, I decided that my final report to Calhoun would concentrate on the deficiencies in his leadership style. As I reported later (Whyte and Hamilton 1965:178):

I came to town to deliver the report in person. Smith (Calhoun) was so eager to get it that he locked himself in his office immediately and read it straight through. When he called me in, it was to express enthusiasm particularly for my analysis of his executive behavior. Later, he called his management group together & told them he had just read my final report. He said further that I had pointed out that he was the main personnel problem of the hotel, and that he intended to profit from the criticisms I had made.

That response made it clear that I should have introduced Calhoun's leadership style into our monthly discussions much earlier. I had no confidence in my skills as a consultant, but I should have given it a try—and learned from the experience.

Wiley remained at the Radisson for two years after the conclusion of our project. Edith wrote a detailed report on our findings, entitled "The Tremont Hotel Study." That manuscript was well worth publication, but it described and analyzed in detail the behavior of individuals in leadership positions. Academic freedom guaranteed our right to publish, but we did not feel we had the right to publish a report that would be embarrassing to some individuals and might damage their careers. We could have changed the names of all the key individuals so that few readers would recognize that the Tremont was the Radisson, but everyone in Radisson management would have been sure to figure out who was who. Although she had the most to lose in delaying publication, Edith decided not to publish her report.

In the 1960s, when I was asked to discuss action research at a management meeting, I reached back to tell the story of the Radisson project. The audience response persuaded me that the Radisson case was still fresh and exciting. I called Edith, now Edith Lentz Hamilton, to suggest that we cooperate on what turned out to be *Action Research for Management* (1965). (Published under a grant to the Academy of Management by the McKinsey Foundation for Management Research, it was honored by the academy as the best management book of that year.)

As I look back on my restaurant and hotel projects, I have mixed feelings. I take pride in what was published, and yet I missed opportunities to contribute more to action research and social theory. This latter deficiency became clear some years after I had published one of my best articles, "The Social Structure of the Restaurant" (1949). In it, I described and analyzed a *sociotechnical system*—but without recognizing the significance of what I had done. As the title of my article indicates, I was still committed to a maxim Burleigh Gardner often pronounced: "A factory [or any work organization] is a social system." I could not yet recognize the limitations of this idea and point to the need for a theoretical framework that linked the social and the technological systems.

In 1951, Eric Trist and K. W. Bamforth published an article entitled "Some Social and Psychological Consequences of the Longwall Method of Coal Getting" in which they demonstrated the intimate interrelation between changes in technology and changes in the social system. In effect, they had created a new theoretical framework and given it a name: *sociotechnical systems*. The idea was simple but basic: A change in technology affects the social system, and a change in the social system affects the operations of the technology. Therefore, to understand and deal effectively with work organizations, one has to recognize and act in response to the interdependence of the *socio-* and the *technical* systems.

Although the *sociotechnical* framework has even now not been recognized by mainstream sociologists, behavioral scientists dedicated to action research have long taken it for granted that their interventions must be guided by a sociotechnical framework.

Bill at 17¹/₂ months behind the Whyte home on Wiegand Place, the Bronx.

Bill with John Whyte in 1920, behind the home on Wiegand Place.

Bill with Isabel Whyte in 1920, on the roof of their Bronx apartment.

BRONXVILLE
SCHOOLS BULLETIN

Number 18 ÷ May 1931

Bill Whyte Visits The Elementary School

"With the responsibility of having four pupils, I became quite adept at my job"—Page 17.

(Picture posed after the event.)

Bronxville school superintendent Willard W. Beatty devoted an issue of the community school bulletin to Bill's weekly newspaper columns on elementary education.

Bill and Bronxville tennis team recruits, Frank Hutson (left) and Edward Macy (right), at Swarthmore, 1935.

Kathleen King in 1933.

Kathleen King and Bill Whyte after their wedding ceremony at the King family home in New Canaan, Connecticut, on May 28, 1938. (From left to right: Clarence King, Alice King, Carrie Baker King, Kathleen, Bill, Isabel Whyte, and John Whyte.)

Bill, Kathleen, and four-month-old Joyce on the Midway in Chicago.

Mama and Papa Orlandi in their North End restaurant in 1937.

*Angelo Ralph Orlandella
("Sam Franco"),
co–participant observer in the
North End study, 1952.*

The original book jacket, designed by Kathleen in 1943.

The North End, 1937.

*Ernest Pecci ("Doc"),
co–participant observer in
the North End study.*

At the Georgia Warm Springs Foundation, Bill and another author proudly display their just-published books (December 1943).

Bill outside of Social Science Building at the University of Chicago in 1944.

Bill and children in Trumansburg, New York, in the winter of 1949. (From left to right: Martin, Bruce, Lucy, and Joyce.)

Bill (with graduate assistant Frank Miller) observing workers in the Steuben Division of Corning Glass Works.

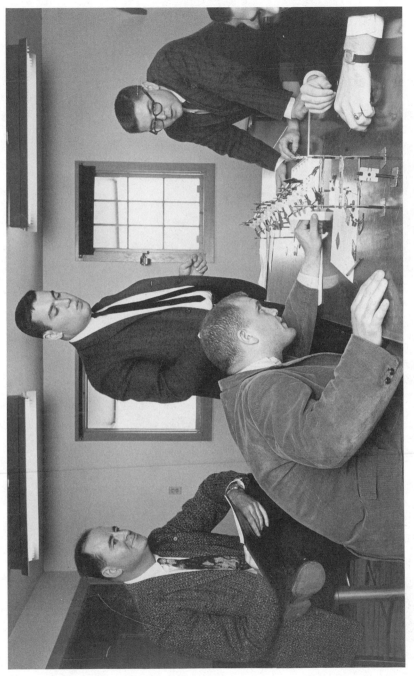

Bill with Cornell undergraduates in the "Group Processes" course in 1961.

Allan Holmberg, Aida Vasquez (wife of Mario Vasquez), and J. Mayone Stycos on the way to Vicos, summer of 1960.

Bill and Oscar Alers with José Matos and other members of the Instituto de Estudios Peruanos team working on the Cornell-IEP program, 1965.

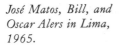

José Matos, Bill, and Oscar Alers in Lima, 1965.

José María Arizmendiarrieta in Mondragón, Spain, 1975.

Bill at Swarthmore's commencement in 1984, when he received an honorary degree in humane letters.

Bill in his ILR office in 1985.

Bill and Kathleen in 1989, at the time of the publication of Making Mondragón.

Golden wedding, May 1988. Left to right, back row: Joyce Wiza, Benito Reyes, Rachel Reyes, Joseph Wiza, Timothy King, Tom Wilson Weinberg, Joseph Wiza (grandson), John Whyte, Lucy Ferguson, Allen Ferguson, Duncan Ferguson, Adam Whyte. Middle row: Tracy Whyte, Frances King, Allison Wiza, Andrea Ferguson, Mark Wiza, Kathleen, Veronica Whyte, Bill, Martin Whyte. Front row: Jason Russo and Blake Ferguson. (Photo © 1988 by Harvey Ferdschneider)

20. Studying Union-Management Cooperation

Fascinated as I was with the restaurant and hotel studies, I felt I was out of the mainstream in industrial research, whose focus I assumed was manufacturing. I was particularly interested in union-management cooperation. I recognized that cooperative relations were rare in the mass-production industries, but it seemed to me important to study such exceptional cases. If labor and management could learn how to work together, the results, I assumed, would be beneficial to both parties and to society. Here I was going against the grain, because most of my colleagues assumed that adversarial relations were inevitable and that conflict might be healthy for society as a whole.

At dinner meetings of the members of the University of Chicago's Industrial Relations Center, I would ask a single question: "Do you have any experience with cooperative relations?" I first put the question to Sidney Garfield, business agent for the International Chemical Workers Union, who later became vice president of its international. His answer led me in 1945 to conduct a case study (with Burleigh Gardner and Andrew H. Whiteford) of S. Buchsbaum and Company, which then had about fifteen hundred workers engaged in producing jewelry and plastic products, particularly rainwear. The firm had broken its union in 1919 and had broken an organizing strike in 1935. In the 1940s, the International Chemical Workers Union had organized a new union drive, culminating in a strike. The settlement of the strike had given birth to an extraordinary cooperative relationship.

Later, William G. Caples, industrial relations manager of Inland Steel Company, led me to the South Chicago plant of a subsidiary, Inland Steel Container Company. The years 1939–46 had been marked by strife, confusion, and rapid management turnover. The conflict reached a climax in a 191-day strike, which ended in July 1946. A year later, the parties had developed a highly cooperative relationship.

When I asked Caples to explain this startling change, he replied, "I guess they learned to trust each other." I wanted to know how that trust had developed.

From Orvis Collins's field study of the Tennessee Valley Authority (TVA), I got some clues to the conditions supporting cooperative union-management relations. In private industry, executives typically staked out a defensive position to protect managerial prerogatives, while union officials were constantly pressing for changes through grievance procedures and other measures. This meant that the official contacts between management and the union were limited largely to initiatives by stewards and higher officials striving to take something away from management. In the TVA, the unions used the grievance procedure, but that challenge to management was balanced by initiatives from supervisors and middle management that called for cooperation from the unions and workers on disciplinary, productivity, and safety problems. This two-way initiation of action between management and the unions was backed up by a number of joint activities in training, safety, and other fields.

This suggested that achieving a balance of initiatives was essential for the building of cooperative union-management relations. But how did the parties establish that balance when management did not want to recognize the union or sought only to defend itself against union challenges? Clearly, now that collective bargaining was the law of the land, the parties were forced to meet, but that was not enough to produce the balance of initiatives between the parties.

At Phillips Petroleum, I had encountered "the watchman statement," which had an enormous negative impact on relations between management and workers. Might there be important *symbols* in these recent cases that encouraged managers to develop favorable conceptions of workers and unions—and that opened the way to initiatives that favored cooperation?

Garfield described a key incident when Buchsbaum's management was trying to bring strikebreakers into the plant. A car bringing in "scabs" drove at high speed right onto the sidewalk by the plant entrance, endangering some of the picketers. They wanted to tip the car over, but Garfield intervened.

> I knew enough to realize that would be a bad move because of the great American tradition of respect for property, so I made them leave the car alone. I don't mean that I was easy. There was one fellow that was trying to sneak in and I pulled him out of his car and just kicked him down the street.

When the company detective told Herbert Buchsbaum about the incident, he was impressed. He contrasted it with the 1935 strike, when workers sabotaged machines and threw rocks through the windows, and he said, "I felt these people were responsible."

Buchsbaum still did not want to meet with the union, but the law required him to do so. First, he met with a business friend who dealt with the union, along with Sam Laderman, Garfield's superior. Buchsbaum had considered union people "a bunch of racketeers," but his friend had assured him that Laderman "was a real human being. He liked opera. He disliked strikes."

Reluctantly, Buchsbaum met with Laderman, Garfield, and a committee of workers. A worker asked Buchsbaum why he was against unions. He replied with the then-standard arguments: that unions held down productivity and would push for wage increases that could drive the company out of business. The workers countered by making suggestions that would save money and increase production. Buchsbaum "took notes that I could see would save the company thousands of dollars annually," he told me. And by the end of the meeting, Buchsbaum had agreed to recognize the union. A contract was quickly negotiated, following the industry pattern. This led to a partnership arrangement, in which management routinely called on the union for help in resolving disciplinary problems and other issues.

In the Inland Steel case, I had access to the court reporter's transcription of the twelve long bargaining sessions leading to the signing of the 1947 contract. They provided essential symbolic clues to how the transition was made from a relationship marked by conflict to one characterized as cooperative.

International representative Jake Shafer was new to this case, so at least he did not bring to it the negative reputation his predecessors had with management. Shafer avoided reviewing the bitter past to focus on future relations. Instead of immediately countering management's arguments, he posed a series of questions that encouraged management to elaborate on its views. His very negotiation style projected cooperation.

When emotional heat threatened the process, Shafer used diversionary tactics. At one meeting, he passed around photographs of a recent hunting and fishing trip and the parties spent a few minutes discussing hunting and fishing. This not only eased tensions but established a bond between Shafer and factory manager Robert Novy, who was to play a major role in establishing the cooperative relationship. As Novy told me, "It's been my experience that whenever you run into a real sportsman, you'll find he is a pretty regular fellow. He's a man you can deal with straight from the shoulder. That's one of the things that sold me on Shafer."

The parties were now able to reach agreement on the most difficult issues and thus to build a cooperative relationship in which management and the union called on one another for help on a wide range of problems.

These forays into studying union-management cooperation produced a number of publications, beginning with one about the Buchsbaum case. During that study, Garfield had discussed a number of other cases he had been involved in. I was fascinated by these tales, and we then got together to coauthor a series of articles entitled "The Collective Bargaining Process" (1950 and 1951). In their path-breaking *Behavioral Theory of Labor Negotiations* (1965), Richard Walton and Robert McKersie made frequent reference to cases in our series.

Also during this time, I laid out my own theoretical analysis of cooperative relations in one of my better articles, "Patterns of Interaction in Union-Management Relations" (1949). Harper and Brothers published my study of the Inland case, *Pattern for Industrial Peace* (1951), with a jacket by Kathleen. (It was translated into German and later into Tamil, an indigenous language of India. In 1987, after the book had gone out of print, Garland Publishing Company reprinted it in their series "Ancestral Books in the Management of Organizations.")

After my first year with the Committee on Human Relations in Industry, I began teaching on a half-time basis at the University of Chicago. I taught a course in industrial sociology, and I worked with some of the graduate students on their thesis research. Kathleen and I held a discussion and reporting meeting in our home every two weeks. Spouses were invited and regularly attended, so this became a function that linked family, studies, and work.

In the summer of 1945, we moved to a house we bought at 5651 South Drexel Avenue, still within walking distance of my office. In December of that year, Bruce, our third child, was born.

Also around this time, Kathleen got back into designing book jackets. The jacket she had done for *Street Corner Society* "as a labor of love" finally paid off. The University of Chicago Press was launching a series of trade books, and Kathleen applied for a job. The press offered her a half-time position, but she arranged to work on a freelance basis, so that she could work at home. With a small baby and two children three and five years old, that meant considerable juggling of work and family responsibilities, especially when she encountered tight press deadlines. Our bedroom was the only space available, and at times that meant Kathleen worked at one end while I tried to get to sleep.

When I had come to Chicago as a graduate student, in 1940, Lloyd Warner and Everett Hughes had treated me as a colleague and included Kathleen and me in social gatherings. I continued to be impressed by Lloyd, not only for each new volume of his Yankee City books but for his ability to fit what he was learning from field studies into his current teaching assignments. I saw him as a major figure in reshaping social anthropology and sociology.

During this period our relationship with Everett and Helen Hughes deepened. They had taken the lead in making arrangements to bring me back to Chicago after I was struck with polio. They were close friends with the Redfields, which led not only to our finding our apartment but also to the rental of a summer cottage on Lake Michigan.

We were in Chicago for only four years (1944–48), but I look back on it as a happy and productive time for me and my family.

21. Moving to Cornell

In 1945, I received a letter from a Bronxville friend of my parents, Edmund Ezra Day, then the president of Cornell University. He wondered if I would be interested in a faculty position in the newly created New York State School of Industrial and Labor Relations (ILR). I was flattered but I could not imagine leaving the industrial heartland of America for the semirural setting of Ithaca, New York.

But in 1946 the Chicago situation changed. Burleigh Gardner, frustrated with the academic bureaucracy that restricted open-ended research, decided to leave to start his own consulting and research organization. Burleigh invited me to join him. I was happy to be asked, but the offer did not tempt me. I had become convinced that the university was the right place for me. I wanted to be in a situation that fostered writing and publishing.

In 1946, I was appointed executive secretary of the committee, which brought no extra pay and much more responsibility. I was particularly troubled by the financing side of the job, as I was not good at raising money from business.

In 1946 Leonard Cottrell, chair of Cornell's Department of Sociology and Anthropology, called me about a possible joint appointment in his department and in the School of Industrial and Labor Relations. I decided to visit Cornell.

I found Cornell, "far above Cayuga's waters" in the Finger Lakes region, a beautiful setting, and it offered ideal conditions for a growing family. Being the first appointment in human relations in industry in the new school seemed an exciting prospect. The school had been created in 1945 in response to legislative hearings and the report of a committee chaired by State Assembly majority leader Irving Ives. The report had stated that labor-management conflict was a major problem with which neither the leaders of labor nor management were prepared to deal effectively. The school provided a four-year college undergraduate degree program and graduate programs leading to M.S. and Ph.D. degrees. All instruction in industrial relations was provided by its own faculty. Other universities followed shortly with graduate degrees in industrial relations, but in those schools instruction was provided by professors based in departments of economics, sociology, or psychology.

I was also attracted by the prospect of joining Cornell's very lively Department of Sociology and Anthropology, which had an outstanding reputation in applied social anthropology. At the time, Morris Opler was conducting research in India and Lauriston Sharpe in Thailand, and Allen R. Holmberg was starting studies in Peru. I was particularly impressed by Robin Williams and his colleagues in sociology, who were planning research on intergroup relations in Elmira, an hour's drive from Ithaca.

After I returned home, Cottrell called with a job offer. The plan was that I would divide my time equally between research and teaching. He promised that the letter of appointment would be sent shortly, but, since it was getting late in the hiring season, could I start at once, to see how Chicago reacted to my Cornell job offer.

I informed my committee and department chairman and dean of the offer, and then waited for the letter from Cornell. Several days later I got a phone call from a very embarrassed Cottrell, informing me that something had gone wrong between ILR and the Department of Sociology and Anthropology and no offer would be forthcoming. I was stunned. I asked him to write a letter stating that he had made what he believed was a firm job offer.

Now what could I do? Kathleen and I talked it over and decided to wait for Cottrell's letter. Before it arrived, my dean Ralph Tyler, told me he was approving a recommendation from the Department of Sociology to offer me a tenured appointment at the associate professor level. When I told him the Cornell story, he did not rescind the offer.

I never did understand the Cornell foul-up, but the outcome was clear. The joint appointment went to Alexander Leighton, a psychiatrist who had done research in social anthropology.

In January 1948, Alex called to offer me a full professorship in ILR. I would have a courtesy appointment in the Department of Sociology and Anthropology, but my office and formal responsibilities would be in ILR. I liked Alex and had a high regard for his work. He had published *The Governing of Men* (1945), an impressive study of a wartime Japanese relocation center, which had received a front-page review in the Sunday *New York Times* book review section.

I was interested, but we were expecting our fourth child in February. I was their first choice, Alex said, but they had to make their move soon. Could I come to Ithaca at the end of February? I agreed.

My mother came for the period while I was away, but I hoped to get back before the baby arrived. I just barely made it. Kathleen had taken a taxi to the hospital a few hours earlier. I found her in the advanced stages of labor. Lucy was born on February 25, 1948.

Once I accepted the appointment, the next question was where to live. Kathleen should have been involved in that decision, but she could not leave the children. I returned to Ithaca alone to look over possibilities with the help of Alex Leighton and Henry Guerlac, my old friend from my junior fellowship days, who was now in Cornell's history department.

Alex interested me in Trumansburg, which offered a much more varied school population than Cayuga Heights, the favorite location of faculty families. In Trumansburg, there were children of farmers, local merchants, factory workers, as well as the families of Cornell and Ithaca College faculty. It was only about a twenty-minute drive from Trumansburg to the Cornell campus, and Alex invited me to join a car pool with him and Jack McConnell. A sociologist trained at Yale, Jack was then teaching and studying social security and protective labor legislation in ILR.

I found an affordable and comfortable house a mile from the center of Trumansburg, right next to the Grove Cemetery, which had tombstones dating back to the early years of the nineteenth century, when the village was first settled. On the other side of the street was Smith Woods, an area set aside by its benefactor to be kept forever wild.

When I phoned Kathleen to tell her about the house, I said it would not need much fixing up. Over the next two years, she found enough to change and rebuild to add substantially to the cost. Her efforts and ingenuity turned it into a much more attractive and useful home.

Kathleen was happy with the move, but it limited her opportunities in commercial art. No longer did she have a regular series of book jacket jobs, although she did pick up some freelance assignments and for about seven years taught adult classes in painting.

Our house was located on a three-quarter-acre lot, on which Kathleen cultivated a varied and beautiful flower garden. I enjoyed being surrounded by flowers, although I could never keep their names straight. Since we were now in the country, I thought we should have a vegetable garden. I got a bulletin from Cooperative Extension and was pleasantly surprised to discover that, if I followed the instructions, the plants really did grow. At the height of this enterprise, we had corn, beans, tomatoes, squash, zucchini, peas, asparagus, rhubarb, cantaloupes, and watermelons. In one memorable two-week period, we had thirty-six melons ripe for picking and were eating them at every meal of the day.

I assumed I could get the children to do some of the gardening. There was no problem getting them to help with the picking, but the chores of planting, fertilizing, and weeding held no appeal. They knew the garden was not necessary to support the family—the value of the crops covered little beyond the expenses of tools, seeds, and fertilizer, and they regarded gardening as my project, not theirs. In the 1960s, when I fell carrying garden tools and broke my leg, I decided that gardening was too much for me and gave it up.

So that the children could have some religious experience, we started going to the Presbyterian church and finally became members. I even became an elder, although I never developed a deep religious commitment.

I had never expected to become a Rotarian, but Alex Leighton and Jack McConnell were members and probably had joined for the same reason I did: to fit into the community. I did not plan to study Trumansburg, but my Rotary experiences did have one incidental payoff for my research.

Rotary met for dinner every Thursday night at Gregory's restaurant. Before dinner, many of the members met at the bar. I liked to have a scotch and soda with them. As I was approaching the bar, a friend would order my drink. At first, that was just a touching expression of friendship, but I did not want to sponge on a friend, so I decided to arrive early. Then, when I saw my friend arrive, I would call in his drink order. But now we finished our drinks earlier than before, and my friend would bang his glass on the bar and order another round for both of us. With this tactic, I ended up paying for two drinks instead of one and having to drink one that I didn't want. There was no escape short of coming in just in time for dinner or moving out of town.

This trivial incident set me thinking of the costs as well as the benefits of interpersonal reciprocity. As some sociologists began to look at exchange theory as the fundamental basis of social relations, I felt a need to go beyond interpersonal reciprocity.

Within a few years, I was elected president of the Trumansburg Parent-Teacher Association and of the Community Council, a local charitable and community improvement organization. This was no tribute to my leadership ability. In a village of about seventeen hundred, the old-timers had long since held such positions, so organizations had to reach out to newcomers, including Kathleen and me.

I became painfully aware of this problem when I was finishing my term as PTA president and headed a committee to recruit my successor. Several potential candidates turned me down, and at last we had to turn to a woman who had no obvious qualifications beyond her willingness to accept. After the election, we learned why she wanted the job: She was trying to organize a campaign to oust the school superintendent. That was not on my personal agenda, so I had to let school people know I was not supporting her campaign.

One of my community projects was to convert a pond adjoining our property into a skating rink. To do so, we needed a small building in which people could change to skates. We acquired an old chicken coop, but we had to get it out to the pond on a flatbed truck. We had a car drive slowly in front of the truck while I formed the rear guard. The distance was not great, but the task was boring, and I was thinking of other things and did not notice when the truck suddenly stopped. I suffered the ignominy of smashing in the front of my car—at five miles an hour.

We did have skating on the pond, but for just one year. Then the owner of the property recognized that, in case of an accident, he would be liable. Since we had no money for insurance, we had to abandon the rink.

I learned from these public service experiences that it is not easy to do good for a community. Willingness to try is not enough. I also learned that, once you get deeply involved in community activities, it is hard to get out. There were so many evening meetings that the children were beginning to complain about our limited home life. The only way to get out gracefully was to leave town. This we did in the summer of 1954, when we took off for a year's sabbatical in Venezuela.

22. *Early Years at Cornell*

The School of Industrial and Labor Relations was in its third year when I arrived in July 1948. Irving Ives, the first dean, had left the New York State Assembly to assume the leadership of the school, which his committee had created. Since he knew little about academic matters, he relied on the first two professors who were appointed: Jean McKelvey, a student of collective bargaining, and Maurice Neufeld, a labor historian.

They told Ives that if he wanted professors to teach extension courses and undergraduate and graduate courses, and do research, two courses or seminars each semester should be the norm. They also suggested a ratio of one secretary for every two professors—at a time when entire departments in the College of Arts and Sciences had to get by with one or two secretaries.

We were also favored by a travel budget for field research. For major projects, we still had to seek outside grants, but all we had to do was request a state car and take off to get fieldwork started.

The teaching faculty was divided into eight small "units": labor market economics, social security and protective labor legislation, labor history, collective bargaining, personnel administration, industrial education, statistics, and human relations. There were three of us in human relations, but I was the only one with a full-time appointment. Alex Leighton divided his time between ILR and Sociology and Anthropology. Alex had recruited Temple Burling, who spent half his time with the university medical clinic. He had been staff psychiatrist for R. H. Macy and Company. Alex had also secured a grant for an industrial psychiatry program.

During this time, the school was developing a statewide extension program. It had been the ideal of the planners to have a faculty of "triple-threat professors." The term was from the sports jargon of the time, when a football player who could kick, pass, and run the ball was called a "triple-threat man." A triple-threat professor was one who was involved in resident teaching, research, and extension. That ideal was never fully realized, but we came closer in the early years of the school than at any time later. With the passing years, the resident faculty felt less commitment to extension, recognizing that, at Cornell as well as elsewhere, the rewards of status and tenure went to those professors judged to be superior performers in research and at least adequate in their resident teaching, whereas what they did for extension received little attention.

In 1948, the resident faculty was small. Academic rivalries and frictions were moderated by a sense that we were pioneers in an exciting new enterprise. There was some sniping at the human relations faculty by those trained in economics, but I did not feel any personal hostilities.

Contrary to the views of the state government, our reception in management circles indicated a widespread belief that there was no need for the ILR school. Some management people referred to the school as the "kardboard Kremlin," the "kardboard" being a reference to the World War II surplus buildings in which we were housed until we moved into a new building in 1962. The Kremlin reference reflected our commitment to collective bargaining, although nothing faintly resembling collective bargaining existed in the Soviet Union.

There was no problem in getting union members and officers interested in our extension courses, seminars, and workshops, but we had to persuade managers that we could offer them something of value. That was particularly difficult for Lois Gray, the extension director of our western district, who was married to Ed Gray, regional director of the United Auto Workers. To open up communication with management people in Buffalo, Lois planned a seminar at which four full professors talked on what she assumed would be the least controversial topic: human relations. I shared that mission with Leighton, Burling, and Ralph Campbell, director of extension.

Some of my students in Chicago had studied the organization drive of the Foreman's Association of America (FAA)—a human relations topic I thought would be interesting. In the mass-production industries, foremen had no influence on management and found themselves caught between management and the unionized workers. In many cases, the president of the company, who had never before given any attention to the foremen, would invite them to dinner and then tell them that they were really key members of management. These pep talks by top management always proved a boon to the FAA. Many foremen signed up afterward, convinced that management was not interested in their problems.

While I was telling this story at the seminar, I was interrupted by a manager who said something like this: "You are telling us that foremen do not really consider themselves members of management? That is an un-American statement. You shouldn't say things like that."

I was startled. I explained that I was not giving my own views but simply reporting how many foremen felt. My critic now shifted his ground to Buffalo. He asked his colleagues, "Do the foremen in your companies think they are not members of management?" He asked for a show of hands of those who would answer in the affirmative. I counted about a third of the hands raised, which I considered a moral victory, but that was not good enough. The controversy upset Lois Gray's objective of selling human relations as a benign and comforting field for management.

~

My first semester at Cornell, I taught introductory undergraduate and graduate courses in human relations and a seminar in fieldwork methods. I used the seminar to get students started on their own field projects.

As Kathleen and I had done in Chicago, Alex Leighton held evening meetings for students working on field projects and their spouses, and Temple Burling and I joined in. Two years after I came to Cornell, Alex moved to a full-time position in the Department of Sociology and Anthropology, leaving me in charge of the human relations unit in ILR. Kathleen and I now hosted the meetings. The meetings turned into an open forum where students did most of the talking and did not hesitate to disagree with the professors. The spouses— including my own—appreciated being included, and they gained a better sense of what we all were doing. Students told us that they often got so involved in our discussions that, after driving back to Ithaca, they would stop for a beer so they could continue talking before going home.

To my surprise Ithaca's semirural location did not turn out to be a disadvantage. A city of about thirty thousand, it had several industrial plants that were informally off-limits for fieldwork so as not to saturate the local area, but it was less than an hour's drive to Elmira and only a little more to Corning. One of the graduate students would take a state car, pick me up at the office, and drive to the plant under study. As we drove through the pleasant countryside, we would discuss what we planned to do that day in the plant. On the way back, we would talk about what we had learned and where that should lead us.

Our first study was carried out in the Elmira plant of Moore Business Forms. We got into that study when personnel manager Hal Ford asked John Thurber in ILR Extension to develop a training program for foremen. As Hal told us later, he had no special expectations regarding human relations. He just needed a vehicle to get the foremen talking to each other—a training course on bird watching would have served that purpose. I agreed to organize the course, provided we had some planning time to get acquainted and develop some sense of what the foremen's problems were.

Graham Taylor, the first trainee in the industrial psychiatry program, shared the course with me, and graduate student Chris Argyris observed and took notes. Later, Chris and Graham reported on that project in the journal *Human Organization*.

Melvin Kohn, my first research assistant, began the research on Moore Business Forms. During the second year of our study, Chris focused particular attention on the plant manager (I'll call him Tom), who cultivated close personal relations with all his four hundred-odd workers. Tom spent much of his time out on the floor, observing and chatting with workers and foremen. He not only knew all the workers' names but also a good deal about their families. The foremen had enormous respect for Tom, who could outsmart and outtalk all of them. But when anything went wrong, Tom wanted to know whom to blame, so the foremen had to devise ways of "throwing the dead cat in somebody else's yard," as they put it.

Chris liked Tom, but Tom did not conform to his ideal of the participative manager. When I read the first draft of Chris's doctoral thesis, I asked him, "What are you—the prosecuting attorney?" In the final draft, Chris modified his accusatory tone, and I did not worry further about that study.

A couple of years later, Chris, then with the Labor-Management Center at Yale, wrote that he had a contract with Harper to publish his first book, *Executive Leadership* (1953), based entirely on the Moore Business Forms study. Here we were facing the same problem Edith Lentz and I had confronted in writing about the Radisson Hotel. It was well known among Moore's management that we had been doing research in the Elmira plant. In fact, the vice president of industrial relations had cited our project to top management as evidence of the forward-looking character of his program. By now, Tom had been promoted to manager of a plant in Moore's regional headquarters that was three times the size of the plant in Elmira. Harper would want to sell the book in the business world, so it was bound to come to the attention of Moore's management.

I telephoned Chris. He was also concerned about our relationship with Moore, and did not want to harm Tom. We agreed to send the manuscript to the vice president of industrial relations. He would judge whether Tom should read it.

Later, I got a call from the vice president. He had read it, Tom had read it, and Tom had risen right up through the roof. I had no power to order Chris not to publish, nor would I have wanted to do so, but I could not imagine a solution to our problem.

Chris and I met the vice president and Tom one morning in the conference room of Moore's headquarters and shook hands—it struck me as the moment in a prizefight when the referee says, "Shake hands and come out fighting." Then Tom laid out the manuscript. He had red-penciled the objectionable passages, and it looked as if there was more red-penciling than not.

Chris handled the situation with consummate skill. Tom would read a passage and state his objections vehemently. Chris would respond with something like, "I understand how you feel about that, but this is the point I am trying to get across. . . . Now, is there some way I can reword it without sacrificing that point?" Then the four of us would grope for words, until Tom was more or less satisfied.

By noon, the tension had subsided. By the afternoon, Tom would read over red-penciled passages, laugh, and say, "Well, I guess that's the way it was." At the end of the day, Tom invited us home for a drink, saying, "I haven't had such a good argument in a long time." Although we drove home much happier, the outcome may have depended as much on luck as on our skill in handling the situation. We were lucky that Tom was able to accept a sometimes critical interpretation of himself.

In another study, I was involved for the first time in survey research. Graduate student Lois Remmers wanted to do a survey of worker reactions to their union. I told her I could not be of much help, but that did not stop her. Her father was a psychologist at Purdue University, and she had learned enough from him to get started. My responsibility would be to help her get the cooperation of local officers of the International Association of Machinists (IAM) at a Remington-Rand plant, so that we could get the names and addresses of its members for a mail survey. The business agent did not want to have such a study done. He said I would have to have the approval of IAM's vice president. I went to New York and got his approval, but the union's business agent and other top officers continued to balk.

The study eventually got done, but the results were hardly worth the effort. I learned that if key people in an organization do not want to have their organization studied, it may be wise to abandon the project and move on to an organization where the key people are more receptive.

In spite of the problems, the project stirred my interest in studies of local unions. Students of labor had so far concentrated on the policies and programs of international union officers. I decided to try to fill this gap in the knowledge by focusing on the local level.

With support from the Grant Foundation, I was able to hire research associates. The first I chose was Leonard Sayles, who was writing his Ph.D. thesis for MIT on how workers decide to file grievances against management.

I assumed it would be useful to start with two cases, to represent major differences in the nature of union-management relations. Lois Gray directed me to Dunkirk, New York, southwest of Buffalo, where the Steelworkers at Allegheny-Ludlum had a history of conflict, in contrast to relations at the American Locomotive Company, which had been much more harmonious.

Leonard and his wife settled down in Dunkirk, where Len gained the support of the leadership of both locals for the study. During that time, relations grew more harmonious at Allegheny-Ludlum and more conflictful at American Locomotive. It didn't matter; the changes illustrated the volatility of labor relations and helped us understand the forces involved in the shifts. The project also provided data on the ethnic rivalries between Polish-Americans and Italian-Americans in contests for local leadership. Up to this time, much research attention had been focused on jurisdictional disputes among craft unions, but now Len was documenting in detail how some of the same economic and social forces produced rivalries and conflicts among workers who were semiskilled.

For the second research associate position, Sayles recommended George Strauss, who was also finishing his doctorate at MIT. His thesis dealt with the unionized linemen who worked for the Boston Edison Company.

George settled down in the Rochester, New York, area and undertook a study of the IAM local at an American Can Company plant in Fairport. The most noteworthy aspect of that study turned out to be a methodological article written by Lois Remmers Dean (1958), who teamed up with George on the study, which combined surveys with participant observation.

The IAM local held its meetings every two weeks, and in the course of a year George attended nearly every meeting. There were about five hundred workers in the plant, but the average attendance was only thirty, so George could identify everyone and thus develop a comprehensive record of attendance. Lois prepared a questionnaire on attitudes toward the union and management and on attendance at union meetings. She mailed the questionnaire to all workers, and, with

George encouraging the workers to respond, got a return rate of more than 50 percent.

Workers were told not to sign their names, but Lois inserted a code on each questionnaire to identify the respondent. This enabled her to check survey responses against observed behavior.

The discrepancies she discovered were quite large. In fact, the number falsely claiming to attend was almost twice as high as the "positive truth tellers" who had been observed at meetings. If the analysis had been made solely on the basis of survey data, there would have been no way to distinguish between the two groups.

Does this mean that self-reports on behavior are not to be trusted? I would not go this far, but it does suggest that when respondents are asked about behavior they believe they have an obligation to perform, they are likely to exaggerate the frequency of performance.

Did we cheat in identifying respondents in an "anonymous" questionnaire? We wondered about that but decided that we could not harm any respondent as long as we kept the codes completely confidential. Furthermore, we felt that there could be much to gain from checking responses against observed behavior.

Ever since they were graduate students, Len and George had been thinking about collaborating on a book about local unions. With their student research, plus what they were learning from their field projects, they were ready to start writing.

Some time later, Dan Katz, of the Institute for Social Research at the University of Michigan, called to ask me to serve as one of the judges of a book award sponsored by the Society for the Psychological Study of Social Issues. We were to select the best book on industrial relations of that or the preceding year. I agreed to be a judge on the condition that I would abstain from voting on the Sayles-Strauss manuscript. Their book, *The Local Union: Its Place in the Industrial Plant* (1953), won the prize.

My own fieldwork at Cornell began in large part because of a celebration of the centennial of the founding of Corning Glass Works. CEO Amory Houghton decided to celebrate with events and projects of major cultural significance, including the formal opening of the Corning Glass Museum, which has since come to be recognized as the finest of its kind in the world—and a major tourist attraction.

Corning financed the conference but turned over its management to the American Council of Learned Societies. An economist with the Stanford Research Institute, Eugene Staley, did the planning. He commissioned four background papers and invited me to write one entitled "The World of Work." (The other background papers were "Leisure in Industrial America," "The Community in Industrial Civilization," and "Personal Morale Today.") I was proud to be selected and yet awed by my prominent role in an assemblage of so many important people in so many fields. I felt under pressure to capitalize on an opportunity that might come only once in my lifetime.

In my paper, I discussed what we were learning about worker participation and participative management. The discussion of my paper went reasonably well, but I was already looking ahead to pursuing research at Corning Glass Works. In the informal conversations over cocktails and at meals, I had concentrated on getting acquainted with the Corning executives.

The company operated worldwide but had its headquarters in the small city of Corning, so, within a short drive of Ithaca, there was a company where I could potentially interview everyone from the bottom to the top of the hierarchy. Since I came certified as a leader in my field, this seemed like a wide open opportunity—but then I blew it!

I assumed it would be hard for management to turn me down, but I did not foresee the possibility that management would sidetrack me. After the conference, I did a little preliminary interviewing, got acquainted with Harry Hosier, vice president of industrial relations, and then found out that to get my research proposal accepted, I had to work through Glen Cole, vice chairman of the board (and a relative of the controlling Houghton family).

Instead of trying to find out what management was interested in, I proposed to launch research on the "meaning of work." As I look back on that proposal, the most charitable thing I could say is that I was twenty years ahead of my time. In the 1970s it became fashionable for management to take an interest in "the quality of work life," a topic that bore some resemblance to what I proposed. I was unable to show management how my research would have any practical payoffs for the company.

After some months of maneuvering, the decision about my proposal came at a luncheon meeting with Cole, President William Decker, and Vice President Harry Hosier. Cole suggested that my research should focus on the Steuben division. He noted that the skilled craftsmen who made the fine glassware for which Steuben was famous were already doing demonstrations for tourists visiting the glass museum. In this showplace, researchers could hardly do any harm. Decker turned to Hosier and asked, "Harry, do you think that would be all right?" What could Harry say but yes?

The project was not a total loss. Working with me in the blowing room, graduate student Frank Miller gathered data for his doctoral thesis, and two graduate fellows, Peter Atteslander from Switzerland and Friedrich Fuerstenberg from Germany, got the field research experience they were seeking in a study of the finishing department, where the glassware was polished and the fine engraving done. Finally, I learned something about "Teams of Artisans," which later became a chapter in the book *Essays on Industrial Research — Problems and Prospects* (1961). Otherwise, what had seemed a great opportunity led me nowhere.

Also during this period, an abandoned Chicago writing project on incentive rates suddenly came back to life. As I wrote in the preface to *Money and Motivation* (1955), after noting the articles on this subject that had been published:

> I rarely take the *American Sociological Review* for bathtub reading, but this time I had it with me because I was interested in an article just published by Roy on "Work Satisfaction and Social Reward in Quota Achievement" (Vol. XVIII, No. 5). I read the piece with mounting excitement and yet with some sense of regret. Wasn't it too bad, I told myself, that we had never been able to push to a conclusion our book on incentives when there was so much rich data available? Suddenly the thought struck me that perhaps the book had already been partially written.

I began by fitting together the various articles by Orvis Collins, Melville Dalton, and Donald Roy on incentive rates and then cast about for ways of presenting important aspects of the incentive problem not covered in their work. I recalled material on interdepartmental and intergroup problems from Sayles's Dunkirk studies. That reminded George Strauss of a case Alex Bavelas had described in an MIT course but had never written up. Serving as consultant to a toy manufacturing company, Bavelas had aimed to demonstrate how the foreman could solve a serious productivity and morale problem among the unskilled young women workers in the painting department through a participatory strategy: involving them in group discussions. The women were paid on a group-bonus basis. The participatory strategy worked so well that soon the women were making more money than the more skilled male workers with longer service records. The reactions from other departments were so severe, however, that management abandoned the group-bonus system, thus sacrificing the gains in productivity and morale.

Bavelas had not published the case because he considered the project a failure. Indeed, it had been, from an action research standpoint, but at the same time, the case had provided one of the most impressive demonstrations of the human problems that arise with the introduction of individual piece rates or narrowly based group-bonus systems. George wrote up the case, and Bavelas reviewed and revised the draft.

Before coming to Cornell, I had carried out a brief field project on a plant-wide incentive system at the main plant of the Bundy Tubing Company. Now I heard that the company had installed a similar system at a branch plant not far from Cornell. Frank Miller worked with Friedrich Fuerstenberg to extend the Bundy study to that plant.

I wrote most of *Money and Motivation*, but nearly all of the case materials were supplied by colleagues, who shared in the royalties. *Money and Motivation* came to be regarded as a basic book for anyone trying to understand worker reactions to incentive systems.

23. A Summer Encounter with Sensitivity Training

During the summer of 1950, I had an intensive exposure to sensitivity training. Some of the disciples of the pioneering social psychologist Kurt Lewin, who were at the Research Center for Group Dynamics at the University of Michigan, had teamed up with the National Education Association to establish the National Training Laboratory (NTL) for Group Development at Bethel, Maine.

Lee Bradford, director of the NTL, had invited me to do a study of the culture of NTL as reflected in the training and research activities carried on at Bethel. I spent five weeks planning and executing that study. Bethel was a pleasant rural community, but my recollections of the town were submerged in the intensive experience of the NTL activities.

Through reading and discussion with Chris Argyris, I had gained some background knowledge of T-groups (the T stands for intragroup training), which had been the NTL's central activity since 1947, when the Bethel program was started. Each group, which involved about twenty members and a discussion leader, met for two hours a day, five days a week, for three weeks to explore the personalities and interpersonal relations within that group. By 1950, the staff had developed some skill in leading T-groups, and members often reported that they learned much about themselves and their relations with others.

In 1950, NTL also experimented with A-groups (the A stands for action). In these groups, the focus was supposed to be on preparing group members to deal with "back-home problems." The six T-groups met in the morning, and the six A-groups met for two hours each afternoon throughout the three-week program. Those from the same organization were divided among the half-dozen T-groups but were assigned to the same A-group, so as to help them figure out what to do about those "back-home problems."

I decided to study the A-groups and lined up five observers to cover the six groups with me. I persuaded Kathleen to take on one group and recruited three visiting social scientists—John Clausen, Stephen Corey, and Rensis Likert—and Winifred Snyder. Having Likert on my team put me in the odd position of supervising the director of the Institute for Social Research, who had general administrative responsibility for the Research Center for Group Dynamics, whose program we were studying.

With a minimum of planning time and with such a distinguished research group, I did not feel I could achieve a uniform standard of data reporting. I decided we would focus only on leadership and on how decisions were made and implemented. This was more complicated than it was in the North End, where a change in the Bennetts' activities was frequently signaled by changes in physical movements. Here, the twenty odd members of each group just sat around a table during each two-hour session. I suggested that we concentrate on who proposed an action, who supported and who opposed it, and whether the proposal led to any action. As we started observing, I realized we needed another category for proposals that were ignored—many just died without eliciting any expressions of support or opposition.

NTL's own research provided a wealth of other data: an initial survey of the opinions and attitudes of the staff and delegates toward group dynamics, a survey late in the program to track any changes, plus daily surveys in each group in which members evaluated that day's discussion. At three times during the summer, members also filled out a sociometric questionnaire that asked each one to name preferred companions for leisure activities and to select individuals playing leadership roles.

I was particularly interested in one item in the initial survey: "An ideal discussion group is one in which an onlooker would be unable to identify the leader." Fifty-nine percent of the delegates strongly or moderately agreed and only 34 percent moderately or strongly disagreed. Among staff members, opinions were more evenly divided: six strongly or moderately agreed, two were undecided, and five moderately or strongly disagreed. For the culture of Bethel, that was a key statement—and I think it is nonsense. If discussion leaders believed in that statement, what were they supposed to do? According to one commonly held assumption, they were expected to transform themselves into "resource persons."

We never observed such a transformation. Five groups went through periods of serious confusion and frustration. In the sixth group, the leader maintained his position throughout.

Many delegates brought to Bethel the assumption that the culture required a completely "democratic" and leaderless group. Therefore, the first task of group members had to be to depose the designated leader.

The first victim of this anti-leadership coup was Charles Loomis, a distinguished sociologist and later president of the American Sociological Association. Seven of the twenty-one members of his group came from two closely related social work organizations in the same city. The evening before the first group meeting, the seven got together to agree on how they would depose Loomis—before they had even met him. They deposed him quickly, but from that point on, confusion, frustration, and factional conflict reigned.

At one point, when general discussion had given way to conversations among pairs and threesomes, Loomis tried to restore order by pounding on a table. That produced a moment of silence, but then he was reprimanded for his "autocratic" act. He asked, "When the discussion breaks up, who is to pound on the table?" He was told, "The group will pound on the table."

Before the group arrived for the final session, Loomis laid out on the blackboard his analysis of the sociometric data. If an analysis of this kind had been done at an early stage of the workshop, it would have helped the group work through its interpersonal and intergroup conflicts. Now, some members asked themselves why they had not recognized the resources Loomis could contribute.

The answer explained why designated leaders never became resource persons. It was against the Bethel culture for the designated leader—or anybody else—to tell the group what resources he or she might be able to contribute. Any such statement was interpreted as an illegitimate bid for leadership.

What should have happened when group discussion broke down because of confusion and frustration? We found two diametrically opposed theories. Some held that the deadlock could be resolved only if each member described how he or she felt about what was going on. Critics referred to this as the "feeling-draining" approach or the "cesspool theory" of group dynamics. They argued that conflicts could be resolved only if the members became actively involved in a course of action. Their critics felt those favoring this approach were afraid to subject themselves to the analysis of their emotions necessary for good group process.

We often observed the feeling-draining process. Facing an impasse, members of a group would spend the rest of the session discussing their feelings. As the session wound up, someone would say, "Well, this has been a painful process, but it has been good for us. We've cleared up our misunderstandings, and we have become a group. Next time we'll be ready to push ahead." There would be general agreement. But next time, after a little preliminary fencing, the members would find that they were stuck at the same old impasse—or had stumbled into a new one. The Bethel experience suggested that it is possible to drain a group's feelings every day and still have feelings left to drain. In the morning T-groups, the discussions proceeded smoothly because there was no agenda other than to explore how members thought and felt about themselves and their relations with each other.

Bethel was a very intense emotional experience for designated staff leaders, as well as members and observers of A-groups. Outside of meetings, we could think and talk about nothing else. As we were meeting, the Korean War was just starting, but compared with what was happening in our groups, that paled into insignificance.

I had never observed such a buildup of emotional tension in such a short time. I feared it might be more than some leaders and members could bear. In the group she observed, Kathleen saw a woman rendered completely unable to carry on normal activity. After the group had struggled in vain to reach a consensus on how to choose a representative to the delegate council, the members fell back on a traditional method: taking a written vote. At this point, the woman's arm became paralyzed so she could not write.

Bethel had a psychiatrist on staff, and some of the delegates did consult him, but I have no idea whether he perceived the psychological problems he encountered to be serious or just temporary reactions to stressful situations.

Bethel was a learning experience for me. I learned about the promise and pitfalls of sensitivity training. It was clear that the leaders of the movement had unleashed a new social technology with the power to move people toward constructive and personally satisfying ends, but a technology that could also expose them to serious emotional risks.

The risks arose because of ideological distortions imposed on the research findings of the original studies of group dynamics conducted by Kurt Lewin and his associates. Those experiments demonstrated that involving people in group discussions was more effective in changing their behavior than lecturing them on the desirability of a particular line of action. There was no question as to who the leader was. He or she was the individual who called the group together and explained the topic to be discussed. The leader sought to encourage members to express themselves freely but made no moves to abandon the role of leader; nor did it occur to anyone that the members of the group were supposed to depose the leader. Further, there was no doubt as to what was to be discussed, since they had all agreed to attend a meeting on a particular topic.

The Bethel experience led me to a new theoretical view of how interactions, activities, and interpersonal sentiments are related. My street corner observations had led me to accept George Homans's theoretical statement in *The Human Group* (1950) that an increase in the frequency of interaction among individuals leads to an increase in favorable interpersonal sentiments, provided an authority relationship is not involved. That position clearly did not fit what I had observed at Bethel, where the high frequency of interaction had increased the *intensity* of interpersonal sentiments but had not predicted whether those sentiments would be positive or negative.

I raised this point in correspondence with Homans, and he responded: "I am inclined to agree with you that a better formulation might be 'The more frequently persons interact with one another the stronger their sentiments toward one another are apt to be.' My formulation is, in fact, a special case of a more general hypothesis."

He then went on to suggest that other variables might determine whether the sentiments were positive or negative: "I have in mind one that sounds very much like yours, which might be stated like this: in a group that is not accomplishing its goals, increased or constant interaction makes for a decreased amount of sentiments of liking."

I was happy with this clarification, but asked myself why had I not seen the fallacies in his earlier formulation. I then realized that the letter formulation applied to informal street corner groups or informal groups anywhere, simply because those who did not fit into the group dropped out, leaving only those who enjoyed associating with the remaining members. At Bethel, no one felt free to drop out. The sentiments members developed toward their group and its members therefore had to depend on other variables.

I began to think of what those other variables might be. That led me to the concept of *transactional relationships*, in which rewards or penalties (or positive or negative reinforcements) arise out of the interactional relationship—in addition to the intrinsic satisfaction or dissatisfaction of the relationship itself. Here I was thinking of relationships characterized by interpersonal reciprocity or the exchange of favors, then becoming prominent in the theorizing of some sociologists, but I did not want to make these central to my theory. I also noted a relationship I called *joint payoff*, in which two or more people join together, not to seek rewards from each other but rather to seek mutual gains in the external environment.

I continued my speculations until I had a total of seven transactional relationships, which, combined with interactions, could shape sentiments and influence other outcomes, such as the progress of a group toward its objectives. I outlined these relationships first in 1969 in *Organizational Behavior: Theory and Application*. These seven, plus one more developed years later, formed the central core of my most ambitious attempt to advance sociological theory in *Social Theory for Action: How Individuals and Organizations Learn to Change* (1991).

My only obligation to the NTL was to submit a report on my findings at Bethel. I thought I had something worth publishing, but I faced a dilemma. I regarded some of the leaders of the NTL as colleagues and friends, and I admired what they were trying to accomplish, yet my research report would inevitably make their A-groups appear to be failures. I decided to publish *Leadership and Group Participation* (1953) but invited Lee Bradford to present a critique of my research in an afterword.

Lee wrote a gracious acknowledgment of the value of my A-group research but placed it in the context of other leadership and group process research sponsored by the NTL and of the changes that had taken place in NTL training programs from 1950 to 1953. He pointed out that the NTL had abandoned the A-group strategy and was experimenting with other approaches to "intergroup training." In conclusion, he wrote: "These, then, are some of the developments NTL has made since Dr. Whyte completed his study in 1950. It is very clear that his study had a major effect on bringing about much of this growth."

The NTL's openness to criticism has moved group dynamics beyond the misguided ideology I observed in 1950. Academicians and private organizational development consultants now take for granted the fundamental assumption supported by the early experiments of Kurt Lewin: If one wants to change behavior, group discussions are more powerful than lectures. Casting aside the cultish belief in the leaderless group and the rotation of leadership, academicians and consultants now try to determine those styles of leadership and group processes that most effectively enhance a group's effectiveness.

24. Family Crises

T he early 1950s were a period of change and reajustment for all the
Whytes. In June 1951, we had lost our five-year-old son, Bruce. I had
taken the family to join other villagers for a swim in a nearby creek.
Kathleen was watching Bruce and Lucy, who had not yet learned to swim, while
they were in the water. I was in the water and thought I was also keeping
track of them. Kathleen was talking with friends while she watched and was
momentarily distracted. Suddenly, we realized we did not know where Bruce
was. In panic, I reacted irrationally. There was a steam shovel working up the
creek, muddying the water. Knowing how fascinated Bruce was with machines,
I thought he might have wandered off to look at the shovel. I sent Joyce and
Martin looking for him. Kathleen shouted for someone to call an ambulance
and jumped into the water. When she encountered Bruce's limp body, she got
him out, and a neighbor struggled to bring Bruce back with artificial resusci-
tation.

Kathleen went on in the ambulance, while I went home to get her dry clothes
and to arrange to have friends stay with the other children. I was with Kathleen
when the doctor came out to tell us that Bruce was dead. We wanted to cry but
could not. I just felt a deep ache in my throat.

Kathleen blamed herself because she had agreed to watch Bruce and Lucy
while I was in the water, and I blamed myself because I thought I was watching
him and then had panicked. Our friends tried to ease the pain, but for many
months it was hard to think of anything but that terrible afternoon.

The loss was hard for all the children, but especially for three-year-old Lucy.
Bruce had been the ideal big brother, her best friend and protector. For some
time thereafter she was not the happy girl we had known; yet, as we learned
later, she did not show us how deeply she felt because she realized how much we

were suffering. In an effort to pull the family together, Kathleen and I worked with Joyce and Martin to build Lucy a dollhouse, complete with furniture and draperies, for Christmas.

With two boys and two girls, our family had seemed complete. Although we could never really make up for losing Bruce, we needed to look ahead to having another child—and hoped it would be a boy. We started trying too soon. Kathleen had a miscarriage.

In 1953, a second blow struck. Early one morning my mother called to tell us that my father had died. He had had a heart attack and been rushed to the hospital. Mother was with him at the hospital and then had gone home. He had died that night. His nurse told her John Whyte's last words: "You know, I have this strange feeling that something important is about to happen to me."

He was sixty-four, just a year from retirement. By this time, he felt worn out from many years of teaching large classes and was looking forward to retirement in a home they had bought on Greensboro Lake in Vermont.

I caught the first plane to LaGuardia Airport. Kathleen followed when Edith Lentz, now at Cornell, agreed to stay with the children.

There was a memorial service in the Brooklyn College chapel, presided over by the president of the university. Several of Father's former students spoke of what they owed to his teaching and personal interest in them. As I listened to those tributes in the well-filled chapel, I felt somewhat guilty that I had not devoted my energies and creativity to trying to be as good a teacher as my father was. Research had always come first.

Mother did not want to remain in the apartment, so we invited her to come back with us to Trumansburg. Driving her car, which I could not manage, fell to Kathleen, who had not driven a car with a stick shift for many years. Starting out in Brooklyn traffic was a harrowing experience for her. As it began to rain heavily and darkness fell, she was afraid of falling asleep. All I could do was watch for road signs and keep talking to her, although we never felt less like conversation.

In Trumansburg, we discussed having Mother live with us. Kathleen and I loved her, but she did not want to be a "burden" and thought she would be happier with her own apartment in Ithaca. To get around, she traded in her car for a Chevrolet—one with an automatic transmission.

Mother generally spent Sundays with us, but she was not dependent on us for her social life or for other activities. She got involved in a peace studies group and became an organizer of Ithaca's Senior Citizens' Program. She joined an amateur theatrical group and had one of the leading roles in a play. We took the children to see it, and we were all impressed with her performance. Over the years, her life had been wrapped up in her husband, but now she was able to branch out on her own.

In January 1953, we had the baby we had hoped for—and it was a boy. We named him John, after my father. When our first son had been born, my parents had been upset that we had not named him after his grandfather—supposedly a family tradition, though it had actually not been started until my generation. As a peace activist, Mother was also upset that we had named Martin after Mars, the god of war. That had not occurred to us; we had just liked the sound of the name. But this time we yielded to tradition and were only sorry my father did not live to see his namesake.

25. Sabbatical in Venezuela

Whatever tales students brought in from the field, Burleigh Gardner had been able to cite parallel cases from his own field experience. By the early 1950s, I found myself in the same position. At first, I took pride in my ability to perceive patterns, but then I got bored with anticipating them. I asked myself, where do I go from here?

One alternative was to examine those perceived patterns in the standard scientific way: by testing hypotheses statistically. That did not appeal to me. I had never been good at hypothesis-testing, and I thought I would get frustrated trying to prove what I already thought I understood.

I began to wonder whether the style of supervisory and managerial leadership that appeared to be effective in the United States would work as well in a country with a markedly different culture. Were there universal principles of "good human relations," or did cultural diversity preclude that possibility?

I looked for foreign opportunities that would enable me to begin this exploration—and that would provide financial support for a full year, supplementing the half year's salary I would receive from Cornell after six years of teaching. For my 1954–55 sabbatical, there were four possibilities worth considering: England, Norway, Quebec, and Venezuela. I ruled out England because it did not offer a culture sufficiently different from our own. I ruled out Norway because I did not speak Norwegian. Nearly all business and professional people spoke English, but I wanted to be able to talk to workers and union leaders in their own language. If I learned Norwegian, it would equip me to do fieldwork in Scandinavia only. Learning French and Spanish would open up much broader horizons.

The opportunities for research in Quebec and Venezuela were similar. At a meeting of the Society for Applied Anthropology, I had met Alec Winn, personnel director for the Aluminum Company of Canada (Alcan). He was well informed about research in organizational behavior—including my own. At the time, he was especially concerned about the Alcan's operations in Arvida, Quebec, where Anglo-Canadian managers were directing the operations of French-Canadian workers and foremen. We discussed the possibility of my doing an organizational study in Arvida.

The Venezuelan project would be with the Creole Petroleum Company, a subsidiary of what was then Standard Oil of New Jersey (now Exxon). There, American managers were supervising Venezuelan workers and *capetaces*, the lowest level of supervisors.

The main difference between the two options was the climate: Arvida is in northern Quebec, where the winters are long and frigid. In Venezuela, I would be in the city of Maracaibo, which is at sea level and close to the equator. The average temperature is eighty-five degrees Fahrenheit all year round. Both options offered generous support for the family and for research assistants and secretarial help. We decided we would rather be hot than cold.

The first order of business was to learn Spanish. When the United States got into World War II, the military leaders recognized that they needed large numbers of people who spoke foreign languages and that they could not wait for them to be trained by conventional methods. They had contracted with Cornell to develop a method to teach people foreign languages in a hurry. That had provided the foundation for the Cornell language training program, which still has an outstanding reputation. The most intensive instruction was crowded into the summer months, when students worked full time with instructors and native speakers learning to speak and to understand. I did not feel I could make a full-time commitment, but I did the next best thing.

The Cornell Spanish course had been published in two volumes, accompanied by records. For six weeks, I devoted two hours a day to learning Spanish. By the time we got to Maracaibo, I was beginning to speak.

We arrived in late August, and about three months later, one of Creole's language instructors came to Maracaibo to administer a language test to all expatriate personnel who had not scored 90 percent or higher in previous tests. As a temporary employee, I was not required to take the test, but I thought it would teach me something about myself and also about Creole.

The test, individually administered to each student, was entirely oral and contained three parts of fifty exercises each. In the first part, the instructor told the student in Spanish to perform certain physical acts and checked whether the instructions were carried out correctly. In the second part, the instructor showed the student drawings of common household objects and asked him to name them. In the third part, the instructor showed the student a set of cards on which there were sentences in English that the student had to translate.

I scored 91 percent, which pleased me, but I was especially interested in the distribution of my grades on the three parts. On the second part, I scored 78 percent—I had not learned the names of many household objects. I scored 96 percent on the first part because I missed two of the fifty instructions. On the third part, which tested grammar, I scored 100 percent. That score surprised me. The Cornell course had emphasized speaking and seemed to tack on grammatical instructions only after the speaking and vocabulary exercises.

When I studied French for four years in high school and one in college, instruction was with the old-fashioned method in which grammar was treated as if it were a puzzle to be solved, rather than a skill to be developed through speaking. After those five years of French, I could read it, but I could not speak it.

Living in Maracaibo was our first experience living under military rule. Juan Vicente Gomez had taken power in 1908 and had established a brutal military government. Upon his death in 1935, the generals who had served under him had begun opening up the country to more democratic ways of life.

In 1945, a junta headed by Romulo Betancourt of the Acción Democrática party took over. Labor unions became legal, and some militant unions were organized, particularly among workers with the foreign oil companies. In 1947, a democratic constitution was enacted, which was followed by the presidential election of Romulo Gallegos, a well-known author. In 1948, he was ousted by a three-man junta, out of which emerged the dictatorship of Marcos Perez Jimenez.

The Perez government did not alter the legal status of unions. In fact, during our year there, an official government bulletin, written in English, announced with pride that the government had demonstrated its support for unions by building the headquarters of the Venezuelan Federation of Labor and donating it to the federation!

We arrived in Maracaibo on a Grace Line ship, which also transported our station wagon. Before we moved into our house, Creole lodged us in the Creole-owned Hotel del Lago. One morning while I was shaving, eighteen-month-old John came into the bathroom. He had never seen a bidet before and asked, "What's this?" Before I could answer, he turned the faucet on full force. The stream of water shot up to the ceiling, inundated me and the bathroom, and spread out into the bedroom. We had to call the maids to clean up. Fortunately, they considered the incident amusing.

The boat trip had been hard on Joyce, our eldest daughter, who got so seasick she could keep little food down. Now the contrast between the outdoor tropical heat and the air-conditioned rooms of the hotel was too much for her. An X ray showed she had a spot on her lung, and the doctor at the Creole clinic thought she had tuberculosis. While we waited for more information, we agonized over what this would do to our family arrangements and my research plans. A couple of days later, we were given the diagnosis: pneumonia. Joyce quickly recovered, so the crisis was over.

Since Creole's operations were concentrated in the Bolivar district on the eastern side of Lake Maracaibo, we should have lived there. But Joyce was to start high school, and the company camps in the Bolivar district provided education only through the eighth grade, so we lived in Maracaibo. There, Creole, Shell, and Gulf had a jointly financed educational program through high school. The language of instruction was English, and Spanish was taught as a foreign language.

Creole offered us a house in the company camp, but that was populated by Americans and a few senior staff Venezuelans, who were all fluent in English. In the hopes of getting to know some Venezuelans, we asked to live outside the camp. Creole rented us a house on the lake, where we had a pleasant view and picked up whatever breezes were blowing. The water looked inviting, but much of Creole's oil drilling was done in the lake, which caused serious pollution. To swim, we had to drive to a pool at the company camp.

Unfortunately, the house opened up no opportunities for social relations with Venezuelans. A Venezuelan family lived next door, and I tried nodding at them when they went by, but they did not nod back. If they had had children around the ages of ours, that might have broken the ice.

The house had one air-conditioned room, the master bedroom. We ran the air conditioner for several hours before bedtime. Then we would turn it off and open doors and windows to pick up the night breezes.

The divisional headquarters was air-conditioned, but my office was in an older building with a high ceiling and an overhead fan. I shared that office with my bilingual secretary, Carlos Diaz.

The working day began early and was broken by a noon siesta of two to three hours. Our house was a few minutes' drive from the office, so I would go home for lunch and a nap. I got to like the siesta custom so well that ever since I have taken a siesta whenever I could fit it in.

I had no problem coming to an agreement with Creole's management on the aims of the research. We decided on two projects, one focusing on company-community relations, the other on the development of Venezuelan supervisors.

Creole was hoping to work its way out of the highly paternalistic relationship the company had built up since oil was discovered in the Bolivar district in 1913. Most of the major oil reserves were in isolated areas, far from towns and cities. The oil companies therefore had to establish company camps for workers, supervisors, and management. There was no possibility of turning over community management to the government. The top local government officials were appointed by the central government and depended on handouts from Caracas to cover whatever limited services were provided. The central government had shown no interest in negotiating with the companies to establish independent and self-governing communities. The Creole manager of each Bolivar district operation was, in effect, mayor of the company camp and responsible for providing the services and facilities required by the residents.

There were three company camps: the "general" camp for workers, the "intermediate" camp for first-line supervisors, and the senior staff camp. The first two camps were populated entirely by Venezuelans. The senior staff camp was populated primarily by U.S. expatriates, but there were a few families of Venezuelan professional men.

All the homes had gas, electricity, and running water, but otherwise they differed according to status. The general camp had row houses in groups of four. The intermediate camp had larger freestanding homes. The senior staff camp had still larger and more opulently designed homes, which were built on stilts so that the family could keep its car sheltered from the oppressive heat.

Management wanted to find out how Venezuelan workers and supervisors felt about living in the company camps and what might encourage them to move out and build or rent their own homes. There were two obstacles to building or renting elsewhere. Instead of charging "realistic rents" for homes at the camps and increasing the wages to cover those costs, Creole paid high wages and charged rents that covered only a fraction of its housing costs. That problem could have been overcome if management had offered large subsidies to workers who moved out—which Creole proposed to do.

The other problem was far more formidable. Close to the Creole camps at La Salina was Cabimas, which in three decades had grown from empty desert land to a city of more than fifty thousand which could provide water, gas, and electricity to only some parts of the city. There was no sewage system, and garbage collection was erratic. Many residents were dependent on water trucks. Outside

Cabimas, water, gas, and electricity were in short supply—although the companies were burning off gas from their wells.

Maintaining the status quo did not seem desirable. When a worker retired, management staged a party his fellow workers and supervisors attended. The manager would present the retiree with his twenty-five-year pin and express the company's appreciation for his contribution, and fellow workers would tell him how they had enjoyed working with him and how they would miss him. The next morning, the camp administration would present the family with an eviction notice, giving it two weeks to move out.

There was another problem in some quarters: There were high-wire fences surrounding each camp. This problem was brought home to me while I was still getting settled in my Creole office. A reporter for *Panorama*, the Maracaibo daily newspaper, telephoned to request an interview. I tried to fend him off, but he persisted and I finally gave in. Fortunately, I had the presence of mind to have the public relations director for the division with me for the interview.

The reporter asked whether the camp study would focus on the fences. I replied that that might be of interest. A friend who had accompanied the reporter proceeded to lecture me on the evils of the fences. He said that for Venezuelans outside the fences, they created "un psicosis popular."

The following morning, *Panorama* printed a story with the headline "North American Sociologist States That Creole Company Camp Fences Create a Popular Psychosis." This was embarrassing, but Creole's PR man reported to his superiors that I had said no such thing.

With the guidance of Creole's industrial relations staff, I selected three fieldworkers. For the community study, I hired Isabel Peraza de Morse, who had graduated from a Venezuelan university with a degree in social work. She was married to an American engineer, and they lived in the La Salina camp, which would be the central focus of my fieldwork. I also signed on Norman Painter, an American sociologist with extensive experience in Venezuela, and Manuel Matienzo, a graduate of a Venezuelan university who had some background in social science. Painter and Matienzo would be based in Judibana, a Creole camp for the recently constructed Amuay refinery on the Paraguana peninsula, a desert area to the north. Their focus would be some of the problems of a company camp still in the early stages of development and also on some of the industrial relations problems in that area.

Besides occasional trips to the refinery to meet with Painter and Matienzo, my regular schedule called for me to spend two days a week doing my own fieldwork, mainly in La Salina, on the Venezuelan supervisors and working with

Isabel on the community study. Getting to the field involved a few minutes' drive, then forty-five minutes on a ferry, followed by about another forty-five minutes' drive to La Salina. I caught the 5:30 A.M. ferry and returned the following day late in the afternoon. The night before, Kathleen fixed sandwiches and a thermos so I could eat breakfast on the ferry while I read that morning's *Panorama*.

The workday at La Salina started at 6:30, and before noon there was a siesta break until 2:30 or 3:00. Everything was shut down for that period except drilling and production, which had to be continuous. For the siesta, the Morses offered me a bedroom in their home.

~

The aim of the community study was to find out how people felt about living in the company camp and whether—and under what conditions—they would move into their own homes. Isabel interviewed the women in their homes and a smaller sample of men at work. She proved to be an ideal research associate: bright, enterprising, and at ease in conversation with all sorts of people.

Isabel began with open-ended interviews, which provided a general view of the workers' problems and attitudes. Having never directed a survey, I hesitated to do one, but clearly numbers were required, so we plunged in. I was pleased to find that our survey yielded a rich harvest of data.

The perceived advantages of living in the company camps were limited to their having running water, gas, electricity, sewage, garbage collection, and very cheap rents. The disadvantages were nearly as uniform. In the general camp, people complained of the poor ventilation, especially if they lived in the middle houses of the row. They resented Creole's ban on keeping chickens, pigs, and other such animals and not being able to choose their neighbors. The homes provided a living room–dining room combination; three out of four respondents would have preferred a combination kitchen–dining room. Three of four respondents living in the camps wanted to keep the high-wire fences—but among those who had already moved out, the votes were evenly split. We found moderate interest in accepting a subsidy to move out. A large majority were ready to move if utilities would be provided.

Our study provided Creole's management with much useful information, but it left the basic problem unresolved. Ideally, as people moved out, local governments would take responsibility for providing utilities and community services, but except in Cabimas, local governments did not exist. There was also the question of how to compare Creole's policies with those of Shell, which was then rebuilding and modernizing some of its company camps while Creole sought to do away with them. Would the union support Creole's policies or push to improve the existing camps?

In my own fieldwork, I concentrated on interviewing Venezuelan *capetaces* and the managers under whom they worked. The *capetaz* had been created by a law that required all those giving orders to workers to be Venezuelans. In the early days of oil drilling, the *capetaz* had simply transmitted orders given him by his expatriate foreman. Now that foreman was supposed to help the *capetaz* assume the full responsibilities of a foreman. But, although there were Venezuelan engineers and geologists working for Creole, with few exceptions, *capetaces* were the highest-ranking Venezuelans in the Bolivar district. In maintenance and construction, I had identified six who claimed they were qualified for promotion and who were judged to be highly promotable by their expatriate supervisors.

When I asked why these men had not been promoted already, I was told they needed more experience. The Americans were unable to specify what experience the *capetaces* needed or how long it would take for them to get it. Ideally, foremen who were good at developing *capetaces* would not lose their jobs but would move up into higher management. At the same time, although the American foremen were well qualified in the technical aspects of their jobs, few had the background or talents to move up. And they were getting more pay and fringe benefits than they could expect to receive in similar jobs at home. Thus, in developing foremen, they could put themselves at risk.

Language was also a major problem. Many foremen acknowledged that they were having difficulties getting beyond what they called "job Spanish." The present tense and the imperative were sufficient when the foremen simply had to transmit orders to workers. To help the *capetaces* plan, anticipate contingencies, and improve their performance and prospects, however, the foremen needed far better Spanish language skills.

In my project report, I proposed that management move at once to establish a pool of *capetaces* judged by their superiors to be promotable, determine specifically what (if any) training or job experience they needed, and then get on with the job of promoting them.

After holding feedback discussions on my research at division headquarters in Maracaibo, I submitted my research reports to Caracas and held discussion meetings with managers in top industrial relations positions there. I had promised Creole reports on its community program and on the advancement of Venezuelan *capetaces*. I not only delivered those reports, written in collaboration with my research staff, but also four reports on other problem areas we had encountered. Of course, I consulted with industrial relations (IR) managers before submitting the additional reports, but what could they say when I appeared to be giving them more than they had counted on? As far as I could tell, some of the reports seemed to be appreciated, but one entitled "The Role of the Industrial Relations Organization" was decidedly unwelcome.

I gave Creole full credit for building outstanding conventional personnel programs; workers had generous fringe benefits, language and other training programs, safety on the job, and so on. But Creole also expected its personnel director to be an adviser and consultant to line management on problems of work organization and human relations. The people in personnel were so occupied with their various programs, however, that they had little time to devote to relations on the job, nor did they have good sources of information and ideas about solving problems.

Unlike the supervisors and middle managers, who had their offices at the job site, the personnel director had his office in district headquarters, close to the district superintendent. If a supervisor consulted the personnel director about an industrial relations problem, information on that problem would reach the superintendent and might have an adverse effect on the supervisor's career.

I had presented Creole with information and ideas they did not want to hear—and certainly that they did not want to have available to top line managers. My report chilled the atmosphere between me and IR. After that I was never called upon to advise Creole.

I had felt compelled to report everything important that I had found out, as if I were writing an academic paper. Instead of submitting a formal report, I could have simply informed the IR authorities that I had some ideas and information on the IR program that I wanted to discuss with them. In that case, the IR people might have given my criticisms some attention. In any event, they would have been more likely to let me know whether any of the recommendations in my other reports had been acted on—and with what results.

∼

Living under a dictatorship made me more aware of the advantages of democracy. In Venezuela, there was no freedom of the press, and any organized opposition had to remain clandestine. Further, the repercussions if one was picked up for some minor legal violation were highly unpredictable. An expatriate neighbor was picked up for what the arresting officer said was drunken driving. Since this occurred on a Friday afternoon as the man was coming directly home from work, he assumed the officer was seeking a bribe, which he did not pay. The judge on duty had gone home for the weekend, so our neighbor was put in jail until Monday morning—and given no opportunity to call a lawyer or his wife. There was, of course, no writ of habeas corpus or any trial by jury, since Venezuela follows the Napoleonic code, which puts all legal decisions in the hands of judges.

Since Creole maintained good relations with the Venezuelan government, we felt somewhat protected from the unpredictability of the legal system—but that protection was not guaranteed. When one of Creole's industrial relations men inadvertently said something to the union lawyer that was deemed to be an aspersion on his honor, Creole had to get the IR man out of the country to avoid his having to serve a jail sentence.

If one's wife got into trouble, the authorities would jail the husband. Once when I was ill, Kathleen was picked up while driving our children. Creole had registered our car but had not informed us that the sticker had to be renewed every three months. Ours had expired long ago and was on a police list of cars in violation. Suddenly, Kathleen heard sirens wailing and was pulled over. Fortunately, the officer did not know what to do with a mother and four children, and Kathleen was able to persuade him to let her drive to Creole's office. She left the car there and got someone to drive the family home. Creole paid the fine and got us a new sticker.

Our biggest scare occurred during the carnival season. The government had decided to get tough on anyone who dropped balloons full of water or less sanitary liquids on passersby and had banned water pistols. I did not know that Martin had a water pistol. While we were driving home from the Creole club, I heard Joyce laugh and say, "Do you know what Martin was shooting at? He just hit the Radio Patrulla!" Then I heard a siren as a police car turned around and caught up with us. The officer demanded the weapon, which we were only too glad to turn over, and proceeded to lecture us about the dangers of shooting water at drivers. I agreed wholeheartedly. The officer hesitated and then let us go. As he drove away, we saw him discharging the pistol on the pavement. Martin was so petrified that we did not punish him.

Of all my early-morning ferry trips, two incidents stand out. On one December morning, *Panorama* carried a front-page picture of George Washington. The story celebrated him not only for liberating the colonies but especially for establishing our great democracy. The article went on to list the rights that went with our form of government—coming about as close as one could in Venezuela to advocating democracy.

That incident made me proud of America. The second incident did not. Several weeks later, *Panorama* carried a front-page story and a picture of the U.S. ambassador pinning an American medal on the chest of Perez Jimenez, the dictator.

26. Cornell: 1955–1961

During the period from 1955 to 1961, my only fieldwork was in Arvida, Quebec. Alec Winn, the personnel director of Alcan, had not given up on me. When we returned from Venezuela, he proposed that we spend the next summer in Arvida, where I could direct a field study of intercultural relations and management development at Alcan. Alec arranged for me to work with three young professors at Laval University in Quebec and also provided me with ample secretarial support and travel funds to cover the family's summer expenses and my trips to Laval to plan the project.

There were no children of my children's ages at the hotel where we stayed, so it was a rather thin summer for my four. I had long felt the handicap of not being able to play outdoor games with the children, so I offered to give Joyce and Martin tennis lessons. They were reluctant pupils. It was much more fun to do what came naturally than to struggle to learn the correct form. Kathleen did some drawing in the countryside, but my research associates did not have their wives with them, so her social life during the day was also limited.

I concentrated on interviewing management people but did want to talk with the chief union leader, who spoke only French. With some trepidation, I prepared myself by writing out my questions. He seemed to understand me, but I did not always understand him. Now I could say that I had carried out interviews in five languages: English, German, Italian, Spanish, and French—if I count that one interview in Quebec and my *Bronxville Press* interviews in Germany.

The study of intercultural relations fitted well with what I had learned in Venezuela. Alcan had advanced further in getting French Canadians into supervisory positions, but at higher levels, the managers were all English Canadian. I found similar problems at Alcan in intercultural communication. Many English speakers acknowledged difficulties in their relations with subordinates when they had to communicate more than job instructions, and subordinates complained about these limitations.

Between August and December 1958, with three associates—André Bisson, Laurent Picard, and Alphonse Riverin—from Laval, I submitted reports on three divisions we had studied and one entitled "Some Aspects of Intergroup Relations in a Quebec Smelter." Since the feedback sessions with management had gone well and Alec Winn was pleased with the reports, I had assumed that I would be able to continue to do research or consulting for Alcan and Laval.

That was not to be, and in this case it was not my fault. During a cost-cutting campaign, the vice president to whom Alec Winn reported was promoted. The new vice president cut out all support for organizational research. Alec's staff was reduced to a half-time secretary.

What happened at Alcan was not so different from what happened in some U.S. companies in the 1950s and 1960s. I would hear about the development of an organizational behavior research program that seemed to be making progress both in research and application, but when top management launched a cost-reduction drive, it would be the end of the research. Clearly, social research was not yet considered essential to the development of North American companies.

∼

Robin Williams was the first director of the Social Science Research Center at Cornell, established with a grant from the Ford Foundation. In 1956, I succeeded Robin as director. This was a half-time job, and I arranged for Henry Landsberger, who had received his Ph.D. in our organizational behavior program, to become assistant director and to devote the rest of his time to the Department of Organizational Behavior. Together, we organized a number of interdisciplinary committees around topics of broad interest, including health and medical care research, problems of communication with the Russians, and "modernization" and economic development in developing nations. We also organized workshops on research methods and set up advisory committees to help junior faculty plan research and secure financing.

Our most memorable project was a faculty seminar on Talcott Parsons, America's leading sociological theorist. It was Landsberger's idea. When he asked me, "Do you think there might be some interest in an interdisciplinary seminar on Parsons's theories?" I replied, "My God, I hope not—but maybe you ought to find out." I had always liked Talcott, but I found his writings almost impossible to understand and not worth the effort. When Henry found there was interest among a very able group of faculty, I felt obliged to participate. Members included Max Black (philosophy), Andrew Hacker (government), Chandler Morse (economics), Robin Williams (sociology), and sociologist Edward C. Devereux and social psychologist Urie Bronfenbrenner, both in the Department of Human Development and Family Studies in the College of Human Ecology.

The seminar went on for two years, meeting every two weeks in the homes of the participating professors. I found the intellectual excitement of these meetings more than enough to repay me for my struggle to understand Parsons. In their evaluation of his work, the members ranged from enthusiastic through skeptical to negative. At one point, Urie Bronfenbrenner said, "This is a great group. Can't we keep the group together and find something else to discuss?"

The project ended with a public meeting featuring Talcott Parsons answering his critics—or dodging their questions. Parsons's appearance attracted a large audience and we had a lively interchange, but the session hardly clarified any issues. Still, I had to admit that Talcott contributed the best line. He pointed out that one of our members, philosopher Max Black, had charged him with operating on too low a level of abstraction whereas I had found him too abstract. "Halfway between Black and Whyte," he said, "I must be on very solid ground."

The project produced a book, edited by Max Black, entitled *The Social Theories of Talcott Parsons*. The main theme of my highly critical chapter was that, although the word *action* appeared in the title of most of Parsons's books, he was not actually focusing on action but rather on the actor's "orientation to the situation." I saw his actors constantly in rehearsal but the curtain never rising.

Also during this period, from 1956 to 1961, I edited the journal *Human Organization*. For several years, Eliot Chapple had served as editor, and the Society for Applied Anthropology, which published the journal, was headquartered in his New York City consulting office. I was aware of the growing dissatisfaction of the members, many of whom felt that control was concentrated in a small "clique" revolving around Chapple and Margaret Mead.

In the business meeting of the society in 1954, a member raised the "clique" issue. Margaret responded angrily, "I am sick and tired of these rumors about some clique controlling the society. The only requirement for playing a leading role is the willingness to do the work."

I replied, "Margaret, suppose you were studying a society on an island in the South Pacific. People there were saying that the society was controlled by a small clique. Suppose you did not believe that was the case. Still, you would not get angry. You would ask your informants what it was that had created that impression."

In all the years I had known Margaret, that was the only time I felt I got the better of her. She fumed, but I don't recall any answer.

Margaret was able to set that interchange aside in 1955 when she telephoned to invite me to take over the editorship of *Human Organization*. She tried to reassure me that the society was financially solvent—which was not true. Margaret was misinformed. Her confusion arose from the fact that the society had support from the Grant Foundation to publish what was called *The Research Clearing House*, which printed abstracts of the most relevant articles related to applied anthropology. Money allocated for that special purpose was in the society's bank account but was not available to finance *Human Organization*.

Getting the society's records to Cornell turned out to be quite a project. One Friday evening, I received a phone call from a truck driver telling me he had a shipment from the society's New York office and would need to receive a certified check for more than three hundred dollars on delivery. Since the banks were closed, there was no way I could comply. I had to ask him to come back on Monday. Since accounts had not yet been transferred from New York, I had to write a personal check.

I found the society's accounting system totally confusing. Max Furman, an accountant friend, volunteered to figure it out and set up a new system. When Max finished, I was relieved to find that, although Chapple had been sloppy about commingling funds from his consulting business with those of the society, he had been honest. Nonetheless, if all the bills were paid, the society would be more than a thousand dollars in debt. I persuaded the foundation officials to allow us to terminate the *Research Clearing House* and use the remaining funds to strengthen the general budget. This relieved the financial crisis, but by now *Human Organization* was more than three issues behind in its schedule.

Since I had already gotten a half-time release from teaching for my job at the Social Science Research Center, I did not ask for any additional release time for the editorship. ILR provided no direct financial subsidy, but the journal operated out of my office and we thus saved the cost of rent. My half-time secretary handled my correspondence for the journal as well as my work at ILR.

The editor was not only responsible for putting out the quarterly journal but also for managing the finances and membership operations. For editorial assistance and help in handling the business affairs, I called on one of Cornell University's hidden resources: talented but underemployed faculty wives.

In my first issue of *Human Organization* I tried to sound a clarion call to the members indicating that the society was beginning a comeback. Nevertheless, improvements would come too slowly to save us unless we undertook some special promotional projects.

The first such project arose out of two summer workshops I conducted with social anthropologist Allan Holmberg entitled "Human Problems of U.S. Enterprise in Latin America," which also became the title of a special issue of *Human Organization*. Included were case materials from our management participants in those workshops along with material by Holmberg on Latin American culture and material from my own research in Venezuela.

We promoted the issue to American companies with major involvement in Latin America, to which we offered a discount on a hundred copies or more. So as to assess the potential market before printing, I called on high-level personnel people in various U.S. firms. Pounding the pavement on Wall Street was exhausting, but it was worth it. I signed up enough orders to justify substantial expansion of our normal press run. Taking a deep breath, I ordered fifty-five hundred copies. (Eventually, we sold almost all of them.) We also circulated the promotional piece for this issue to former subscribers, and that brought back some we had lost.

I look back on this project with mixed feelings. It was vital to the survival of the society, but the implicit message was that if the leading executives of American-owned firms understood the culture and developed good human relations with the nationals inside and outside their companies, the companies and the host nations could live happily ever after. I realized later that foreign domination of the industry of a nation constitutes a political problem that good human relations cannot resolve.

We followed the same formula several times later—but without special promotions to business. With each special issue, we sought to enhance the value of membership to those already with us and at the same time tried to sell individual copies and gain new members. Later we added a monograph series, which was distributed free to members and used to promote the sales of individual copies of the journal and new memberships to the society. We also secured a grant from the New World Foundation to finance a special issue celebrating the twenty-fifth anniversary of the founding of the society.

One of the most enjoyable aspects of my editorship was the opportunity to express my views on social research. Probably the most noteworthy of my editorials was entitled "Freedom and Responsibility in Research: The 'Springdale' Case" (1958), in which I entered a controversy that had erupted in my own university following publication of *Small Town in Mass Society* by Arthur Vidich and Joseph Bensman. It provoked a storm of protest in the village of "Spring-dale" and also a dispute between Urie Bronfenbrenner, director of the Spring-dale project, and Vidich, a former project member. My editorial set off a contin-uing exchange of views in *Human Organization* and led to the establishment of a committee in the Society for Applied Anthropology to draft a statement on professional ethics, dealing particularly with the relations between researchers and the people we study.

My editorship ended in mid-1961. I was happy *Human Organization* was on schedule and had a balance of more than eleven thousand dollars in its account. I enjoyed being editor, but I was glad to move on to other things.

∿

The period of 1948 through 1958 in ILR had been a happy and productive time for me, with one major exception: my relations with the dean, Martin P. Catherwood, who wielded more power and authority than I thought was appropriate. Many in the faculty shared this view, but I had the most serious clashes with him.

At one point, a group of faculty had proposed establishing a committee on faculty personnel policies to set up standards and procedures to limit the power of the dean to act against prevailing sentiment. Catherwood did not like the idea, but the faculty voted to set up the committee, which became an established part of the governance of ILR.

When the teaching faculty was divided into eight so-called units, it was not clear what authority each unit head had, and the dean could decide into which unit a new appointee would go. I was actively involved in a successful move resulting in the consolidation of the eight units into four departments, thus enhancing the power of department heads.

In the course of arguing about these issues, I became identified as the dean's chief opponent. This became clear in a faculty meeting that I can no longer place in time or even in terms of the issue that provoked the dean's wrath. But I shall never forget the tone of the argument or Catherwood's words. He got very angry and announced, "I appoint Professor Whyte chairman of a committee to investigate the dean."

I was stunned. I accepted the challenge because I did not know what else to do. Then I went home and worried about it with Kathleen. I was in an untenable situation. The outcome would have to be that either Catherwood or I would leave Cornell. On rare occasions, there have been cases in which a faculty has mobilized itself sufficiently against a dean to force him out, but I did not see that happening at ILR. I also recognized that Catherwood had built up a substantial reputation on his ability to get funds from the state government. If the scenario laid out by the dean reached its predictable conclusion, I would be the one to leave.

The showdown never came. Within a day or two, some of the senior professors talked to Catherwood and persuaded him to forget about forming the committee to investigate him.

Still, I was sufficiently concerned about my relations with Catherwood to consider whether I would be better off elsewhere. An opportunity seemed to have presented itself in November 1957, when I received an offer from the Department of Sociology at the University of Wisconsin. It involved a substantial increase in salary for the academic year, plus a guaranteed summer salary for five years, with no teaching responsibilities in the summer. The teaching requirements otherwise were similar to those at Cornell.

With the existing salary classifications in New York State, it was nearly impossible for the dean to match the Wisconsin offer, but other factors were also involved. At the end of that academic year, I would have eight thousand dollars invested in my state pension, and all that would have been lost if I left. Also, I had enrolled in a new program entitling me to retire at fifty-five, at a somewhat reduced pension. I did not expect to stop working then, but that program would have allowed me to work full time except on the state payroll. And, in contrast to some of my fellow sociologists, I liked working in an interdisciplinary program. Finally, our son Martin wanted to go to Cornell, where my position would give him free tuition.

Kathleen got Catherwood's response to my offer from Wisconsin while I was off on a trip to Alcan, and she wrote to my mother:

> After consulting all the faculty and getting strong and unanimous demands to keep Bill here, the dean has made proposals which make it look fairly certain that we will stay. . . . I think the faculty stand is important. Where else would you find even those who disagree with you demanding that you must stay?

I am sure the dean did not consult *all* the faculty, but it was reassuring that those he particularly respected gave me strong support. The dean's decision eased my relations with him. I was happy at ILR and Cornell, and it seemed to me that the Ithaca area was ideal for my family.

I look back now on my relations with the dean with somewhat mixed feelings.

I continue to believe that he sought to wield more authority than was good for the school, but I also recognize my own shortcomings. In my research, I had been concentrating on ways to build effective relations with those one supervised without focusing on how one deals with a boss who is too bossy.

In a move that may have been designed to improve relations between us, Catherwood wrote me a note saying that he was to deliver a talk on human relations and would like me to respond with a memo on some aspect of the field. Instead of encouraging that rapprochement, I selected a theme that would enable me to criticize him. I had noted his tendency to make decisions without consulting with those who would be affected. In research, I had come across two cases that neatly illustrated this point. In dealing with similar types of problems, one manager had decided how to proceed without consulting anyone, while the other had worked the issues over in consultation with subordinates before taking action. His decisions were implemented much more smoothly. As I read over the memo later, I still thought my analysis was correct, but Catherwood could hardly have failed to note the malice that underlay my response to his call for help.

How should I have responded? Certainly not by making a veiled attack. I could have tried to handle the dean's problem of making decisions without consulting anyone by keeping the dean thoroughly informed about what I wanted to do and why, instead of meeting with him only when I had to get his approval. If I had viewed him as someone I needed to work with instead of as an obstacle to get around, our relations might have been more harmonious.

I never solved the problem of working with Catherwood, but it was solved for me. On December 31, 1958, he resigned to accept an appointment from Governor Nelson Rockefeller as industrial commissioner of New York State.

27. *Introduction to Peru*

What became my central professional and personal interest for fifteen years began during my sabbatical (1961–62) in Peru simply as another cross-cultural study of supervision. That study, called "Human Problems of Industrial Development," was made possible by a Fulbright fellowship and a research grant from the National Institute of Mental Health (NIMH) to cover research assistants, secretaries, and other field expenses.

In Venezuela, I had studied relations between U.S. managers and Latin American first-line supervisors and workers. Now I wanted to study supervisory relations where Latin American managers were directing the work of Latin American supervisors and workers.

I was impressed by Allan Holmberg's project in Vicos, Peru, which seemed to me the most exciting case of applied anthropology then in existence. That project had captured the interest of some prominent Peruvians, which meant that Allan already had strong ties and could help me get started. During exploratory visits for two weeks in the summers of 1959 and 1960, Allan introduced me to some of his key contacts and then drove me to Vicos, in a valley between two ranges of the Andes in the department of Ancash.

Allan had done some preliminary research in the region around Vicos in anticipation of economic and social changes that would follow the completion of a massive hydroelectric project. When a flood wiped that out, it became clear that a government project was not going to produce the social changes Allan had hoped to study. A Peruvian graduate student working with Allan, Mario Vazquez, learned that the firm that had leased the Vicos hacienda had gone bankrupt, and the final five years on the lease were available. Mario suggested that Cornell bid on the lease and take over control of the two thousand Vicosinos living there.

Dr. Carlos Monge, a remarkable Peruvian who later became a good friend, had been appointed director of the Indigenous Institute, a government agency designed to serve the interests of the indigenous Peruvian population—or at least give that impression. Carlos Monge's father had died when he was very young, and his mother struggled to support him and his brothers by giving piano lessons. He studied medicine and had had a distinguished career during which he had treated some of the most prominent Peruvians. He had also done basic research, which had won him international recognition, on the human ability to adapt to high altitudes. Without funds to finance expensive laboratories, he had capitalized on the physical environment of Peru, where the indigenous population lives and works at altitudes of up to fifteen thousand feet above sea level. His work in the highlands exposed him to the poverty of the Indians and to their exploitation by the mestizos.

Dr. Monge was a small man with gray hair and a complexion that reflected his mix of European and Indian ancestry. He stated proudly "I am a mestizo," yet he identified himself with the Indians rather than with their oppressors. He was committed to social and economic reform but was frustrated because the Indigenous Institute had no budget to support field projects.

Holmberg told Dr. Monge about the possibility that Cornell would take over the lease and start an applied anthropology project. Dr. Monge was enthusiastic, and he and Holmberg approached Cornell to establish the Cornell-Peru Project to be based on a *convenio* (contractual agreement) between the university and the institute. Cornell would manage the project and would hire and train Peruvian students to do applied research. Mario Vazquez was the first Peruvian hired. He became a key man on the project and went on to a distinguished career in research and application. In the 1970s, Vazquez became director of the land reform program for the Peruvian military government then in power.

The aim of the Vicos project was to transform a semifeudal hacienda into a democratic and self-governing community. The government of Peru had signed all the democratic provisions of policies laid down by the International Labor Organization, and the Peruvian constitution embodied those same concepts, yet the prevailing conditions of the Indians had long violated such principles.

In the typical highlands hacienda, the owner or renter required the adult males to work his land three to four days a week in return for the right to farm their own plots, generally in the least fertile areas, plus daily token payments of coca leaves to chew and pay of less than two cents. In addition, the Indian women were required to do housework for the *hacendado*, or owner.

The project eliminated all of these nearly free services and converted the hacienda into a farmers' cooperative. Project leaders helped the Vicosinos set up their community government and plan capital investments, paid for by the surplus gained from selling the food produced on their communal land. The project also helped the Indians get help from agricultural research and extension services, thereby enabling them to increase their potato yields significantly.

By 1959, the Vicosinos had built a community center; a house for schoolteachers, Cornell staff, and visitors; and a well-equipped elementary school for up to four hundred pupils. (The Vicos school contrasted with what *hacendados* traditionally provided: a dilapidated one-room building large enough to accommodate only one class, because it was assumed that Indian children would not go to school beyond the first grade.)

An architect who was working with the U.S. embassy heard about the plan to build the school and volunteered to draw up plans. He designed a building whose construction would have cost $250,000. The actual cost of construction was $6,000, which was used to buy essential materials, such as windows and plumbing fixtures, not available locally. Otherwise, the Vicosinos volunteered their labor. They made adobe bricks for the walls and fired tiles for the roofs.

According to a government commitment, Vicos was to be sold to its inhabitants in 1956, at the end of Cornell's lease. The conservative government of President Manuel Prado and Prime Minister Pedro Beltran was then in power. The Indigenous Institute and Cornell appealed in vain to the government to honor its commitment. Henry Dobyns, who then represented Holmberg, asked Beltran: "Will your government honor the commitment to the people of Vicos?" Beltran gave an honest answer: "Certainly not. That would create a terrible precedent."

Every year, in his report to the congress and the people, President Prado included several paragraphs on the achievements of Vicos. It was clear that the government regarded the community as a showcase, but it could not be allowed to have any wider repercussions. Government officials talked about land reform, but their version involved resettling highland Indians in the high areas of the jungle to the east of the Andes.

The political sensitivity of Vicos was illustrated by an event that occurred on August 10, 1960, in Huapra, an indigenous community just up the valley from Vicos and related to Vicos through family ties. Huapra was owned by the Mutual Benefit Society of Huaras, a Catholic organization controlled by the bishop of Huaras (the city nearest to Vicos). This organization also owned Vicos. Huapra had been rented to a man named Lopez. After Lopez had failed to pay rent for three years, the bishop of Huaras had suggested to the Huaprinos that by paying rent directly to the church, they could take over the property. The Huaprinos approached the delegate council of Vicos for help, and the Vicosinos lent them money to buy seed, fertilizer, and so on and also provided technical advice.

Lopez decided to reassert his rights to the hacienda and called on the prefect of the department of Ancash for help. The prefect supplied him with fifteen policemen armed with rifles.

The road from Huaras to Huapra ends at the Vicos community square, at which point the police and Lopez had to leave their truck and walk the rest of the way. This procession was observed by Mario Vazquez and several North Americans, who were there to study child development and family relations. They followed with cameras. At Huapra, Lopez and the police came upon thirty-five Indians cultivating their fields. The police rounded up the group and announced that they were going to arrest the two ringleaders. The other Huaprinos protested, saying they were as much involved as the two, and suggested that if the police were going to shoot anybody, they should shoot them all. In the next few seconds, more than forty shells were fired into the crowd. (The shells were found later in the ground or in the Indians.) Casualties: four dead, four wounded. The police then left.

The witnesses had a remarkable pictorial record of the events: pictures of thirty-five Indians at work, of the discussion preceding the shooting, and of the dead and their widows and children. The police cut the telephone lines, but not before Mario Vazquez had reached Allan Holmberg in Lima. Allan immediately informed Dr. Monge, the minister of government (responsible for the police) and the minister of labor and indigenous affairs.

Meanwhile, the prefect was circulating his story, that 150 Indians had illegally deprived the renter of his property. Ten policemen had tried to reason with them, the Indians had been drunk and had attacked them with agricultural tools and stones, and the police had fired in self-defense.

The government investigating commission spent some time at Vicos, apparently trying to blame the massacre on the Vicosinos, but that theory did not hold up in the face of the pictorial documentation and the eyewitness accounts. Although similar events had often occurred in the highlands, Dr. Monge told me that this was the first incident that had been described in the Lima press as a massacre. (One of his former patients was a prominent senator on the commission. Dr. Monge had urged him to be an honest man and describe the killings in this way.)

The Vicosinos did not provoke the event, but their assistance to Huapra encouraged the Huaprinos to effect their own land reform. How far from Vicos could this indigenous resistance spread?

Although officials of several European governments had made pilgrimages to Vicos, until 1961 no U.S. ambassador had shown any interest in the community. Early that year, James L. Loeb, President Kennedy's ambassador to Peru, had made the first official U.S. visit and was deeply impressed. Later that year, he was called upon to plan a three-day visit to Peru for Edward Kennedy. The president's youngest brother held no official government position, but the family relationship made it an important event for the embassy and the Peruvian government. Loeb was instructed that the schedule was not to follow the usual pattern: meetings limited to important government and business leaders and exposure only to those sights they considered important. Edward Kennedy insisted on making contact with the common people.

Besides arranging for Kennedy to see the sprawling *barriadas* (shantytowns) that had grown up around Lima, Loeb scheduled a trip to the highlands, ending at Vicos. The first stop in the highlands was the village of Huaylas, where Paul Doughty, one of Holmberg's students, was doing a study.

Kennedy asked the village officials what they wanted from the United States. They replied that they wanted support for a rural development project, led by Paul Doughty. That indicated to Kennedy that Doughty was a real man of the people. Abandoning his official party, Kennedy arranged for Doughty to drive him to Vicos.

Paul found that Kennedy had almost no knowledge whatsoever of Peru, but he was interested and willing to listen. On several occasions when Kennedy spotted a group of Indians walking along the road, he jumped out, shook hands, and asked them questions. He wanted to know their reaction to the United States, to President Kennedy, and to democracy and communism. Kennedy's questions were translated into Spanish and then into Quechua, and the answers were translated from Quechua to Spanish and English. Thanks to the imagination of the interpreters, Kennedy got all his questions answered. By the time Doughty and Kennedy reached Vicos, Paul had provided a detailed history of the Vicos project and particularly the struggle to get the government to honor its commitment to sell Vicos to its inhabitants.

Before leaving Peru, Kennedy had an audience with President Prado. Kennedy emphasized the president's support of land reform and rural development in Latin America and spoke of how impressed he was by the Vicos project. Then he put the question bluntly: "Mr. President, when does your government propose to honor its commitment to allow the inhabitants to purchase Vicos?"

President Prado was taken by surprise. He assured Kennedy that the matter would be taken care of. Kennedy said he hoped it could be done soon because President Kennedy would consider the handling of Vicos a test of Peru's commitment to land reform and rural development.

In 1962 — five years after the commitment should have been honored — the contract that turned over Vicos to its Indian inhabitants was signed in the offices of the Ministry of Labor. Since Holmberg had given me a courtesy appointment as a member of the Cornell-Peru Project, Kathleen and I had the privilege of attending the contract-signing ceremony.

There was more than an hour's delay as we all waited for the delegation from Vicos. There had been heavy rains in the highlands and some roads were washed out. Finally, the minister's office decided to go ahead with the signing without them. As we went to the elevator to head upstairs for the ceremony, the door opened and four Vicosinos stepped out. They were dressed in their customary ponchos and *chullos* (knitted caps), and they were covered with mud to the knees.

Kathleen and I were moved by the ceremony. There were official photographs taken of the signing and of the Indians viewing the title to their property. They presented a check as down payment for the purchase. (They wanted to pay in cash directly to the bishop of Huaras to show that they had the money, but the government believed the chance of robbery was too great.)

Vicos still seems a great achievement in applied anthropology. It showed that, in just a few years, a poverty-stricken, exploited, and disorganized population could be transformed into a democratically governed and economically progressing community.

Could it have served as a model for broader-scale land reform and rural development? Only if it had served to persuade national political leaders of the falsity of stereotypes that the Indians are too apathetic and ignorant to take advantage of opportunities that might be opened to them.

Otherwise, the terms under which the Vicosinos gained their independence suggest that simply extending such terms on a regional or national basis would have been out of the question. The annual rent Cornell paid for the property was five hundred dollars. What would have been a fair purchase price? One would think a sum that, if invested, would have yielded an income of between five hundred and one thousand dollars. Because of the capital improvements created by the Vicosinos and Cornell, the Public Benefit Society of Huaras first set a price of 4 million soles (then about $264,000, or about 528 times the annual rent.) The government got that price cut to 2 million soles. The Vicosinos paid 500,000 soles out of their savings, were obligated to pay another

500,000 within three years, and the balance of one million in twenty years, on a no-interest loan. Even so, the final price was 149 times the annual rent—and the government sweetened the deal by pledging to build a hospital for the Mutual Benefit Society of Huaras. The Vicosinos were happy, but the figures suggest that widespread land reform could have been achieved only if the government had had the power and the will to transfer ownership on a far less costly basis.

28. Our Year in Peru

D r. Carlos Monge attended the twenty-fifth anniversary meeting of the Society for Applied Anthropology. From that meeting in Massachusetts, he was to fly to Ithaca, but, with a long-standing spinal problem, he could not manage the steps to get on the plane. We were delighted to have the opportunity of spending a long day's trip driving him to Cornell. In the two week-long exploratory trips in 1959 and 1960 I visited him in Lima.

On one of those trips, I had my first successful experience with bargaining in Peruvian stores. I had no intention of buying anything, but I was attracted by two solid-silver fighting cocks, one crouched as if to defend itself, the other poised to attack. I went in and asked the price. The proprietor quoted me a figure in American money: one hundred dollars. My curiosity satisfied, I thanked him and turned to walk out. I had taken only two or three steps when he called after me: "Ninety dollars." I hesitated a moment and then resumed walking. He called out "Eighty dollars." I continued until he finally called out "Seventy-five." I turned back and said, "I'll take it." It was only later that the proprietor realized that I had thought I was pricing one bird rather than the pair. We had a deal, and I brought home the fighting cocks, which have been on our dining room table ever since.

We booked passage on the Grace Line to Peru and shipped our trunks ahead. With Lucy and John, we drove to the Grace Line docks in New York.

Lucy, John, Kathleen, and I arrived in Lima for my sabbatical in June 1961, right at the start of Lima's winter season. (Joyce was at Swarthmore, and Martin was at Cornell.) From October until May, the weather in Lima is delightful. It almost never rains, and the daytime temperatures are in the mid-seventies to the mid-eighties. In the winter, Lima is nearly always under a heavy cloud cover. It doesn't really rain, but often there is a light drizzle. The daytime temperature hovers in the fifties and low sixties. It is not wet enough for a raincoat, but you need windshield wipers—which you take off when you park, so they won't be stolen.

We called Dr. Monge shortly after our arrival, and he arranged to have his daughter, Christina Temple, drive us around to look for a house to rent. She already had a lead on one belonging to a Peruvian anthropologist in San Isidro, a middle-class district. It turned out to suit us very well. There was a living room, dining room, and kitchen and toilet on the ground floor and three bedrooms and a bathroom above. There was also a backyard bedroom and a toilet for a maid—as was customary for maids, with no toilet seat, and the bed had only ropes to support the mattress. Kathleen hired a very large black woman named Maria. She was pleasant, dependable, and a good cook. She had only one complaint, which she voiced very hesitantly several days after we hired her. The first night, one of the bed legs had broken, and she had slept on her mattress on the floor until she had gotten up the nerve to tell us about it. Kathleen wanted to buy her a new bed from Sears, but Maria would not hear of it. She guided Kathleen to a store that made a larger and stronger version of the bed that had broken.

Lima had two private Peruvian-American schools, Roosevelt and Lincoln. In Roosevelt, most of the classes were taught in English, and it enjoyed a higher status. In Lincoln, most of the classes were taught in Spanish. Most of the playground conversation was in English at Roosevelt and in Spanish at Lincoln. We chose Lincoln.

Lucy, who by now was fourteen and a half, fitted in quickly. Within several months, she was completely bilingual, and she ended the year with the highest grade in her class in Spanish language and literature. An attractive girl with coal-black hair, she could easily be taken for a Peruvian, which indeed did happen on the occasion of her most prominent public performance. At the time, the twist was all the rage in the United States. Lucy had not learned the dance, but all her friends insisted that she must know it, so she taught herself and then others.

A TV program called *High Life*, which featured scenes from society, showed films of the best twist dancers at parties and then invited them to a studio competition. Not only was Lucy shown at a party, but she and her partner won the contest. After stating that all the contestants were Peruvian, the announcer introduced her as "*la encantadora Lucy Whyte, la reina de las damas twisteras de Lima*" (the enchanting Lucy Whyte, the queen of the twisting ladies of Lima). We worried what this sudden fame would do to our daughter, but it had no effects beyond adding to her enjoyment of Lima.

Lucy attracted lots of attention from the boys, partly because she took a keen interest in the 1962 campaign for the president of Peru, and many of them were strongly committed to one or another candidate. Most of the Peruvian girls paid little attention to politics and confined their conversations with boys to small talk. For a time, we were holding open house most nights as boys dropped by to tell Lucy the latest political gossip and to argue with each other.

John, who was eight and a half, had a more difficult time. The Peruvian elementary school system has one grade between our kindergarten and first grade, so John was placed in a second-grade class. When he was assigned a book he had already studied, we arranged to have him moved to the next higher class, but John had problems keeping up with the work. When the school year ended in December, the teacher recommended that he go back to his former class for the new school year. We and he agreed, but his friends in the higher grade now shunned him for having been left back.

Since San Marcos National University was then a center of political radicalism, directed particularly at "U.S. imperialism," the Fulbright Commission had arranged for me to have my offices in the Department of Industrial Engineering in the Engineering University. The budget provided for four research assistants and two bilingual secretaries to handle correspondence and transcribe research notes dictated on tape.

I had assumed we would hire graduate students for the research, but all of them were either working for the government or studying abroad. We had to settle for advanced undergraduates and were pleasantly surprised by how well they performed. In Peru, the undergraduate program takes five years, and the fifth year requires presentation of a thesis. We found several of the fifth-year students mature and able to do their own work and assume responsibility for guiding others. Even some of the third- and fourth-year students developed into first-rate field-workers.

Through leads from Allan Holmberg, I hired Hernan Castillo and Mario Vallejos. Hernan had already been involved with research at Vicos. I hired the third assistant on the recommendation of a U.S. professor who had been teaching at the University of Huamonga at Ayacucho in the highlands. Of Victor Cardenas, she said, "He is brilliant, but he needs close supervision." I should have known that I am not capable of exercising close supervision. I am at my best guiding independent-minded and self-motivated students and tend to assume they are all that way. As it turned out, he did as little as possible. When I recognized the problem and threatened to let him go, he promised to reform, but it never happened. I also hired Graciela Flores, on the recommendation of the director of industrial engineering, and she turned out to be a real find.

Lining up field sites for our industrial case studies was an early and continuing problem. I got guidance and help from Norman King of Cerro de Pasco, a U.S.-owned firm, and then had the great good fortune to meet Robert Braun. Born in Vienna, Braun had followed an older brother to Peru after graduating from high school. Later, he had become a partner in a U.S. accounting firm in Peru and had also been a management consultant to English-, American-, and German-owned firms. He was fluent in four languages: German, English, French, and Spanish.

I met Braun when he was interim director of IPAE, the Peruvian management association. Some of its members had formed a group they called "Miembros y Amigos de IPAE" (Members and Friends of IPAE), which met every two weeks for lunch and discussion with an invited speaker. Somehow I got myself invited to one of these lunches. Before lunch, during drinks, Braun took me aside to pump me about my proposed research. Later we always talked in English, since his English was better than my Spanish, but on this occasion he sounded me out in Spanish. "That is very interesting," he said. "My job with IPAE and my management consulting do not fill up all my time. I would be happy to work with you. Call on me at any time when you think I can be helpful."

Bob Braun was a first-rate natural observer of people, groups, and organizations. Talking with him, I picked up many shrewd observations regarding the cultural differences among English-, American-, German-, and Peruvian-managed companies.

He made his first contribution by helping me prepare a statement to explain my project to Peruvian management people. I had written a first draft myself and then had had my secretary, Sheila Campion, go over it to be sure my Spanish was correct. I showed my draft to Bob, and, without changing the meaning, he rewrote it to fit the culture of Peruvian management.

Later, Bob pushed me to expand the project to include survey research on a number of companies. I thought that overly ambitious, but I agreed to do one study if he could line up the site. He had strong connections to the Swiss-owned Empresas Electricas (Lima Light and Power Company). Lawrence K. Williams had recently been hired by the Department of Organizational Behavior in ILR at Cornell, and he had had a major responsibility in the University of Michigan surveys of Detroit Edison. I wrote Larry, and he supplied me with the questionnaire used in the Detroit study. We translated and adapted it, and added items that might reflect Peruvian culture.

When I returned to Cornell, Larry did a comparative analysis of the Lima data and the data from Detroit. This began a collaboration that continued for more than a decade.

I collaborated with Bob Braun on several writing projects. The most interesting for me was an article entitled "On Language and Culture" (1968), which grew out of discussions with him on how best to communicate to Peruvian management people in Spanish. My Spanish was now good enough that when I was stuck for the right word for an American concept, there was a fair chance there was indeed a problem in finding an exact Spanish equivalent. For example, there are no exact Spanish equivalents for *achieve* and *achievement*. In English, these words mean not only an important, successful result but also one that is arrived at through one's own persistent efforts. In Spanish, there are several words for having a successful result, but they do not distinguish between what happens by luck or influence and what comes about through one's own efforts.

I came upon a newspaper story that commented that Spanish has no exact equivalent to the German *gründlichkeit*, which does have an exact English equivalent: *thoroughness*. The writer went on to note that Peruvians often speak of doing things *a la criolla*, which means just well enough to escape serious criticism. I thought I was observing many *a la criolla* performances.

There are also words that appear to have exact equivalents but that have different meanings because of Peruvian custom. For example, the Spanish for *negotiate* is *negociar*, but in the 1960s, in customary Peruvian usage, that word carried the implication that one party was taking advantage of the other party. When Peruvians wished to avoid that implication, they spoke of *trato directo*, emphasizing that the dealings between the parties were direct.

Then there was the simple word *no*, which is spelled the same in Spanish as in English and appears to have the same meaning. In genteel Peruvian society of that era, *no* was seldom heard. Bob Braun told me that when he heard it, he was startled. To judge whether a Peruvian really meant to do something, one had to listen to "the music" in his words, as he said *si* (yes). In time, I developed better judgment of "the music," but I was never fully confident of my interpretations.

With Bob's guidance, I set up a management advisory committee for my project. Bob was a member, but he played a more active role behind the scenes, interpreting what went on in committee meetings. On one occasion, the meeting had seemed to go very well up to a point, but then it fell apart. When I was describing what we were doing in the field, I got supportive nods and comments, but then I asked which company to choose for the next field site. At this point, the members seemed confused, and I was puzzled by their reactions. Bob explained later that I had given them the impression that I had a very solid understanding of what I was doing; they had assumed that, given my expertise, I would have known which site to choose. If I had told them which company I wanted to study next, they would have been happy to advise me on how to work out the necessary arrangements.

My studies of industrial relations led to some conclusions regarding intercultural differences between Peruvian and U.S. firms, but I found my interests shifting toward a different type of study.

I had planned to study the relations between Peruvian managers and workers and labor unions, but I became fascinated with the apparent bias in Peruvian culture against industrial entrepreneurship. With few exceptions, the important companies had been founded by immigrants or sons of immigrants. For example, Antonio D'Onofrio had come from Italy as a small child. From a start selling ice cream on street corners, he had built up Peru's largest producer and distributor of ice cream, chocolates, and cookies. Oscar Ferrand was born in Peru, the son of a French immigrant who had owned a grocery store. Ferrand had built up Peru's most successful firm in the glass industry and also had the Ford Motors franchise in Lima. The son of an Italian immigrant, Luis Banchero had started as a gasoline station attendant while going through the university. He had gone on to become the leading entrepreneur in Peru's booming fish meal business. It seemed that, for the second generation of men born in Peru, the appeal of industrial entrepreneurship had died out. (Decades later I learned, through the research of Hernando de Soto [1989] that the Peruvian entrepreneurs who were not immigrants or sons of immigrants were with the small firms in the "clandestine economy," operating without government sanction or support.)

What was it about Peruvian culture that militated against industrial entrepreneurship? I consulted the academic literature and read widely in Peruvian newspapers and magazines. I also consulted children's history books to see what role models they provided. I found no mention of industrialists or inventors. The most prominent role models were military men who had won their fame in the disastrous War of the Pacific, in which Peru was defeated by Chile.

These men all displayed great courage and patriotism, but they achieved nothing. Among Peruvian heroes, the only one who can be credited with an achievement is Jorge Chavez, and even in his case the claim was ambiguous. Chavez was the first man to fly over the Alps, but he crashed upon landing and died.

Newspapers covered the current business news of Peruvian industrialists, but I found a complete absence of feature stories telling readers about the humble origins of men such as D'Onofrio, Ferrand, and Banchero.

Later, when I collaborated with Graciela Flores on "Culture, Industrial Relations, and Economic Development: The Case of Peru" (1963), she persuaded me to leave out any references to the humble beginnings of men such as D'Onofrio, Ferrand, and Banchero in the Spanish translation of the article. I asked her, "Aren't those origins well known in Lima?" That did not make any difference, she replied. The children and grandchildren of the entrepreneurs would be embarrassed by public references to their humble origins.

Could I go beyond casual interpretations of culture and pursue a study systematically? In the 1950s, Cornell sociologists had surveyed the attitudes and values of college students. I wrote sociologist Rose Goldsen, who sent me a copy of the survey, along with some of the research reports. Graciela and I selected those items that seemed relevant to Peru, and she translated them. We also devised a number of items especially for Peru.

Since we were interested in career choices, and students in Peru generally chose their careers by the time they entered the university, we decided to survey students in their final year of high school. For guidance on differences in status among the various private high schools, I called upon the director of the Instituto Psicopedagógico Nacional in the Ministry of Education. He had a very small staff and no budget for research, so he was delighted when I proposed that the survey be jointly sponsored by Cornell and his institute.

We started our project by studying large public high schools and three status levels of private schools in Lima. The data-gathering process went much faster than I had anticipated. The director of the institute personally called each school director to make arrangements for the survey. In each case, he asked to have a senior class available for the survey on a particular day. The most resistant director said that it would be more convenient if Graciela could distribute the questionnaires at 10 o'clock instead of 9.

Within three weeks, Graciela had completed surveys of boys in twelve Lima high schools. (In the United States, arranging such a survey would have required much more field time and diplomacy in dealing with school boards, school principals, and teachers.)

Since we were about to undertake factory studies in the provinces, I arranged to have our field-worker distribute the questionnaire in several of those cities.

All the IBM data cards were punched in the Ministry of Health, and Graciela brought them back to Cornell. She worked with Rose Goldsen and me on the Peruvian school surveys and on the Peru-U.S. comparisons.

The most striking difference was in a dimension we called "faith in people" or "interpersonal trust." We measured this with several items. One asked students to choose between the following two statements: "Some people say that most people can be trusted. Others say you can't be too careful in your dealings with people." The optimistic response drew an average of 79 percent among the eleven U.S. colleges sampled. By comparison, in our twelve Lima schools, the response drew only between 30 percent and 45 percent. A similar contrast existed between employees of Sears Roebuck in the United States and Peru.

Our findings indicated that Peru's prevailing low level of trust was a serious barrier to economic progress. If people don't trust other people, they hesitate to delegate responsibility and authority. They also try to control the flow of information to prevent potential enemies from using it against them.

In the U.S. study, the social backgrounds of the students' families appeared to make little difference in their responses. In contrast, the responses of the Lima students exhibited enormous differences by social class. We decided to concentrate our analysis on this finding.

We found that boys in the elite schools of Lima were much more inclined to choose industrial careers than students in the public schools, who preferred government jobs. For these potential leaders of Peruvian industry, their own interpretations of their motivation and that of their fellow students presented a discouraging picture of Peru's industrial future. Compared with the public school students, the private school students saw themselves as less inclined to persist in efforts to overcome obstacles, more inclined to cheat in class, and more inclined to prefer a teacher who did not require them to study hard but who was sure to give them good grades.

One novel feature of our survey was a projective item Graciela adapted from surveys used at the Centro de Altos Estudios Militares (Center of Higher Military Studies): "Supposing you hadn't been a man, which of the following animals would you have preferred to be?" The choices were ant, sheep, wild horse, llama, turkey, fox, tiger, dog, lion, and elephant. Three of the choices showed marked differences between the students in the public and elite schools. The ant was most chosen by the public school boys (32.1 percent) but got a much lower rating (6.18 percent) among those in the elite schools. The lion was the most popular choice in the elite schools (25.7 percent), whereas it drew only 14.2 percent of the choices in the public schools. The wild horse was chosen by 19.5

percent of the boys in the elite schools, whereas it drew only 7.7 percent in the public schools. The boys in the public schools chose the hard-working and cooperative ant, yet they were not thinking of industrial careers. The choices of the elite boys suggested a desire to dominate or to be entirely free of any controls, neither of which boded well for effective industrial leadership.

Among the public school boys, only those in the industrial arts program showed any interest in industrial careers. Since Peru was suffering from a shortage of skilled workers, this seemed an encouraging finding. But when we asked them to choose between *obrero* (blue-collar worker) and *empleado* (white-collar worker), only 13.3 percent chose *obrero* with equal pay and two-thirds chose *obrero* only under conditions that were extremely unlikely to arise.

Before leaving Peru, I arranged for a feedback presentation on my study for my Peruvian friends and sponsors. I decided to base my talk on our school surveys. I spoke for only about fifteen minutes, yet the impact was striking. My comments on the low level of interpersonal trust hit particularly hard, although no one challenged this conclusion. Bob Braun made this comment to Kathleen: "It was like being in your own home at night, without the lights being on. You know where all the furniture is, so you can get around in the dark, but then Bill turns the lights on, and you see everything more clearly."

29. *From Industrial to Rural Research*

I n 1964, I launched my most far-reaching and ambitious research program. I had become fascinated by Peru. The patterns of social stratification were so clear-cut that they led me to believe that I understood the dynamics of Peruvian society better than I did those of my own country. As I applied for an NIMH Career Research Award, I visualized my industrial studies fitting in with Allan Holmberg's Vicos project and other rural research and becoming the foundation for a book on the social and economic development of Peru. My vision expanded in response to events involving Holmberg, Cornell graduate student John Hickman, and Fernando Beláunde Terry, the president of Peru from 1963 to 1968. By 1964, Allan was dying of leukemia. Since I could not work with him, I wondered whether I should get into rural research myself.

John Hickman nudged me in that direction when he adapted some of the high school survey items Graciela and I had developed, added his own, had the Spanish translated into the indigenous languages of Quechua and Aymara, and surveyed adults in half a dozen Peruvian villages.

A further nudge was provided by the 1962 presidential campaign of Fernando Beláunde Terry. He visited more remote rural areas than any candidate before him, and land reform and rural development were major planks in his campaign. The campaign ended in a virtual dead heat between Victor Raul Haya de la Torre and Beláunde, at which point a military junta took control and held a new election in 1963, under revised ground rules. Beláunde won and became president.

Beláunde's victory inspired me to plan a longitudinal study that combined surveys with anthropological studies in a number of villages. If the government was planning to launch a major rural development program, it was important to start the surveys as soon as possible, so as to lay down a baseline against which to compare the survey findings in those same villages three to five years later.

While visiting Lima shortly after the 1963 election, I looked up Dr. José Matos Mar of San Marcos National University, who was generally regarded by foreign scholars as Peru's most distinguished social anthropologist. I had met him earlier through Holmberg, and he had invited me to talk to a class about my industrial and cultural studies. Now he was serving as a consultant to Belaúnde on his rural development plans.

Matos planned for a group of students to study villages in the Chancay Valley, on the coast about an hour's drive north of Lima, during the university's vacation period (January through March). I described my vision of the new research program, and, since I could bring in modest funding to pay the students, they could work with me on the Chancay Valley surveys. I asked Larry Williams to assume primary responsibility for the surveys, and we began to work together to design the questionnaire. We had a draft translated into Spanish, and I took it with me when I joined Matos and the students in January in the Chancay Valley, where we all lived and worked together in a school building.

Many of the villages in the Chancay Valley are at altitudes of between six thousand and eleven thousand feet. There are also villages and haciendas on the coastal delta. After revising the draft of the questionnaire with Matos and the students, I went to one of the delta villages to pretest the interview questions; I then made further revisions.

My statistical consultant suggested interviewing all the male adult inhabitants in 20 percent of the households; he said we would be wasting our time with the females because they would answer the same as the men. We decided to include both men and women—and, in fact, the results showed some marked differences by gender.

Peruvian students are so conscious of Peru's history that they are inclined to trace the development of any area back to the Spanish conquest. I made what I thought was a big concession by suggesting they trace the history of the villages back fifty years. Fortunately, they did not accept that limitation. Instead, they traced events back more than one hundred years, which distinguished one village from another. Later, in the Mantaro Valley, they traced developments to the first century after the Spanish conquest.

Several students had been studying Pacaraos, an indigenous community at an altitude of ten thousand feet. If we selected another highland community, which one was likely to provide an interesting contrast? They had found Pacaraos to be a very poor community with a small affluent class dedicated to trucking and other commercial enterprises. Most of the inhabitants were subsistence farmers who cultivated the traditional crops of corn and potatoes. The students reported that there was a low level of cooperation and a high incidence of conflict.

Information was vague on the villages at an altitude of about six thousand feet, but some of these communities, which had begun cultivating tropical fruits, were much more affluent than Pacaraos. The leader in this economic shift had been the village of Huayopampa. The students and I became fascinated with Huayopampa, whose strong economic foundation was its extraordinarily effective community organization.

The first impulse toward change and development in Huayopampa had occurred in 1850 with the founding of a Catholic missionary school. The school was short-lived, but it had a lasting impact. In 1886, Huayopampa took matters into its own hands and built its own school and hired a teacher. None of the other villages in the area would have its own school until 1922.

In 1904, Huayopampa built a new school and attracted a married couple, the Ceferino Villars, who were remarkable teachers. Their two sons succeeded them as teachers, so that the community remained under the influence of the Villars family until 1925. This was in striking contrast to what we found in other rural areas, where schoolteachers were alienated from the villagers.

Even from the perspective of the 1990s, the Villars's educational model seems strikingly progressive. The teachers integrated their instruction with the life of the area. They got the children to study local plant diseases and prevention and regional archaeology—from a book by Pedro Villars Cordova, son of the pioneering schoolteachers.

In 1940, 1943, and 1945, the teachers persuaded the community to cede plots of land for experimental gardens and a reforestation project. From this, the children (and indirectly their parents) learned modern methods of agriculture and control of soil erosion.

Migrants from Huayopampa to the coastal delta had learned about the economic potential of tropical fruits, but it was impossible to transport such delicate crops to coastal markets without a road connecting Huayopampa with the cities of Huaral and Chancay. Huayopampa completed that road in 1948.

To guide the shift to growing tropical fruits, schoolteachers provided information and linked the village with professors in the National Agrarian University, with extension agents, and with officials of the Agricultural Development Bank. The rapidly growing demand for credit and a good repayment record led to the establishment of a branch office of the bank in Huayopampa.

Huayopampa had built its social and economic development on a base of collective solidarity. Thus, by 1964, the village had several cooperative enterprises: a store, a trucking firm, a bus line to the coast, a system of potable water, and an electric power plant. The villagers of Huayopampa had learned that depending on the government cost more than the results were worth. By the early 1960s, Huayopampa was hiring its own engineers, buying its own raw materials, and controlling village projects from start to finish.

The social and economic results were spectacular. Huayopampa had the highest educational level of the twelve villages in our study. Those in the lowest income stratum earned the equivalent of a reasonably good white-collar job in Lima, and those in the top income stratum earned only four times more than those in the bottom stratum, whereas in Pacaraos the ratio was eighteen to one. And half the families in Huayopampa also owned homes in Lima.

~

The Career Research Award funds, available beginning July 1, 1964, made it possible to expand the research program. In the eight months of the year when I was not teaching, I was free to take field trips to Peru.

I had been regarding any administrative duties as necessary evils, tasks that had to be accomplished to get on with the fieldwork. To manage the expanded program, I would have to create a research design in which working out the arrangements provided intellectual excitement comparable to the adventure of the fieldwork.

Expanding the program involved working out collaborative arrangements with increasing numbers of Peruvians and Peruvian institutions. Since the funds I could raise were limited, what inducements could I offer? Trying to answer that question led me to devise an organizational model based on what I called *multiobjective planning* and *joint-payoff* relations.

Sociologists had long recognized the "unanticipated consequences of planned social actions." Why couldn't we anticipate some of those consequences and make them part of the project design? Focusing on the economics of scarcity, economists speak of *opportunity costs*: when you are doing one thing, you can't do something else. The opportunity costs are what you give up by not doing something else. But that principle holds only for particular actions and not for the objectives sought through a given line of action. In fact, the same line of action can lead to two or more objectives. Implicitly, economists recognize this distinction when they refer to *externalities*—benefits gained incidentally beyond the progress made toward your principal objective. We decided to locate our field sites in areas accessible to regional universities, so that the program could become part of their research and teaching programs. Thus, we would be training their students in survey research and in anthropological field methods.

At Cornell, we used our Peruvian data in seminars, concentrating on the integration of surveys with anthropological methods. Our work could strengthen Cornell in Latin American Studies and particularly in Andean studies, where the University was already well known.

In the spring of 1964, Matos informed me that the Instituto de Estudios Peruanos (IEP) had been established with a grant from the Ministry of Education. As director, he had brought together a distinguished group of social scientists and humanists to serve on its board. Matos invited me to make IEP the headquarters of our research program, and I happily accepted.

Larry Williams and I asked Matos to be co-director of the Cornell-IEP program, and strengthening IEP now became one of our principal objectives. My relations with Matos changed as we worked more closely together. At first, Larry and I would decide what we wanted to do, and it was up to me to persuade Matos to accept our plan. Since Cornell retained financial control of the research, I had some power to force decisions if we did not agree. With further experience, our relationship moved toward a full partnership. I would tell Matos what Larry and I were thinking of doing, outline the dilemmas our program was facing, and then ask for his views.

As support from the Peruvian government declined year after year, IEP became increasingly dependent on Cornell. Matos was not happy about this development and was energetically pursuing other funds. I assured him that the dependence was not one-sided, insofar as Cornell was becoming increasingly dependent on IEP for the administration of our joint research program.

I started the survey expansion with Oscar Nuñez del Prado at the University of Cuzco. Earlier, he had worked with Holmberg on a study of the village of Virú on the north coast, and that experience had gotten him interested in applied anthropology. He was a professor and also regional director of the National Plan for Integration of the Indian Population, an agency coordinated by the Ministry of Labor and Indian Affairs. The National Plan was also sponsored by the Ministries of War, Education, and Agriculture; the Agrarian Reform Institute; and the Agricultural Development Bank.

Oscar was in a precarious position. He had been an active member of the political party APRA, which was identified with the labor movement and with rural land reform. When the leaders of the Cuzco APRA party ordered him to beat up a former schoolteacher, Oscar broke with APRA and denounced its increasing use of strong-arm tactics. He joined no other party and found himself

227

without political allies in the university. Like other Peruvian universities, Cuzco was highly politicized, as Apristas and Communists struggled for control. A political conflict had deprived Oscar of his university salary, but he was managing to survive on the meager pay he received from the National Plan.

Oscar was a physically slight man who was endowed with enormous drive and courage. He had become known as a friend of the Indians and therefore as an enemy of their mestizo oppressors. His home had been stoned, and once he had been visited by a lawyer bearing the message that it would be dangerous to his health if he appeared in the village of Paucartambo. He thanked the emissary and told him that on the following Sunday he would be in Paucartambo all day. He spent the day taking pictures of village activities. Nothing happened, but he knew that his life could have been at stake.

Oscar had started an applied anthropology project in the Indian community of Kuyo Chico, in an area dominated by the mestizo town of Pisaq. We wanted to do studies in Kuyo Chico and Pisaq and several other Indian villages in the area. Oscar became field director of those studies.

Like the Vicos project, the Kuyo Chico project represented one of those rare applied anthropology projects in which the principal objective was to transform the local power structure. In Vicos, that was accomplished when Cornell bought the lease on the hacienda. In Kuyo Chico, the task was more difficult. As he wrote later (Nuñez del Prado 1973: 47), "We had decided to oppose power with power, but had no power at our disposal, and so had to create the appearance of power."

After establishing relations with key people in Kuyo Chico, Oscar called a community meeting to announce the beginning of the development project, sponsored by the National Plan for the Integration of the Indian Population. He saw to it that the meeting was well publicized in Pisaq, as well as in neighboring villages. Posters announcing the meeting prominently displayed the names of the various government ministries and agencies that were official sponsors of the National Plan—although Oscar knew that this represented nominal rather than highly committed support.

As a result of the publicity, some of the leading mestizo officials of Pisaq and of the Department of Cuzco came to the meeting. Speaking in Quechua, Oscar began by telling the Indians their rights according to the laws and constitution of Peru. He told them that no one had the right to draft them for public works projects; that they could not be pressed into service on haciendas, which were often far from their communities; and that their men and women could not be required to spend a day a week performing community cleanup and household duties in Pisaq. After enumerating each of these customary but illegal practices, he turned to the mestizo authorities to ask them if he had indeed correctly interpreted the villagers' legal protections. They could not deny the facts. Now the Indians of Kuyo Chico ceased providing free services to the mestizo authorities in Pisaq, and other Indian villages rapidly followed suit.

During this time, a general in charge of a road-building project let it be known that he wanted to talk to Oscar about getting the Indians to do the work. Oscar sent back word that he would be glad to meet the general in the Kuyo Chico project office.

When the general announced his plans, Oscar replied, "That's fine. How much do you propose to pay them?"

The general replied that this would be a voluntary public service and added, "It is their civic duty."

Oscar cited the laws and constitutional provisions that outlawed such free services. The general left in high dudgeon and went to Lima to denounce Oscar as a Communist. Oscar was called to Lima by Román Pelegrin, the director of the Indigenous Institute, a government agency. When Oscar told him the story of the encounter, Pelegrin just shrugged and let the matter drop.

A short time later, Oscar and an agricultural engineer were driving from Kuyo Chico to Pisaq when they noticed a group of Indian men and women standing forlornly by the side of the road, and some of the women were crying. When they stopped to inquire, the Indians told them that the lieutenant governor of the district had confiscated the crops they were taking to market and paid them extremely low prices. When Oscar asked the lieutenant governor to explain, he said, "These Indians are monopolizers and speculators," whereupon he produced a newspaper article about government measures to crack down on monopolies and speculators.

Oscar told him that was nonsense and demanded that the produce be returned. When Oscar tried to enter the house where the produce was located, the lieutenant governor barred the door, and then, Oscar writes, "I found myself obliged to hit him, and he fell down inside the house." As Oscar entered the house, the governor of the district arrived and attempted to enter, but the engineer barred the way. Now Oscar called out to the Indians to rush the house and pick up their produce. In a few seconds, the Indians were gone.

The next day, Oscar was summoned to the office of the prefect of Cuzco, the officer over the district governor and lieutenant governor, to answer a variety of charges. Oscar came armed with a document incriminating the prefect and the governor in a plan to press Indians into service on a hacienda owned by the prefect. The document was signed by the governor and was sent to a local official of Kuyo Grande, a neighboring Indian community, who was to be the recruiting agent.

The governor had sent a member of the Kuyo Chico community as a runner to carry the document to Kuyo Grande. The runner had shown the envelope to Oscar and asked, "Wouldn't it be good to know what the message is?" Oscar had steamed the envelope open and photographed the message.

Oscar defended his actions and then brought out his photographic bombshell. As he pointed out, this reference to illegal activities could have put the prefect in legal jeopardy. The prefect was alarmed. As Oscar wrote, "I suggested that the prefect dismiss these authorities, and permitted myself to propose as a replacement for the governor a man over whom we had some influence." About a week later, the governor and lieutenant governor were discharged.

Having established a firm power base, Oscar and his associates were now free to work with Kuyo Chico on the community development project. With our surveys and anthropological case studies, we would eventually tell much of the Kuyo Chico story, but it seemed important that Oscar write his own version. I wrote an application for research support for Oscar from the Wenner-Gren Foundation. The support was limited to small grants, but I hoped the twenty-five hundred dollars would encourage him to write.

Months passed, and I wondered if the writing would ever get done. Larry Williams suggested I interview Oscar. I suggested Matos go with me. We arranged to spend a week with Oscar at a location far from the distractions of his work.

Oscar took us to a small country hotel in Urubamba that was suitably isolated. It even lacked telephones; transistor radios were the only connection with the outside world—except for a group of travel agents who were meeting there. While Oscar, Matos, and I were piecing together the story of a remote highlands village, in the background we heard discussions of how to get from Lima to Hong Kong or other international destinations.

When Oscar received the transcription of the interview, he was energized to write his own story, and he prepared a document much richer than what we had sent. My daughter Lucy was spending some weeks in Peru, and she translated it into English. At Oscar's request, I wrote an introduction, "The Context of Kuyo Chico," relating his project to Vicos. He also asked me to do a chapter entitled "The Evidence from the Surveys" and to collaborate with him on a final chapter, "Lessons for Applied Anthropology." The dedication reads "To the memory of Allan R. Holmberg, pioneer in applied anthropology in Peru and unforgettable friend." I was happy to see this tribute to the man who had led me to Peru and who had inspired so many of us to expand our vision of applied anthropology. *Kuyo Chico: Applied Anthropology in an Indian Community* was published in 1973.

30. *Political Crisis*

The Chancay Valley surveys encouraged us to extend our research to other regions. We had laid down our baseline for the Chancay Valley early in 1964. To get comparable data from other villages, we would have to complete those surveys by the end of that year. I had already worked out arrangements with Oscar Nuñez del Prado to do work in Cuzco, but I had to make arrangements with professors in Arequipa, Huancayo, and Ayacucho in the highlands and in Trujillo on the north coast.

We realized that we had undertaken far more than we could manage without additional funds and staff. Using Ministry of Health machines, we got the survey data on punch cards, but the analysis and report writing would have to be done at Cornell. This would put us in the role of "academic imperialists," using the natives simply to provide us with raw materials while we creamed off the benefits of research and publication.

Matos argued that two survey research professionals should be located with the institute, one representing Cornell, the other representing IEP. He had a Peruvian candidate in mind, his brother-in-law Julio Cotler, then with an MIT research group analyzing surveys carried out in Venezuela. Larry Williams and I had interviewed Julio at Cornell and been impressed with him. J. Oscar Alers, who was finishing his Ph.D. at Cornell, was our choice for the field director to represent Cornell.

We agreed to spend our grant money far faster than originally planned to ensure that we could do the surveys by the end of 1964, but worried whether we could get the additional funds we needed fast enough to build on the momentum we were generating.

I presented a report on the Chancay Valley project at an American Anthropological Association meeting in November 1964, and Lee Huff, director of the

Advanced Research Projects Agency (ARPA) in the Pentagon, was present. He wrote that he had found my report very interesting and asked if I knew of any other projects like ours that needed financing. In January 1965, on my way to Peru, I stopped off in Washington to talk with Huff. I would have preferred almost any other source of funds, but I wanted to see whether the conditions of an ARPA grant might be acceptable.

Huff told me that ARPA was committed to supporting basic research. No secrecy was required; we would be free to publish as we saw fit, and ARPA would exercise no control over any aspect of the research. He said it never took more than sixty days following the receipt of a proposal for ARPA to make its decision. By contrast, it could take up to nine months for a major private foundation to decide on a proposal. The National Science Foundation (NSF) or NIMH would take that long—even to consider financing a program it was already supporting.

Matos said the IEP would have no problem accepting Ford Foundation or other U.S. foundation grants or NSF or NIMH grants. Support from the Agency for International Development (AID) was less desirable but probably acceptable. Support from ARPA raised more serious questions, since the Pentagon was the key symbol of U.S. imperialism. We wrestled with the issue and finally Matos suggested that an ARPA grant could be used to pay the salaries and expenses of Cornell researchers, while our NSF grant would support IEP activities.

We submitted the ARPA proposal on March 1, 1965. Huff phoned on March 30 to tell me the grant had been approved. We appointed Alers as Cornell field director and Cotler as field director for IEP.

In the summer of 1965, the Camelot scandal broke in Chile. The Pentagon had contracted with the Special Operations Research Office (SORO) at American University for a large research program to assess the conditions favoring counterinsurgency in developing countries. While the project director, Rex Hopper, was considering possible target countries, Hugo Nutini, an assistant professor of anthropology at the University of Pittsburgh, told Hopper that he planned to visit his native Chile and proposed that he sound out officials at the national university about their interest in SORO's research program.

In discussing the project, now known as Camelot, with officials in Chile, Nutini did not reveal that the Pentagon was financing it. Johan Galtung, a Norwegian sociologist, was then in Chile with the Latin American Faculty of Social Science. Earlier he had been invited to an exploratory meeting about Camelot. He declined to attend, but the background papers provided full information on the financing. Galtung informed officials at the National University in Chile of the Pentagon's involvement.

They expressed their outrage at the attempt to trick them into serving Pentagon interests, and this resulted in cancellation of Camelot. The scandal was widely reported in the press in Latin America.

Our research program was quite different from Camelot. We had no interest in insurgency or counterinsurgency. Whereas Camelot was initiated by the Pentagon, our ARPA grant simply supported work already well under way. Nevertheless, we knew the scandal would heighten political sensitivities in Peru.

I had planned to be in Peru during July and August 1964, but I fell and broke a leg and had to postpone the trip until October. I found Matos very worried. He had not told any of his board of directors except the chairman of IEP, Luis Valcarcel, about the ARPA grant. Sooner or later news of the grant would leak out. What then? I suggested a typical American solution: Call a meeting of the members of the board, give them a full story of what we were doing, and ask for their advice.

Matos scheduled a luncheon meeting, to proceed in two acts. He would introduce me to the board (many of whose members I had already met). I would describe our research program, particularly the IEP-Cornell partnership, and our plans not only to publish our research but also to contribute to the development of Peruvian students and institutions. Later, during the coffee hour, I would give them a full account of our financing.

As we anticipated, the mood during the two acts was quite different. During my talk it was enthusiastic. Several members stated that a full-scale collaboration among equal partners was just what Peru needed. During the coffee hour, however, members expressed their worries. Two said they wished they had not been informed of the ARPA grant so that, when the news got out, they could claim to have known nothing about it. The former minister of education, Francisco Miro Quesada, who had authorized the government grant to establish the IEP, led the discussion. Acknowledging their political concerns, he suggested that we could use the ARPA money so long as it was not going to IEP personnel—the solution Matos had already suggested.

On my next trip to Peru, in January 1966, Matos was even more concerned. One of the men who had been at the board meeting had told some of his friends about the ARPA financing, and the news was spreading. Matos said, "Years ago, when I wasn't working with North Americans, I was accused of being a Communist. Now that I am working with North Americans, Julio [Cotler] and I are both being accused of being Camelot agents."

Soon after, Dr. Monge called to say he had heard that Matos and Cotler were working for Camelot. That same day, Matos told me that five people had come up to him at a funeral to ask about the report that he was involved with Camelot.

The storm broke in the press on February 11 with a front-page story in *La Tribuna*, the official organ of the APRA party. It focused particularly on Matos and some of his associates. They had been active with the Social Progresista party, a small socialist party of intellectuals, well known for its attacks on APRA. The story linked us all to Camelot and included the following statement:

> This institute was working with juicy subsidies from an analogous institution in France . . . and with dollars that it is said were being delivered by a Yankee citizen named White [sic]. The self-sacrificing research men of the "left" were getting paid succulent salaries. But, upon the death of Mr. White, it is said to have been discovered that what was providing the golden dollars was the Pentagon—the Ministry of Defense of the United States.

La Tribuna continued hammering away on the same theme in stories that appeared on February 12, 13, 18, and 19. The February 18 report concluded with this paragraph: "Meanwhile efforts are being made to locate White, a foreigner who does not represent any university of his country, so that he may provide information on the origin of the dollars that he is delivering to Peruvian communists."

On February 19, *La Tribuna* published a letter from Luis Valcarcel. He denied that IEP had received any Pentagon money, and then went on to give a description of IEP's relations with Cornell. The letter devoted a paragraph to "the distinguished North American sociologist, William F. Whyte," listed my books, and noted that I had been president of the Society for Applied Anthropology and editor of *Human Organization*. The letter also mentioned Cornell's contribution to Peru through the Vicos project.

Matos felt that we had to return the unused funds (by far the largest part) from the ARPA grant so that we could honestly state that IEP was not benefiting from Pentagon money. I agreed, even if it meant the end of our program.

On my return home, I consulted with David G. Moore, the dean of ILR and an old friend, and with Cornell's vice president for research, Franklin Long, about returning the ARPA money. They arranged it, to the surprise and anger of Lee Huff, the director of ARPA.

There would be no ARPA funds after February 15, 1966, and our remaining grant money would carry us only into the following September. To give us breathing space until the end of the year, Dean Moore committed funds from ILR, and I later learned that Frank Long would have drawn on university funds if necessary. It was gratifying to have such support, but that would serve no purpose unless we could secure new grants before the end of December.

Matos was receiving no money from Cornell, but Julio Cotler's salary came entirely from the university. Since we could not expect him to wait until December to look for another job, I secured a ten-thousand-dollar grant from the Agricultural Development Council to study the agricultural impact of a program sponsored by Peru's leading brewery to get farmers to grow malting barley. It had little relationship to our program, but investigating industry involvement in agricultural development was an interesting idea, and we needed that ten thousand dollars, which paid Julio's salary for several months into the next year.

We then asked the NSF and NIMH to allow us to apply for funds to replace the ARPA grant. Both agreed, although we still had to go through the peer review process, and no decision would be made until early December.

We hurried to put together proposals while I checked into the possibility of securing an AID grant. An official told me, "Your project is so good, if you weren't doing it, we should be out trying to persuade other people to do something like this." Nonetheless, our ambassador to Peru, J. Wesley Jones, vetoed the idea. He had nothing against the IEP, but our involvement had become controversial. He referred us to Peter Frankel of the Ford Foundation. Frankel told me that our project was the kind the AID should support.

Subsequently, I discovered that an AID grant involving the IEP would have required Matos and Cotler to get U.S. security clearances! No such clearance had been required by ARPA. Apparently the State Department was still suffering from the McCarthy-period suspicion of being "soft on Communism," whereas the Pentagon was above such suspicion. I did not even ask Matos and Cotler to consider going through security checks. Being certified as not constituting a danger to U.S. security would have forever branded them as lackeys of the Yankees.

In November 1966, I made what I thought might be my last trip to Peru. I told Matos how happy I had been to work with him and the IEP and how sad I was that we could not continue. He said that working with Cornell was the most rewarding experience of his many international collaborations. He also said that the end of Cornell's financial support would probably mean the end of the IEP. The Beláunde government, under increasing financial pressures, had reduced the IEP's subsidy by two-thirds, and the next year the institute would probably get no government money.

Around December 1, I got a call from the NSF. Our grant had been approved, but, the caller added, "There is a problem."

While I held my breath, he explained that the NIMH had also approved our proposal. Which grant would we accept? Never before had I experienced such an overwhelming vote of confidence in our work by funding agencies. Larry and I decided to choose the NIMH for one reason: the NSF was limited to two years of support, whereas the NIMH granted us the three years we needed.

~

Some weeks after the initial salvo against us and the IEP, the attacks died down and it became clear that our program would survive. I would like to think we survived because we were good for Peru, but clearly that would not have been enough. *La Tribuna* was owned by the APRA party and did not enjoy the journalistic reputations of *La Prensa* or *El Comercio*, which were not owned by any political party and had much larger circulations.

The political motivation behind the attacks was clear. There had been a long feud between APRA and Matos and his associates in national and university politics. Matos and some of his fellow intellectuals in the Social Progresista party or with Acción Popular (President Belaúnde's party) had been attacking APRA for selling out to conservative interests. In the 1962 campaign, Matos had been a Social Progresista candidate for congress. Although he was not going to get a large vote, people in APRA roughed him up at a campaign rally.

According to Matos, the key man behind the IEP attacks was Luis Alberto Sanchez, one of the original supporters of Haya de la Torre and the APRA party's leading intellectual. Sanchez had been rector of San Marcos. When he was elected to the national senate in 1963, he had to resign his university position.

APRA had formed an alliance with the party of General Manuel Odria, the former dictator, and that alliance had won control of the legislature. Sanchez got the law changed so that a senator could run for rector. His leading opponents were Agusto Salazar Bondy and Francisco Miro Quesada, both members of the board of the IEP. Earlier, Sanchez had supported instituting a program of general studies in San Marcos. Now the leading proponents of that reform were Salazar Bondy and Miro Quesada. Since his opponents were backing general studies, Sanchez turned against it. APRA cultivated support on the left, particularly from the Peking communist faction, charging that general studies was a plot to introduce "Kansas-style" education into San Marcos. (The Ford Foundation had been supporting the planning for the general studies program, and the consultant was from the University of Kansas.)

This campaign got Sanchez elected rector. Matos spoke grudgingly of Sanchez as "the old master." After the election, the attacks on our program faded away.

Finally, for all the political furor accompanying the attacks, we had the firm support of two old men of enormous intellectual prestige who were detached from political battles—Luis Valcarcel and Dr. Carlos Monge—and we were fortunate to be associated with Cornell, which had established such a good reputation through the Vicos project.

31. *Winding Up the Rural Research Program in Peru*

For his sabbatical year, 1967–68, Larry Williams was Cornell's field director. Larry had been working hard on his Spanish, so he could participate fully in planning discussions. He also collaborated with Cotler on field work in the highlands.

In 1968, Giorgio Alberti became Cornell's field director. He had come from Italy to Cornell to do graduate work in the Department of Sociology and then had shifted to Organizational Behavior. He was interested in a methodology for studying intervillage systems, developed by Frank Young in the Department of Rural Sociology. Giorgio asked if he could do a study of intervillage systems in Peru for his doctoral thesis. It seemed only tangentially related to our program, but Larry and I encouraged him to go ahead.

Giorgio decided to work in Huancayo in the Mantaro Valley. We supplied him with contacts at the IEP and with Huancayo students who had worked on our 1964 surveys.

In Huancayo, Giorgio met LaMond Tullis, a student from another U.S. university. Tullis had vague ideas of what he wanted to study and no money for student assistants, but he had one important asset: a Volkswagen station wagon.

Giorgio persuaded LaMond to join him in a study of intervillage systems. LaMond provided transportation, and Giorgio provided the student assistants, and jointly they taught informal seminars on research methods and social theories.

On each field trip, the VW would drop off the students in a village and Giorgio and LaMond would go on and do their own fieldwork. On the way out, they would discuss plans, and on the way back, they would discuss what they had found out. This arrangement worked so well that they soon exhausted the villages in the Mantaro Valley and moved on to the neighboring Yanamarca Valley.

During 1969, as we began planning our resurveys, we recognized that we had become seriously overextended. We had 1964 data on twenty-six villages in six regions. The more intensive anthropological studies were far behind. Further, we had been too ambitious in trying to work with six universities. The rising influence of communism in the university had made it impossible to continue in Arequipa. Our most spectacular fiasco, however, had been in Ayacucho. The professor in charge—let's call him Sanchez—had previously been assigned to direct the Mantaro Valley surveys. He had been recommended as one of the best scholars in Peru, but he just handed out the questionnaires to the fieldworkers and collected them afterward, paying no attention to the sampling design and neglecting to check on how the surveys were filled out. Nevertheless, the enterprising students surveyed such a large sample in the villages that we decided, after throwing out some unusable surveys, that we could continue to work with the data.

Sanchez was to be a visiting professor at the University of Huamonga in Ayacucho. I told him we were dissatisfied with his performance, and he promised to do better. The Ayacucho surveys were to be done in December 1964. We had translated the survey into Quechua for the Cuzco studies, but all the adults in the Chancay and Mantaro valleys spoke Spanish. I thought we might need a translation into the Quechua dialect spoken around Ayacucho. Sanchez assured me that "everyone around Ayacucho speaks Spanish." I told him he should do some pretesting to check that assumption.

Sanchez claimed he had encountered bureaucratic delays at the University, so the fieldwork could not begin before Christmas vacation. He handed out the forms to the students before he left to spend the holidays in another city. When he returned, he collected the filled-out questionnaires.

In January, I was in Ayacucho to conduct a feedback discussion with Sanchez and his student assistants. When I asked if they had had any problems, one student said, "Some of the people we interviewed did not understand Spanish."

I looked at Sanchez. He laughed nervously and said, "That surprised us all." I hesitated but then asked the obvious question: "How many people did not speak Spanish?" The answer: "I would say about 95 percent."

Students who spoke no Quechua had simply to drop out. The others improvised their own translations.

Not knowing what else to do, we put the Ayacucho surveys on IBM data cards at Cornell. This led to a discovery Larry Williams and I called "the Swiss cheese phenomenon." Looking at the stack of cards against a window, he could see all the way through them at a number of points. Perhaps for the first time in survey history, we had encountered populations who all shared exactly the same opinions on various questions!

I should have just dropped Ayacucho from the research design, but I would not admit defeat. Instead, I arranged with a Cornell graduate student from Argentina who was planning to return home to go first to Ayacucho. That did not work out either, so we wasted still more money.

When we eliminated Arequipa and Ayacucho and dropped several other villages where our anthropological studies were inadequate, we were left with twelve villages, four in the Chancay Valley, three in the Mantaro Valley, four in the Cuzco area, and Virú, on the north coast. Oscar Nuñez del Prado continued to be a tower of strength, and we were able to maintain working relations with professors in the universities of Huancayo and Trujillo.

For the resurveys in 1969, we decided to rely much more heavily on the IEP than we had for the 1964 surveys. Giorgio and Julio Cotler were in charge overall. In each region, an IEP staff member who had performed well on the 1964 surveys took charge of recruiting and training survey interviewers and supervised the whole process.

After the resurveys were conducted, I suggested to Giorgio that he and I write a book on our village study program (Whyte and Alberti 1976). We were pleased to find how well the surveys and anthropological studies fitted together. In case after case, we found the survey data helped us understand what the anthropological studies told us was going on in the community, and the anthropological data helped us interpret the surveys. This integration also led us to a theoretical breakthrough on the perceptions of conflict and cooperation in communities. It happened when I was reading the anthropological report on the village of Mito in the Mantaro Valley.

The report stated that Mito was low in both conflict and cooperation. That struck me as odd. Could it possibly be true? I pulled out the survey data for both 1964 and 1969 and discovered that indeed Mito respondents rated their village lower than average on levels of conflict and cooperation.

Based on the academic literature, I had assumed that conflict and cooperation were at opposite ends of the same dimension, that a village that was low in conflict would be high in cooperation. In other words, I expected a high *negative* correlation between these variables.

We then ran the correlations of the two variables for the twelve villages for both 1964 and 1969. The correlations were as close to *zero* as one could get without cooking the data. Here was a rare case of a zero correlation that was statistically significant in proving that what had been assumed was false.

By lining up one dimension perpendicular to the other, we created a four-box framework: high cooperation and low conflict, high cooperation and high conflict, high conflict and low cooperation, and low conflict and low cooperation. At least one of our villages fell into each of those four boxes. Furthermore, five of the twelve villages moved from one box to another from 1964 to 1969. That movement helped explain what had happened in the intervening years.

As I worked my way through from problem diagnosis to the discovery of the solution, I felt a sense of elation that tempted me to shout "EUREKA." Like my colleagues, I had assumed that combining surveys with anthropological methods would be useful in some general way, but now I had demonstrated that the combination was *essential* for solving some important problems. Before that discovery, I had not considered that I had any skill in interpreting survey data, but now, although I did not do the correlation calculations myself, I had the idea that led to the solution.

Without this combination of research methods, it is hard to imagine how this theoretical advance could have been achieved. If I had only relied on the anthropological studies, I would not have believed a student's report when professional anthropologists provided conflicting interpretations of the same community. Relying on the survey data alone, it would not have occurred to me to check the correlations between perceptions of conflict and perceptions of cooperation. If I had found a zero correlation, I would not have known how to interpret it.

There was also a payoff I did not expect from the historical research. It had been well known that Mantaro Valley villages were more dynamic and democratic than most in the highlands and that this was in part because there were no large land holdings, but how that had come about was not clear until a Peruvian historian (Espinoza 1973) traced the history of the valley back to the first century after the Spanish conquest. As Francisco Pizarro and his small band of conquerors approached the Mantaro Valley, they were alarmed to see thousands of Huancas lined up. About fifty years earlier, the Incas had conquered the Huancas, and the Huancas were there to enlist the Spaniards as allies against the Incas. After some days of ceremonies, the two parties signed a treaty. In return for acknowledging Spanish sovereignty, the Huancas retained control of their lands and local affairs.

The treaty was violated as Spaniards began taking over large areas and making the Indians work for them. Decades later, two Huancas managed to get aboard a ship to Spain. At the royal court, they displayed their document and demanded restoration of their rights. Surprised and impressed, the monarch ordered his viceroy in Lima to oust the usurpers from the Mantaro Valley. That secured the valley for small farmers and merchants. Economic activities were further stimulated by the development of mining companies in the mountains just west of the valley in the late nineteenth century and the construction of the Central Railroad from Lima to Huancayo and the Central Highway in the early years of the twentieth century.

This account came from secondary sources, but students researched the histories of the villages in the Chancay Valley. They discovered documents going back to the 1850s. Even when few of the villagers were literate, there always was at least one person who could keep records.

Our experience supported *multiobjective planning* and *joint payoffs* as the bases of our success in carrying out an extraordinarily ambitious research program, in the face of tremendous obstacles, over more than a decade. We did not reach all our objectives, but we kept moving toward those that were still reachable.

By the late 1960s, the IEP had become the leading Peruvian producer of social research and publications. Too heavily dependent on Cornell in the early years, the IEP had major support within Peru by the 1970s. This began when a friend introduced José Matos Mar to Luis Banchero, the fish meal king. Over a long dinner and discussion, Banchero offered the IEP a grant.

Matos consulted me about an unfamiliar dilemma. A new Ford Foundation official had told Matos that Ford would now be happy to receive a proposal from the IEP. Should he take the Ford grant or Banquero's offer? I advised him to take the Peruvian money, which he probably would have done anyway.

After supporting the IEP for a year, Banchero invited Matos to come to his office the day after New Year's to agree on the terms for an expanded grant. On New Year's Day, Luis Banchero was murdered. Although that ended Banchero's support, Matos was now able to go back to Ford for a substantial grant—and others followed from international sources.

The IEP also managed to survive serious internal problems for many years. The first crisis occurred in 1970 in the weeks following the International Congress of Americanists, which met every two years, alternating between Europe and the Western Hemisphere. Matos had won this year's congress over a U.S. city, a great honor for the IEP and Peru but also a very heavy responsibility for an institution that had no organizational infrastructure to manage such large meetings.

For many months before the congress, Matos was completely occupied with planning and organizing. He made Fernando Fuenzalida secretary of the congress, which meant Matos was constantly calling on him to attend to congress business. Fuenzalida had been the leader of the group studying Huayopampa and was writing a book on that village. He was widely regarded as the most able of those working with Matos.

Over lunch, Fuenzalida told me he was unhappy about his relations with Matos. He recognized that his responsibilities with the congress had given him important international contacts, but he was chafing under Matos's domination. I urged him to sit down with Matos to discuss their relationship. Fuenzalida said he would.

He never did. Fernando persuaded some of the young IEP staff members that Matos was exploiting them and they therefore should establish their own institute. To secure financing, Fernando had talked to Carlos Delgado, (a former Cornell fellowship student), who was a chief adviser to General Juan Velasco Alvarado, the president of the military government. This was done secretly so they could remain on the IEP's payroll until the plot succeeded.

Delgado informed Luis Soberón, who had played a leading role in our survey program, of the plot, and Soberón told Matos, who thereupon fired Fernando and his followers. The uprising was a terrible shock to Matos, who felt he had given this younger generation opportunities to establish themselves in field research and to publish their reports.

Matos had had similar problems with protégées in the past. He was known for getting very good people to work with him, but many felt that if they were not under his thumb, they would never have a chance to win the international fellowships they were all seeking. Some of those who gained career opportunities through Matos looked forward to the time when they would no longer be under his domination. At the same time, friends of his told me that, after some of these younger people abandoned Matos to go out on their own, they never accomplished anything that lived up to the promise they had shown while working with him.

Shortly after this blow, Matos was hit with another. Julio Cotler had teamed up with Anibal Quijano to publish a journal called *Sociedad y Política*. The journal carried on the back cover of its first issue a woodcut of Karl Marx. The leading editorial stated that the journal was fulfilling a great need in Peru by providing a Marxist critique of current political and economic affairs. I wrote Julio that this was the last thing Peru needed. Matos had not been consulted and was very upset.

The political leaders of the time claimed that theirs was a revolutionary government of the armed forces, but a Marxist revolution was not what they had in mind. They tolerated the journal for a while but then exiled Julio.

Giorgio Alberti had stood by Matos in the Fuenzalida crisis, and now Matos came to depend on him more and more. After our joint program ended, Giorgio continued on salary with the IEP until he returned to Italy as a professor at the University of Bologna.

Six of our field-workers went on to gain master's or Ph.D. degrees abroad, three at Cornell, three at British universities. They were able to move faster than native students because they began with their own research reports from our program. Five returned to pursue academic careers in Peru. Fitting in academically was not difficult because they were known for the research and writing they had done before going abroad and had already begun to focus their research careers on Peruvian materials and problems. Cornell did not finance these fellowships, but it was our program in Peru that enabled students to win them.

The program had reshaped my own theories about rural development. We had thought that some outside force was needed to modernize traditional villages. That outside force never materialized. Nevertheless, we traced major changes, largely generated internally, in many of our twelve villages in just a five-year period. I now referred to what we earlier had believed as "the myth of the passive peasant."

This reorientation led us to expand the coverage of the book Giorgio and I were writing. We would still focus primarily on our twelve village studies, but we also included treatments of two regional peasant movements. The story of the Yanamarca Valley movement was based on fieldwork for Giorgio's doctoral thesis, during which he and the students had extended their Mantaro Valley studies into the neighboring valley. There, they found themselves studying villages that only a few years earlier had been haciendas, dominated by large landowners. The Convencion Valley movement had been much in the Lima press during 1961–62. It was led by Hugo Blanco, a colorful, folk-singing Trotskyite who eluded the police and the army for several years. By 1970, that valley, which had been dominated by haciendas, had been transformed into independent villages.

We had to abandon the objective of strengthening six Peruvian universities in teaching and research in anthropology and sociology, but we were successful in strengthening the IEP during the 1960s and 1970s.

On our objective to demonstrate the potential scientific and practical gains achievable through integrating surveys and anthropological methods, we did not convince our Peruvian collaborators. Our first publication in Spanish, on the Chancay Valley project, jointly written by Matos, me, Cotler, Williams, Alers, Fuenzalida, and Alberti (1969), states the case for our methodological and theoretical approach. I contributed the last two chapters, one on our orientation to social theory, the other on our integrated and interdisciplinary methodology.

When Fuenzalida and his coauthors were writing their book on Huayo-pampa, I pointed out that they made no reference to the survey data, even though some of them had done survey interviews there. Why did they leave out the surveys? Fuenzalida said, "We didn't think the answers to those questions meant anything."

I asked them if they had noted at how many points the survey responses fitted perfectly with their anthropological interpretations. They agreed that this was true. I tried to suggest that they were behaving unscientifically by neglecting to include the survey data in their analysis. They went ahead and published an excellent, but purely anthropological, study.

I suspect that Matos went along with our research design because he saw the Cornell-IEP program as an opportunity to support further anthropological studies and publications and needed the money to support the institute. He followed through on all his commitments when we worked together, but other-wise continued with solely anthropological studies. At the same time, our pro-gram had produced anthropological studies that were being widely used in uni-versity teaching.

I was disappointed in the review of *Power, Politics and Progress: Social Change in Rural Peru* (Whyte and Alberti 1976) by Paul Doughty in the *American Anthropologist*. Besides charging us (incorrectly) with mixing up the geographi-cal locations of the Departments of Cuzco and Junin, he reviewed the book as if it were based entirely on survey research. In fact, only five of twenty-two chap-ters present any survey data whatsoever. Nor does Doughty make any reference to our uses of history. In other words, he simply ignores our claim that anthro-pological studies can be enriched by the integration of surveys and historical data.

In two articles, in the *American Ethnologist* (1975) and the *American Sociologist* (1976), I made further attempts to interest anthropologists and sociologists in methods for studying conflict and cooperation, and those articles did draw some requests for reprints. In recent years, I have noted among sociologists a growing disillusionment with survey research as *the* sociological method and an increasing openness to qualitative research. Perhaps some of them will now be persuaded not to give up on surveys but to integrate them with anthropological methods.

32. *Finding a New Focus*

The Peruvian program was my longest lasting and, after the North End, my most intense field experience. I had mixed feelings about ending the program. The collaborative relations with Matos were ideal. Kathleen and I enjoyed living in Lima, especially from 1971 to 1975. By then, the children were on their own, so we could get away for two months each year during the period from January to March—the middle of Peru's summer—thus missing much of the northern winter. As time went on and acquaintances turned into friends, we felt at home.

I had met some of the leading figures in management and labor during my early trips, and the rural research program introduced me to the villagers. In the 1962 presidential campaign, I had met the leading candidates. With the Members and Friends of IPAE, I sat in on dinner and evening discussions with Victor Raul Haya de la Torre and with Fernando Beláunde Terry, who became president in 1963.

I had also met some of the members of the traditional social and economic oligarchy and of the military government, which took power from 1962 to 1963, and of those who called themselves "the Revolutionary Government of the Armed Forces," who were in control for eleven years beginning in 1968.

It was a heady feeling to have such far-reaching contacts with such *important* people. I saw myself as tuning in to the major trends in Peru's social and economic structures. But still I recognized that I was only a spectator and not actually involved with large-scale changes or really studying them. I realized that I had completed the work I set out to do in Peru and now I was just marking time. It was time to move on.

My experience in Peru had had a major impact on my teaching. For several years Larry Williams and I taught a seminar based on our studies there. We focused on our survey data and the anthropological studies—for those who could read Spanish.

Larry Williams was an imaginative and gifted interpreter of survey data. The students and I learned much from him, and my own teaching performance was enhanced by the collaboration as we relived the intellectual excitement of our Peruvian program. Several students later told us that their trial runs on live data in this seminar had done more than any other studies to prepare them for their doctoral research in the field.

The Peruvian experience also led me to develop two new courses. In "Government Bureaucracy and Social and Economic Development," I combined an organizational behavior analysis of large government organizations with an emphasis on problems of rural development. Our study of the industrial community in Peru turned my attention to "Systems of Labor Participation in Management," which I taught until I retired.

The villages had been in the foreground of my studies and agricultural extension and research in the background, noticed only when they affected the villagers. Now I brought agricultural research and extension into the foreground.

Three developments led me in this direction. The first was when a former student, Douglas Horton, the head of the economics unit of the International Potato Center (IPC), headquartered in Peru, invited me to accompany him to Colombia to advise its national research program on its so far unsuccessful effort to develop a dependable supply of disease-free seed potatoes.

Some of the professors in the College of Agriculture and Life Sciences had already become concerned with the limited impact "the green revolution" was having on small farmers. The spectacular development of new higher-yielding seed varieties, especially for wheat and rice, had produced enormous gains in yields, but the gains had been primarily by farmers on large, irrigated lands. Studies were now indicating that small farmers, who depended on rainfall, had hardly benefited from the scientific breakthroughs. Concerned about these findings, the Cornell professors had formed a group to exchange information and ideas on ways to help small farmers gain access to the fruits of scientific research.

At the same time, the Rural Development Committee in the Center for International Studies, under the leadership of political scientist Norman Uphoff, had begun paying special attention to the problems of small farmers and their families. The committee attracted an interdisciplinary group in the social and agricultural sciences, and the agricultural scientists and the social scientists were recognizing that they needed each other.

Vice President Long of Cornell secured a grant from the AID to set up the Program for Policies for Science and Technology in Developing Nations (PPSTDN) within the Center for International Studies. Long was chairman of the executive committee for the program, and Edward Cranch, dean of the College of Engineering, served as director. Long invited me to join the executive committee. I admired Frank Long. Highly regarded in his own field of chemistry, he had been slated to become head of the National Science Foundation until President Richard Nixon blocked the appointment because of Long's active involvement in the anti–Vietnam War movement.

I decided to focus on the organizational aspects of agricultural research and development. In that way, I could build on my background of rural community research and my years studying organizations in industry. As far as I knew, no one before me had designed such a study.

This new direction produced a marked change in my relations with Kathleen. She had always been interested in my research, and we had often discussed what I was doing. In this new stage, we were together on nearly all my field activities. I depended on her to do all the driving of rental cars, which I could not safely drive. Having her along added interest and enjoyment to our marriage. While I took the lead in interviews, Kathleen often thought of questions I had failed to ask, and discussions with her helped me get my ideas in order.

PPSTDN financed study visits to CIMMYT, the International Center for Maize and Wheat Improvement in Mexico, and to CIAT, the International Center for Tropical Agriculture in Colombia, and field studies carried out in Guatemala, Honduras, and Costa Rica. The visit to CIMMYT provided the basic framework for everything else I did in agricultural research and development.

CIMMYT and the International Rice Research Institute (IRRI) in the Philippines were known throughout the world for developing the higher-yielding wheat and rice that gave rise to "the green revolution." Norman Borlaug, director of the CIMMYT wheat program, had been awarded a Nobel Prize.

CIMMYT headquarters was at El Batán, about an hour's drive from Mexico City, but the center for Mexican wheat production and research was in the northwest, on large land holdings supported by a government-financed irrigation system. In the center's guest house, we met Borlaug and spent an evening interviewing him, but my interest was drawn more to the maize program, particularly the project under way in the state of Puebla.

The work of Ernest Sprague, the director of CIMMYT's maize program, had been overshadowed by Borlaug's spectacular achievements. Mexico's maize was grown by thousands of small farmers, and, although CIMMYT had not been able to develop new varieties of maize that substantially improved yields, Sprague assumed that major gains could be achieved through a scientific program of cultivation and fertilization.

When I was visiting CIMMYT in 1975, I read its official report, *The Puebla Project: Seven Years of Experience, 1967–1973*. Puebla was a demonstration project whose planners were committed to the concept of *technology transfer*, the idea that the technology already existed to bring about substantial improvements. The problem was to make it possible for small farmers to adopt the methods available. Since the improved methods could not be applied without more fertilizer, the project made arrangements with the Agricultural Bank of Mexico to facilitate crop loans to farmers who committed themselves to farming according to project instructions.

Participating farmers achieved substantial yield increases (about 30 percent), but they were still far below the increases in wheat. Furthermore, the planners were disappointed when the percentage of participants leveled off at about 25 percent of the total number of maize farmers in the state of Puebla.

These results led Mexican staff members to go into the field to interview farmers who had not adopted the project methodology. And this led to a startling discovery: *Some of the more successful nonadopters were achieving total crop yields of twice the value of the adopters!*

How could this be possible? The nonadopters were cultivating beans in the corn rows, thus making much more efficient use of the same space and fertilizer. The adopters had left fallow the space between the rows of corn, as Iowa corn farmers do. But Iowans farm large tracts of land and drive tractors through those fallow spaces. Where land and money are scarce and ample labor is available as in Puebla, tractors are out of the question.

The planners in Puebla had failed to recognize that the logic of the Iowa system did not apply to Puebla, where farmers could do better with intercropping. Instead, they had promoted the conventional crop-specialization system of agricultural experiment stations.

How could the ablest American and Mexican agricultural scientists have made such a basic error? We got the answer from Mauro Gomez, the general coordinator of the Puebla Project from 1970 to 1973, in one of those rare but treasured interviews when the informant makes a statement that suddenly propels us toward a new theoretical framework. According to Gomez,

In Mexico we have been mentally deformed by our professional education. Without realizing what was happening to us, in the classroom and in the laboratories we were learning that scientists knew all that had so far been learned about agriculture and that the small farmers did not know anything. Finally, we had to realize that there was much we could learn from the small farmers.

His comment led me to an analysis of the common thoughtways of professionally trained agricultural scientists relative to the thoughtways of peasant farmers. The framework I was developing viewed the research and development process as involving two-way communication and the initiation of action between professional experts and small farmers. This framework laid out the agenda for what would become my studies of the agricultural R&D process.

~

The mission of PPSTDN required participants to do research and consult with one or more national governments on their policies for the development of science and technology. Where we worked depended on the answers to two questions: What governments were interested in working with us, and on what basis were we choosing where to work.

I thought the executive committee had decided that we would not provide advice to a highly repressive government. When it was reported that the government of Guatemala had expressed a strong interest in our program, I raised the political issue. Guatemala's government had a terrible reputation for political repression and the violation of human rights. I urged that, before any decision was made, we seek up-to-date information and suggested calling anthropologist Richard N. Adams, who had studied Guatemala and whose wife was Guatemalan. As I understood it, the decision was put off for later consideration.

At the next executive committee meeting, I was shocked to learn that a letter of agreement had been signed and that a delegation of Guatemalan officials would be meeting with PPSTDN at Cornell several weeks later. I resigned from PPSTDN in protest.

At the time, program director Edward Cranch was traveling in Europe, but program chairman Frank Long decided to reverse the decision and informed AID that we were not accepting the invitation to Guatemala and were asking AID's help in finding another potential partner. This created an awkward problem not only for our relations with AID and Guatemala, but also for the relations between the program chairman and the program director because Long had not been able to communicate with Cranch before reversing the decision. I was awed by Long's audacity. He recognized that a serious mistake had been made, and he thought it was important to get me back into the program. A decision was made to work with Costa Rica, and I did get involved in that project, but the most interesting research site during my association with PPS-TDN turned out to be in—of all places—Guatemala.

I had heard that a highly innovative program was developing in Guatemala supported partially by the Rockefeller Foundation but with strong leadership by Guatemalans. Would doing this research violate the principle I was upholding in protesting PPSTDN's involvement with the Guatemalan government? I got around this concern by reasoning that I would only be studying this innovative research and development program and would not be advising the government.

We made several study trips to Guatemala, and during one I worked with graduate student Lynn Gostyla documenting the historical development of the Instituto de Ciencia y Tecnologia Agricolas (Institute for Agricultural Science and Technology, or ICTA) and focusing on how agricultural researchers worked with small farmers, integrating their experience-based information and ideas into the R&D process.

Guatemala offered many attractions besides research. We managed to combine research trips with sightseeing and visits to village markets to enjoy the wonderful woven textiles, which were Kathleen's special interest. We had mixed reactions to the country: wonderful people, terrible government—partially foisted on the people when the Eisenhower administration sponsored a CIA-directed coup to oust the democratically elected government of Jacobo Arbenz, who was thought to be "soft on communism."

When we arrived in Quezaltenango, the second largest city, I was eager to get to the offices of DIGESA, the agricultural extension agency, before closing time so I could set up interviews for the following morning. We had the address and a city map but still got lost. At last we saw a man and woman on the sidewalk and called out for help. The woman did not know where the DIGESA offices were, so I tried another approach. I showed her the city map and asked, "Can you tell me where we are?"

"Yes," she replied, "You are in Quezaltenango, Guatemala, Central America." We thanked her and went on our way. Fortunately, DIGESA's offices were around the next corner.

In Mexico and Central America, I was getting in on the early stages of major changes in research and development strategies that put new focus on the practices, interests, and needs of small farmers. Up to this point, agricultural experiment stations had been operated to serve the interests of large farmers, who generally specialized on one particular crop. Agricultural planners were now recognizing that small farmers did not specialize, that generally they cultivated several crops, and that usually they also raised livestock. This had led to a new research focus on *farming systems*. Since there was no research background on farming systems, researchers had to begin by studying what small farmers were doing and in effect, to learn from them. This new focus also led to a shift in the location of research, so that increasing numbers of projects were carried out on farmers' fields, with the active participation of the farmers.

The involvement of farmers also stimulated the broadening of the research base of agricultural programs. They had begun with a strictly technological focus on how changes in the application of the plant, soil, and animal sciences could increase agricultural productivity. Economics was the first social science discipline to be included in the broader base, since the agricultural experimenters needed new and better ways of measuring the impact of their programs. With increasing attention to small farmers and the development of farming systems research came a recognition of the need to broaden the research base even further to include anthropology, sociology, and political science.

I was fortunate to link up with Douglas Horton, who was the first person in all the international agricultural research centers to adopt a more participatory, broader approach to research. Beginning as the head of the economics unit of the ICP, he transformed it into the Social Science Program, in which anthropologists and sociologists became actively involved.

33. Cornell in the 1960s

T he 1960s started off tranquilly for me. In 1963, I became president of the Industrial Relations Research Association (IRRA). The next year, I became president of the Society for Applied Anthropology. Although the title sounded impressive, the most important figure in the organization was the editor of *Human Organization*. Since I had already held that position, this was an anticlimax.

From 1960 to 1964, I served on the President's Committee on Research for the Prudential Insurance Company. Membership included economists John Kenneth Galbraith and William Baumol, political scientist Harold Lasswell, sociologist Paul Lazarsfeld, and behavioral scientist Chris Argyris. We were asked to discuss trends that could affect the insurance industry—and since any important social and economic change could have an impact, this was a license for far-reaching reflections.

Also beginning in the 1960s, I worked with the U.S. Department of Labor as a member of the subcommittee on Research of the National Manpower Advisory Committee, chaired by Eli Ginzberg, a Columbia University economist. I was the first noneconomist to serve on the subcommittee. Social psychologist Richard Shore had somehow managed to get a staff position in a department dominated by economists, and he had proposed that I be asked to join. Later, from 1968 to 1972, I was its chairman. By this time the membership had been broadened to include other sociologists and psychologists.

I did not have to persuade Ginzberg and Howard Rosen (staff director of research at the Department of Labor) to broaden the disciplinary base of research. They wanted to find ways to integrate studies of sociological and psychological factors with economic variables. That experience made me optimistic about the future of Department of Labor research, but that judgment was soon proved wrong. In the 1980s, Ronald Reagan's first Secretary of Labor is reported to have told his staff, "I don't want research. I want action."

By the 1960s, I also felt ready to write a textbook on organizational behavior. To get students involved, I organized a weekly seminar in my home. I handed out drafts of the various chapters and asked for criticism and advice on how to relate the topic under discussion to the research literature. Students enjoyed the seminar and seemed to take pride in contributing to my book.

Men at Work was published in 1965. The sexist title embarrasses me, particularly since the book also deals with women workers and supervisors. It never sold well and soon went out of print. Still, I decided to take one more try. The revisions seemed major enough to justify calling this a new book with the title of *Organizational Behavior: Theory and Application* (1969).

The indifference of my academic colleagues fully matched their reception to *Men at Work*. Some greeted both books with enthusiasm, but they were not numerous enough to keep either book alive. Although I was considered an important contributor to the literature on organizational behavior, I had proved that I could not write a successful textbook.

I had aimed to give professors and students a sense of what working life was like in factories, oil fields, restaurants, hotels, and so on. I relied primarily on case studies (particularly my own). Although my field experience was unusually broad, it did not cover all the topics customarily found in an organizational behavior text. As Kathleen has reminded me, I neglected certain topics because they did not interest me. Then too, I was always falling between two stools. I wanted to produce a book that would be read with pleasure not only by students majoring in the behavioral sciences but also by anyone interested in the situations described. I accomplished that feat with *Street Corner Society* but not with any book later on.

I drew on other researchers' survey findings on some of the issues, but surveys did not bulk large in the text. Mainstream sociologists were doing surveys and testing hypotheses statistically, which had come to be *the scientific method*. I had learned to value surveys, but reliance on that method alone failed to reflect the complex realities I encountered as I interviewed workers, union leaders, and managers and observed them in action.

～

The decade of the 1960s was marked by two major protest movements: the campaign for civil rights and the resistance to our involvement in the Vietnam

War. I believed in both movements and saw them come together at Cornell. Among the students, the leading war protest organization was Students for a Democratic Society (SDS).

The debate on Vietnam split the Cornell community. I felt it most vividly in my car pool, which at the time consisted of Bob Ferguson, Duncan Macintyre, and me. Bob was an agonizing supporter of the war and Duncan was an all-out hawk. So as to maintain some semblance of peace, we had to agree not to discuss the war. Since I found it hard to think of anything else during those drives, this was a difficult truce to maintain. What had been a pleasant experience was now becoming just a necessary trip.

In June 1966, I slipped and fell in the kitchen and broke my left leg. We had planned to spend some weeks in Peru, but that had to be put off until fall. We had already rented our house for the summer school period and were therefore grateful when two organizational behavior professors, Ned Rosen and Leo Gruenfeld, offered us their homes in the Cayuga Heights area of Ithaca for a month each when they would be away.

For some time, we had planned to move nearer to Cornell after the children finished high school, and John was now in his sophomore year. Trumansburg life revolved around families, and we felt it would be less appealing when we were alone. Breaking my leg made us realize we needed a house that better accommodated my needs.

While staying in Cayuga Heights that summer, we saw a two-and-a-half-acre plot of land in Lansing, a little north of Cornell, on a hillside overlooking Lake Cayuga. We were lucky to find an architect who was willing to let Kathleen be involved in every detail of the plans. We had three principal requirements: (1) the house had to be all on one floor, since stairs were becoming difficult for me; (2) there had to be an enclosed pool, since swimming was my only exercise, especially in winter; and (3) it had to have an attached apartment. Both sets of our parents had had to give up their homes late in life when they could not manage them alone. At some point, we might need live-in help. Meanwhile, we would rent our apartment to graduate student couples.

The architect was endlessly patient as Kathleen redrew his plans to make them "handicap accessible." She checked for wheelchair accessibility everywhere. I cannot bend my knees without falling, so electric outlets were set high, and the dishwasher was raised so I could reach both shelves—which turned out to be better for everyone. Many small details were included, such as grab bars in the bathroom and phone jacks in every room. We also installed roll-down screens and thermopane windows so we wouldn't have to change storm windows and screens.

We had to move out of our Trumansburg home on September 1, 1968, but an exceptionally rainy spring had delayed construction of the new home into the late fall. We rented an eight-by-thirty-foot trailer, which was trucked to our lot. (Lucy was now in a Cornell dormitory.) Kathleen, John, and I, plus a cat that delivered a batch of kittens, lived in that cramped space until mid-December. I spent much more time than usual at the office, and I was in Peru in November and early December. In late November, the hose supplying water to the trailer froze, and Kathleen, John, and the cats had to move into a half-finished house where the temperature never got above fifty.

Since Kathleen was now on the spot, she began supervising most of the job. Once, without calling the architect, she countermanded his plans just as the carpenters were about to drill holes for electric lights ten feet above the middle of the pool. She ordered them to place the fixtures on the walls. When the architect questioned her decision, she agreed that the lights in the ceiling would be more attractive but asked, "What will we do then when we need to change a bulb?"

With beds for plants, pots on the floor, and hanging baskets, we had a year-round garden in our pool room. In the warm weather, we could leave the windows open on two sides, which made the room seem as if it were outdoors. In colder weather, to cut down on the condensation, we kept the pool covered. With a winch and three ropes and pulleys, Kathleen devised a system that enabled me to crank the plastic cover high above the pool or lower it in a minute or so, with very little effort.

Shortly after we moved into our new house, colleges throughout the United States struggled in the wake of the student uprisings. The story of Cornell's uprising is worth telling because the crisis and its aftermath directly affected my life, and I also played a minor role in the events leading up to the crisis.

James Perkins became president of Cornell in 1963. He had graduated from Swarthmore College two years ahead of me. He greeted me as "my oldest friend at Cornell." A more accurate statement would have been "my oldest acquaintance at Cornell," but I did not object since I had always thought well of him. He had been second in command at the Carnegie Corporation and chairman of the board of trustees of the United Negro College Fund.

In 1963, among Cornell's approximately fifteen thousand students, there were fewer than twenty blacks, and of those there were, many were from abroad. Perkins made it a priority to recruit increasingly more blacks from America.

Other universities were moving in the same direction, but Cornell appeared to be out in front. Perkins even had the strong moral and financial support of board chairman Robert Purcell. From 1965 through 1968, Cornell's annual admission of American blacks rose from thirty-seven to forty-nine to sixty-seven, and then to ninety-four.

During this period, Cornell's black students were increasingly influenced by national civil rights developments. Although Martin Luther King, Jr., was revered by most blacks, a growing number followed the more militant strategy espoused by Malcolm X and responded to the "black power" slogan proclaimed by Stokely Carmichael, leader of the Student Non-Violent Coordinating Committee. The most militant black students were in the Afro-American Society (AAS).

The first black-white confrontation occurred in the spring of 1968 in an introductory economics class taught by a visiting professor. The professor made some remark about urban slum conditions that a black student considered racist, and he raised his hand to object. The professor ignored him. After class, the student confronted the professor and demanded an apology. The professor apologized, but that was not enough. The student demanded that he apologize to the whole class, which he did during the following class. Also during that class, several of the black students informed the professor that they had a written statement that they wanted to read to the class. The professor asked to see the statement. When the students refused, the professor dismissed the class.

Sixty black students converged on the office of Tom Davis, chairman of the Department of Economics, and held him hostage for six and a half hours. Eventually, an agreement was worked out between the students and the provost and the dean of the college. The university would pay the expenses for someone the students chose to come to Cornell and speak in the professor's class. Although violence was avoided, the deal upset some faculty members, who considered it a serious violation of the professor's academic freedom.

In the fall of 1968, President Perkins established the Afro-American Studies Program under the temporary chairmanship of economics professor Chandler Morse, who also chaired an advisory committee to the program. The main business of the committee was to select and recruit a black scholar to direct the program.

The committee consisted of eight black students and nine members of the faculty or administration. When Chan Morse asked me to join the committee, I realized that I would be getting into the middle of very highly charged issues, but I thought being a member was important and that the experience would be interesting—which indeed it was.

Except for one professor in the School of Hotel Administration, Cornell had no blacks on the faculty or in the administration. Since the lone black professor was not on the committee, any disagreement between students and faculty/administration was likely to be seen in racial terms rather than in terms of functions and status.

Further, there was an ideological split among the black students on campus. The black members of the committee believed in negotiating issues, but they also had to be on guard against saying anything that could be interpreted as yielding to the whites, particularly since the more militant blacks were well represented as observers at our meetings.

I thought Chan was handling a highly charged situation exceedingly well. He provided ample opportunity for the black students to air their grievances and yet managed to steer the discussion toward action.

The student members of the committee seemed determined to give us a hard time, yet we did make progress. In our next-to-last meeting, we came to a unanimous agreement that James Turner, a doctoral student in anthropology at Northwestern University, would be our first choice for director of the Afro-American Studies Program. Turner was a militant leader among the black students at Northwestern, but he also had strong recommendations from several of his professors. Chan announced that he would telephone Turner and invite him to come to Cornell to discuss the terms of his appointment.

At our last meeting, on December 6, four black students, dressed in black suits, came to our committee meeting and stood silently by the wall. A student member of the committee asked them if they had something to say. Their spokesman told us that Cornell should abandon the nonsense of negotiations, disband the committee, immediately establish a black college, and give it a building and a million dollars. A student committee member asked, "Will you take questions?" The spokesman said, "No," and the four students walked out.

Steven Muller, the vice president for public affairs, and Chan Morse met with leaders of the AAS in a vain effort to reestablish negotiations. On December 12, President Perkins rejected the demand for an autonomous black college. In response, members of AAS marched through several buildings, damaged some property, and then converged on President Perkins's office to deliver a letter reaffirming their demands. They occupied his office and conducted a "seminar" that consisted of playing bongo drums and reading black poetry. They also overturned a cart of refreshments that Perkins had provided for them.

Next, they went to Cornell's medical clinic to demand appointments with a nonexistent black psychiatrist. And from there, they went to a dining room in the student union, where they played musical instruments and shouted. About thirty of them danced on tables, upsetting some lunches. Finally, they marched through three of Cornell's libraries and dumped an estimated three thousand books on the floor as they announced, "These books have no relevance to me as a black student."

Such disturbances invited punishment by the Student-Faculty Board on Student Conduct (SFBSC), consisting of five students and four professors, and six students were accused of misconduct. When the board met on February 13, 1969, the six failed to appear. The AAS protested the "selective reprisals," charged that the university was in no position to judge "political acts" against it, and that the SFBSC was a racist body because it had no black members. (Tom Jones would have been chairman of the board in 1969, but he had resigned during a dispute in 1968).

Up to this point, the leading group protesting the Vietnam War, Students for a Democratic Society (SDS), and the AAS had been on separate tracks. Now both the AAS and SDS demanded that Cornell divest itself of stocks in banks that had lent money to South Africa. Perkins agreed to address their concerns in an open meeting, but just as he was about to talk, a black student leaped to the stage, grabbed Perkins by the collar, and lifted him slightly, while another black student stood by, holding a wooden two-by-four. Perkins was released shortly, whereupon he declared the meeting canceled and left the hall. The leaders of the AAS condemned the actions of the student who grabbed Perkins and expelled him from their organization.

Now that it had found common ground with the AAS on South Africa, SDS adopted the AAS campus struggle. SDS played a major role in the developments that followed.

The SFBSC was meeting again on March 13. If the six black students again refused to appear, the board proposed to suspend them. The students did not appear. SDS and the AAS came out against the board's sanction. In the largest faculty meeting in Cornell's history, more than six hundred professors voted to support the SFBSC.

On April 15, after a 6½-hour meeting, the SFBSC decided to impose a penalty on the accused black students: a letter of reprimand would be sent to their parents and to the deans of their colleges. AAS challenged even this slap on the wrist.

Late that night, a cross was set afire in front of the black women's residence.

The incident was condemned by the Cornell administration, but the perpetrators were not apprehended, and there were rumors that the fire had been set by male black students.

Early on the morning of April 19, during Parents' Weekend, about one hundred male black students marched into the student union, Willard Straight Hall, and ordered the parents who were staying there out of the building. Meanwhile, some white student members of a fraternity got into the building through an open window. They claimed that they only wanted to talk with the black students, but their entry was treated as a hostile act and a scuffle ensued. The white students were ejected, but according to the blacks, they believed that the whites would return armed. With help from black students outside and SDS, the black students inside got guns themselves.

In a downtown Ithaca parking lot, several hundred sheriffs' deputies from several counties were mobilizing as Cornell's administration strove to keep the crisis from exploding into armed struggle. Finally, Dean Robert Miller got into the student union to negotiate with the black students. After considerable discussion, he agreed that if they would leave the building peaceably, he would recommend that the faculty rescind the disciplinary measures imposed by the SFBSC and the administration would impose no penalties for the takeover.

Before a horde of national TV and newspaper reporters, the students marched out with rifles slung over their shoulders, wearing bandoliers containing cartridges. That scene appeared in many newspapers and on the cover of *LIFE* magazine, giving Cornell instant fame as the most violent campus in the nation.

After considerable heated debate, the faculty rejected Dean Miller's offer to the students, which meant that the disciplinary penalties remained in effect. SDS responded by calling a mass meeting, at which an estimated ten thousand members of the Cornell community turned out, to discuss the next steps. President Perkins addressed the meeting and then opened it to all speakers. The meeting ended with an overwhelming vote to rescind the penalties. The vote had no legal standing, but it indicated that a substantial proportion of Cornell's students and faculty were now in favor of Dean Miller's recommendation.

At six o'clock that evening, Tom Jones, a leader of the black students, spoke on the Cornell radio station. He denounced as racists President Perkins, Provost Dale Corson, two other administrators, and several prominent professors. He concluded with the announcement that "they will be dealt with. Cornell has only three hours to live."

Jones's statement sent shock waves through the Cornell community. Several professors and their families abandoned their homes and spent the night in local motels.

Events followed rapidly as students and faculty became involved en masse. On April 23, four days after the takeover of the student union, the faculty held an emergency meeting. After an impassioned debate, they voted about seven hundred to three hundred to rescind the penalties, reversing their earlier vote.

The vote brought widespread claims that the faculty had capitulated in the face of threats and violence. Three professors in the government department resigned, and fifteen law school professors signed a letter attacking President Perkins for not defending academic freedom. These charges were too much for Perkins. On May 31, he resigned and was succeeded by Dale Corson.

Did Cornell capitulate? Cornell did give in under the threats of further violence. What was the alternative? The administration managed to defuse the crisis without calling in the police and sheriffs' deputies. If Cornell had met the force by the black students with force by outside authorities, we might well have had far worse carnage than occurred when Kent State University called in the National Guard to deal with its war protesters.

I was worried and upset by the crisis. It seemed to have provoked paranoia and apocalyptic fantasies. Some professors said "Cornell had lost its soul." I could not figure out what that meant. An ILR professor told a colleague that President Perkins had entered into a conspiracy to turn control of the university over to SDS. But by the fall of 1969, SDS at Cornell had disintegrated and was nowhere to be seen.

Perhaps the best explanation for the Cornell crisis was offered by militant leader Tom Jones in an article in the *Cornell Daily Sun*, the university's student-run newspaper, on the tenth anniversary of the takeover. Jones wrote:

> Many black students had an emotional need for a "victorious" confrontation with a powerful white institution. . . . Many black students were emotionally primed for a confrontation even though, in my view, negotiations with the Administration for a substantial Black Studies program could have been concluded successfully without such action.

In fact, before the takeover, the AAS had "demanded" that Cornell appoint James Turner, who had been the first choice of the nominating committee, as head of the new program. After the crisis, that appointment was made, and the Africana Studies and Research Center was established.

At the time of the takeover, I supported Perkins. In both faculty meetings during the crisis, I voted to rescind the penalties. Looking back, it seems as if a collective fever had swept the campus—and other campuses. The blacks had to have their "victorious confrontation." It was accomplished without bloodshed, and the university did recover. To be sure, there was a brief period when some professors changed their lecture plans for fear of provoking black student protests, but that soon passed. In the weeks after the crisis, I served on a faculty committee on the state of academic freedom at Cornell. I joined the majority in finding some temporary damage, but we did not call for any action. We offered to convene faculty discussions on the topic during the fall semester but had no requests to do so. The issue seemed no longer of major concern.

Perhaps the most lasting damage was the polarization that occurred among faculty. I noted this within ILR. Before the crisis, I would go into faculty meetings without any fixed position on issues, expecting to listen to the discussion before making up my mind. After the crisis, many faculty came to meetings with what seemed like fixed positions and categorized their colleagues as liberals, radicals, or conservatives, or sound or unsound thinkers.

34. *From Research to Practice*

ornell's 1969 crisis gave me a sense of urgency—a feeling that something had to be done and soon. I felt guilty because I had been aware
of growing student unrest, yet I had minimized my involvement in
teaching, especially of undergraduates. I had developed one undergraduate
elective in group processes but otherwise was teaching only graduate students.
When I thought about social and economic changes, I thought more of Peru
than of the United States.

I believed that the student unrest was due in part to the isolation of the university from what some students called "the real world." I saw no way of combining
a university education with active involvement in the civil rights movement or
in the political struggles over the war in Vietnam, but it seemed to me that it
might be possible to build a bridge to "the real world" on a foundation of
fieldwork on the social and economic problems of Cornell's surrounding communities.

In the standard teaching and research program in the behavioral sciences, a
student does four years of undergraduate work plus a year toward a master's
degree before getting into research. I began to think about developing a one-year
course that would march undergraduate students to the frontiers of knowledge of
individual, group, and organizational behavior. In a university faculty discussion of how to improve the undergraduate program, I stated that I could design
such a course—in fact, I added, it might be possible to design a one-semester
program. I argued that this was not a superhuman task because the "frontiers"
of the behavioral sciences were not far away. That offended some of my colleagues, but I argued that students would learn most effectively if they were in
a program that combined fieldwork with in-class study. I supported that argument by noting the experience Larry Williams and I had had with the Peruvian

undergraduates. If Peruvians could accelerate their learning through field research experience, why couldn't Cornell undergraduates?

Before 1969, such ideas had remained entirely in the discussion stage—except for one undergraduate summer field project developed by organizational behavior professor William Friedland with Dorothy Nelkin. Bill was interested in studying migrant farm labor in New York State and for his research selected a large farm that had been willed to Cornell by an alumnus. Supported by a small grant, Bill and Dorothy worked for two summers with about fifteen undergraduates as participant observers, studying conditions and labor relations on the farm.

Our daughter Lucy was one of them. She found the project her most valuable college learning experience. In fact, it prepared her so well to conduct research that she was able to take on a professional research job right after college. Bill Friedland recommended Lucy for the job, which was with an Office of Economic Opportunity project in Rochester, New York, that was developing a health outreach program in a predominantly black and Hispanic slum district. The clinic doctors had been relying on women from the district with paraprofessional training to advise families about health problems and link them to the health care system. The project directors needed a participant observer to accompany the paraprofessionals during their house calls and to report and consult with the doctors and nurses at the clinic.

The doctors were impressed with Lucy's fieldwork experience and her fluency in Spanish but hesitated to hire someone without graduate training. They wanted a University of Rochester sociologist to assume supervisory responsibility but found that they did nothing but questionnaires. Lucy suggested that she could consult with me from time to time, and they settled for that. With just minimal guidance from me, Lucy carried out an excellent study.

Bill Friedland's program lasted for only two years, until he left Cornell for a position at the University of California at Santa Cruz. Bill had tried to persuade the College of Agriculture and Life Sciences to convert the Cornell farm to a sociotechnical experiment station for the purposes of determining whether it would be possible to produce an adequate financial return while creating more humane conditions for the migrant laborers. Instead, the college decided to solve its labor relations problems by selling the farm.

~

In the late afternoon of the day in 1969 when ten thousand Cornellians turned out for the crisis meeting, Donald Hayes in the Department of Sociology invited me to a meeting at his home. It was to be that evening. In ordinary times, no professor would invite colleagues to an evening meeting on such short notice, but these were not ordinary times, and I agreed to attend.

At the meeting that night, Don explained that he had a vision of Cornell creating a human engineering college where the emphasis would be on applied research.

There was no consensus among the five or six of us about how to proceed, but I was moved that night to pursue my own vision of developing a program of fieldwork for undergraduates. I began to look for potential collaborators. I found some support and interest in the Department of Rural Sociology in the College of Agriculture and Life Sciences and in the extension divisions of ILR, the College of Agriculture, and the College of Human Ecology. I also recruited a maverick professor of electrical engineering, Ben Nichols, who became a key member of the organization we created.

Several of us met with President Perkins to seek the administration's support to start what we were calling the Human Affairs Program (HAP), to be set up by a faculty committee that would assume overall responsibility for the program. Students would work in field projects guided by section leaders who had some experience in working with poor and working-class people. The plan also called for the development of a behavioral science course integrating the study of individuals, groups, and organizations so as to provide background for the fieldwork. This commitment was never fulfilled, since those of us who were involved were too occupied with planning, organizing, and defending HAP. Also during this time, I had applied for a fifty thousand dollar Ford Foundation grant to start the program. Ford responded quickly, and we had the grant in time to spend the summer in detailed planning and in recruiting and orienting section leaders.

Since I had taken the lead in establishing HAP, I was the obvious choice for director, but my Career Research Award barred me from assuming administrative responsibilities. For the first year, we settled on Theodore Reid, an assistant professor of organizational behavior in ILR. Even if the professors who would vote on his reappointment and tenure would not hold this unorthodox activity against him, the job of director was bound to be so absorbing as to slow down his research and publication. I felt uneasy about offering the directorship to Ted, but he understood the problems and decided to take the risk.

Ideally, the section leaders should have been faculty members. Unfortunately, no faculty were available. We therefore had to settle for able and dedicated people with rich backgrounds in community experience but with limited academic credentials.

Most undergraduate courses at Cornell are for three or four course credit hours. Since doing well in fieldwork and writing up notes and a final paper plus doing the assigned background reading takes more time than the average course, we planned to make each course worth six credits. To get that approved, we had to persuade the various committees on approving curriculum plans in ILR and the Colleges of Art and Sciences, Agriculture and Life Sciences, and Human Ecology.

To legitimate the courses, we recruited professors who were sympathetic with our objectives and willing to assume nominal responsibility for each six-hour course. That meant conferring with the section leader on plans for the course, reviewing progress during the course, and approving the final grades proposed by the section leader.

The fifty thousand-dollar grant from Ford did not go very far so we asked each dean to commit some thousands of dollars. In each case, we had a member of our faculty committee make the pitch to his dean.

As I look back now, it seems remarkable that we were able to work through so many problems in time to start the Human Affairs Program in the fall of 1970. This was due to the dedication of our group and the sudden openness of Cornell. We were all living with a sense of crisis. There was no consensus as to what should be done, but there was a widespread feeling that something had to change.

HAP set up offices in a building just off the Cornell campus and rented a storefront in downtown Ithaca, readily accessible to the people we were trying to reach. The storefront served as a meeting place and referral center for information on welfare, health, criminal justice, and housing. Several HAP sections used the storefront as their headquarters. There were also other sections: the Blue Bus, which brought library books to poor people who did not have transportation; a project to help inmates of the Elmira prison on their studies; and a project to develop an alternative junior high school.

HAP lasted for four academic years. It gained strong support from participating students, some of whom said it was the most valuable part of their Cornell education.

A number of factors worked against HAP. For one, it never gained academic legitimacy. Ted Reid was not reappointed at the end of his three-year term as assistant professor. Perhaps his involvement with HAP weighed against him — it certainly did not count in his favor.

Ted left in June, and I took his place as director in July and August. I arranged with the NIMH to give up my Career Award temporarily and to be reinstated in September. By this time, my ILR salary had risen well beyond the $25,000 subsidy from NIMH.

Daniel Leahy, who had been a section leader, became director in September 1971. Dan had a background in community organizing and had done well as a section leader. He was not a faculty member and had only a master's degree. He wore his hair long and, to some faculty people, appeared to be a "hippie."

Some Ithaca residents complained that HAP students interfered in their lives. Further, there was mounting criticism by the faculty that HAP slanted toward radical ideologies and that the students did not learn enough to justify six hours' credit. Some of that criticism was directed at me. To some of my colleagues, I had become an unsound fellow who was unwilling to stand up for academic freedom, undermining academic standards, and bent on trying to radicalize the students.

In the crisis atmosphere of 1969, it was relatively easy to get the deans of the various colleges to commit money for HAP. As time went on and other plans and projects competed for the administration's support, getting those commitments became increasingly difficult.

In 1974, the ILR faculty voted to set up a committee to evaluate HAP. George Brooks, chairman of the committee, had a joint appointment in extension and the Department of Collective Bargaining. The committee took its responsibilities seriously. After George had interviewed section leaders and students, the committee suggested some improvements and recommended that HAP remain open to ILR students. The leaders of the opposition moved that only a course taught by a Cornell professor should count for ILR course credit. George argued that the effect of the motion would be to bar ILR students from studying with HAP. That was what the opponents wanted, and their votes prevailed. Since HAP had drawn a large number of ILR students, the vote was its deathblow.

The Human Affairs Program did not sink without a trace. An alternative school was started by two graduate students in the Department of Education, who worked on plans with several junior high school teachers. I led the negotiations between Ithaca's superintendent of schools, Roger Bardwell, and the school board to gain acceptance of the idea for the school within the public school system. Bardwell was committed to exploring new directions, but the school board was reluctant to accept experimentation. Our strongest critic was a Cornell professor of education.

We worked out a program for the first year that would not cost taxpayers any more than a conventional junior high school. Bardwell appointed as principal a teacher who had worked with HAP, and as assistant principal one of the graduate students of education who had been involved in the planning process. The graduate student was paid by Cornell from money for an assistantship.

The new school was housed in a warehouse owned by the school system. Teachers, junior high pupils and their parents, and Cornell students reconditioned the building.

The school attracted a diverse population: children of professional parents looking for innovative education, and low-income children who were having trouble in regular school programs. This mix, together with an administrative commitment to involve pupils in managing the program, made the school exciting but at times unruly. As the unruly aspects were sometimes played out in the surrounding neighborhood, the school continued to be attacked by some community people but vigorously defended by some of the pupils' parents.

For the second year, Superintendent Bardwell proposed to recruit a new principal. I was involved in the recruiting and selection process. Furthermore, since a Cornell assistantship would no longer support the school, I was asked to commit the salary for the new principal from the HAP budget, which I agreed to do.

My decision created an uproar among HAP's section leaders. One afternoon in the summer of 1971, I got an urgent call from the HAP office, informing me that the section leaders were in revolt against my leadership and I'd better come right over to meet with them.

I invited them to vent their grievances, and they needed no encouragement. The section leaders had come to consider themselves participants in a social movement to democraticize society. They met frequently at the HAP office or at the downtown storefront and had become a cohesive group. By contrast, the education graduate students involved with the school spent no time at the HAP office or at the storefront.

The section leaders believed that HAP was a participative organization and that important decisions had to be made by the group. What right did I have to determine that using HAP funds to support the school was more important than using it for other projects?

I apologized for failing to consult them but argued that, as temporary director of HAP, I was the only one who had the legal right to commit Cornell funds. I told them that HAP had achieved a breakthrough in linking the university with the community through the school, and I believed it was important to support the project through this critical testing period. I can't say that the section leaders accepted this defense, but at least they had the satisfaction of getting their complaints heard.

For the school year 1971–72, the Ithaca School Board called for an evaluation study of Markles Flats, as the alternative school was called. Jason Millman, a Cornell professor of educational research methodology, directed the study. Also on the study committee were two Cornell professors, two Ithaca teachers, and one member who was described as a "Markles Flats volunteer." A thoroughly professional job, the study was based on classroom observation and interviews, comparative achievement scores between Markles Flats and the two regular junior high schools, as well as surveys of the attitudes of pupils at the same three schools. As evidence of the communitywide interest in the school, the committee's final report was printed in full (except for the appendixes) in the *Ithaca Journal* on May 17–19, 1972.

The study found that Markles Flats pupils were slightly behind students at the other two schools on standard achievement tests. The students at Markles Flat scored much higher, however, in their attitudes toward school. On an item that asked whether school was "exciting" or "dull," 78 percent of the Markles Flats pupils chose "exciting" versus only 37 percent in the other schools. On an item that asked whether the material they studied was important or not important, 90 percent at Markles Flats chose important versus 54 percent at the other schools. The study pointed out that Cornell had contributed $7,250 for that year but that even without that subsidy, Markles Flats would have cost less per pupil than one of the two schools chosen for comparison.

On the basis of the study, the school board voted to continue Markles Flats but recommended that efforts be made to boost the standard achievement scores. That ended the public controversy over alternative education in Ithaca. Twenty years later, the program has been extended through high school and is now called the Alternative Community School. Its current principal is one of the most widely respected educational administrators in the region.

I found the HAP experience exciting. I took pride in having mobilized part of the university to undertake a program of change that was intellectually stimulating and emotionally rewarding to the students and that had a lasting impact on public education in Ithaca.

35. Focusing on Employee Ownership

Before going to Peru, I had assumed there were just two ownership options: government ownership and private ownership. My work in Peru suggested another possibility: that workers could share ownership with private investors. The Peruvian program clearly was not working, but that did not mean that a system under which workers shared in ownership could not be feasible.

I had been aware that other options existed. Under the Yugoslavian system, for example, firms were self-managed and elected worker representatives held nominal control. Furthermore, worker cooperatives in the U.S. plywood industry were thought to be highly successful, although few social scientists had paid any attention to them. Perhaps we had ignored worker cooperatives because of Beatrice and Sidney Webb, two prestigious English social scientists, who had concluded in the early 1900s that worker cooperatives had poor prospects for long-term survival. If they failed, they went out of business like private firms. If they succeeded financially, the original worker-owners would take in additional personnel as hired labor, and eventually the cooperative would become privately owned.

The leading American authority on the Yugoslavian system, economist Jaroslav Vanek, was at Cornell. He believed that that system had been successful socially and economically in the 1950s and 1960s.

Vanek had a missionary's zeal for worker self-management, and he attracted many student converts, particularly those from Third World countries. In the early 1970s, Jaroslav invited a small group of professors to meet in his home.

We moved from discussions toward a series of action initiatives. First, we set up the Organizing and Supporting Agency (OSA) with Vanek as president and Chandler Morse as executive vice president. With some small grants and a lot of volunteer effort, we set out to establish a worker-managed firm that would employ black workers to do home repairs and construct homes for middle-and low-income people. This project generated a lot of activity, and, although we were short on entrepreneurial talent and financing, we even built one house.

I served on the Executive Committee of Vanek's Program on Participation and Labor-Managed Systems, which generated another organizational by-product in 1974, which we called the Federation for Economic Democracy (FEDO). I took over as chairman of FEDO when Jaroslav was on sabbatical leave. Encouraged by media accounts of the drama of workers who had saved their jobs by buying a firm threatened by a shutdown, we hoped to build a national organization dedicated to the cause of employee ownership, combined with an active program of worker participation in decision-making. FEDO began with the Ithaca chapter and grew to include chapters around Boston, Philadelphia, New York City, and Washington D.C., and at the University of Connecticut.

Under my leadership, FEDO fell apart. Beyond our lack of entrepreneurial talent and business experience, we were defeated by an unrealistic development plan. We aimed to build a national organization that would concentrate on two objectives: (1) providing technical assistance and training to actual or potential employee-owned firms and (2) assuming responsibility for organizing and supporting such firms. We could work on the first objective in our planning and study discussions. To accomplish the second objective, FEDO needed funds.

At first, FEDO had what seemed to be a stroke of good financial fortune, but it may also have led to our undoing. Vanek introduced me to George Benello, who was wealthy enough that he did not need to work for a living and who seemed as dedicated as we were to our goals. George did not have substantial capital to invest or loan, but he knew other rich people and had contacts with officials of foundations. Furthermore, he was willing to devote full time to our cause.

· There were two obvious routes we could follow: a grassroots strategy, which would facilitate the development of a local group, which would then start up a firm; or a strategy whereby we supported worker buyouts of plants facing shutdowns. I led those pushing the buyout option. I was too impatient to take what seemed to me the slow route of building from the ground up. I was also influenced by the excitement that comes with helping workers and union leaders struggle to save their jobs.

The struggle between those favoring the grassroots initiative and those favoring the buyout route came to a head over a decision the executive committee made to hire someone with entrepreneurial experience to work with unions trying to buy plants threatened with closing. The grassroots people were outraged that we would decide to put so much of our limited funds into this person's salary. The executive committee of FEDO had arguments in which I was bitterly attacked. I remember this as a very painful time, as it seemed that I was presiding over the fracturing of the committee.

As things turned out, I made the wrong judgment. Although each worker buyout got lots of media attention, in fact, buyouts were not occurring often. Furthermore, many potential firms were far from our chapters, making FEDO's involvement impractical. When FEDO did work on an attempted buyout, more often than not, the project would fail because it lacked equity or could not finance a loan.

When foundation grants ran out and we had no evidence that we could do better in the future, FEDO died. Spin-offs have survived, however. The Industrial Cooperative Association (ICA) grew from the nucleus of the Boston chapter, and the Philadelphia chapter gave birth to the Philadelphia Area Cooperative Enterprise (PACE). At this writing, those two organizations are still doing interesting and useful work. They have found, however, that they cannot confine their activities to worker buyouts or other such projects. They have had to adopt a more general community economic development strategy.

One of the greatest benefits of my association with Vanek was my discovery of the Mondragón worker cooperatives. One day I had noticed a feature story from the *London Observer* of January 21, 1973, on the bulletin board outside his office. The headline read "Mondragón: Spain's Oasis of Democracy." Journalist Robert Oakeshott had been looking through the files of the Centre de Recherches Cooperatives in Paris when he had come upon a 1967 report on Mondragón by F. Aldabaldetrecu and J. Gray.

Oakeshott had decided that he had to see Mondragón. The complex, in the heart of the Basque country, then included forty-seven industrial cooperatives. Ulgor, the first and largest firm, employed more than twenty-five hundred people.

Oakeshott's article convinced me that Mondragón was new and important. Its success suggested that the Basques had discovered ways to overcome the limitations that had stood in the way of the development of other worker cooperatives.

Vanek had visited Mondragón in 1974, and his enthusiasm reinforced my interest. He set up my first contact through Javier Retegui, who was then director of the Escuela Politécnica Profesional, the technical school that formed the educational base for the complex.

Indebted as I was to Oakeshott and Vanek for leading me to Mondragón, I recognized that I would have a comparative advantage. Speaking Spanish, Kathleen and I could pursue the Mondragón story in greater depth.

Our opportunity came in April 1975. I had accepted an invitation to speak and lead discussions in a management training program at an Israeli university. We arranged to spend two weeks in Mondragón, on the way to Israel. I had not wanted to go to Spain while Franco was in power, but now the dictator was reported to be dying, and the lure of Mondragón was too strong to resist.

The man who picked us up at the airport in Bilbao was no ordinary chauffeur. Manuel Quevedo had been a teacher in the Escuela Politécnica Profesional and was now director of Ikerlan, the cooperative's applied research and development unit.

During the drive to Mondragón, I remarked that I had not expected to find such a progressive and imaginative development in Spain under Franco. Quevedo laughed and replied, "We are Basques." When Quevedo dropped us at the Hostal Txirrita, just outside Mondragón, he offered to bring the founder of the cooperative complex, Father José María Arizmendiarrieta, to talk with us that afternoon. Don José María had never held an executive position in any of the cooperatives, yet he had guided and structured the Mondragón movement in ways that avoided the pitfalls that had undermined worker cooperatives elsewhere.

By the time we met him, Don José María was slim and frail. He had sparse, receding gray hair, sunken cheeks, and a sallow complexion. He was approaching the last year of his life and depended on a pacemaker, but those who had known him in the early days of Mondragón had always found it difficult to reconcile his inexhaustible energy with his frail body. When we settled down in the hostal's living room, he seemed to recede into the upholstered chair. His dark glasses, which he had worn since losing an eye in a childhood accident, made him seem even more retiring.

He spoke softly, hesitating as if searching for just the right words to express his thoughts. Our most vivid impression from that first meeting was of his hands—the long, thin El Greco fingers—constantly moving as if to shape his thoughts.

The founder of an important social movement may be called a charismatic figure, but that suggests an eloquent public speaker. That did not fit Don José María. Parishioners found his sermons uninspiring and hard to follow. His great strength was in dialogue, in thinking and getting others to think and plan with him.

The son of farmers, Don José María was studying for the priesthood when the Spanish Civil War broke out. He wrote for and edited the Basque army newspaper. When the Basques were finally defeated, he surrendered to the Franco forces. Along with a colleague, he was on a list to be executed. His colleague identified himself as a journalist and was shot. Don José María identified himself as a solider and became a prisoner of war.

Returning to the seminary after the war, he read in areas far beyond traditional theological studies. He developed a particular interest in worker cooperatives. He read about the nineteenth-century social reforms of Robert Owen and learned how Owen's once successful worker cooperative degenerated into a firm controlled by outside investors.

When Don José María was ordained in 1941, he asked to be sent to the University of Louvain for graduate work in sociology. Instead, he was dispatched to the small city of Mondragón, whose population was about eight thousand, where he became one of the most effective applied sociologists anywhere at any time.

He arrived in Mondragón in what was later called "the hunger period." The Basques lived under military occupation, unemployment was high, and many people had lost hope for a better future.

He began working with the young people, especially those from blue-collar families, organizing projects to improve health conditions and to build a sports field. He gave religious instruction in the vocational education classes the leading private firm offered employees' children. When management turned down his request to extend the classes to all the youth of Mondragón, Don José María organized blue-collar youths and their families to start their own technical school. The Escuela Politécnica Profesional began with young men ages fourteen to sixteen and has since grown to include the equivalent of a junior college program. That school became the first engine of growth for the cooperative movement.

Following completion of the studies then available in the school, some of its graduates went to work for the leading private firm, but Don José María continued his association with them through weekly discussions on social values and economic development. No son of a blue-collar worker had ever gone to college, but Don José María worked out an arrangement with the University of Zaragosa so that students from Mondragón could study engineering in absentia, while working to support themselves.

When five of his disciples wanted to start a cooperative, he worked with them to raise the money to add to their personal savings. The first firm, Ulgor, was started in 1956. For its first two years, Ulgor was registered as a private firm in the name of one of its founders, while the five founders and their eighteen fellow workers met after work to study and discuss with Don José María its constitution and bylaws.

Don José María worked out a novel financing arrangement for Ulgor. Instead of buying stock, the members agreed to *lend* money to the firm. They set up a capital account for each member on the basis of the initial loan, and those capital accounts grew through annual profit-sharing. Because it had no stock, the cooperative could not be taken over by outside investors unless the worker-owners themselves voted to sell.

Shortly after Ulgor was founded, Don José María began talking with its leaders about establishing a cooperative bank. At first, they would not listen. When they were still learning how to manage a factory, how could they take on a bank? He persisted, and, for the first and last time in his career, Don José María made the decision for them. Spanish banking law required the report of a preorganization meeting, signed by two of the proposed founders. Don José María wrote a report on an imaginary meeting and he signed the names of two of Ulgor's executives.

I asked my informant, "Weren't they upset that he did that?"

"They were a bit annoyed," he replied, "but they thought it would never amount to anything."

The bank, the Caja Laboral Popular, was started in 1960 in a small office in a church and grew rapidly. By the 1990s, it was the most prosperous savings bank in the Basque provinces.

The Caja channeled workers' savings into financing cooperatives. Its Entrepreneurial Division helped groups organize and plan for the establishment of new cooperatives and also provided consulting and technical assistance on a broad range of business and legal problems.

As new cooperatives sprang up, Don José María encouraged them to form groups to share the costs of personnel administration, accounting, financial planning, research, and legal matters. In this way, they achieved economies of scale while maintaining lean manufacturing organizations.

When a group of industrial arts teachers were concerned about making their instruction more useful to the cooperatives, he encouraged them to enlarge their vision to include research and development. He also persuaded Escuela authorities to finance the teachers' study trips to applied industrial research centers in France. Under the leadership of Manuel Quevedo, they then organized a small applied research unit within the Escuela.

In 1974, Don José María surprised even his closest associates by suggesting that they were ready to launch a more ambitious industrial research program. The cooperative leaders resisted the idea, but he persuaded them. They authorized an investment of $2 million dollars for a new building with offices, laboratories, and shops to house Ikerlan, their applied research unit. By the 1990s, still led by Quevedo, a former high school teacher with the equivalent of only a junior college degree in engineering, Ikerlan had become one of Spain's leading applied research institutes and was joining other European research units in collaborative projects.

Philosophically, Don José María could best be described as a pragmatist. He had a vision of society that did not conform to any established political ideologies. He believed in a peaceful moral revolution in which economic progress would coexist with mutually rewarding relations among members of different socioeconomic strata. To anchor that lofty vision in current realities, he always emphasized the need to arrive at an *equilibrio* or balance between social interests and ideals and economic and technological requirements. In planning discussions and the documents of the cooperatives, Mondragón members constantly speak of the quest for *equilibrio*.

Don José María warned his followers against the dangers of complacency and encouraged a spirit of collective self-criticism. We were impressed with the ways in which this self-critical spirit and the quest for *equilibrio* had become institutionalized in the structures and social processes of the Mondragón complex. Never content with the present, he guided them toward the future. As Javier Retegui said, "He sees the future and makes us face it."

A day after our encounter with Don José María, ILR graduate student Ana Gutiérrez-Johnson joined us for two weeks and stayed on for five weeks more. A Peruvian citizen who was married to an American, she had been attracted to Cornell by what she had heard of our program with the Instituto de Estudios Peruanos.

Ana joined us for our second interview with Don José María, which he allowed us to tape, but after that he banned the recorder, saying it gave too much weight to him. He insisted that he had been involved only in a collective achievement. "I have no power," he said. If power means holding an executive position that gives one the right to make decisions, his statement was accurate—except for his decision to create the bank. At the same time, he had enormous influence over an expanding circle of people and organizations.

Ana wrote her master's thesis on Mondragón and arranged to return there in 1977 for nine weeks to gather material for her doctoral thesis. Largely on the basis of her 1975 field reports, she and I wrote the first research article in English on Mondragón, "The Mondragón System of Worker Production Cooperatives" (Johnson and Whyte 1977).

I remarked to Ana that, following her second study trip, she would have enough data for a book. Without weighing my words carefully, I said the book could be either a joint publication with her as the first author or done in collaboration with me. That decision would depend on how much I was able to contribute. Ana finished her Ph.D. in 1982 and went to Costa Rica to take a job for which I had recommended her.

By 1982, I had finished the Peruvian writing, and the visits to Cornell by several Mondragón members had reinforced my interest in the cooperatives. I now felt the most important thing I could do was a book on the complex. I wrote Ana, proposing that we write the book jointly but that her name would appear first. In correspondence, she raised no objection.

On returning from Costa Rica, Ana told me somewhat hesitantly that she objected to the joint authorship arrangement. She wanted to be sole author and suggested that I write only a final chapter on the implications of Mondragón for the United States.

I was stunned. I had already sent her my drafts of the first eight chapters. Furthermore, in all of my previous writing projects with students or younger colleagues, I had never encountered someone whose reaction implied that I was treating him or her unfairly.

Ana believed that since I already had an established reputation, readers would credit me with the book even if her name came first. I failed to persuade her that the arrangement I had proposed would be best for her as well as for me.

I told her to go ahead and write her book, and I would write mine. To implement that decision, however, I would have to do substantially more research in Mondragón, given the changing situation in the 1980s. Our data had all been gathered when the complex was growing and prospering. The recession of the 1980s had hit Spain earlier than other industrialized countries and had caused Mondragón serious difficulties, leading to retrenchment and readjustment. If Kathleen and I went back, we could study how Mondragón was coping with adversity. We arranged to spend three weeks in Mondragón in the spring of 1983.

At this point, a new idea regarding collaboration occurred to me. Kathleen had been my editor and critic beginning with *Street Corner Society*. She had joined me at all the group meetings I had for students in our home. In Peru, she was with me on some of the field trips. Finally, in my studies of agricultural research and development in Mexico, Colombia, and Central America, she was a full participant.

Our collaboration had been formalized in *Learning from the Field*, published in 1984. While I was writing it Kathleen kept reminding me of field research experiences I had told her about but had not written up. Her advice probably delayed the book's publication by six months, but the book was much better as a result, and she appears as a collaborating author. Further, she had been with me on all my Mondragón interviews, and I had gained much from her occasional questions and from discussing the interviews later. Why not ask her now to be a coauthor of my Mondragón book?

The 1983 trip to Mondragón was a rich field experience. Growth had come to a halt, but although unemployment in the Basque country was more than 25 percent, the Mondragón complex had managed to keep its rate below 1 percent. We were fascinated by the ways in which the complex kept unemployment down by transferring members from one cooperative to another, by retraining, and by enabling the Caja Laboral Popular and its Entrepreneurial Division to refinance debt and guide a failing cooperative through financial sacrifices to survival. In a period when American workers were being laid off with little or no advance notice or assistance, we were moved by the infinite pains and humane manner in which Mondragón was coping with its economic crisis.

With the 1983 data, we had ample material for our book. To reciprocate for the help we had received, I presented some of our observations to a small group of informants. When I concluded, José Luis González, the personnel director of the FAGOR group of cooperatives, responded, "Why don't you propose that you do a new research project and request a budget to do that research?" That took me by surprise. At age sixty-nine, I was not prepared to accept such a large commitment. Nevertheless, I could not just forget about Mondragón.

Back at Cornell, I consulted with Davydd Greenwood, a professor of anthropology, director of Cornell's Center for International Studies, and an authority on the Basques. He suggested enthusiastically that we broaden the project to include other Cornellians, including himself, in an interinstitutional collaboration.

After additional field trips to Mondragón, Kathleen and I produced *Making Mondragón: The Growth and Dynamics of the Worker Cooperative Complex*, which was published in 1988. (A Spanish edition was published in 1990.) As reviews and reader responses indicated that our book provided the best description and interpretation yet available, we went back for a final time in 1990. Based on this visit, we revised the book to take into account the tremendous period of adjustment as Mondragón prepared to cope with the advent of the European Common Market. The revised second edition (1991) brings the Mondragón story into the 1990s.

As painful as it was to discontinue the collaboration with Ana, I now regard the break as one of the most fortunate events of my academic career. If she had accepted the arrangement I had proposed, we would presumably have written a book about Mondragón that would have been limited largely to the periods of strong growth. Her decision plunged me back into following the complex during its stressful struggle for survival in the early 1980s and during its major restructuring, as it prepared to compete in the European Common Market.

36. The New Systems of Work and Participation Program

In December 1974, Kathleen and I made our last trip to visit my mother in California. We had planned our trip to Peru, Spain, and Israel and would be away from early January until late June. Mother was eighty-six and in the final stages of illness and had ordered the medical staff to take no measures to prolong her life. She wanted to be buried beside her husband in Greensboro, Vermont, and had made the necessary arrangements.

Mother made us promise not to delay our trip abroad. That thoughtfulness was typical. As we sat with her, we would hear her mumble from time to time, "Let me go, let me go." We were saddened to see her slipping away, but we could not ask the doctors to prolong her life. She died in early January 1975, shortly before we were to leave the country.

The semester away from home gave me time to think about new directions in research. I decided to set aside my interest in rural development to concentrate on employee ownership and worker participation in U.S. industry.

Upon my return to the United States, I consulted with colleagues about possible developments to study. Through them, I learned about the Jamestown Area Labor-Management Committee (JALMC), a program that linked leaders of organized labor and management in an effort to save jobs through cooperative activities and through employee buyouts of plants facing shutdowns. Earlier community labor-management committees had limited their functions to mediation. JALMC left this to the New York State and federal mediation services in order to concentrate on community economic development. This sounded novel and interesting.

A new trend was emerging in management strategies. Earlier, the fad had been diversification. Corporations had become conglomerates as top management bought up locally owned plants outside their main lines of business. Now the fashion was for top management to strive to achieve leaner organizations by dumping plants that were unprofitable or only marginally profitable. This created a scramble as local citizens sought to save jobs through employee buyouts or by making local investments and establishing local management.

Dean Robert McKersie encouraged me to organize what we were calling the New Systems of Work and Participation Program (NSWPP). We would do case studies of labor-management cooperative activities in Jamestown and several of the employee buyouts.

Although NSF and NIMH program directors personally approved of my interest in action research, they felt required to consider only the "scientific" merits of a project in awarding grants. I therefore submitted proposals to NIMH for support of the "scientific aspects" of my work and to the Economic Development Administration (EDA), which had played a major role in supporting the Jamestown Area Labor-Management Committee, for support of the action research.

While I was visiting employee buyout cases, Elliot Liebow called to tell me that EDA had turned down its part of the proposal on the grounds that the agency could not justify putting more of its funds into Jamestown. At the same time, an NIMH review committee had voted to support the "scientific aspects." I told NIMH I would take the money and deliver a report on the "scientific aspects" and find other ways to move ahead on the action research.

The NIMH grant attracted into the project three colleagues from ILR's Department of Organizational Behavior. Tove Hammer and Robert Stern got involved in the study of employee buyout cases, and Howard Aldrich joined Stern in a historical study of worker cooperatives from 1840 to 1940.

I took charge of finding cases to study, making the initial contacts, and getting my colleagues and students involved in those cases. Much of the fieldwork arose out of a class I began teaching in the fall of 1975 called "Systems of Worker Participation and Ownership." Christopher Meek was my teaching assistant and became one of my chief collaborators. I encouraged students to find cases for field study. One picked Byers' Transport Limited, a firm headquartered in his hometown of Edmonton, Canada, which had undergone a worker buyout. Another began a doctoral project on the Saratoga Knitting Mills in Saratoga, New York. And another pursued the story of the Vermont Asbestos Group.

Chris Meek and I studied the Jamestown Area Labor-Management Committee. The Jamestown venture introduced me to one of the more memorable figures in my experience, Congressman Stanley N. Lundine (lieutenant governor of New York State at this writing). The first Democrat in forty years to be elected mayor of Jamestown, Lundine had begun by trying to revive his depressed manufacturing city by persuading big companies to move into abandoned industrial buildings. Frustrated by Jamestown's reputation as having a "poor labor climate," he had shifted his strategy to the development of local resources. Through his family, Lundine had ties with leading local figures in management and unions. After meeting separately with some of these people, he called them together to create the Jamestown Area Labor-Management Committee.

Lundine turned to Eric Trist, then with the Wharton School of the University of Pennsylvania, for advice on planning and staffing the program. Trist began consulting with the JALMC in May 1973. In the late spring of 1975, EDA funds became available, and two of Trist's graduate students, John Eldred and Robert Keidel, also joined the project.

When Chris Meek and I made our first visit to Jamestown in January 1976, a number of joint projects were under way. Trist had found that managers in the area's woodworking and metal-fabricating plants were worried about losing their most highly skilled workers through retirement. JALMC coordinator James Schmatz had been organizing a communitywide skill training program. Eldred and Keidel had helped companies and unions in ten plants set up joint labor-management committees. Four of these committees had been abandoned, one each on the initiative of the union or of management and two on the recommendation of consultants, who had found too many barriers to progress.

When Chris and I met with Eric Trist, John Eldred, and Bob Keidel, the Wharton team was still trying to overcome management resistance to its involvement in the JALMC. Was Cornell now coming in to reap the fruits of its efforts? I considered it an honor to work with Eric and tried to make it clear that we wanted to learn from them and to fit in any way that they would find helpful. Eric welcomed us from the outset, but others clearly had reservations about our intentions. After lengthy discussions, we agreed that Chris would spend half his graduate study time for the second semester with the JALMC, first observing and learning and then seeing if he could find ways to be helpful. Chris began patiently on the fringes of JALMC and gradually won the confidence of Bob Keidel, who invited him to collaborate on a project. They worked well together, and eventually John Eldred began to think of Chris as member of the team.

During this time, the JALMC became involved in some impressive projects. When the Carborundum Company rejected the $10 million plan of a consulting firm to modernize and expand an old plant, John Eldred led the plant labor-management committee in a study that produced a $5.8 million design that management accepted. This saved an old plant from shutdown.

Hopes Windows was a job shop that depended on competitive bidding to bring in orders. When engineers and supervisors made the estimates, Hopes secured the contracts on only 10 percent of its bids—and found it lost money on some bids it won. With the assistance of Bob Keidel, committees of workers, union officers, foremen, and engineers were set up to work together on preparing the bids. This raised the success rate to 50 percent—and the company made money on the bids it won.

Toward the end of 1977, Keidel returned to Wharton to complete his Ph.D. with Trist, while Eldred was promoted to coordinator of the JALMC with the departure of James Schmatz. Chris Meek moved up from research assistant to research associate and remained with JALMC, living in Jamestown, until June 1981. Through most of this period, the JALMC paid half his salary. I continued to make periodic visits to Jamestown.

Worker Participation and Ownership: Cooperative Strategies for Strengthening Local Economies (1983), which I wrote with other members of the NSWPP team, presents the JALMC story and that of several employee ownership cases.

∾

My involvement with the employee buyout at the Rath Packing Company began in 1979 when I got a call from Randy Barber, an old friend from my days with the Federation for Economic Democracy and then with the Citizens' Business Commission in Washington, D.C.

> I've been out to Waterloo [Iowa] where something exciting is happening. I talked to Lyle Taylor, president of Local 46 of the United Food and Commercial Workers Union, and Chuck Mueller, chief steward. They are trying to buy Rath Packing Company to keep it from going down the tube, and they're interested in control as well as ownership, and they need all the help they can get. Could you do something?

Up to this point, workers and union leaders had been passive in employee buyouts. The initiative had come from plant managers and local citizens. High-level union leaders had been confused as to what their policies should be. We found them asking, "How can you bargain with yourself?" This meant that management controlled the planning and implementation of ESOPS.

On April 16, 1979, I wrote Lyle Taylor, congratulating him on his efforts and offering whatever assistance we could provide. Chief steward Charles Mueller read the research reports I sent.

Tove Hammer and Bob Stern were planning a study of worker members on the boards of directors of companies. They decided to fly to Waterloo in May to talk with the Rath union leaders.

Tove and Bob were met at the airport by Chuck Mueller. While he was driving them into town, he told them:

> We're at a critical point—the ten members of the negotiating team are trying to decide today what form of ownership and control we will accept. The company lawyer and our own lawyer have advised us that the only practical way to go is with the conventional stock ownership arrangement: one share of stock, one vote, no trust, no way of consolidating worker voting power. The negotiating committee stands nine to one for going this way, and I'm the one that's holding out. Can you come in and talk the negotiating committee out of that decision?

Tove and Bob did not want to get involved in internal union politics, but they offered to talk with the negotiating committee about what they had learned from other cases of worker ownership and control.

Neither Tove nor Bob had shown any inclination toward applied research, but this unexpected event captured them. They did not exhort the negotiating committee to do anything. They simply laid out how workers inevitably lost control when an ESOP was structured along what were then conventional lines.

Following this discussion, the negotiating committee reversed its position and committed the union to an ESOP structure in which all employee stockholders would elect a board of trustees, which would vote the 60 percent of employee-held stock and thereby control the company. Furthermore, the committee decided to allocate all employee stock on an equal basis, contrary to the conventional practice of allocating stock in relation to pay levels. To our knowledge, this structure had never before been implemented in any ESOP. In my dealings with Congress, I had met Jack Curtis when he was staff assistant to Senator Russell Long, father of the major ESOP legislation. Now that Jack was in private law practice, I suggested the union hire him to put into legal form the ESOP structure the committee desired. Jack worked out what came to be known as the democratic ESOP model. When this model became known among advocates of worker cooperatives, they recognized the possibility of creating "democratic ESOPs" that reflected the egalitarian principles embodied in cooperatives.

President Lyle Taylor telephoned Tove to ask her to represent the union and the workers on the newly reconstituted board of directors of Rath Packing Company. The negotiating committee had chosen several workers for board positions, but it wanted some outside expertise. Among the outsiders who were already chosen were former U.S. senator Richard C. Clark and Ralph Helstein, former president of the United Packinghouse Workers Union, to which Rath workers belonged before the merger into the United Food and Commercial Workers Union.

The invitation took Tove by surprise. Joining the board meant abandoning her role as detached social scientist. Bob and I urged her to accept. He could assume the role of the detached social scientist, while she would have an unprecedented opportunity to be a participant observer on the board of a major company. Furthermore, she could take shorthand—a rare skill for a professor—which would enable her to record the board discussions very fully except when she was speaking. (She enlisted the secretary of the board to make notes on her own comments.)

Tove soon won the confidence of the other board members, including the minority representing private investors. With Ralph Helstein, she became the principal adviser to the union leaders on all matters coming before the board. Dictating from her shorthand notes, she accumulated an enormous volume of data on board meetings. A subsequent small-group analysis kept her busy for many months.

My other involvement with employee ownership arose when I was asked to join the board of trustees of the O&O Investment Fund in Philadelphia. The fund arose out of an innovative contract between Local 1357 of the United Food and Commercial Workers Union, under the leadership of President Wendell W. Young III, and the A&P food chain in the Philadelphia area.

In the spring of 1982, A&P had announced its intention to close seventy stores in the Philadelphia area. Young, a graduate of St. Joseph's College, had anticipated this decision, and his union had contracted with the Wharton School and with the St. Joseph's College Food Marketing Institute for technical assistance.

Young presented a counterproposal. The union would agree to pay cuts if A&P would reopen many of these stores under a new plan that provided training for managers and workers in participative management and if A&P would sell two of the stores it had shut down to the employees and give the union the right of first refusal to purchase any of the other stores.

In May 1982, A&P reopened many of the stores under the logo of Super Fresh Food Centers. Management also agreed to set aside the equivalent of 1 percent of gross sales for its employees. Forty percent of that figure would be used to pay incentive bonuses to store employees, and the balance would go to the O&O Investment Fund, to be established by the union. ("O&O" stands for employee owned and operated, so that the bulk of those funds would be used to finance and develop other worker cooperative enterprises.)

Young had contracted with two nongovernment organizations, Gray Areas and the Philadelphia Area Cooperative Enterprise, to develop a training program for the laid-off employees who would own and operate the former two A&P stores. (The credit union of the United Food and Commercial Workers granted a loan of five thousand dollars to each prospective employee-owner toward the purchase.)

The payoffs from my involvement in the employee buyouts were clear for me personally but much more ambiguous for the people I was trying to help. In the Rath case, through the work of Chris Meek and Warner Woodworth (of Brigham Young University) we were able to stimulate and guide many improvements in manufacturing, but that was not enough to make the company economically viable. There were serious deficiencies in top management we were not able to reverse. The moral of the Rath story is that whatever money can be saved through improvements in production can be lost through incompetent management. Good industrial relations is no cure-all.

In spite of these weaknesses, the Rath buyout kept the company alive from 1980 to 1985, during which some of the older workers were able to retire on pensions, and the local economy benefited. Furthermore, Rath was a landmark case for the employee ownership movement, demonstrating that it is possible to design a democratically structured ESOP in which all the employee-owners have equal voting rights.

My involvement with the O&O Investment Fund provided me with the wonderful learning experience of being able to follow an innovative worker cooperative development program led by one of the most creative union leaders I had ever encountered.

When the fund was established, the organizers assumed that it would have an annual income of about $500,000, coming from the fund's share of 1 percent of the gross revenues of the reopened A&P stores. But then employees of some of the most profitable stores hired a lawyer who threatened to bring suit against Local 1357 of the United Food and Commercial Workers Union, claiming that contributions to the fund could be made only on a voluntary basis, after each employee signed a personal authorization.

Wendell Young believed the union would win such a suit, but he decided—

probably wisely—that the costs of winning an internal conflict were too heavy to bear. The union backed off and simply urged members to pledge 10 percent of their bonus money to the O&O Investment Fund. That was far less than what had been planned for in the contract, but members had agreed to that amount when they were all unemployed and were much more willing to give up money they were not receiving. Now even 10 percent of their bonus seemed too much for workers earning eight dollars per hour. Thus, the anticipated $500,000 per year quickly turned into a mere trickle.

To pursue its original objectives, the fund had to raise money from foundation grants and government subsidies. This brought the fund, directed by Jay Guben of Gray Areas, into direct competition with PACE, directed by Sherman Kreiner.

I should have realized that there would not be enough employee ownership activities developing in Philadelphia for two competing organizations. I also failed to discharge my fiduciary responsibilities as a trustee by not keeping close track of the finances of the O&O Fund. It should have been obvious that the fund was not going to be able to continue at its current level of activities with any grant income that could reasonably be expected. The end came when the money in the fund ran out and the trustees voted to turn over responsibility for the fund to PACE.

My experience with the fund paid off for me in what I learned ("The Philadelphia Story," 1986), but I could see no benefits to the people I was trying to help. Whatever I was able to do for the fund was not worth what my services cost. I received no fees, but travel expenses for quarterly visits to Philadelphia mounted up to sums the fund could hardly afford.

37. *Working with Congress*

My involvement with Congress began with my work for Congressman, Matthew F. McHugh. Matt had been born and raised in Brooklyn but after law school had settled in Ithaca. In 1974, he won a congressional seat that had been held by Republicans for decades.

Kathleen and I were enthusiastic supporters of Matt in his 1974 campaign, and I attended a reelection meeting in the fall of 1976 to see what we could do to help. During that campaign, I told Matt that through the New Systems of Work and Participation Program, several of us at Cornell had seen opportunities to save jobs through employee buyouts of plants being shut down. I said we did not yet have definite ideas of what the government should do, but that if he wanted to work on this, we would be glad to work with him and his staff.

Matt's legislative assistant was Gary Bombardier, who had been doing research with the Brookings Institution. Matt suggested Gary and I discuss how we might work together. Matt also mentioned that I take the issue to his "best friend in Congress, Stan Lundine."

I was on the executive council of the American Sociological Association and a member of a review committee for the Center for the Study of Metropolitan Problems of NIMH, and those two assignments brought me to Washington every few months. I would usually fly down early in the morning on the day before our 9 AM meeting and use the balance of the day to work on my congressional project. Stan Lundine needed no persuasion to sign on. He introduced me to his legislative assistant, Mary Eccles, and I began working with her.

I was not planning to involve another congressman, but a stroke of luck brought that about. In a coffee break during an NIMH committee meeting, I told a staff member of the NIMH about my congressional project. He said, "You should meet my friend Joseph Blasi" from the staff of Congressman Peter Kostmayer of Pennsylvania.

The next day, Joseph and I had lunch. There was a perfect match between his objectives and mine. For his doctoral thesis in education at Harvard, he had been a participant observer in an Israeli kibbutz. Returning to Harvard, he had organized the Project for Kibbutz Studies, which he continued to direct while teaching in the Department of Social Relations.

Both Blasi and Kostmayer had grown up in a suburb of Scranton. When Peter was elected to Congress, he offered Joseph a staff job. Joseph made a counterproposal, which Kostmayer accepted: Joseph would serve as social policy adviser, spending one day a week in Washington, providing the congressman with ideas and information—without any responsibility for the routine functions of the office.

Although Joseph was in Washington only one day a week, within a short time he emerged as the key organizer for my congressional project. The other staff assistants had to fit the project among many competing activities. At first, Joseph got permission to spend half his time in Washington on the project, but then, as we gathered momentum, Kostmayer encouraged Joseph to give it his full time there. Because employee ownership was Joseph's principal research interest at Harvard, his commitment extended far beyond the one day a week in Washington.

Thinking we might accelerate progress if the three congressmen could get together away from the distractions of Washington, I proposed a luncheon meeting at Cornell during the August recess. Dean Robert McKersie extended the invitation. I had been keeping my NSWPP colleagues informed about my project, and they agreed to join us at lunch—although I suspect they were uneasy about this nonacademic project.

I had announced that the lunch would be a planning meeting and had sent the congressmen an outline of the topics we might want to discuss. Little actual planning got done, but we had a lively discussion. Probably the main value of the meeting was that the three congressmen consolidated their commitment to the project.

Gary Bombardier advised me that drafting a bill to support our employee-ownership initiative would require the concentrated time of the three staff assistants and me for several days in November when Congress would not be in session.

Since the Economic Development Administration had the most experience with employee ownership of any government agency, we agreed that the EDA should administer the funds provided in our bill. We set the appropriation level at $100 million for the first year. The goal was that the funds would cover information-gathering and dissemination on plant shutdowns and potential employee buyouts as well as provide direct support to groups involved in employee ownership to save jobs. The direct support was to come in various forms: information, technical assistance on feasibility studies and in establishing and managing an employee-owned firm, and loans to the firm and to individual workers to finance their purchase of stock.

We called our bill the Voluntary Job Preservation and Community Stabilization Act, with the hope that it would have a broad bipartisan appeal. The bill opened with this statement of purpose: "To preserve jobs and stabilize communities by facilitating employee, or employee-community, ownership of concerns that would otherwise close down or move out of the community, and for other purposes."

Peter Kostmayer introduced the bill as H.R. 12870 on May 25, 1978, with twenty-three cosponsors, including McHugh and Lundine. The June 19 *Congressional Record* contains supporting statements by Kostmayer, Lundine, and McHugh. It also contains a two-page supporting statement that Kostmayer asked me to write. I drew upon NSWPP research on plant shutdowns and employee ownership, thus indicating to Congress our knowledge in this field.

Up to this point, I would not call my congressional involvement lobbying. I saw myself as organizing a participatory study and action project to which the NSWPP would contribute ideas and information and learn from the congressmen and their staffers how such materials could be used to draft legislation.

When I was working with FEDO, I had met Sister Madeleva Roarke, who worked in Washington with Network, a lobbying organization for social justice. She and two other nuns worked out of a small office and were supported by contributions from nuns all over the country. Network worked closely with the American Friends Service Committee and with Protestant church organizations, so they were able to bring to bear on Congress the initiatives of a broad religious community.

Sister Madeleva was interested in employee ownership and offered to help us generate support. By the time the Ninety-fifth Congress finished its work, our bill had been cosponsored by one out of every six congressmen. I suspect the nuns and their religious allies were responsible for most of these sponsors.

It was Corey Rosen who got our project into the Senate. With his wife, Karen Young, Corey had been appointed by Senator Gaylord Nelson of Wisconsin to a staff position on the Senate Select Committee on Small Business. Reading the June 19 issue of the *Congressional Record*, Corey happened upon the story of the introduction of the Voluntary Job Preservation and Community Stabilization

Act. He was fascinated and called Kostmayer's office and talked to Joseph Blasi, who sent him copies of Blasi's employee ownership files—which were largely ones I had sent him from Cornell.

By keeping Joseph informed of all employee ownership activities in the Senate, Corey became a key member of our team. He once told me, "We have so many routine duties taking care of constituents' interests, it's great to have an opportunity to work for something you really believe in."

Our bill died with the end of the Ninety-fifth Congress. It was reintroduced in the Ninety-sixth but never got beyond committee hearings. Nevertheless, the initiative bore fruit by paving the way for new employee ownership legislation. The Small Business Administration (SBA) had been refusing to make loans to employee stock ownership trusts on the grounds that the trusts were not small businesses. Corey drafted a bill directing the SBA to abandon this restriction. Corey also arranged to have his committee hold hearings on employee ownership. I was called to testify, along with some employee-owners drawn from cases in our research files. By the time the hearings were held, the SBA administrator announced that the SBA had decided it could loan to employee stock ownership trusts. To fix this in law, the committee introduced the Small Business Employee Ownership Act (S388), which passed in the Senate and in the House. President Jimmy Carter signed it in the summer of 1980.

Another spin-off to our work occurred during the debates over whether Congress should guarantee bank loans to the Chrysler Corporation to save it from bankruptcy. Since the Chrysler employees were being required to sacrifice some of their pay to save the company, Corey suggested that Chrysler give them ownership shares in the company in return. He drafted a letter that was sent to two hundred newspapers, which was signed in the Senate by Charles McC. Mathias, Jr., a Republican from Maryland, and the following Democratic senators: Robert C. Byrd, majority leader from West Virginia, Russell B. Long of Louisiana (the leading power in Congress for employee ownership legislation), Gaylord Nelson of Wisconsin, Donald W. Stewart of Alabama, and Mike Gravel of Alaska. It was signed in the House by Kostmayer and McHugh.

Lundine did not sign because he was on the House committee dealing with the Chrysler bailout. He introduced an amendment to establish employee ownership shares as part of the buyout package. Senator Donald Stewart introduced the same amendment into the Senate bill.

The letter was featured in the *New York Times* letters column of October 24, 1979, under a three-column headline: "If Chrysler Workers Were Chrysler Stockholders." This alarmed the company's lobbyists, who tried to see Senator

Stewart. He refused to meet with them and instead sent this message: "If you want the bailout, you'll take employee ownership."

Chrysler thus suddenly became the largest American company sharing ownership with its employees. The 15 percent of stock going to the employees was estimated to be worth about $162 million.

Where was the AFL-CIO leadership while the discussions in Congress were going on? In one word, absent. When the Voluntary Job Preservation and Community Stabilization Act was picking up cosponsors in the House, Blasi heard rumors that the AFL-CIO was about to blast the bill, but no such attack ever came. When a Swedish visitor interviewed the AFL-CIO director of public relations, he asked what position the organization had taken on the bill. The official could only say, "I wish it would go away."

The leaders of organized labor were unsympathetic to employee ownership, yet they were hearing from some local unions of cases in which jobs had been saved through employee buyouts. Where employee ownership presented the only hope of saving jobs, the AFL-CIO could hardly take a public position against it.

In the case of the Chrysler bailout, the UAW leadership regarded employee ownership as a distraction that could threaten the bill guaranteeing bank loans or delay its passage. A UAW lobbyist told Blasi, "If you delay by one hour passage of the Chrysler bailout bill, we'll kill you!"

As organized labor gained more experience with employee ownership, the leadership of some unions shifted to a more pragmatic position. Recognizing that employee ownership could be beneficial to workers, attention turned to how to structure ESOPs to safeguard workers' interests and promote worker participation in decision-making. In 1983, when I met with members of the UAW research department, they were skeptical but interested in discussing how the central staff and regional officials could help the locals deal with employee ownership. Some time later, the top leaders of the United Steel Workers were taking the position that employee ownership might be necessary to ensure continued American ownership of the steel industry.

As far as the general public was concerned, employee ownership at Chrysler passed by almost unnoticed. For weeks the press carried daily stories about the Chrysler debates in Congress, focusing on whether the federal government should subsidize a private company and on the novel element in the buyout package—Douglas Fraser, president of the UAW and also a member of the Chrysler board of directors. Even in the *New York Times*, the first and only mention of sharing ownership with the workers was in the last paragraph of a long front-page story continued on an inside page.

In the Reagan landslide of 1980, Senator Gaylord Nelson and Representative Peter Kostmayer lost their seats in Congress. (Peter won his back in 1982.) That ended the congressional careers of Corey Rosen, Karen Young, and Joseph Blasi. Although this seemed a severe blow to the employee ownership movement, it did not turn out that way. Corey and Karen transferred their activities to their home in Arlington, Virginia, and established the National Center for Employee Ownership (NCEO), which publishes the bimonthly *Employee Ownership Report*, conducts research on employee ownership, and sponsors regional and local conferences and workshops as well as an annual national meeting. Now located in Oakland, California, the NCEO is increasingly well financed by membership and conference fees and research grants. NCEO has come to be recognized as the prime source for information and ideas on employee ownership. I was on its board of directors for the first several years after its founding.

Joseph Blasi has intensified his commitment to employee ownership. Now at Rutgers University, he has gone far beyond me in researching and publishing on this topic. He is a member of the board of NCEO and of the employee-owned Northwestern Steel Company.

Getting around the halls of Congress on crutches was always a physical struggle, so I sometimes wondered, "Why am I doing this in my old age?" Still I found it exciting. Although I was concentrating on employee ownership, my involvement with Congress led me into other advisory and lobbying activities. I did some lobbying against U.S. military and financial support to the repressive government of El Salvador—without any noticeable effect. And, as my work on employee ownership became known in Congress, I testified on hearings on somewhat related issues, such as the dangers of conglomerate mergers and plant closings.

The Senate's growing interest in employee ownership led to an invitation to meet with Senator Russell Long and his staff assistants on the Senate Finance Committee, first Jack Curtis and later Jeffrey Gates. Before we met, Jack had described the Voluntary Job Preservation and Community Stabilization Act in a speech at Princeton University as "the most creative legislative initiative to come out of the Ninety-fifth Congress." Now in private practice, both Curtis and Gates have become leading figures in the employee ownership movement.

I am proud of what I accomplished in working with Congress. Without any previous experience, I designed a strategy and social process that worked. I began with the assumption that I was dealing with intelligent and well-meaning congressmen and their staff assistants. Since I had no idea of how to draft a bill that would fit my objectives and theirs, I proposed a participative approach to the analysis of problems and the legislative design for their solution. I had the backing of my academic-activist network. Although this network existed only in the minds of some of its members, I knew most of these people personally, and those I did not know responded when I called for their help. I was not asking for personal favors but to contribute to a cause we all believed in.

I admired our three congressmen, and I am proud of my relationship with Corey Rosen and Joseph Blasi, who not only became my friends but carried on action research in employee ownership far beyond where I left off. In the acknowledgments to their book *Understanding Employee Ownership* (1991), Corey Rosen and Karen Young wrote: "William Foote Whyte provided the initial inspiration for the founders of the center to get involved in employee ownership and offered a model of how research can be used to help encourage social change."

38. *Becoming Professor Emeritus*

I reached Cornell's official retirement age of sixty-five in June 1979. Robin Williams and some others had challenged that policy and managed to continue teaching until seventy, but I regarded retirement as an opportunity to reflect on what I had learned in the field and to try to put it into some systematic form.

I planned to divide my time between research and writing on agriculture and on industrial relations. I figured that with my pensions, I could maintain my preretirement income if Cornell would pay me half my former salary. I arranged to get one-quarter each from ILR and the Rural Development Committee in the Center for International Studies. That arrangement worked for the first two years, but then the available money ran out from both sources. Fortunately, a grant from the Economic Development Administration for a follow-up study of employee buyouts restored part of my lost income and provided a basis for keeping me on partial salary through ILR Extension when the grant ran out.

There was also the question of my office, which was in the main building of the School of Industrial and Labor Relations. With new professors being hired, I did not feel I could claim I had to keep it. I arranged with Dean McKersie to move into the extension offices, as long as I could keep a half-time secretary. Since I was then doing all my writing by dictation, the secretary was more important than the money.

Through the Rural Development Committee, I organized a faculty seminar on agricultural research and development, focusing on the problems of small farmers. This brought together professors in sociology, economics, political science, and the plant, animal, and soil sciences. At the suggestion of committee director Norman Uphoff, plant scientist Damon Boynton and I co-edited the book *Higher Yielding Human Systems for Agriculture* (Whyte and Boynton, eds.

1983). Kathleen was hired to edit that book, assuring that none of our co-authors used technical jargon, and seeing that it all fitted together without repetition.

Although I had served on several committees of the American Sociological Association (ASA), I had never run for president. In 1979, some of my younger colleagues organized a petition drive that brought in more than the required number of signatures to get me on the ballot. I had a high regard for both of the candidates selected by the nominating committee and wrote them that running was not my idea. I won the three-way contest and thus became president-elect in 1980 and president in 1981.

I was gratified by the honor and felt that I now had a chance to advance the cause of applied sociology. I believed that the leading figures in sociology had been misled by the false dichotomy between *pure or basic sociology* and *applied sociology*. Underlying that dichotomy was a status distinction. Those who pursued basic sociology regarded themselves as pure scientists and looked upon applied sociologists as nothing more than craftspeople. The purists cherished the illusion that if they continued to test specific hypotheses, those that turned out to be statistically significant would fit into an evolving theoretical framework, which would *eventually* make it possible to bring sociological knowledge to bear on practical problems.

Applied sociologists turned these assumptions upside-down. They assumed that focusing first on a practical problem and designing research strategies that led to the solution of the problem was more likely to advance sociological knowledge.

The administration of ASA is in the hands of the executive officer, who is chosen for a five-year term by a vote of the executive council, whose members are elected. The president can exert some influence as the leading member of the council, particularly at the annual meeting. The president chooses and chairs the program committee and establishes the "theme" for the meeting. This committee schedules a number of "thematic sessions," which are especially featured on the program.

For my theme, I chose "Social Inventions for Solving Human Problems." I defined a social invention as

- a new element in organizational structure or interorganizational relations;
- new sets of procedures for shaping human interactions and activities and the relations of humans to the natural and social environment;
- a new policy in action (that is, not just on paper); or
- a new role or set of roles.

297

I claimed that social inventions could be as important as technological inventions in advancing human progress. In my presidential address (Whyte 1982) I stated that, although a social scientist could devise a social invention, members of communities or organizations often did their own social inventing. To illustrate, I provided examples from the Mondragón cooperatives and from studies of agricultural research and development.

For years I had done all my public speaking on the basis of detailed notes. For this occasion, I took special pains. I rehearsed in front of Kathleen and then revised my notes on the basis of her evaluations. I recorded the speech as well. As I listened to the tape, I made further notes on points to emphasize and ways to smooth out transitions. Finally, I recorded myself once more.

The annual meeting was held in Toronto. As we drove up, I listened to the tape with Kathleen, who assured me that this version was much better than my first.

The talk went very well, but my selection of the theme for the meeting may have been a mistake. Although I did not invent the concept, few of my colleagues were thinking in terms of social inventions.

I was particularly proud of a plenary session I arranged entitled "New Perspectives on the World of Work: Organizational Innovations Enhancing the Quality of Working Life." I got Eric Trist, inventor of the sociotechnical systems framework for studying and influencing organizational change, to plan and chair the session. He brought Richard Walton of Harvard Business School, Einar Thorsrud of the Work Research Institutes in Norway, and Fred Emery from Australia, who had worked with Eric at the Tavistock Institute. This brought to the same platform the internationally recognized leaders in promoting innovations in organizational behavior. I had expected a full house and was disappointed to see many empty seats. Since most sociologists were not familiar with sociotechnical ways of thinking, none of these four men were well known to them.

In planning the annual meeting, I had circulated "Guidelines for Speakers and Session Organizers." Arguing that "the reading aloud of scientific papers is the dullest form of public performance yet invented by man," I instructed the presenters to speak rather than read. Although each speaker had to submit a written paper to get on the program, that did not mean he or she had to read the paper aloud. I added some elementary instructions on how to prepare an oral presentation.

The January 1981 issue of *Footnotes*, which was mailed to all ASA members, contained my "report" on the cultural patterns of the ASA annual meeting, supported by bogus measures of behavior. Allowed twenty minutes on the program, the typical male professor writes a twenty-page paper. He does not rehearse his presentation, even by reading aloud to himself. If he did, he would discover that the paper takes close to forty minutes to read. When he has to confront reality, he speeds up, and the audience shifts attention from the contents of the paper to his race against time. Or he tries to make instant decisions on what to cut. He finds those decisions so painful that he must summarize what he is leaving out, thus consuming most of the time gained by cutting. The typical professor presents more ideas and more quantitative data than his audience can absorb from an oral presentation. I argued that the purpose should be to interest the audience in the ideas and information presented and not to *prove* scientific points. No serious social scientist should be convinced by facts and figures presented orally, even with the backup of audiovisual aids. If the talk is interesting, the sociologist can get a copy of the paper to study. I also argued against putting discussants on the program, claiming that their customary function was to consume so much time that there was none left for audience participation.

Finally, I called for chairpersons to hold speakers to their allotted times. Since I had found them unwilling or unable to do this, I devised a technological solution, which I called FAST (Fanny-Activated Speech Terminator).

> The FAST is built on a base of upholstered chairs for the chairperson and the speakers on the platform. At the side of the chairperson's chair is a control panel with dials that can be set for the time allotted to each speaker. . . . Before introducing the speaker, the chairperson sets the dial for twenty minutes. When he sits down, the pressure of his body on the seat triggers the mechanism and the timing operation gets under way. . . . Once the timing mechanism is released, it ticks away to its inexorable conclusion. At two minutes before the end of the allotted time, the ticking becomes audible to the speaker. . . . When time runs out, an alarm begins sounding . . . and FAST provides for only one way in which it can be shut off. When the speaker returns to his seat, the pressure of his body upon sitting down triggers a mechanism that shuts off the alarm.

Colleagues enjoyed the essay, and no one questioned the conclusions from my imaginary data.

Did my reform efforts do any good? Temporarily, perhaps. About half the presenters actually spoke. But my guidelines were not continued by presidents who succeeded me.

My essay "On the Culture of the Academic Meeting" reached beyond ASA. For its next meeting, the Southern Sociological Society reprinted the essay and included it in the information packets for all registrants. A year later, the Canadian Society of Anthropology and Sociology distributed it at its annual meeting. Finally, in May 1984, the *Rural Sociologist* reprinted a condensed version of the essay, along with two essays supporting my thesis with their own imaginary data.

In advancing the cause of applied sociology, I may have made a bit of progress. I was fortunate in following Peter Rossi as ASA president. His survey research style was quite different from mine, but I had a high regard for him, and he was as dedicated as I to applied sociology.

Strongly supported by Howard Freeman and executive officer Russell Dynes, Rossi and I planned to conduct a conference on applied sociology, to be followed by a book illustrating its scientific and practical value. Peter suggested that he and I write a chapter describing the research methods a prospective applied sociologist should be required to learn. Though I had some doubts about whether we could fit our two quite different approaches together, the collaboration worked out well for both of us. I was already on record as advocating a combination of survey research and more intensive interviewing and observation, and Peter had no problems with this position.

We got financial support from ASA for the conference and the book. The book (Freeman et al., eds. 1983) was probably worth doing, but the product was not as impressive as we had hoped. All of us still had much to learn about doing applied sociology and communicating what we knew.

While I was trying to reform sociology, I found myself caught up in the struggle to save federal funding of social research from the onslaughts of the Reagan administration. Ronald Reagan was said to believe that sociology and other social science disciplines were contaminated by subversive ideologies. Leaders of the various disciplines joined forces to convert a very loose federation, without any central staff, into the Consortium of Social Science Associations (COSSA), with a small staff led by the very able Roberta Miller.

ASA executive officer Russell Dynes played a leading role in advancing COSSA, and I did my best to support the cause. As the political struggle was getting under way, I got a call from a *New York Times* reporter, who asked me to comment on the belief of Reaganites that social scientists did not have any political clout. I replied, "That remains to be seen."

I was pleasantly surprised to find that there were indeed influential members of Congress willing and able to fight for our cause. Working with the executive officers of the professional associations and some of the prominent social scientists involved in research that should be of interest to the government, Roberta Miller organized a campaign to put social science information and ideas into the hands of receptive members of Congress. She also began a series of meetings at which social scientists could report on research relevant to congressional committees. COSSA has continued its activities, playing an important role in strengthening the relationships between social scientists and the government—and ASA has continued to provide strong support for COSSA's efforts.

39. *Programs for Employment and Workplace Systems*

How does an emeritus professor find a new role for himself? During my early months in ILR's Extension Division I felt at sea without a compass. Then I got involved in the creation and development of Programs for Employment and Workplace Systems (PEWS), which turned out to be one of the most gratifying experiences of my long years at Cornell.

Donald Kane, the director of Statewide Management Programs, led me in the new direction. Teams from the personnel department of Xerox and the Amalgamated Clothing and Textile Workers Union (ACTWU) were in the ILR Conference Center for off-site training for Xerox's quality of work life (QWL) program. Social psychologist Peter Lazes was Xerox's chief trainer and consultant.

I realized at once that something exceptional was going on at Xerox. The company had started its QWL program with the goal of focusing solely on improving shop-floor relations. Matters covered in the labor contract and managerial prerogatives were off-limits. After some initial successes, the program had bogged down because work groups had been unable to deal with structural and policy issues.

The breakthrough had come when Xerox and ACTWU confronted "the wire-harness crisis." The company that created the xerography process was now losing market share and profits to Japanese competitors. That had led to the launching of an ambitious worker participation program. But it also had led to an effort to cut costs by competitive benchmarking—finding a vendor that could supply good-quality components at a lower price.

Xerox had found a vendor who could supply wire harnesses at an annual saving of $3.2 million. Management planned to close its wire harness department six months later and lay off 180 workers. The announcement sent shock waves through the plants. Using these competitive benchmarking studies, other departments could be shut down until Xerox was doing little manufacturing. The shock extended to management people in personnel, many of whom were strongly committed to worker participation. They did not see how they could continue to improve efficiency through worker involvement in the face of major layoffs.

Peter Lazes had gone back and forth between the union and management to find an alternative to the layoffs. After weeks of discussions, the parties had arrived at a social invention that we call cost study teams (CST). Management was persuaded to make an extraordinary commitment to allow a joint team of six wire harness workers and their supervisor and an engineer to devote six months at full-time pay to determining if there was any way the department could reduce its costs by $3.2 million and thus save the jobs. Management agreed to provide the team with any financial and operating data it requested. The union leaders agreed that the team could consider changes in the union contract, which could then be renegotiated. The parties agreed that if the CST did not produce a viable plan to meet the vendor's bid, Xerox would shut down the department.

Toward the end of the six-month period, the CST presented a detailed plan for saving slightly more than $3.2 million. No one in management had thought this possible, and the union leaders had considered it a very long shot.

CSTs were subsequently established for four more departments whose costs were far higher than those of outside vendors. Those CSTs either met their targets or came close enough to persuade management to keep the products in-house.

Xerox management estimates that these CSTs saved more than nine hundred jobs. Equally important, the CSTs' successes transformed managers' views of the intellectual abilities of workers. This led to worker involvement in planning the construction of a new plant and in research and development projects. It also led to an extraordinary employment security clause in the 1983 labor contract (renewed in 1986 and 1989): No worker with at least three years of continuous employment can be laid off.

I had never heard of anything that involved workers and union leaders in such far-reaching strategic issues. Nor could I think of other cases in which worker participation had such spectacular outcomes.

Peter and Don wanted to bring Xerox-style participatory systems into Cornell. Did I want to help them set up an organization to accomplish that objective? I was delighted.

First, we had to find funds to enable Peter to abandon his consulting jobs. Extension director Lois Gray liked the idea of the program but could promise no financial support. Instead, Lois invited Peter, who lived in Manhattan, to work in the ILR extension offices in New York.

Second, there was the matter of what to call our new program. We finally settled on Programs for Employment and Workplace Systems. We used the plural to indicate that we did not have a standard program to sell to every client organization but would develop programs designed to meet particular needs. We have never been satisfied with our name, but at least PEWS sounded better than one alternative we considered: Programs for Employment and Workplace Changes (PEWC). We began PEWS with Don, Peter, and me as codirectors, no staff, and no money beyond what Don could channel out of the surpluses of his Statewide Management Program.

State financing came to us in a very roundabout way. Bethlehem Steel Company had announced plans to shut down its extensive operations in Lackawanna, a city near Buffalo. Steven Allinger, staff director of the New York State Assembly's Higher Education Committee, had been born and raised near Lackawanna. The shutdown was unrelated to the business of his committee, but Steve felt he had to do something to confront the emergency in his home area.

He had read newspaper accounts of plants where jobs had been saved through employee buyouts, so he wanted to locate somebody who knew something about employee ownership. He checked the computer personnel files of the State University of New York (SUNY), but that led him to only one name, which turned out to be in there because of a computer error. At that time, the Cornell personnel files were not on the computer files, although our statutory colleges were part of the SUNY system. Steve called an old friend, Kurt Edelman, an ILR graduate living in Ithaca, and he led Steve to me.

I arranged to fly to Albany to meet with a group of assembly staffers to discuss employee ownership. I took Edwin (Wynn) Hausser with me. He was working on a thesis study of employee-owned Hyatt-Clark Industries. No one at Cornell was an expert on the economics of the steel industry, but I got names of professors elsewhere and began calling for information and advice. I learned one critical fact: Except for routine maintenance, Bethlehem's management had not invested anything in Lackawanna since 1935. To make these facilities competitive again would take an enormous investment, so an employee buyout was out of the question.

Steve met us at the airport. We agreed we would use the meeting primarily to provide the staffers with a general orientation to employee ownership, rather than concentrate on the Lackawanna emergency. We had a lively meeting with an apparently interested group, but I expected nothing to come of it.

Shortly afterward, I got a call from Steve requesting to visit Cornell with a fellow staffer for further discussions. I arranged a lunch with a professor of metallurgy, Lois Gray, Don Kane, Wynn, and me.

The discussion moved quickly beyond Lackawanna. "The state is always drawn in when disaster strikes," Steve said. "Wouldn't it be better if the state were prepared to anticipate disasters so as to take some preventive action?" Steve said he would go back to Albany and work on that idea.

A few days later, Steve called to tell me he was drafting a bill to provide PEWS with $200,000. On March 1, 1984, that bill was introduced in the assembly. PEWS was directed to study the causes of plant closings and contractions, to analyze the roles of state and local government and of labor, management, and community organizations in responding to these events, and to assess "the viability of alternate ownership and management of plants threatened by future shutdowns, such as employee and/or community ownership plans."

When I saw the draft of the bill, I called Steve to tell him that he had promised much more than PEWS could deliver in a year. He told me that bills always promised more than could be expected. If we did something useful along these lines, our program would be considered successful.

The bill stirred up interest but did not pass during the 1984 legislative session. In the meantime, PEWS had not been simply standing by. Peter offered to make trips to Albany to discuss PEWS plans with political leaders and with key officials in the state bureaucracy. I welcomed his offer, and Don arranged to pay his travel expenses.

Peter's lobbying may have been vital in keeping PEWS alive. The $200,000 appropriation for PEWS was included in the governor's 1985 budget.

Peter arranged with state officials for PEWS to charge clients for its services. This made it possible to build a larger and more effective program than would have been possible if we had been limited to state appropriations. We have worked primarily (but not exclusively) within New York State, charging top rates to industrial management and less to unions, schools, and hospitals. So far, we have been financed well enough to give us the flexibility to take on some projects for no fee and others for substantially reduced rates when there was an important social need or a staff member wanted to pursue a particular research interest.

Beyond its value to management and labor in New York State, PEWS serves to change existing patterns of research, teaching, and extension in ILR and

Cornell. The founders of ILR had a vision whereby teaching, research, and extension would be closely linked. In the early years, some professors had joint appointments in extension and in one of the resident teaching departments. Over the years, those links have been broken. Professors have concentrated more on on-campus teaching and on research. Furthermore, the emphasis has been on *pure* or *basic* research, which wins recognition from one's professional colleagues. *Applied research* has been discounted as not really scientific. The gulf between extension and resident instruction was formalized when the resident faculty passed a resolution banning future joint appointments between the two units.

Since I believed that applied research could advance scientific knowledge as well as serve practical ends, I wanted to promote this emphasis within ILR. I hoped that PEWS' close involvement with client needs and interests would lead some of us to develop research projects and publications out of our consulting and training activities. Our staff members would be in much closer touch with emerging trends in industrial relations than members of the resident faculty. It seemed unfortunate to me that faculty in extension could not teach in the resident program, no matter what they had to offer students.

The first opening came when we recruited Michael Gaffney, who was guiding a study of the U.S. shipping industry. Particularly through the pioneering work of Einar Thorsrud and his associates in Norway, that industry had become known for developing new sociotechnical systems that increased productivity and seamen's job satisfaction. Mike met Peter Lazes, who introduced him to Don Kane. They managed to persuade Mike to shift his base from the National Academy of Sciences and a naval architecture program at the University of Michigan to PEWS.

Mike had received a B.S. degree in nautical science from the U.S. Merchant Marine Academy and was a licensed officer and pilot for deep-sea and Great Lakes ships. He also had a Ph.D. from Ohio State in anthropology and had published some of his research.

I saw Mike's appointment as an opportunity for extension faculty to break into on-campus teaching. He and I designed a course that became ILR 675: "Cooperative Strategies for Strengthening Organizational Performance." After all my years of teaching in the Department of Organizational Behavior, they could not turn me down.

For two years, Mike and I taught the course together. We included case presentations from PEWS' fieldwork, and student interest was high. I sat in on most of Mike's sessions and was convinced that he could do a first-rate job on his own, perhaps even better without me. After the second year, Mike applied to do the course by himself, and the department accepted his proposal.

In the early years of PEWS, we had two tasks: to develop an effective organization and to find out how to fulfill our commitments. Fieldwork was now too strenuous for me, but I tried to learn from the experience of my colleagues.

Bringing in Mike Gaffney was the first step in PEWS' organizational development program. The next recruits were Ann Martin and Sally Klingel. Ann got involved through a field project in ILR 675 while she was pursuing a master's degree in ILR. She had been a member of the Ithaca School Board and was a practitioner of interpersonal conflict resolution. Sally had been a graduate research assistant with PEWS and in 1986 had spent several months at the Mondragón cooperatives while working on her master's.

Peter Lazes was the only one of us with experience in facilitating joint union-management programs. We all had to learn from Peter what was intended to be PEWS' main line of field intervention.

Our first step in going beyond what Peter could teach us arose out of our first fiasco, involving a large clothing manufacturer. PEWS had a contract to do a "needs assessment" preliminary to our presenting a proposal for an extended program of intervention. The PEWS team wrote a report diagnosing the organization's problems and proposing a course of treatment. The union leaders were pleased, but the plant manager rejected the diagnosis and the proposed treatment. End of project.

What went wrong? My associates had the good sense not to blame the plant manager but ourselves for this failure. We concluded that we had failed primarily because the researchers had acted like a professional elite. We had to find ways to get the leaders of the union and management involved both in making the diagnosis and deciding on the course of treatment.

Some of us had read about search conferences, and they showed us a new way to begin a field intervention, but we needed help to get started. That came from Morten Levin, a visiting scholar from the Norwegian Institute of Technology in Trondheim, Norway, who spent several months with PEWS.

Search conferences provide a means of getting key representatives of groups involved in discussions aimed at identifying their important problems and prioritizing them so as to decide which problem to work on first and how further studies and actions will be carried out.

We learned about mutual gains bargaining (also known as interest bargaining or win-win bargaining) through Bernard Flaherty, ILR's extension director of the Central District. Mike Gaffney and Ann Martin had sat in on Bernie's joint union-management workshops and learned the technique. Soon, everyone in extension was learning it, including our new extension director, Ronald Seeber, who sat in on one of Mike's workshops and then tried it out himself.

The popularity of mutual gains bargaining (MGB) arises from the recognition by unions and management that fighting among themselves can lead to serious weakening of a company's competitive position. They learn how to identify and solve problems rather than concentrating on issues.

Through a professor of education at Cornell, Joseph Novak, we learned concept mapping, a technique to help people visualize the concepts they are implicitly using so as to map out the way the organization looks to them. As group members compare their individual concept maps, they learn to understand and deal with some of their problems.

I had learned that a Xerox program that trained in-house facilitators had gone so well that more facilitators were available than were needed. Was there a way we in PEWS could take advantage of this highly skilled talent? The facilitators in management could potentially move into higher management positions, but the surplus union facilitators had nowhere to go but back to production work. Some were happy to do so, but others felt frustrated. Larry Pace in the Xerox personnel department came up with the idea of contracting out the services of some of them to other companies.

That sounded like a great idea, and I took the first steps to put it into practice. With support from the dean of ILR, Robert Doherty, and my PEWS associates, I organized a day-long meeting in the Rochester district offices of the Amalgamated Clothing and Textile Workers Union. We sent out invitations to labor and management officials in western New York State, and I persuaded Lieutenant Governor Stan Lundine to be our keynote speaker, which helped bring in a large crowd. He drew on his experience with the Jamestown Area Labor-Management Committee to support our new initiative. Some of the Xerox facilitators spoke about their experiences with cost study teams, and then they helped facilitate small-group discussions.

The meeting stirred up a lot of interest—but not for what we were trying to promote. From managers, I heard the standard claim that "our company is unique"—which implied that they could learn little from Xerox. Representatives of small companies voiced a more solid objection: Their firms did not have the resources to pay the full salaries of CST members for one month, let alone six. Nevertheless, they wanted to pursue CSTs in another form: to have Cornell develop training and discussion meetings that would generate cooperative labor-management activities.

Don Kane followed up by organizing the New York State Manufacturers' Network, a group of management and union officials. Each year, three day-and-a-half meetings are held on campus to provide members with a presentation by some recognized expert and a forum to present their problems and solutions that have been attempted. Through this growing program, practitioners learn from each other while they learn from PEWS and guest speakers, and while those in PEWS learn from them.

Ann Martin has organized a public schools network to facilitate a mutual learning process for school reform efforts. PEWS has also begun working with hospitals.

∽

The first structural change in PEWS occurred when I demoted myself from codirector to research director. That left us with Don Kane and Peter Lazes as codirectors.

The next change was precipitated by Don's decision in 1989 to become dean of academic and graduate studies at Tusculum College in Tennessee. Peter assumed that that would make him the sole director.

With Don, I organized a committee to do some long-range planning. We found ourselves concentrating almost entirely on the question of who should be the director. I believed Peter was a highly gifted consultant, but the other members of PEWS strongly resisted his appointment as sole director—and I shared some of their reservations. We proposed that Peter and Mike Gaffney should be codirectors. Extension director Ronald Seeber and Dean David Lipsky accepted our recommendation, but Peter rejected it. He dropped out of PEWS but remained in ILR Extension in the New York City office.

The ILR administration appointed Gaffney director. After the many weeks of discussions and negotiations on the directorship issue, the members of PEWS settled down with a sense of relief and turned their energies back to project development and recruiting replacements for Don and Peter.

The first appointment, in 1990, went to Frank Wayno, who had a strong record as a private consultant and who welcomed the opportunity to work with a university group. He had an undergraduate degree from Cornell's College of Engineering and a Ph.D. in sociology from Princeton.

In 1991, Edward Cohen-Rosenthal joined us. He had served on the staff of the Bricklayers, Masons and Plasterers' International Union, and had run his own consulting firm, whose focus was labor-management relations. Through his consulting and publications, he had built strong relations with unions, and he had shown that he could work effectively with management.

Frank Wayno and Mike Gaffney co-taught ILR 675, "Cooperative Strategies for Strengthening Organizational Performance." When Cornell's engineering college decided to institute a new master's program in manufacturing engineering, a business school professor suggested that ILR 675 might be a useful course to include in the program. The planners asked Mike and Frank to adapt it as a required course for them. When it went well, Frank took over the engineering course, and Mike became sole teacher for the original ILR 675.

Frank's success persuaded some of the engineering professors of the importance of visualizing manufacturing in terms of sociotechnical systems. To expand his own background in these ideas, Albert R. George, director of the Cornell Manufacturing Engineering and Productivity Program (COMEPP), arranged to co-teach ILR 675e with Frank in the fall of 1992. At the same time, Mark A. Turnquist, a professor of civil and environmental engineering, invited Frank to co-teach project management with him.

As Frank was fitting into the engineering teaching program, Albert George was exploring the possibility of developing a universitywide program of teaching and research in manufacturing. The engineers and the business school already had a joint master's program, and now PEWS and ILR were recognized as important contributors.

In January 1993, Cornell's board of trustees approved the establishment of the Center for Manufacturing Enterprise (CME). Albert George was appointed director, and Frank Wayno was named executive director. Membership is open to all professors and research associates, and representation in the governing structure is roughly proportional to the number of members with teaching and research interests in manufacturing.

Frank has a half-time commitment to CME, which means he devotes the other half to PEWS. Frank sees PEWS as having a major involvement with CME. In fact, PEWS' New York State Network could become a major component of CME.

In 1990, I established an academic advisory council to PEWS as a means of becoming more closely involved with the resident faculty. I invited professors who were sympathetic to PEWS but who also carried weight in their own departments. We selected one member from each of ILR's four main departments, a professor from Cornell's business school who had strong links with the College of Engineering, and a professor from the Department of City and Regional

Planning in the College of Architecture, Art and Planning. In 1992, we invited Albert George, the director of CME, to join the committee.

In our first meeting, Lee Dyer, head of the Department of Personnel and Human Resources in ILR, expressed a tentative interest in a proposed study of the role of company and union facilitators in cooperative union-management activities. We proposed to start this project with Xerox.

Lee's department had set up the Center for Advanced Human Resources Studies (CAHRS), financed by more than fifty large companies, to support research of interest to the corporate sponsors and to the professors involved and to improve communication between the worlds of business and Cornell University. After the committee meeting, Lee said that, although CAHRS might support the proposed project with Xerox, he was much more interested in a study of how Xerox escaped financial disaster and restructured itself so as to win the Baldrige Award for highest-quality organizational performance.

Ann Martin wanted to do the project on facilitators, and Frank Wayno had a strong interest in studying the overall process of how Xerox transformed itself in the years 1978 to 1989. I then drafted the research proposal for CAHRS.

The grant was approved, and I was named as the principal investigator, even though I had made it clear that I would not be doing any fieldwork. Perhaps that was necessary to give the project academic legitimacy.

Frank's report on Xerox received an enthusiastic reception from our academic advisory committee and from CAHRS. CAHRS devoted a whole day of briefings for its member companies to discussions of the study. CAHRS was now eager to discuss further research Frank wanted to do, and he no longer needed me to provide academic legitimacy.

David Lipsky, dean of ILR, and extension director Ronald Seeber have told us in PEWS that the program is their strongest evidence that ILR is committed to contributing to the state. We cannot claim that our long-term position is secure, but we have established PEWS as an organization that bridges the gap between "pure," but often sterile, academic research and teaching, and applied research and consulting. Professors elsewhere are beginning to look to PEWS as representing a model for applying teaching and research to the practical problems of the organizational world — an ideal often stated for a university but rarely represented in practice.

I cannot claim that I anticipated all the major contributions PEWS has made. In my original vision for PEWS, I never imagined we would become increasingly involved with Cornell's engineering and business schools. In this, we built on trends on the Cornell campus and in the nation. In the 1940s and 1950s, when Allan Holmberg tried to interest professors in agriculture through his Vicos project, he got no response. By the 1980s, Cornell had developed active collaborative relations between agricultural and social scientists. In earlier decades, I had seen no interest among engineering professors in involving behavioral scientists in their work, whereas now many of them recognize the role of sociotechnical systems in industry. The federal government's shift to a more active economic and industrial development policy is likely to further these trends. In the competition for federal industrial development support, Cornell has an important competitive advantage. Many universities have colleges of engineering and business administration, but only Cornell has a School of Industrial and Labor Relations.

40. Participatory Action Research

Since my initial introduction to cost study teams at Xerox, they have excited my interest. They arose out of an unusual collaboration of practitioners with a behavioral scientist. The behavioral scientist/facilitator led union and management to agree to set up the CSTs and helped them develop methods of study and group discussion, but the practitioners (six production workers and two members of management) did the research in accounting and engineering to show how Xerox could cut its costs by more than the $3.2 million target amount. In my publications, I suggested that this methodology be called participatory action research (PAR).

I defined PAR as the active participation of one or more of the practitioners working with a consultant/researcher on a project and the actions arising out of it. When the first application of PAR took place, I cannot say, but the most impressive early case involved the Norwegian Industrial Democracy Program, led by social psychologist Einar Thorsrud in the 1960s. The goal of this program, undertaken by the Work Research Institute and shipping companies, unions, and ship officers and seamen, was to improve the competitive position of Norwegian shipping and the quality of the work lives of seamen. The behavioral scientists structured the discussion and experimentation, but it was practitioners, from management officials to seamen, who provided the essential technical and social information used to redesign the ships and make the necessary social changes. The program led to major changes in Norwegian shipping and stimulated similar changes in the fleets of other nations.

At Xerox, it was not only the practical results that impressed me. PAR produced what I called "creative surprises": theoretical advances that would not have arisen out of a conventional social research process. It led to a reconceptualization of one of the most studied problems in organizational behavior: the relationship between worker participation and productivity. It also demonstrated that the way indirect or administrative costs are allocated can have an enormous impact on how management measures labor costs—and on the actions taken regarding labor.

Davydd Greenwood's involvement with PAR arose while he was working with the Mondragón cooperatives. With José Luis González, personnel manager of the FAGOR group of twelve cooperatives, he spent the month of July 1985 in morning meetings for fifteen members of the personnel department of FAGOR and its constituent cooperatives discussing social research methods and theories. The aim was to help the members understand the culture of the cooperatives so as to enable them to improve the performance of the personnel department. As he wrote to me: "We did not start out to do PAR. I simply believed that they know much more about the organization than I and that I was there to help them, not simply to instruct them. It developed into PAR later."

The seminar members arrived with notebooks and pencils, expecting to take complete notes on what Davydd said. Davydd did some lecturing, but he also stimulated participation in the personnel project by encouraging the group to study the culture of Ulgor, the oldest and largest of their cooperatives. Most of them had worked in Ulgor, so they could draw on experience, as well as on extensive documentary records. They read what had been published about the Mondragón cooperatives, and Kathleen and I shared the first draft of our manuscript on Mondragón (1988) with Davydd. Alex Goiricelaya, of the seminar group, read them, and he went over his detailed criticisms and suggestions with us. Thus, what had been our personal research became part of the developing PAR project, to our great advantage because we were able to correct factual errors and incorporate important new material.

At Davydd's suggestion, the group decided to crystallize its interpretation of the culture of Ulgor by writing a monograph. Davydd worked with José Luis González and four other members of the group to write what became a 116-page paper, which they delivered to Javier Mongelos, general manager of the FAGOR group.

Mongelos was impressed and urged the group to continue to study the culture of FAGOR. At this point, the project advanced beyond personal recollections and the analysis of documents to include fieldwork. They interviewed members of the cooperative representing different educational backgrounds, work positions, and tenure. They also conducted small-group discussions of members with various backgrounds and experiences.

The 1986 summer project led to more months of analysis and writing that culminated in a book (Greenwood et al. 1991). It also led to several members carrying out their own PAR projects in some of the cooperatives.

In 1988, while I was planning a session on PAR for the annual meeting of the Eastern Sociological Society (ESS), Mitchell Allen, executive editor of Sage Publications, called to say that my session looked interesting. Would participatory action research be a good topic for a special issue of *American Behavioral Scientist*, for which he was general editor? If so, would I like to edit it?

I had been working with Davydd Greenwood and Peter Lazes on an article on PAR. We were stuck with drafts too long for journal articles but too short for a book. With the option of the special issue, we could use as much space as we needed.

Our issue came out in May 1989, under the provocative title "Action Research for the Twenty-First Century: Participation, Reflection, and Practice" and stirred up interest among our social science colleagues, which suggested expanding it to a book. In the *American Behavioral Scientist*, we had limited ourselves to industrial cases. Now I realized that I had been studying PAR projects in agricultural research and development. A book dealing with cases in both industry and agriculture would emphasize the power and range of PAR.

The volume I edited, *Participatory Action Research* (1990), attracted more attention than the special issue of *American Behavioral Scientist*, and working on that book propelled me to write my next: *Social Theory for Action: How Individuals and Organizations Learn to Change* (1991). I wanted to make the case that applied social research could yield advances in scientific knowledge as well as practical results. I also felt that I had developed theoretical ideas in my textbook, *Organizational Behavior: Theory and Application* (1969), that had not gained the scholarly attention they deserved. If I restated those ideas in a new context, perhaps they would catch on. The edited book suggested the context: participatory processes in agriculture as well as in industry.

While I was working on my book, I received a letter from Sheldon Hackney, president of the University of Pennsylvania, informing me of the applications of the PAR strategy in a program the university was pursuing in the poverty-stricken neighborhood surrounding it. His letter thanked me for providing some of the inspiration guiding Penn's program.

That a president of a major university should take such an interest in a neighborhood program struck me as unusual and exciting. The program was an essential part of his university development strategy. Before Hackney's arrival at Penn, the university had been in an increasingly adversarial relationship with its surrounding slum community, as Penn expanded without regard to the impact on the neighborhoods. Hackney announced that Penn would seek to develop a harmonious relationship with its city and particularly with the neighborhoods surrounding the university. He did not visualize university experts trying to do good things to the community. Rather, he had a vision of university and neighborhood people jointly studying and solving community problems.

Putting that vision into practice depended on the leadership of Ira Harkavy, vice dean of the School of Arts and Sciences and director of the Penn Program for Public Service (PPPS), and Lee Benson, a professor of history. A novel feature of the Penn PAR program is that all three of these men are historians, although Benson has made the history of the social sciences one of his specialties. This represents a significant expansion of PAR strategies beyond the behavioral sciences.

The Penn program began with interdisciplinary summer seminars taught by Hackney, Harkavy, and Benson on the problems of Philadelphia. Each undergraduate was required to pick a problem, analyze it, and write a paper on what might be done to solve it.

The professors found these seminars interesting, and they were impressed by the student papers. Still, the seminars were only an academic enterprise. Students were dealing with such a wide variety of topics in such a large urban area that there was no way to move toward action.

Harkavy and Benson decided to sharpen the focus by concentrating on the area surrounding the university. In consultation with community people, they organized the West Philadelphia Improvement Corps (WEPIC) to link the neighborhood and the university. To involve local people in an expanding series of projects, a local resident was appointed executive director of WEPIC, while the Penn Program for Public Service (PPPS) served as the means to attract undergraduate and graduate students and professors into community projects. Without pushing an explicitly race relations program, WEPIC and PPPS projects got both black and white students and professors working on the same projects.

The Penn program established a strong base in the community through the Turner Middle School, whose principal welcomed PPPS and appointed a teacher as a liaison between the university and the school. In one project, Penn students worked with Turner pupils on refurbishing and redecorating the school. Meanwhile, Jack Ende, director of ambulatory care education in Penn's medical school, mobilized a group of students to teach middle school pupils how to do blood pressure readings. The Turner pupils and staff then organized free blood pressure screenings for their parents and other adults.

Turner teachers also developed a health improvement course, emphasizing preventive measures. And the dean of the medical school is now working with PPPS and WEPIC on a project to develop and finance a community health maintenance facility.

Kathleen and I visited Philadelphia in April 1990. Ira Harkavy convened a group of deans and professors from various parts of the university to discuss PAR. Ira credited me with providing essential guidance for PPPS. I was not convinced that I had done more than provide a good rationale for what they were doing.

When many university presidents are so preoccupied with raising money, I was happy to find one who had a vision for his university and the capacity to inspire professors and students to pursue that vision. It was also exciting to get to know so creative, energetic, and resourceful a leader as Ira Harkavy. As time passes, more and more students and professors from the various faculties of the University of Pennsylvania are responding to the invitation to work with WEPIC to revitalize the neighborhood.

Ira is so dedicated to PAR that he is determined to spread the message of its value beyond Cornell and Penn. In February 1992, he talked us into staging a conference on PAR at the University of Pennsylvania, sponsored jointly by Cornell and Penn and organized by Davydd and Ira. The idea was to bring together a small group of people already involved in PAR-like activities to exchange ideas. As word of the conference spread, the list of potential participants kept growing. Ira and Davydd had to stop accepting attendees at fifty, but that included strong representation from Cornell and Penn, as well as from Britain, Norway, the Netherlands, Israel, and Canada.

Besides generating interest and enthusiasm, the Penn meeting stirred up controversy over the definition and use of the term "participatory action research." I never claimed to have invented the term and had pointed out that my definition also applied to many other projects whose methodologies had been given other names by their directors. Nevertheless, some saw us as trying to impose our terminology and definitions on anyone trying to engage in participatory research. They claimed that PAR was originally used to describe a *radical* organizing strategy developing in the Third World and was being corrupted by *liberal* researchers in the industrially developed nations.

∼

The months following publication of *Participatory Action Research* yielded many indications that PAR was catching on in the United States. In 1991, Mitch Allen of Sage called to tell me about a conference at which the Sage exhibit was besieged with people wanting to buy *Participatory Action Research*. Robert Graves, director of the National Institute of Disabilities and Rehabilitation, had been the principal speaker. Graves had brandished a copy of the book, as he announced that his institute had decided to support research projects designed along PAR lines.

In 1992, I was invited by James Coleman, president of ASA, to give a "didactic seminar" on PAR at the organization's annual meeting in Pittsburgh. In contrast to the regular sessions, in which each speaker has about twenty minutes and there are scheduled discussants, a didactic seminar gives a recognized expert full freedom to plan an hour and fifty minutes as he or she wishes.

I seem to be emerging, at least temporarily, as the "guru" of PAR. The reputation is more than I deserve. I only claim credit for popularizing the concept and clarifying the terminology.

Confusion has prevailed regarding how PAR is related to *action research* and *participatory research*. There can be action research without participation and participatory research without action. In fact, until recently, in the most common type of action research, the professional researcher sought to maintain as much control as possible over the research and the actions that flowed from it.

There is also participatory research in which individuals in a community or organization participate in a research process that is not designed to lead to action. For example, the men I called Doc and Sam Franco in *Street Corner Society*, played active roles in guiding the research process. We all hoped the book would someday benefit poor urban people somewhere, but such a vague objective can hardly be called action. I suspect this process often occurs in social anthropological studies. Individuals who begin by being informants become key informants and even informal collaborators.

It is important to reserve the term "participatory action research" only for projects in which individuals among the population studied *participate* actively in the research process and help generate *action* that grows out of the research. There are indeed important issues regarding "liberal" or "radical" plans for social change that deserve study, but questions of political ideology should not be confused with descriptions of the relations between professional researchers and the organizations they study.

41. The Book That Would Not Die

W hen I finished *Street Corner Society*, I thought I had accomplished
something important. Early reactions of my sociological colleagues,
however, were disappointing. The official journal of the American
Sociological Society, the *American Sociological Review*, did not review the book.
A distinguished criminologist did give me a favorable review in the *American
Journal of Sociology*, but he called the book just another good slum study.

At first, the book got a better reception outside the academic world. In early
1944, Harry Hansen, a nationally syndicated columnist, devoted one column to
Street Corner Society. He concluded, the book "offers fresh material on the ever
important subject of American community life, presenting it eloquently from
the human angle."

The book was reviewed in several newspapers but not in Boston. The reviewer
in the neighboring city of Providence guessed the study had taken place in
Chicago.

At first, sales seemed to confirm the pessimistic prediction of the publisher's
business manager. The book was published in December 1943. By 1945, sales
had declined to a trickle.

My 1946 royalty check, which reflected a tripling of sales over the previous
year, came as a happy surprise. World War II veterans were flocking back into
colleges and graduate schools, and their GI benefits provided generous allow-
ances for the purchase of books. At the same time, many teachers of sociology
were becoming dissatisfied with simply assigning textbooks and were requiring
students to read research monographs.

By the early 1950s, sales were again declining, and once again the book
appeared to be about to go out of print. Alex Morin, an editor at the University
of Chicago Press, told me that he had reread *Street Corner Society* in the hope of

getting ideas for a revision that might justify a new edition and keep the book alive. He could not think of anything to suggest, but the conversation set me thinking.

While I was director of Cornell's Social Science Research Center, I worked with colleagues on improving training in research methods for students in the behavioral sciences. When I taught a seminar on field methods, I oriented students to participant observation on the basis of my own experience. To make the method accessible to other students and professors, I wanted to draw up a list of readings.

A canvass of the literature revealed practically nothing worth considering. It seemed as if the academic world had imposed a conspiracy of silence regarding the personal experiences of field-workers. The authors had written what read like statements of what they would have done if they had known at the outset what the study was going to reveal. It was impossible to find accounts that described the errors and confusions and the personal dilemmas a field-worker encounters.

I decided to do my bit to fill this gap. In so doing, I resolved to be as honest about myself as possible. That meant not suppressing foolish incidents, such as my abortive attempt to pick up a girl in a tavern or my involvement in a federal crime—voting four times in a congressional election—although several colleagues advised me not to make such a confession. I wrote as I did to help future field-workers understand that, although some mistakes are inevitable, it is possible to produce a valuable study.

The 1955 edition, with an appendix on my field experiences, gave *Street Corner Society* a new lease on life. In the 1960s, the publication of a paperback edition boosted sales to a new high. Adding the appendix also appears to have had a more general effect. After its publication, other behavioral scientists began publishing their own personal accounts of field experiences.

I had no thought of a third edition until the ceremonies marking my retirement in 1980. Robert Doherty, dean of ILR, invited me to ask seven collaborators to make remarks at the ceremonies. I asked six behavioral science colleagues—Margaret Chandler, Melvin Kohn, Chris Argyris, Leonard Sayles, George Strauss, and Joseph Blasi—and my North End collaborator, Angelo Ralph Orlandella.

Much as I treasured the remarks by my old friends, it was Ralph's talk that inspired me to do the third edition. Several members of the audience said that his talk had to be published. That gave me the idea to make "The Whyte Impact on an Underdog" appendix B. For the third edition (1981), I also added an account of how I got *Street Corner Society* accepted by the University of Chicago sociology department as a Ph.D. thesis without the customary review of the literature, without footnotes, and without that final obligatory sentence: "More research is needed on this topic."

Since more than forty years had passed since I left the North End, I could see no harm now in identifying the city as Boston and in using the actual names of some of the leading characters. (Doc had died in 1967.) I also thought this might add interest to the book.

In 1991, five behavioral scientists co-edited a book entitled *Reframing Organizational Culture* (Frost et al. 1991). They devoted a section to *Street Corner Society* as "an exemplar of organizational culture research." That section was followed by essays by four behavioral scientists on the book and my responses. Since all the critics hailed the book as a classic, I could hardly object, but there were some points of disagreement worth discussing.

The editors of the *Journal of Contemporary Ethnography* told me the journal was considering doing a special issue on *Street Corner Society*. The idea had come up as a result of an article by W. A. Marianne Boelen that had been submitted to the journal. She had gone back to the North End on several occasions thirty to forty-five years after I left, had interviewed some of the people I knew and some others, and had written an interpretation quite different from mine. The journal would print Boelen's article only if I agreed to write a rejoinder and if the editors could recruit three behavioral scientists to serve as critics.

The editors told me that the decision to print Boelen's article could not be made until the journal had a lawyer read the manuscript. That suggested the possibility of libel. It took several months to resolve *that* issue, and, in the meantime, while I was trying to fall asleep at night, I would sometimes worry as I tried to imagine what Boelen wanted to print about me.

When I finally received Boelen's fifty-seven-page article, I found it to be a sloppy hatchet job. I was inclined simply to report that my field notes told a different story. But then Kathleen persuaded me to take Boelen's challenge seriously. She reminded me of Derek Freeman's attack on Margaret Mead, to which Harvard University Press had lent credibility by publishing as a purported restudy. When Freeman's book appeared, Margaret Mead was dead. I had the advantage of being able to defend myself.

My Boston field notes had been stored in the ILR library, and now I got them out again. Kathleen spent about two weeks organizing the notes and letters to and from North End friends. I spent some of that time looking for evidence to refute Boelen's most serious charges.

I sent a copy of Boelen's article to Angelo Ralph Orlandella. He called me in high dudgeon over what he considered Boelen's misguided and mean-spirited attack. I encouraged him to write me his comments. Ralph entitled his paper "Boelen May Know Holland, Boelen May Know Barzini, But Boelen 'Doesn't Know Diddle about the North End.' " I sent it to the editor of the journal, who published it along with my paper, "In Defense of *Street Corner Society*."

When I agreed to answer Boelen's attack, I assumed the three behavioral scientists the journal editors were asking to serve as critics would judge whether my account or Boelen's was more likely the accurate portrayal of the North End in the late 1930s. None of the three took a position on that issue. Social anthropologist Arthur Vidich simply stated that "readers may draw their own conclusions about the issues raised in these essays" (80), but he then paid tribute to the continuing value of *Street Corner Society* for social theory and practice in urban slum areas.

Sociologists Laurel Richardson and Norman Denzin did not deal with the issue because for them the nature of the critical game had changed since I did the study. Richardson (103–4) stated that she writes about *Street Corner Society*

now in a radically different context from that in which it was produced. Some refer to the present intellectual context as "postfoundational." The core of this postfoundational climate is *doubt* that any discourse has a privileged place, any text an authoritative "corner" on the truth.

Denzin called me a "positivist-social realist" (130) and stated that

today, social realism is under attack. It is now seen as but one narrative strategy for telling stories about the world out there. (126)

As the 20th century is now in its last decade, it is appropriate to ask if we any longer want this kind of social science that Whyte produced and Boelen, in her own negative way, endorses? (131)

These critiques took me by surprise. I had been vaguely aware of the rise of deconstructionism in literary criticism and the appeal of its offshoots in critical epistemology among some behavioral scientists, but I did not see how it was relevant to someone striving to produce scientific studies of social relations.

Although I found it hard to take critical epistemology seriously, some of my colleagues saw merits in it, so I clearly needed to learn more. Guided by Davydd Greenwood, I began reading up on the literature. Unable to find anything of lasting value in it, I concluded that critical epistemology was bound to be a passing fad.

I could not imagine how Boelen had become so dedicated to attacking me. Herbert Gans, of Columbia University, where Boelen got her M.A. degree, and the author of the classic study *Urban Villagers*, wrote to tell me he had tried to persuade Boelen not to pursue her attack against me but that she had seemed obsessed with trying to make her case.

I wondered how I could get even with Boelen for all the anxiety she had caused me. Never before had I felt as if I wanted to get even with anybody, so I dropped that tack and began thinking about how I could turn all the pain to my advantage.

I decided to propose to the University of Chicago Press that it publish a fiftieth anniversary edition of *Street Corner Society*. I informed the editor of the extraordinary revival of scholarly interest in the book and suggested that I could add to the appendix on my fieldwork experiences a commentary on the issues raised around the book. Associate editor Penelope Kaiserlian happily accepted this idea. (I also discussed some of these issues in *Sociological Forum* in June 1993.)

By a happy coincidence, I got a notice from the Eastern Sociological Society as I was working on the anniversary edition informing me that the annual meeting in 1993 would be on March 26–29 in Boston. What could be more fitting than to celebrate the fiftieth anniversary of the book where it took place? I wrote the president of ESS, Doris Wilkinson, to suggest an author-meets-critics session at that meeting. She agreed and told me that ESS was planning such a session with Herb Gans on *Urban Villagers*, but he had said priority should be given to *Street Corner Society* since it was the fiftieth anniversary and the thirty-ninth for his book. (Both sessions were held.)

Normally, the author has no say in the design of a book jacket, but I pointed out that Kathleen had provided the design for the 1943 and 1955 editions. (That jacket also appears on the cover of the October 1993 issue of *Qualitative Sociology*.) The press had used its own artist for the paperback edition in the 1960s, but he had depicted the corner boys in a garb unlike anything I had ever seen on the corner. For the cover of the 1981 edition, the press used a photograph Ralph Orlandella had taken of his gang in the mid-1930s. Ralph supplied a newspaper photograph which shows our protest march on city hall. (I am in that picture, behind the leaders, as I preferred to be.)

Ralph was excited about the fiftieth anniversary edition and my session at the Boston meeting. He called to suggest an addition to the celebration. Years earlier, his son, Frank, had won a four thousand–dollar scholarship to Holy Cross College. Now Ralph wanted to donate five thousand dollars to the Eastern Sociological Society to support a student doing field research in a depressed urban area. Kathleen and I were overwhelmed that a man of modest means would give ESS such a generous gift. This may be a unique case in which a subject of social research who became a co-researcher put up money for a grant to support social problems research. I wrote to Doris Wilkinson. She arranged for ESS to set up a committee to work out the rules for administering the grant.

In organizing the plenary session on *Street Corner Society*, Doris Wilkinson allowed me the unusual privilege of choosing my critics. I wanted one to be a skillful and experienced participant observer, so I asked Elijah Anderson of the University of Pennsylvania, author of *Streetwise*, a study of adjoining city districts, one predominantly black and one predominantly white. Although I did not accept the "postfoundational critique," I felt bound to have it represented, and for that I chose Patricia Clough of Fordham University, author of *The End(s) of Ethnography*. As presider, I chose Peter Rose of Smith College, immediate past president of ESS and an old friend with whom I had served on the executive council of ASA. Doris encouraged him to provide his own interpretation, while he set the program up for others—and he did a beautiful job.

I had told Peter that Ralph Orlandella could not serve as a critic since he was a co–participant observer but that I hoped he would join in the discussion from the floor. I was happy when Peter overruled me and invited Ralph to speak from the platform. He also asked Herbert Gans to speak.

Elliot Liebow, author of *Talley's Corner*, wrote me that he was not able to attend, but he sent this statement, which he wanted read into the record:

> Quite apart from its extraordinary execution, *Street Corner Society* was startling in its distinctive methodology. Indeed, it is *Street Corner Society* that defines participant observation in the present day, and *Street Corner Society* that sets the standard by which all subsequent participant observation research is to be measured.

Peter read and endorsed that statement, and similar judgments were echoed by Elijah and Herb. Patricia Clough spoke along different lines, but she did not give me a hard time. Ralph did not know he would be called on, but he was a big hit with the audience.

When the session was all over and I was getting my notes together, I suddenly realized that five hundred people were on their feet, clapping. That was a wonderful surprise. Never before had I received a standing ovation.

What followed was almost as exciting as the session itself. Sociologist John Hudson invited Ralph to speak in April at the annual meeting of the New England Sociological Association at Bryant College in Rhode Island. His talk, "A More Effective Strategy for Dealing with Inner City Street Corner Gangs," described how what he and I had learned together through interviewing and observation could help those trying to deal with corner gangs. The message was simple but basic: To work effectively with street corner gangs, you must first identify and work with their informal leaders.

He explained that in a group of three or more, the leader is the one who frequently (but not always) initiates a change in group activity. When anyone else proposes a change, it does not happen unless the leader supports it. Gaining the leader's support is only the beginning, but it is a necessary first step toward bridging the gap between the gang and middle-class and professional people who might be able to help the group find new activities that would have a long-term payoff.

Ralph's talk was a big hit at the Bryant College meeting, which encouraged him to put it in writing. I provided some editorial assistance, but the ideas were his own. (Ralph's article is to be published in a forthcoming issue of *The Gang Journal*, which seeks to reach people in law enforcement as well as sociologists.)

How does an author of many books feel when his first book is hailed as a sociological classic and none of his later books receives such scholarly (and popular) recognition? I have mixed feelings. I like to think I have written other important books. Still, I cannot resent the recognition *Street Corner Society* continues to receive. I have a special warm spot in my heart for it.

I lived that book longer and more intensively than any others, a year and a half alone and then with Kathleen for the final two years. What did it do for me? Besides the professional recognition I received and the income from the sales of 160,000 copies, the book had a profound effect on me. Up to the point of writing it, I had been on a fast track academically, even though I did not know where I was going. From *Bill Whyte Visits the Elementary School* to *Financing New York City*, my intellectual achievements had come unusually early. Nevertheless, I was concerned by the lack of fit between my social values and the comfortable life I was living. Like many other liberal middle-class Americans, my sympathies were with the poor and unemployed, but I felt somewhat hypocritical for not truly understanding their lives. In writing *Street Corner Society*, I was beginning to put the two parts of my life together.

In college, I had progressed by expressing myself well orally and especially in writing. In the North End, I had to learn to listen to others, to draw out their life experiences and views, and eighteen months had passed before I knew what to write. That long dormant period troubled me, but through it I learned the virtue of patience, which I had never had before. During later projects, I came to expect that when I did not understand what I was observing, the underlying pattern would reveal itself if I just kept active in the field and kept on writing.

The North End was not only an intellectual challenge. I had to win the friendship and respect of people with a far different background from my own. In that process, I came to like and respect myself more. When I left the North End, I at last knew where I was going.

42. Adjusting to Retirement and Aging

A s a child of eight, as I thought about life and death, I noted that both my parents and grandparents had lived through the dawn of the twentieth century, and I thought it would be a good idea to live to usher in the twenty-first. Subtracting 1914 from 2000, that meant living to the age of eighty-six.

As I reached retirement age in 1979, I wondered how much time I had left. My four grandparents had lived into their early or mid-seventies. My mother had died at eighty-six. My father had been struck down by a heart attack at sixty-four. I reassured myself that I did not have his health risks. He had smoked for many years, whereas I quit smoking after that half a pack at age eleven. My father was also quite different from me temperamentally. In layman's terms, he was high-strung and I am more calm. That suggested I would have a good chance to live into my seventies. I had no guarantee that I would see the new century, so I wanted to try to finish my personal agenda in the 1990s.

Adjusting to retirement was easy. After moving into ILR Extension, I settled into a working pattern that has been ideal. As research director of PEWS, I keep close to the research and action, without getting involved in field projects.

In sheer volume of output, my years since retirement have been the most productive of my life. Besides various articles, I have written or coauthored or edited *Worker Participation and Ownership: Cooperative Strategies for Strengthening Local Economies* (1983), *Higher Yielding Human Systems for Agriculture* (1983), *Learning from the Field* (1984), *Industrial Democracy: Strategies for Community Revitalization* (1985), *Making Mondragón: The Growth and Dynamics of the Worker Cooperative Complex* (1988), *Participatory Action Research* (1990), *Social Theory for Action: How Individuals and Organizations Learn to Change* (1991), and now this autobiography.

Advancing age brought other pleasures. In May 1988, Kathleen and I celebrated our fiftieth wedding anniversary, surrounded by our extended family.
There were my daughter Joyce and son-in-law Joseph Wiza and their four children from Derry, New Hampshire. Joyce is a stained-glass designer and active
with the National Organization for Women. Joe was a physicist and engineer
with an electronics firm. Martin came with his wife, Veronica, and their two
children from Ann Arbor, Michigan. A sociologist, Martin has become an
authority on China and on family studies. Lucy and her husband, Allen Ferguson, came with their four children from Silver Spring, Maryland. Lucy has
built a very successful chiropractic practice, and Allen is a lawyer with special
expertise in labor relations. John came with his companion, Tom Wilson Weinberg, from Boston. With his M.D. and Ph.D. in psychology, John is engaged
in brain injury research and rehabilitation. We were also joined by Kathleen's
brother, Timothy King, and his wife, Frances, from Washington, D.C.

It was a happy event. We all felt we were among nice people, caring people,
interesting people whom we could admire as well as enjoy.

I felt that this day belonged particularly to Kathleen. Lucy had told us a story
that I often think of when I remember our anniversary party. Her twelve-year-
old son, Blake, had been going steady with his first girl. Then suddenly he
stopped seeing her. Lucy asked him what had happened. He replied, "You
know, Mom, love does not last forever." I can't testify about "forever," but I can
say that I am much more in love with Kathleen now than when we were married.

If adjusting to retirement was easy, aging presented more problems. I knew
that advancing age would mean some loss of strength. I first noticed it when I
was out in the garden. Kathleen had always done far more of that work, but I
had tried to help and get some exercise while doing the unskilled job of weeding.
I had no trouble getting down on the ground, but it was more and more of a
strain to push my body up, reach down to pick up one crutch, push up on that
crutch to a standing position, and lean on it while I bent down to pick up the
second. In my early seventies, I had to give it up.

For exercise, I was now limited to some walking and a half-hour or so of
swimming every day. When my right leg was no longer strong enough to lift
me straight up the pool ladder, I had to lean to the left and push up with my
left hand. That helped bring on carpal tunnel syndrome, and I required an
operation. Fortunately, our pool man discovered the Nolan chair lift, a remarkable chair that turns and eases me down into the water and then lifts me back
up, operating entirely on water power from a hose.

In June 1989, I fell and broke my left thigh bone. That was the third time I broke a leg, the first two times having been in the 1960s. Since it would be some weeks before I was able to get back to the office, my friends arranged to have PEWS buy me a computer and a printer. I had been dictating or typing most of what I wrote, and at first I did not know how I would adapt to this new technology. As I got used to it, I became addicted to the computer and dictated only brief letters.

When I had recovered enough to put weight on my left leg, I found I was weaker than before and was walking more awkwardly. Lucy gave me some exercises to build up my legs. Then John arranged for me to have my walking gait and strength evaluated at the Moss Rehabilitation Hospital in Philadelphia, where he was now in charge of head injury research. The doctor who tested me commented, "It is remarkable what you can do with what you haven't got." He prescribed a full-length brace for my right leg. For years I had worn a left leg brace that extended from below the knee to the foot.

In the past, we had rented wheelchairs for emergency use. Now we needed one of our own. Since I had poor circulation, I had to elevate my feet when I sat for any length of time. At Moss, I was measured for a custom-made chair that has leg supports that lengthen when lifted and contract when lowered.

The new plastic brace under my right foot required more strength to operate my car's brake and accelerator, making driving exhausting and unsafe. We solved that problem by buying a Dodge Caravan, which has ample space for the wheelchair, and had hand controls installed.

I assumed that, as I walked more and did Lucy's exercises, I would get back the strength I had before I broke the leg. Instead, distances I had walked without difficulty were now too exhausting. At last I had to recognize that postpolio syndrome had caught up with me. I had been reading reports on other old polio patients, some of whom had gained back much more strength than I, whose overused muscles had given out. For years I had prided myself on doing as much as I could. Now I realized that pushing myself may well have contributed to my muscle deterioration.

In August 1990, I suffered a minor stroke. When I woke up one morning, I could not talk straight. I knew what I wanted to say, but, as much as I tried, I could say no nouns. Kathleen and I had a frightening time. She brought me a pad and asked me to write. What I wrote was completely incoherent. After about twelve hours, the words began to come back. The following day, with some hesitation, I could speak intelligibly, but I was still at a loss for some words.

Hospital tests showed I had a small blood clot in the part of the brain that controls speech. Gradually, I regained my facility to speak and write, but for a month or two I would sometimes find myself blocked on words that I had known well. That posed a problem since I was scheduled to speak at a University of Pennsylvania conference on the state of social sciences. For years I had spoken from detailed notes and had argued against the common practice of reading speeches. Would I now find myself blocked in the middle of my talk? I rehearsed especially thoroughly. When the talk went well, I took it as a sign of full recovery.

I realized, of course, that I could have another stroke at any time, and the next time I might not be so lucky. I went for neurological and cardiological examinations. The heart can sometimes be involved in precipitating a stroke, but the tests indicated that my heart had not been affected.

Since the stroke, I have taken extra precautions. For a time, I did not drive alone except once or twice a week to my office, five miles away. I still do not go into the pool unless Kathleen is with me or within earshot. When she is elsewhere in the house, I call out the numbers of each of the laps I customarily swim so that she will know at once if something has happened to me.

Otherwise, life returned to its former pattern, except that I continued to lose more strength in my legs. That limited what I could do and put a further burden on Kathleen.

Besides cooking and housekeeping and working on the grounds, with only occasional part-time help, Kathleen had kept all our financial records, done our income tax returns with the help of an accountant, taken care of nearly all the shopping, and maintained the house—all in addition to participating actively in the editing and writing of my books.

When our tenants moved out in March 1992, we decided to use the apartment as we had originally planned: as a home for a live-in couple who could take over much of the house and grounds work and be available in emergencies. Through the informal network of Peruvian immigrants in Ithaca, we found what we needed in the Loayzas from Lima. So far this arrangement has been close to ideal. When they started with us, the Loayzas spoke little English. Since we speak Spanish to them, that is no big problem, and they are taking English lessons.

The only other alternative would be to move into a retirement home where all services are provided. It is a great satisfaction to be able to remain in our own home with its pool, to enjoy the garden and the view of Cayuga Lake, and to keep involved in Cornell life through PEWS.

This is a time for nostalgia—or at least reflection on my life so far. I have been blessed with a happy family life. As my legs have grown weaker, long-distance travel to see children and grandchildren, spread out from New Hampshire to New Mexico, has become too difficult for me, but they come to see us when they can. In 1993, we had a visit from our first great-grandchild, Joëlle, the granddaughter of our first-born, Joyce.

How do I look upon my work life? I enjoyed teaching, even though I tried to limit my teaching time so I could concentrate on research. How good a teacher was I? In teaching undergraduates, I could not match the performance of my father. When he was teaching at City College, he got his students excited over German by turning his classes into a glee club and singing German lieder. In undergraduate and graduate classes, I was probably at least average. On the one hand, I was not content to use the same set of notes from one year to the next, without making substantial revisions. On the other hand, I was never able later to put into teaching the creativity I showed in my first summer school course for schoolteachers.

I did my best teaching in seminars on research methods and on fieldwork. I did not want to build a Bill Whyte School of Social Research; I tried to help students discover what they really wanted to do and to progress toward their personal goals. Some very able students have worked with me, but they have developed their own styles of research and writing.

I am recognized as a major figure in sociology and social anthropology, yet I have never received the highest scholarly awards in the American Sociological Society or the Society for Applied Anthropology. I was pleased, however, when Swarthmore College awarded me an honorary degree in 1984, and in 1992, when the Society for Applied Anthropology gave me its first Career Achievement Award.

I never achieved my ambition of becoming a successful writer of fiction, but I transformed that goal into one of writing social research in ways that would be understandable and interesting to people without advanced technical education. A young Italian-American professor of sociology once told me how he had suggested his father read *Street Corner Society*. The old man had replied that he only had an eighth-grade education, so he would not understand it. The son persisted, and the father read the book and enjoyed it.

When I started writing *Participant Observer*, I thought it would be the last item on my work agenda, and I hoped to live to finish it. As I approached the end of my manuscript, Kathleen began worrying that after it was finished, I would just wither away. I assured her that I would still write some articles, but that was not good enough. While awaiting the ILR Press readers' reports on this autobiography, I started an essay entitled "Rethinking Sociology." Over the years, I had written various pieces on what was wrong with sociology, but now I found myself working out a strategy that would improve the discipline and enhance its value to society. It soon became evident that I could not say all I wanted to in an essay, so I told Kathleen that "Rethinking Sociology" was turning into a book. Now she was reassured, assuming I would always find one more book to write.

References

Books by William Foote Whyte

(in chronological order)

Street Corner Society. 1943. Chicago: University of Chicago Press Reprint, Chicago: University of Chicago Press, 1955, 1981, 1993.

Industry and Society, ed. 1946. McGraw-Hill.

Human Relations in the Restaurant Industry. 1948. McGraw-Hill.

Pattern for Industrial Peace. 1951. New York: Harper and Brothers.

Money and Motivation. 1955. New York: Harper and Brothers.

Men at Work. 1965. Homewood, Ill.: Irwin-Dorsey.

Action Research for Management. 1965. Coauthor with Edith Lentz Hamilton. Homewood, Ill.: Irwin-Dorsey.

Toward an Integrated Theory of Development: Economic and Non-Economic Variables in Rural Development. 1968. Coauthor with Lawrence K. Williams. Ithaca: New York State School of Industrial and Labor Relations.

Organizational Behavior: Theory and Application. 1969. Homewood, Ill.: Irwin-Dorsey.

Dominación y Cambios en el Perú Rural 1969. Coauthor with José Matos Mar, Julio Cotler, Lawrence K. Williams, J. Oscar Alers, Giorgio Alberti, and Fernando Fuenzalida. Instituto de Estudios Peruanos.

Organizing for Agricultural Development: Human Aspects in the Utilization of Science and Technology. 1975. New Brunswick, N.J.: Transaction Books.

Power, Politics, and Progress: Social Change in Rural Peru. 1976. Coauthor with Giorgio Alberti. New York: Elsevier.

Participatory Approaches to Agricultural Research and Development. 1981. Ithaca: Rural Development Committee, Cornell University.

Applied Sociology: Roles and Activities of Sociologists in Divers Settings. 1983. Coedited with Howard E. Freeman, Russell R. Dynes, and Peter H. Rossi. San Francisco: Jossey-Bass.

Higher Yielding Human Systems for Agriculture. 1983. Coedited with Damon Boynton. Ithaca: Cornell University Press.

Worker Participation and Ownership: Cooperative Strategies for Strengthening Local Economies. 1983. Coauthor with Tove Helland Hammer, Christopher B. Meek, Reed Nelson, and Robert N. Stern. Ithaca: ILR Press.

Learning from the Field: A Guide from Experience. 1984. With the collaboration of Kathleen King Whyte. Beverly Hills: Sage.

Industrial Democracy: Strategies for Community Revitalization. 1985. Coedited with Christopher B. Meek and Warner Woodworth. Beverly Hills: Sage.

References

Making Mondragón: The Growth and Dynamics of the Worker Cooperative Complex. 1988. Coauthor with Kathleen King Whyte. Ithaca: ILR Press. Rev. ed., 1991. Ithaca: ILR Press.

Participatory Action Research, ed. 1990. Newbury Park, Calif.: Sage.

Social Theory for Action: How Individuals and Organizations Learn to Change. 1991. Newbury Park, Calif.: Sage.

Articles by William Foote Whyte
(in chronological order)

"Bill Whyte Visits the Elementary School." 1931. *Bronxville Schools Bulletin* 18.

Financing New York City. 1935. *The American Academy of Political and Social Science Bulletin* no. 2.

"The Social Role of the Settlement House." 1941. *Applied Anthropology* 1 (1): 14–19.

"A Challenge to Political Scientists." 1943. *American Political Science Review* 37 (4): 692–97. (Bobbs-Merrill Reprint Series no. 117.)

"A Slum Sex Code." 1943. *American Journal of Sociology* 49 (1): 24–31. (Bobbs-Merrill Reprint Series no. 312.)

"Social Organization in the Slums." 1943. *American Sociological Review* 8: 34–39.

"Age-Grading of the Plains Indians." 1944. *Man* (54): 53–72.

"Pity the Personnel Man." 1944. *Advanced Management* 9 (4): 154–58.

"Sicilian Peasant Society." 1944. *American Anthropologist* 46 (1): 65–74.

"Who Goes Union and Why?" 1944. *Personnel Journal* 23 (6): 215–30.

"From Conflict to Cooperation." 1946. Coauthor with Burleigh B. Gardner and Andrew H. Whiteford. *Applied Anthropology* 5 (4): special issue devoted to Buchsbaum case.

"Patterns of Interaction in Union-Management Relations." 1949. *Human Organization* 8 (4): 13–19.

"The Social Structure of the Restaurant." 1949. *The American Journal of Sociology* 54 (1): 302–8. (Bobbs Merrill Reprint Series no. 314.)

"The Collective Bargaining Process: A Human Relations Analysis." 1950–51. Coauthor with Sidney Garfield. *Human Organization* 9 (2): 5–10; 9 (3): 10–16; 9 (4): 25–29; 10 (1): 28–34.

Leadership and Group Participation. 1953. New York State School of Industrial and Labor Relations Bulletin no. 21.

"Human Problems of U.S. Enterprise in Latin America." 1956. Coauthor with Allen R. Holmberg. *Human Organization* 15 (3): 1–40.

"Freedom and Responsibility in Research: The 'Springdale' Case" 1958. *Human Organization* 17 (2): 1–2.

"Needs and Opportunities for Industrial Relations Research." 1961. In *Essays on Indus-*

References

trial Relations Research—Problems and Prospects: A Series of Lectures Designed to Stimulate Research in Industrial Relations. 1961. Ann Arbor: Institute of Labor and Industrial Relations, University of Michigan-Wayne State University.

"Culture, Industrial Relations, and Economic Development: The Case of Peru." 1963.
Industrial and Labor Relations Review 16 (4): 583–93.

"Supervisory Leadership: An International Comparison." 1963. Coauthor with Lawrence K. Williams. Symposium 33, 1–8. C.I.O.S. International Management Congress 13.

"Toward an Integrated Approach for Research in Organizational Behavior." 1963.
(Presidential address to the Industrial Relations Research Association.) *IRRA Proceed-
ings* 32: 2–20.

"Do Cultural Differences Affect Workers' Attitudes?" 1966. Coauthor with Lawrence
K. Williams and C. S. Green. *Industrial Relations* 5 (3): 105–17.

"On Language and Culture." 1968. Coauthor with Robert Braun. In *Institutions and the
Person*, edited by H. E. Becker, 19–38. Chicago: Aldine.

"Rural Peru—Peasants as Activists." 1969. *Transaction* 7 (1): 37–47.

"Pigeons, Persons, and Piece Rates." 1972. *Psychology Today* (April): 68–69, 98–99.

"Conflict and Cooperation in Andean Communities." 1975. *American Ethnologist* 2 (2):
373–92.

"Methods for the Study of Conflict and Cooperation." 1976. *American Sociologist* 2
(4): 208–16.

"The Industrial Community in Peru." 1977. *The Annals of the American Academy of
Political and Social Science* 431: 103–12.

"The Mondragón System of Worker Production Cooperatives." 1977. Coauthor with
Ana Gutierrez-Johnson. *Industrial and Labor Relations Review* 31 (1): 18–30.

"Potatoes, Peasants, and Professors: A Development Strategy for Peru." 1977. *Sociological Practice* 2 (10): 7–23.

Review of *The Elusive Phenomena* by Fritz J. Roethlisberger. 1978. *Human Organization*
37 (4): 412–19.

"Social Inventions for Solving Human Problems." 1982. [Presidential address to the
American Sociological Association.] *American Sociological Review* 47 (1): 1–13.

"Philadelphia Story." 1986. *Society* (March-April): 36–44.

"Advancing Scientific Knowledge through Participatory Action Research." 1989. *Sociological Forum* 4 (3): 367–85.

"Participatory Action Research: Through Practice to Science in Social Research." 1989.
Coauthor with Davyyd J. Greenwood. *American Behavioral Scientist* 32 (5): 513–51.

Works by Others Cited in Text

Aldabaletrecu, F., and J. Gray. 1967. *De l'artisanat industriel au complexe coopératif:
L'experience de Mondragón.* Paris: Centre de Recherces Cooperatives.

References

Arensberg, Conrad M. 1951. "Behavior and Organization: Industrial Studies." In *Social Psychology at the Crossroads,* edited by John Rohrer and Muzafir Sherif, 324–52. New York: Harper and Brothers.

Argyris, Chris, and Graham Taylor. 1950. "The Member-centered Conference as a Research Method." *Applied Anthropology* 9 (4): 5–14.

———. 1951. "The Member-centered Conference as a Research Method: Part Two." *Applied Anthropology* 10 (1): 22–27.

Barnard, Chester I. 1938. *The Functions of the Executive.* Cambridge, Mass.: Harvard University Press.

Black, Max, ed. 1961. *The Social Theories of Talcott Parsons: A Critical Examination.* Englewood Cliffs, N.J.: Prentice-Hall. 1976. Reprint, with an afterword by Talcott Parsons. Carbondale, Ill.: Southern Illinois University Press.

CIMMYT. 1974. *The Puebla Project: Seven Years of Experience, 1967–73.* Mexico, D.F., Mexico: CIMMYT.

Davis, Allison, Burleigh Gardner, and Mary R. Gardner. 1941. *Deep South.* Chicago: University of Chicago Press.

Dean, Lois Remmers. 1958. "Interaction Reported and Observed: The Case of One Local Union." *Human Organization* 17 (3): 36–44.

Dickson, William J., and Fritz J. Roethlisberger. *Counseling in an Organization: A Sequel to the Hawthorne Researches.* 1966. Boston: Division of Research, Graduate School of Business Administration, Harvard University.

Espinosa, Waldemar. 1973. *Los Huancas, Aliados de la Conquista.* Lima: Casa de la Cultura.

Frost, Peter J., Larry F. Moore, Meryl Reis Louis, Craig C. Lundberg, and Joanne Martin, eds. 1991. *Reframing Organizational Culture.* Newbury Park, Calif.: Sage.

Fuenzalida, Fernando, with José Luis Villaran, Jürgen Golte, and Teresa Valienta. 1968. *Estructuras Tradicionales y Economia de Mercado: La Comunidad Indigena de Huayopampa.* Lima: Instituto de Estudios Peruanos.

Gardner, Burleigh. 1946. *Human Relations in Industry.* Homewood, Ill.: Richard D. Irwin.

Greenwood, Davydd J., et al. *Industrial Democracy as Process: Participatory Action Research in the Fagor Cooperative Group of Mondragón.* 1991. Assen/Maastricht: Van Gorcum.

Homans, George C. 1941. *English Villagers of the Thirteenth Century.* Cambridge, Mass.: Harvard University Press.

———. 1950. *The Human Group.* New York: Harcourt-Brace.

Homans, George C., and Orville T. Bailey. 1959. In *The Society of Fellows,* edited by Crane Brinton. Cambridge, Mass.: Harvard University Press.

Hughes, Everett C. 1943. *French Canada in Transition.* Chicago: University of Chicago Press.

References

Journal of Contemporary Ethnography 21 (1). 1992. Patricia Adler and Peter Adler, eds. Special issue: *"Street Corner Society* Revisited." April.

Leighton, Alexander H. 1945. *The Governing of Men.* Princeton: Princeton University Press.

Mead, Margaret. 1928. *Coming of Age in Samoa.* New York: Morrow.

Muhs, William, ed. 1989. *Symposium on Committee on Human Relations in Industry at the University of Chicago.* Bozeman, Mont.: College of Business, Montana State University.

Nuñez del Prado, Oscar, with the collaboration of William Foote Whyte. 1973. *Kuyo Chico: Applied Anthropology in an Indian Community.* Chicago: University of Chicago Press.

Orlandella, Angelo Ralph. 1992. "Boelen May Know Holland, Boelen May Know Barzini, but Boelen Doesn't Know Diddle about the North End." *Journal of Contemporary Ethnography* 21 (1): 69–79.

———. Forthcoming. "A More Effective Strategy for Dealing with Inner-City Street Gangs." *The Gang Journal.*

Roethlisberger, Fritz J. 1977. *The Elusive Phenomena: An Autobiographical Account of My Work in the Field of Organizational Behavior at the Harvard Business School.* Cambridge, Mass.: Harvard University Press.

———, and William J. Dickson. 1939. *Management and the Worker.* Cambridge, Mass.: Harvard University Press.

Rosen, Corey, and Karen M. Young, Eds. *Understanding Employee Ownership.* 1991. Ithaca.: ILR Press.

Roy, Donald. 1959. "Banana Time." *Human Organization* 18 (4): 158–68.

Soto, Hernando de. 1989. *The Other Path: The Invisible Revolution in the Third World.* Translated by June Abbot. With a foreword by Mario Vargas Llosa. New York: Harper and Row.

Strauss, George, and Leonard Sayles. 1953. *The Local Union.* New York: Harper and Brothers.

Trist, Eric, and K. W. Banforth. 1951. "Some Social and Psychological Consequences of the Longwall Method of Coal Getting." *Human Relations* 4: 3–38.

Vidich, Arthur J., and Joseph Bensman. 1958. *Small Town in Mass Society: Class, Power, and Religion in a Rural Community.* Princeton: Princeton University Press.

Walton, Richard E., and Robert B. McKersie. 1965. *A Behavioral Theory of Labor Negotiations: An Analysis of a Social Interaction System.* New York: McGraw-Hill. Reprint, Ithaca: ILR Press, 1991.

Warner, W. Lloyd. 1959. *The Living and the Dead: A Study in the Symbolic Life of Americans.* Vol. 5 of the Yankee City Series. New Haven: Yale University Press.

Warner, W. Lloyd, and J. O. Low. 1947. *The Social System of the Modern Factory.* Vol. 4 of the Yankee City Series. New Haven: Yale University Press.

References

Warner, W. Lloyd, and Paul S. Lunt. 1941. *The Social Life of a Modern Community.* Vol. 1 of the Yankee City Series. New Haven: Yale University Press.

———. 1942. *The Status System of a Modern Community.* Vol. 2 of the Yankee City Series. New Haven: Yale University Press.

Index

Index

Schlesinger, Arthur, Jr., 59
Schmatz, James, 284
Schuyler, Belle, 12
Schuyler, Irwin, 12
search conferences, 307
Seeber, Ronald, 308, 309, 311
Senate Select Committee on Small Business, 291
Seybold, John, 37–38, 42, 43, 44, 64
Shafer, Jake, 161–63
Sharpe, Lauriston, 165
Shaw, Clifford, 111
Slim (Bennetts), 99–100
Sloan, Joe, 125
Small Business Administration, 292
Small Business Employee Ownership Act (S388), 292
Smith, Al, 8
Snyder, Winifred, 180
"Social Inventions for Solving Human Problems," 297–98
Social Progresista party, 237
Social Science Research Center, 200, 320
Sociedad y Política, 244
Society for Applied Anthropology, 254, 331
Society for the Psychological Study of Social Issues, 175
Sociological Forum, 323
sociotechnical systems, 157–58, 298, 312
Sorokin, Pitrim, 65, 108
Special Operations Research Office (SORO), 233
Spiller, Robert E., 42, 45
spindle, 151
Sprague, Ernest, 249–50
Staley, Eugene, 175–76
Stern, Robert, 282, 285, 286
Stewart, Donald, 292
St. Joseph's College, 286
Stouffer, Sam, 110
Stouffer, Vernon, 150
Strauss, George, 174–75, 177, 320
Street Corner Society, 319–26
Student-Faculty Board on Student Conduct (SFBSC), 260
Students for a Democratic Society (SDS), 256, 260–62

Taubeneck, Ignatius D., 34
Taylor, Frederick W., 146
Taylor, Graham, 172
Taylor, Lyle, 284–86
technology transfer, 250

Temple, Christina, 215
Tennesee Valley Authority (TVA), 160
Thorsrud, Einar, 298, 306, 313
Thurber, John, 171
Tilden, Bill, 23
transactional relationships, 183
Tribuna, La, 235, 237
Trist, Eric, 158, 283–84, 298
Trujillo, 232, 241
Tullis, LaMond, 239
Turner, James, 259
Turner Middle School, 316–17
Turnquist, Mark A., 310
Tyler, Ralph, 165

Ulgor, 275–76, 314–15
United Food and Commercial Workers Union, 284–88
Uphoff, Norman, 248, 296
U.S. Department of Labor, 254

Valcarcel, Luis, 234–35, 238
Vallejos, Mario, 216
Vanek, Jaroslav, 271–74
Van Sickle, James H., 7, 13, 21, 44
Vazquez, Mario, 207–10
Vermont Asbestos Group, 282
Vicos, 223, 235, 238
Vidich, Arthur, 203–4, 322
Vietnam War issue, 255–57
Villars, Ceferino, and family, 225
Virú, 241
Vitale, George, 83
Vogel, Robert, 8, 22, 24
Voluntary Job Preservation and Community Stabilization Act, 291
Von Hausen family, 32
Von Klenze, Camilo, 29

Wagner Act, 124
Walling, Tom, 127, 128
Walton, Richard, 162, 298
Warner, W. Lloyd, 108–10, 112, 139, 142, 144, 153
Watt, Effie, 13–15
Watt, Homer, 13
Wayno, Frank, 309–11
Webb, Beatrice and Sidney, 271
Weber, Max, 147
Wenner-Gren Foundation, 230
Wenzel, Al, 122–23, 127–28
Western Electric research program, 142
West Philadelphia Improvement Corps (WEPIC), 316–17